STANLEY YOUNG
Professor of Management, School of Business Administration,
University of Massachusetts

CHARLES E. SUMMER, JR.
Columbia University
Consulting Editor to Scott, Foresman and Company in Management

SCOTT, FORESMAN AND COMPANY

MANAGEMENT: A SYSTEMS ANALYSIS

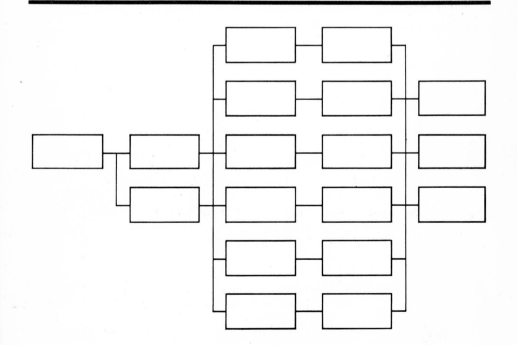

To Eleanor

Library of Congress Catalog Card No. 66-20354

Copyright © 1966 by Scott, Foresman and Company, Glenview, Illinois

All rights reserved. Printed in the United States of America.

Regional offices of Scott, Foresman and Company are located in Atlanta, Dallas, Glenview, Palo Alto, and Oakland, N.J.

FOREWORD

Management, the problem solving or decision making segment of an organization, is currently undergoing a fundamental transition both in practice and in theory. With the introduction of the computer, the increased use of quantitative methods, and the application of the findings of the behavioral sciences, a trend has developed toward viewing organizational decision making as an identifiable, observable, and measurable process—rather than as one which is essentially covert and unplanned and which relies on managerial "intuition" or "judgment." The deliberate formalization of this process makes it increasingly possible to introduce and use conceptual tools which will ensure more effective decision results. While one can speculate upon the ultimate effect of this trend, there is little doubt that it will be extended and will achieve predominance.

Management: A Systems Analysis is another effort in this conceptual movement. Its primary focus is upon the problem of integrating the new managerial techniques, or sciences, into a single, effective operating system—not only for the individual manager but also for the organization as a whole. Managerial tools tend to be developed and applied in a piecemeal fashion. For example, because of the capability of the computer, effort has—by and large—been directed to those organizational activities wherein the computer can be applied. Although it uses the systems approach, this study demonstrates the feasibility of designing a *total management system* which effectively incorporates the various components of a management system.

Rather than attach the new techniques to the existing management structure, it is possible, and highly desirable, for us to view management as a specific subsystem of the organization, a subsystem which has its own inputs, outputs, and processes. In the development of any technology, the initial tendency is to incorporate the latest tools into the existing vehicle; but a point of development is reached when the basic vehicle must be modified if continued improvements are to be made.

The growing trend toward an explicit decision making process has been viewed by some with apprehension, and concern has been expressed about its effects on the individual. Although granting that the transition will be an uneven process, I believe we are at a stage of having developed conceptual tools which, when applied, will result in organizational processes that will significantly increase human dignity and satisfaction. On the theoretical level, it is already possible to envisage the organization as a self-adapting and self-motivating organism which optimizes the human welfare of the organizational participants as it eliminates the coercive, inefficient, frustrating, "noisy" aspects of the organization that currently exist. Moreover, if most aspects of an individual's life are to be organizationally determined, it is imperative that organizations be made as human as possible. Let us hope, then, that the true potential of the cybernetic revolution, as envisioned by its progenitor, Norbert Wiener, will be achieved: the bringing about of "a more human use of human beings."

I am indebted to many people for their help in making this book possible. Among those who offered strong encouragement are Professor Joseph Litterer of the University of Illinois; Professors Richard Johnson and James Rosenzweig of the University of Washington; Professor G. D. Hanrahan of St. Louis University; Mr. Michael Witunski, Director of Long-Range Planning, McDonnell Aircraft Corporation; Sister Mary Edelburg, Administrator of St. Mary of Nazareth Hospital, Chicago; and Mr. Thomas Stark, Assistant Administrator of St. Mary of Nazareth Hospital. The following graduate students helped gather material for the cases in Chapter 16: Messrs. Brandenburg, Moroney, Vogel, Gumper, Chalet, Johnson, Dienstbach, and Danes.

Finally, the author is especially indebted to Professor Charles E. Summer, Jr., of Columbia University, who provided insight and guidance in the endeavor; and to the editors of Scott, Foresman and Company, who offered their able support throughout the writing of this book.

S. Y.

CONTENTS

ment system; performance standards; sensory devices; comparison of actual and expected performance; sources of system breakdown; actuation; evaluation of the control mechanisms; control from the submanagerial viewpoint; summary; questions for discussion; suggested readings

PART ONE

MANAGEMENT, SYSTEMS, ORGANIZATIONS, AND DECISION MAKING

1

THE MANAGEMENT OF THE DECISION MAKING PROCESS

As organizations greatly expand in size it becomes increasingly unfeasible for a few individuals to make all of the decisions, and top management thus must increasingly delegate its decision making duties to subordinate managers. However, because top management continues to be responsible and accountable for all of the decisions that are made, the character of its organizational role changes from that of *making* the actual operating decisions to that of *managing* the decision making activities.

This increase in the size of organizations also necessitates a division of managerial effort, and two sets of managers emerge. One is top management, whose organizational role or function comprises the primary authority and responsibility for determining the *nature* of the management system, the process by which organizational problems are to be solved.[1] The other group of managers is subordinate to the top managers, and its members constitute the human components of the management system; their primary function or responsibility is *decision making.*

THE OBJECTIVES AND SCOPE OF THIS BOOK

The first objective of this study is to show how top management can meaningfully *administer* the decision making function

[1] "Management system" frequently refers to the procedures of collecting, recording, processing, and retrieving information, but its use in this study will relate almost entirely to the organizational decision making process. See Chapter 2, The Management System and the Meaning of Organization, for an elaboration of the nature of management systems.

and, more specifically, how it can *design, install, direct, maintain, and control a total, integrated management system.*

In the creation of such a system, we will consider the following questions in detail:

How does one actually plan an organizational decision making system?

What decision making tasks should be considered, and why?

What techniques should be utilized in the execution of these tasks?

How are these tasks to be incorporated into an operating plan?

How are these activities to be executed in the organization?

Who shall perform which tasks, and where and when?

What staffing and motivation problems exist?

What control mechanisms are required to assure that sub-managers are performing their duties as specified?

In view of the changes in managerial technology and the problems which may arise to affect an existing system, how should top management redesign and improve its present system?

Some examples of decision making systems will be reviewed and the applications of planned decision making, both within and between organizations, will be explored, particularly with respect to the economic and political areas. Current principles and practices in top management's administration of the decision making function will also be examined.

To illustrate system design, a particular model will be constructed. This model is not intended to have universal application but only to demonstrate how system design can be accomplished in the ongoing organization by top management or by the designer. Decision making is not yet an established science; therefore there may be differences of opinion on the content of such a system. Then too, because top managers hold definite views of how decisions should be made by their subordinates, our analysis will focus on the methods by which these concepts can be converted into an operating system.

AN INTEGRATED MANAGEMENT SYSTEM

The second purpose of this study relates to the problem of designing a total, integrated management system. Unless all segments of a system are properly interrelated, overall results will be deficient even though specific parts are highly sophisticated.

The function of organizational decision making can be approached through different disciplines, and concentration can be centered on any of its many subparts. Statisticians and mathematicians may be concerned with applying quantitative tools to assist in organizational problem solving; they may construct quantitative models for simulating the operation of various facets of organizational operations, such as inventory control or advertising media selection. Behavioral scientists, such as economists or sociologists, may devote their efforts to the environment of the firm: economists may attempt to forecast the future demand of a product and sociologists may delve into changes in consumer aspirations. Still other specialists may consider parts of the decision making process, or only a single subprocess, such as the exercise of authority; some analysts, for example, are concerned with the modification of managerial prerogatives in the collective bargaining relationship. Those closest to the computer may explore the informational requirements of the problem-solver; and some psychologists may emphasize the human components of the system while others will concentrate upon its control aspects.

Analysis of the subfeatures of the decision making system is important, but the extent of this importance becomes most meaningful only when each feature is evaluated in the context of the total operating system. It is generally recognized that all parts of a system must be effectively integrated, but, except for the broad recommendation that a manager should know the advantages of various tools or processes, and that he should consider them in the context of his work, specific recommendations for achieving total integration of the parts have not yet been advanced.

We can assume that the student of business will study the management function in great detail and in the terms of a variety of disciplines, but the student must also understand how all facets of the managerial function interrelate. Without this comprehension, his specialized information will be disconnected and will therefore lose much of its real significance.

Accordingly, our analysis will focus upon solving the problem

4

of combining these many disparate elements of decision making into a total, integrated management system. The methodological device will be systems analysis.

Richard Johnson (among others) defines a system as "an organized or complex whole; an assemblage or combination of things or parts forming a complex or unitary whole."[2] In essence, the systems approach provides the designer with analytical devices for simultaneously identifying and determining a large number of processes and components, as well as the interrelationships which make up the system. In other words, the systems approach enables the designer to maintain a concept of "the complex," or the whole operation, while he analyzes its parts.[3] An evaluation can then be made of the way in which all subparts should be united into the whole—into the total system.

For the most part, the systems concept (in terms of design) has emerged from the engineering discipline, for it was the increasing complexity of communications and weapons systems that necessitated—and produced—a methodology for helping to integrate all parts of these operations.[4] As Professor Johnson has noted:

> In particular, military and space programs are becoming increasingly complex, thus indicating the need for integrating various elements of the total system. Manufacturing the product itself (a vehicle or other hardware) is quite complex, often involving problems of producibility with requirements of extremely high reliability. This is difficult to ensure for individual components or subsystems. In addition each subsystem also must be reliable in its interrelationship with all other subsystems. Successful integration of subcomponents, and hence successful performance of a particular product, must also be integrated with other elements of the total system. For example, the functioning of the Nike-Zeus antimissile missile must be coordinated with the early warning system, ground facilities, and operating personnel. All elements must function as an operating, integrated whole.[5]

[2] Richard Johnson, Fremont Kast, and James Rosenzweig, *The Theory and Management of Systems* (New York: McGraw-Hill Book Company, 1963), p. 4.

[3] See Chapter 2, The Management System and the Meaning of Organization (pp. 18–19), for an explanation of the design process.

[4] See Arthur Hall, *A Methodology for Systems Engineering* (Princeton, N.J.: D. Van Nostrand Co., Inc., 1962), pp. 5–7.

[5] Johnson *et al., op. cit.,* pp. 16–17.

UNDERSTANDING THE MANAGERIAL PROCESS

A third major purpose of this analysis is to recast the traditional treatment of the managerial function into a systems context in the hope of thereby providing a better understanding for the student—but this does not mean that the accepted analysis of the managerial function, which is generally viewed as a set of tasks such as planning, organizing, staffing, and control, is not valid. In this study, although these tasks are integrated into a single process of organizational problem solving, the essential characteristics of the tasks will be reviewed as we cover some of the material that is considered in nonsystems treatments.

Because the systems approach imposes a specific discipline upon the analyst, this book will present the functions of management in a more explicit, interconnected, and operational way. By "operational" we mean that the phenomena under study are reduced to identifiable, observable, and measurable entities. Although such concepts as employee morale, managerial responsibility, and organizational survival may be significant ideas, they cannot be used in a systems framework until they have been reduced to operational form.

The operational aspect is of great assistance in learning about the managerial function because many abstract features are thereby made more concrete. In presenting the material in this text to a classroom of undergraduates, graduate students, and operating managers, the author has urged his students to work with ideas which are identifiable and measurable. And, to emphasize this aspect, students have been asked to graph or simulate the decision making processes of organizations with which they are most familiar: the various subprocesses and their sequence of use, the information that was needed and collected for each subprocess, and the decision criteria, information manipulation, and tools of analysis. When the student is required to analyze an organization on a behavioral or observable level, he will find that the managerial process becomes more explicit, meaningful, and precise.

ORGANIZATIONAL DECISION MAKING MODELS

A fourth objective of this study is to suggest, and perhaps stimulate, further improvements in the formulation of organizational decision making models. A decision making model is a construct or a representation which shows how decisions should be made; and an example of such a model is the United States Constitution, which represents a political decision making system. The manner in which federal legislation is to be formulated, enacted, and executed is predetermined. Major national problems (and suggested solutions) are often raised by the executive branch of the government. A bill is formulated and introduced in Congress, and the problem is then cleared to the appropriate committee of one or both houses of Congress, where the problem is investigated and where alternative solutions are considered. After a committee has approved a solution, it is voted on (with or without modifications) by both houses, and, if approved, is sent to the President, who may sign it or veto it. If the bill is signed (or authorized) it becomes law, and the appropriate executive department will then execute it. The Supreme Court acts as a (delayed) control device by declaring a law unconstitutional if it should violate the Constitution.

Although improvements could probably be made in this system (particularly in the executive branch of the government), there is little question that it operates as a planned system. One can usually predict the legislative course that a government proposal must follow.

The effectiveness of decision output is in large measure determined by the particular decision making model that is utilized, and the importance of a good model or plan has been empirically established. One aspect or purpose of planning is therefore the search for the optimum decision making model — for the model which will provide the greatest number of solutions, with the highest output per solution, at the least cost, over a specific time period. The measure of the output or value of a decision can be defined as the extent to which that decision increases organizational goal achievement when it is used by the operating units.

Additional advantages are obtained from effective decision models because they assure an integration of managerial activities so that these efforts will be directed toward a common purpose; and order in managerial endeavor is provided in the form of consistent, predictable behavior. Finally, whenever new and proved decision techniques are developed (as is presently happening in the statistical, mathematical, and behavioral sciences), these techniques can be incorporated into the operating model and managers can be trained (or retrained) in their application.

In the past, however, top management has relied almost exclusively upon the bureaucratic model as the guide for structuring the work of submanagers, and this study will suggest that, as a decision making model, the bureaucratic form is at best an incomplete plan. Furthermore, because this model is the type most

7

widely employed, it will be used in this study primarily as a basis for comparison with the model that will be proposed, in order to better illustrate the advantages of systematic decision making.

Although the bureaucratic model will be analyzed in detail in Chapter 15 (Redesigning the Bureaucratic System), it will help at this point in our discussion if the salient decision making features of this traditional model are briefly described. Under the bureaucratic model, the planning of the decision making function, or "organizational planning," is restricted to defining the authority and responsibility of submanagers. The primary concern in the bureaucratic model is merely the allocation of authority within the organization, and an organizational chart or table is drawn up which designates the number of submanagers and the perimeters of their authority. The establishment of the lines of authority and responsibilities, centralization versus decentralization of authority, and so forth, are regarded as the major problems to be solved, and, in the typical program, each manager is delegated the authority to determine how his particular organizational unit will function. The schematic representation of all this is the familiar hierarchical or pyramidal chart, with authority flowing downward from the president to the first line-manager. Lower management, in turn, must follow the instructions of its superiors, and staff officials are frequently provided to assist line managers in the performance of their tasks. Once these authority relationships have been defined (perhaps in considerable detail), it is assumed that an effective decision making system has been planned. However, only the organizational area in which the manager is to perform has been defined, and even then guidelines or principles for his performance may be lacking.

In reviewing either the organizational chart or the procedural manual of the bureaucratic model, one fails to find a detailed plan of how organizational decisions are to be made. Usually there is no advance determination of the decision making tasks to be carried out, nor is there a plan of when, where, how, why, and by whom these tasks are to be performed; and generally one does not find a written, operational, decision making manual. The reason why decision making remains unplanned is found in the delegation of authority. In the bureaucratic system, the manager, within his assigned authority, is free to do whatever in his judgment will be necessary to accomplish his objectives. Each submanager is granted the permission to plan, execute, control, and, to a certain extent, evaluate his own activities and those of the employees who are within the limits of his delegated authority.

8

Planning, however, means that objectives are to be achieved by a predetermined program of action to which each manager is expected to conform.[6] But planning and delegating authority are contradictory processes for structuring organizational work: one cannot plan the work of submanagers while simultaneously granting them the right to determine their own duties.

Top managers are daily made aware of instances in which submanagers make poor decisions—with consequences which they, as top managers, have to correct. Consider, for instance, this report about one company president:

"I don't know whether my organization [its decision making system in particular] is good, bad or indifferent because I don't know with what to compare it," he said. He had investigated an "organization planning" program [design of a decision making system] in one company which was devoted exclusively to employee counseling and coaching and the interpretation of color-coded organization charts for management inventory purposes. In another company he had found the "organization planning" staff department primarily concerned with wage and salary matters; in still another, as he put it, they were "keepers of the organization charts." In a fourth instance, the [organization planning] function reported to the auditor and was responsible for procedures.[7]

Our study will show that when the top manager is confronted with poor submanagerial performance the systems approach will provide techniques for isolating and correcting the problem encountered above.

On the other hand, although the traditional model is deficient as an information-based decision making system, it has advantageous organizational attributes; for example, it encourages a measure of organizational individualism for the middle manager[8] and it provides for a division of labor. The argument of this analysis does not imply that the traditional view of management's performance of a set of tasks is incorrect; it is rather the manner in which these tasks are organizationally arranged—and

---

[6] Preston P. Le Breton and Dale A. Henning define an organization plan as a "predetermined course of action," in *Planning Theory* (Englewood Cliffs, N.J.: Prentice-Hall, Inc., 1961), p. 7.

[7] Louis A. Allen, *Management and Organization* (New York: McGraw-Hill Book Company, 1958), p. 51.

[8] See Chapter 14, Individualism Within the Organization, for a discussion of the ideological aspects of organizational decision making.

the absence of a plan which converts these tasks into an operating system — that will be critically assessed.

MANAGEMENT TRENDS

There is a deepening disenchantment with the traditional guides for organizing the work of managers. Along with the increased complexity of operations (which requires a broader range of skills), with the wider acceptance of the manager as a problem-solver, with the emergence of multinational cooperation, with the widespread use of the computer and a greater use of quantitative and analytical tools, and with greater emphasis on systems analysis, there is a growing realization that the customary methods for arranging the work of managers may now be inadequate, although they were quite satisfactory when an organization was smaller and when the productive process was more routinized.[9]

As Professor Peter Drucker has observed:

> . . . *authority and responsibility may well be the wrong principles of organization. It may well be that we will have to learn to organize not a system of authority and responsibility — a system of command — but an information and decision system — a system of judgment, knowledge, and expectations.*[10]

Firms are indeed beginning to redesign their information and decision requirements; systems personnel are exercising broader influence in the planning of organizations;[11] and Professor Thomas Whisler suggests "there may be some 'hair-raising transitions' in management."[12]

[9] For examples, see Melvin Anshen and George Bach (eds.), *Management and Corporations: 1985* (New York: McGraw-Hill Book Company, 1960); Johnson *et al., op. cit.,* pp. 22–25; Herbert A. Simon, *The New Science of Management Decision* (New York: Harper & Row, 1960); and Harold J. Leavitt and Thomas L. Whisler, "Management in the 1980's," *Harvard Business Review* (November-December, 1958), 41–48.

[10] Peter F. Drucker, "Managing the Educated," in *Management's Mission in a New Society,* Dan H. Fenn (ed.) (New York: McGraw-Hill Book Company, 1959), p. 174.

[11] "The Cybernated Generation," *Time* (April 2, 1965), pp. 84–91; "The Computer's Newest Conquest: Marketing," *Business Week* (April 17, 1965), pp. 114–138 (special report); Gilbert Burck, "Management Will Never Be the Same Again," *Fortune* (August, 1964), pp. 124–126+; and "The Information Revolution," a pamphlet issued by the American Federation of Information Processing Societies (211 E. 43d St., New York).

[12] "The Challenge of Automation," *Newsweek* (January 25, 1965), pp. 73–78+.

[13] For a review of this hospital project, see Chapter 12, A Hospital Case Study (pp. 290–325); also see Stanley Young, "Designing the Management System," *Academy of Management Journal,* 7 (June, 1964), 137–148.

Although the problem of the design of a management system is fairly recent, our study will demonstrate that sufficient research and analysis have taken place so that an operational system can now be formulated. Moreover, during the past four years the author has participated in the design and operation of a management system—in a hospital context—and many of the examples used in this book will relate to this project.[13]

Even though there is always a risk in predicting the nature of the corporation of the future, there can be little doubt that because of the rapid changes which are presently taking place it is incumbent upon the student of management to become familiar with his future organizational role and with the environment in which he will be expected to perform. If, as we have suggested, he will be a part of a management system, he should understand the nature of that system and he should also have the capability of designing improved models.

THE ROLE OF TOP MANAGEMENT

The need for managing the activities of submanagers in a way that is similar to the method employed for managing other organizational participants is not always recognized. Nor, at times, is a clear, functional distinction drawn between top and middle managers; nor has organizational decision making generally been viewed as a distinct and unique function which itself requires management, just as do marketing, production, finance, or personnel. The final objective of this study is therefore to develop a more rigorous concept of the top management role.

Top management is often believed to be only a part of the organization's decision making function, and only over a given operating area; it is, for example, the vice-president of sales who is expected to decide how the marketing function will be conducted. The functions of top, middle, and lower management are often assumed to differ only in the methods by which decisions are reached or in the aspects of organizational problems which the managers at each level will consider. Top management is expected to formulate broad policies, middle management to interpret these policies, and lower management to implement them. Top management is therefore seen as a participant in the decision making function rather than as the proper manager of it.

It is important for top management to perceive that its true organizational role is the management of the entire decision making function. Once it is accepted that decision making is a

11

distinct organizational function, but one which must be managed as are the other functions of the organization, those techniques of management which have proved effective with other functions can then be advantageously applied to decision making. If, on the other hand, top management's role is construed as only the administration of *non*decision making .functions, top management will then devote its energy to the management of such functions as sales or production, neglecting the decision making function because the need to administer it will not have been recognized. Another important and almost corollary perception is that it does not necessarily follow that because a middle manager was a successful decision-maker he will, upon promotion to the top managerial position, be able to administer the decision making function effectively. As Herbert Simon points out:

> *The executive's job involves not only making decisions himself, but also seeing that the organization, or part of an organization, that he directs makes decisions effectively. The vast bulk of the decision-making activity for which he is responsible is not his personal activity, but the activity of his subordinates. . . .*
>
> *There is no reason to expect that a man who has acquired a fairly high level of personal skill in decision-making activity will have a corresponding high skill in designing efficient decision-making systems. To imagine that there is such a connection is like supposing that a man who is a good weight lifter can therefore design cranes.*[14]

The administration of the decision making function is unlike that of any other organizational function; its processes, tools, relationships to other functions, human components, and environment all are different (as will be indicated in this book).

THE PLAN OF THE BOOK

This book is separated into five major sections. Part One (Chapters 1 and 2, The Management of the Decision Making Process and The Management System and the Meaning of Organization) is introductory. Chapter 2—which reviews the systems approach, its components, and the nature of the decision making function in any organization—also considers why organized activity exists, the necessity for decision making, the relationship of the decision making function to other organizational functions, a definition of the decision making process, and the nature of the management discipline.

[14] Herbert A. Simon, *The New Science of Management Decision* (New York: Harper & Row, 1960), pp. 4–5.

Part Two (Chapters 3 through 8) is concerned with the process of designing a management system. In Chapter 3 (Designing a Management System) a model of an integrated management system is presented, and Chapters 4 to 8 analyze this model in terms of its subprocesses and tools. Chapter 4 (Organizational Objectives) relates to the defining of organizational goals, and Chapter 5 (Devising Organizational Solutions) to raising and diagnosing organizational problems and to searching for and evaluating solutions. Chapter 6 (Organizational Consensus) considers the achievement of organizational agreement upon the proposed solution. Chapter 7 (Effectuating the Decision) reviews the authorization, implementation, utilization, and audit of the organizational solution. Chapter 8 (Decision Making Technology) discusses the selection and integration of decision making tools and processes.

Part Three (Chapters 9, 10, and 11) studies the administration of the management system. Chapter 9 (Selecting the Management System) is concerned with using selective criteria for choosing among alternative models of management systems. After the best design has been selected, Chapter 10 (Installation, Operation, and Maintenance of the System) demonstrates how it can be installed and utilized. Chapter 11 (Control of the System) examines the control aspects of the management system's administration.

Part Four (Chapters 12, 13, and 14) considers the implications of our study. Chapter 12 (A Hospital Case Study) reviews a four-year operation of an integrated management design and cites some of the interpersonal difficulties that might be encountered by higher executives. Chapter 13 (Interorganizational Cooperation) extends the conceptual tools developed in the study to the design of interorganizational decision making systems which may require greater attention in the future. Chapter 14 (Individualism Within the Organization) explores the personal consequences of planned decision making and shows that the process will result in greater organizational individuality for the middle manager.

Part Five (Chapters 15 and 16) is concerned with a critique of the bureaucratic model. Chapter 15 (Redesigning the Bureaucratic System) examines the traditional model, and Chapter 16 (Cases) evaluates this system in ongoing organizations. Part Five is basically a by-product of the previous chapters, intended only to assist in the identification of management problem areas which may be present in ongoing organizations. If effective use would be made of this study, it is important to recognize the areas that are in need of correction, a matter of primary concern to the operating manager. Each group of top managers must ultimately select that management system which each believes is best for its particular organization.

QUESTIONS FOR DISCUSSION

1. As organizations increase in size, what management problems will arise?
2. How have these problems usually been met?
3. How can one determine to what extent a given organizational activity or function is planned?
4. When an organizational function — such as sales or production — is unplanned, what consequences might be expected?
5. Why is the decision making function only partially planned in many organizations?
6. What is the difference between the planning and the delegation device?
7. How might one measure the effectiveness of an organizational decision making system?
8. Would you consider the Constitution a political decision making plan? Explain.
9. Why is it important to study the interrelationship between the parts of an organizational operation?
10. Speculate upon the nature of the middle manager's role in the large corporation twenty-five years from now.

SUGGESTED READINGS

CHAPPLE, ELIOT D., and SAYLES, LEONARD R. *The Measurement of Management.* New York: The Macmillan Company, 1961.

DALE, ERNEST. *The Great Organizers.* New York: McGraw-Hill Book Company, 1960.

DRUCKER, PETER F. *Landmarks of Tomorrow.* New York: Harper & Row, 1959 (chapters 2 and 3).

ETZIONI, AMITAI. *Complex Organizations: A Sociological Reader.* New York: Holt, Rinehart & Winston, Inc., 1961.

HAIRE, MASON (ed.). *Modern Organization Theory.* New York: John Wiley & Sons, Inc., 1959.

NEWMAN, WILLIAM H., and SUMMER, CHARLES E., JR. *The Process of Management: Concepts, Behavior and Practice.* Englewood Cliffs, N.J.: Prentice-Hall, Inc., 1961.

SPIER, LEO. "Graph Theory as a Method for Exploring Business Behavior," *Interdisciplinary Studies in Business Behavior,* Joseph McGuire (ed.). Cincinnati: South Western Publishing Co., 1962 (pp. 70-98).

2

THE MANAGEMENT SYSTEM AND THE MEANING OF ORGANIZATION

Because the ultimate responsibility of top management is to administer the management system, it is obviously essential that we establish the nature of this system at the outset. This chapter will therefore define the management system[1] and will then explore the characteristics of such a system.

A management system can be defined as that subsystem of the organization whose components consist of a subset of individuals (man to man) whose duties are to receive certain organizational problems (inputs) and thereupon to execute a set of activities (process) which will produce organizational solutions (output) for either increasing the value or return of the total organizational activity (satisficing) or for optimizing some function of the total organizational inputs and outputs. Let us now consider some aspects of this definition in detail.

Management systems can be viewed as being essentially normative, and, although there is no uniform agreement on the definition of a normative system, the following construction by Richard Kershner is nevertheless representative:

A system is a collection of entities or things (animate or inanimate) which receives certain inputs and is constrained to act

[1]The author wishes to thank the Academy of Management for permission to reproduce material in this chapter which appeared initially in Stanley Young, "Designing a Behavioral System," *Academy of Management Proceedings, 1963,* pp. 76–83.

15

concertedly upon them to produce certain outputs, with the objective of maximizing some function of inputs and outputs.[2]

Systems are man-created inventions for serving specific human objectives; they are purposeful, deliberate, and rational, and they are also subject to modification so that their value may be increased.

Normative systems can be broadly classified, in terms of their components or entities, as (1) machine to machine, (2) man to machine, and (3) man to man. This study is concerned with the third classification, but the terms "man to man" and "behavioral" systems will be used interchangeably. Meredith Crawford has observed that a football team can be designated a man to man system in which man supplies the power, movement, striking force, information processing, memory and decision making. He further notes that a guided-missile battery consists of machines which perform these same operations.[3]

Thus in a man to man system the "hardware" of the system is man himself. Moreover, by analogy with machine systems, human behavioral systems can be construed as social inventions. Social, economic, and political institutions can be so construed and categorized, as can organizational policies, procedures, or methods. This complex of social innovation and construction, we should remember, is presumed to lead to greater human satisfaction.

Systems are typically represented by flow charts or block diagrams, and the elementary system generally takes the following form:

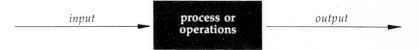

The basic parts of the system, then, are the *input*, the *process* or *operations*, and the *output*.

Inputs have been classified by their relation to the operation of the system. One input is that which actually enters the process, upon which some operation is to be performed, and this input is,

[2] Richard B. Kershner, "A Survey of Systems Engineering Tools and Techniques," *Operations Research and Systems Engineering,* Charles D. Flagle, William H. Huggins, and Robert H. Roy (eds.) (Baltimore: The Johns Hopkins Press, 1960), p. 41.

[3] Meredith Crawford, "Concepts of Training," *Psychological Principles in System Development,* Robert Gagné et al. (eds.) (New York: Holt, Rinehart & Winston, Inc., 1962), pp. 304–305.

16

or will affect, the "load" of the system. A second input is environmental, and this affects the operation of the system.[4] A third input relates to component placement and replacement. Inputs are also classified in terms of their content: material, energy, or information, or any combination of these. In a man to man system the material entering the system is men: a patient admitted to a hospital or a potential customer who enters a marketing system. Law can be viewed as an environmental input in the form of human force, or as a constraint, which may affect, say, the operation of a business system. When human components leave a system, and have to be replaced, the replacement becomes the input.

The second part of the system is the operations, process, or channels through which the inputs must pass. A system must be so arranged that the proper process acts upon each input, at the appropriate time, to achieve the desired output.[5] If the input is a patient in a hospital, this "material" will be passed along a channel from human operator to human operator, and these operators represent the hardware of the system in performing the work or set of acts which has been assigned to them.

In general a set of acts can be said to constitute an operation if each act is necessary for the occurrence of a desired output and if these acts are interdependent.[6]

And Russell Ackoff says:

The acts are interdependent relative to the outcome if the rate of change of any outcome variable affected by change in any variable describing one of the acts depends on (i.e., is a function of) all the other relevant act variables.[7]

The third component of the system is its output, the system's product or accomplishment, and two operational criteria warrant attention here: the stability and the reliability requirements of the system. Requirements imply the performance standards which the system must meet, stability relates to the continuity of output, and reliability refers to the operational consistency of

[4] Harry H. Goode and Robert E. Machol, *System Engineering* (New York: McGraw-Hill Book Company, 1957), p. 99.

[5] *Ibid.,* p. 38.

[6] L. F. Robinson and J. E. Beavers, "A Presentation, Analysis and Evaluation of the Admissions Sub-System at the University of Illinois" (unpublished paper [January, 1965]), pp. 27–28.

[7] R. L. Ackoff, "Systems, Organizations, and Interdisciplinary Research," *Systems: Research and Design,* Donald P. Eckman (ed.) (New York: John Wiley & Sons, Inc., 1961), p. 28.

components, or the error rate. Given various inputs to which the system cannot adjust, the output would be adversely affected.

Systems, as we have seen, can be categorized in terms of their inputs, processes, outputs, and components, and, because the purpose of a management system is to provide solutions to organizational problems, we can represent this process as follows:

organizational problems → management process → organizational solutions

Organizational problems are the inputs into a problem solving process or mechanism that produces organizational solutions as its output. The components that make up our process are usually human components, the submanagers.

The management model that we will develop is essentially "satisficing"; it will produce solutions which will provide an increment in organizational payoff. However, if a manager is aware of all possible alternative solutions to a problem input, and if he can select with certainty the one with the greatest payoff, an optimum solution would be produced.

THE DESIGN PROCESS

Given these characteristics of a management system, what general process should top management employ in designing its system? Let us follow Harry Goode's suggestion that the design process consists of (1) the statement of the problem, (2) the formulation of a model, and (3) the collection and application of data.

In stating the problem one would sketch the proposed system, whether he is starting with an existing system or beginning anew, and generally this means that, from the beginning, we must consider the system's output and payoff. (Payoff is the human utility or satisfaction that will result from the system's operation, or that which the system is to optimize. In a man to man system, payoff is usually described in a cost ratio; for example, an educational system might be measured in terms of its graduates [the output] per cost per student [the organizational resource used to achieve this output]).

Other problem-statement considerations are the description of the environment, the general area of permissible or acceptable solutions, and the measures of effectiveness. Description of the environment means noting the different expected inputs that will enter or affect the system. The area of permissible or acceptable

18

solutions essentially relates to a review of the present technology relative to the system's operation. And the measurement of effectiveness determines how various parts of the system are to be evaluated.

The second step in the design process is the formulation of a model, or the representation of the proposed system, and the key to effective design is the ability to simulate the system. The development of a model serves as a conceptual link between the operation of the system and its environment; it can be a relatively simple flow chart, or a highly sophisticated mathematical model, or something in between.

The block diagram or flow chart, however, is probably the most basic tool in systems design. An initial schematic might reflect the system in considerable detail, including the subsystems that comprise the total system, so that each subsystem could be analyzed for the form of its input, operation, and output. Or a single-thread schematic, depicting the functional specifications of what occurs to a representative input, would be a helpful starting point. Or the schematic could be further reduced to an equipment block diagram which details the operational interrelationships between specific human components and every other component.[8]

The third phase in the design of a management system is simulating the system's operation in order to determine its strengths and shortcomings. With a measure of operating experience, data can be collected which will enable the redesign of the system. For the most part, a constant feedback should exist between the collection and analysis of data and the completeness of the model.

METHOD OF ANALYSIS

Systems analysis will be the methodology utilized in this study, and this means that the system with which one is concerned is broken into increasingly smaller subsystems until one arrives at the system's basic components. Ideally, at this stage one would have a model and would be able "to state exactly what will happen to every possible input at every stage of its passage through the system, or to describe every response which it will evoke in the system."[9] If, in other words, we view the organization as a total operating system, we must also think of it as constituting a

---

[8] Goode and Machol, *op. cit.*, pp. 305–306.
[9] *Ibid.*, p. 305.

series of subsystems; and, to better understand a complete system, systems analysis is the actual procedure that is usually used for subdividing a system into its subparts or subsystems.[10] (Combining the parts into a whole is called systems synthesis.[11])

Therefore, when we turn to the total management system, recall the basic diagram:

and that this system can then be broken into subsystems. Because decision making is specialized on the basis of the specific organizational areas to be managed, we may have sales decision making, production decision making, and personnel decision making, which could be represented as in this parallel diagram:

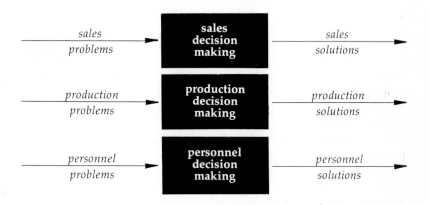

The decision making function can of course be further specialized according to the task to be performed within the decision process itself, and thus we find that an organization may have submanagers who will perform only a segment or minor portion of the decision making function that is necessary for producing a decision.

In this study the decision making process will be broken into a series of sequentially integrated processes, which would be diagrammed as a serial analysis:

[10] Arthur Hall, *A Methodology for Systems Engineering* (Princeton, N.J.: D. Van Nostrand Co., Inc., 1962), p. 346.
[11] *Ibid.*, p. 109.

20

What, then, is the significance of the decision making function in terms of organizational adjustment to the external-internal environment? The answer is simply that an organization must be acutely aware of all environmental changes, must interpret them according to their significance to the organization, and must choose the best reactions for furthering its objectives. In short, it must react effectively to the stimuli of the environment—and not unlike the manner in which an individual responds. If an individual is to achieve his personal goals he will have to adjust successfully to his environment because it is the environment that sustains him, and, unless there is this harmonious, working relationship, his very sustenance will be threatened. The maintenance and increase of food, shelter, recognition, or affection obviously must be acquired from our external environment, the only source.

Changing external events provide stimuli or cues which are perceived by the senses and which are then interpreted; and the individual next selects the appropriate response to these changing external events. A suitable response is that which results in the greatest reward or "payoff" to the individual, and this response can best be explained by the learning process. On the basis of the various rewards which result from the utilization of specific responses to various stimuli, the individual accepts or rejects certain programs of action, and this action usually represents his learned behavior. If, for example, a baby is fed whenever he cries, he will continue to cry whenever he is hungry because he has "learned" that he will be fed.

Organizations can be similarly viewed; all are subject to external inputs and all must depend upon them for their continued well-being, just as consumers provide the income for a business organization. Even organizations which produce and consume their own product or service, and which are relatively self-contained, such as recreational organizations (the country club or bridge club), even these must operate within their environmental constraints.

Therefore, if organizations adjust effectively to their environment, the welfare of the individual contributors will be increased. But if an organization is relatively insensitive to its environment, or unrealistic, or if it responds improperly to changes in its environment, it may become unproductive, or it may fail altogether.

The significant fact here is that the output of any one subprocess becomes the input of the next process. This ability to analyze the total set of inputs and outputs gives systems analysis an integrated characteristic, and the analyst will continue to break each process down until a final set of actions is obtained. Block A can be further divided into:

and block A_1 can then be divided into:

and so forth. Each box represents a set of instructions (to a human operator) that tells how a specific operation is to be executed, given a particular input and an expected output that will result from each operation. The purpose of so close an analysis, given the expected inputs, is to devise a set of operations or instructions which will produce the best—or an improved—output.

In a management system, optional programmed instructions would be provided for the problem-solver. Or, given various inputs, the problem-solver, on his own initiative, can select from a set of alternative instructions the techniques that he will utilize. The detail and the extent of the analysis will depend upon the nature of the output that the designer is receiving. For example, if a management system is expected to produce solutions which attain a specific average value, and if this output is not being obtained, more detailed programming is indicated.

Having a complete model which graphically locates all parts of the system, the designer can then concentrate upon the analysis of even the smallest subparts of the total system and can still maintain the relationship of the parts to the whole. After the process has been analyzed, he could synthesize the system, and it might appear as follows:

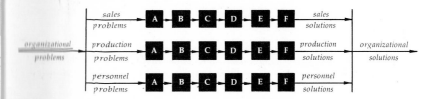

THE NATURE AND PURPOSE OF
ORGANIZED GROUP ACTION

In evaluating the significance of the management system we must necessarily consider the aim of organized group action. Organizations are purposeful systems of cooperation among individuals for increasing personal welfare, and therefore organizational goals should represent the collective welfare of the component individuals. Moreover, if an organization does not accomplish this goal, there is little reason for its existence or for individuals to join it. Organizational goals inhere in the personal objectives of the members,[12] and the advantage of organized group effort is that, collectively, man can accomplish his goals more satisfactorily than he can individually. He has, accordingly, developed cooperative, integrated systems of behavior for performing his activities.

The factors that make group efforts more productive than individual efforts are (1) biological limitations, (2) the advantages in a division of labor, and (3) the growth of modern technology. The individual can see only a limited distance, or lift or push or carry only a limited weight, but he knows that "the organization" can extend his physical capabilities in many and various ways. Individuals, through organization, can also take advantage of specialization. One benefit is that by repeatedly performing uniform tasks a person becomes increasingly adept. Specialization also takes advantage of the distribution of talent that is found in the population, so that an individual can be placed in a job which utilizes his unique aptitudes. Finally, through specialization the individual saves time by not having to move from task to task.

Current technology requires that activities be carried out in an organized group context rather than by an individual. If, for example, we are to utilize the knowledge for producing steel most efficiently, we require a plant organization of many individuals who perform predetermined, interdependent, coordinated, and specialized tasks. When individuals combine their efforts rationally, they find that the productivity per individual is much greater than it would be if each person worked separately.

[12] There are several exceptions to this general rule: prisoners, for example, constitute an involuntary membership, and penal institutions are therefore largely custodial; the welfare of the prisoners may not be an objective of such an organization.

Organizations can therefore be viewed as systems, which, their most general form, appear as follows:

It is also apparent that the individual holds membership in ma organizational systems. The business organization satisfies individual's economic needs, his church membership serves F spiritual needs, government provides for his political needs. A member of the community his social needs are satisfied; as member of a family his needs of affection will be met.

THE REASONS FOR PROBLEM SOLVING

How does the problem solving function arise within the organ zation, or, to rephrase this question upon our welfare premi what can an organization's membership do to maintain a increase its collective welfare? This latter question, it wou seem, involves two subquestions: How can the productivity the group be increased, and how should this increment be d tributed among the membership?

There are many different ways in which an organization c utilize its resources, but all are not equally productive. It mu therefore be determined which process will render the greate unit-productivity and, in turn, most enhance the individu welfare. Since human components can be arranged and c operate in a wide range of patterns, a pattern of human behavi must be developed that will optimize or more closely approa the particular goal, and the extent to which human welfare achieved in the operation of a particular man to man system is, great part, a function of how well that system is designed.

Besides enlarging its welfare, the membership of an organiz tion also wants to maintain this flow. Therefore, because t business organization provides human welfare in a series individual benefits, such as income, interesting work, and sati factory social interaction, and because its collapse would destr this series, the ability of the overall organization to achieve t dual objectives of increased welfare and its continuance will als depend upon its skill in adjusting to the changes in its extern and internal environments.

THE FUNCTION OF DECISION MAKING
IN ORGANIZATIONAL ADJUSTMENT

Again, what role does the decision making function perform? To understand more clearly the mechanics of the adjusting process we can reconsider the individual: when his environment changes he finds that he must devise a new program of action for deriving satisfaction. As he matures over the years, and is faced with new environmental situations, he acquires a diversified set of reactions, which we will call programs. These are stored in his mind, and he will select an applicable program (or response) for a particular situation. This response can become habitual. For example, if cleanliness is an objective, a daily shower might become part of an individual's learned program, and if this program remains satisfactory, he will continue to use it. However, if the plumbing should fail, or if some other change should occur in this environment, the individual is required to devise a new program for achieving the goal of cleanliness.

The same is true for organizations. Programs of organizational behavior are designed to achieve certain ends (within the constraints of an organization's environment), and these programs are effective if these ends are obtained. Whenever comparable situations arise, the programs will be repeated and will become habitual. But there is always the danger that a large organization will be unresponsive; it may be unable to change rapidly, or, for that matter, it may be unable to change at all: although changes occur in the organization's environment, the organization itself may remain static. For example, after the Second World War some major department stores were reluctant to move to the mushrooming suburbs. Another example is General Billy Mitchell's unsuccessful appeals to the military leadership in the 1920's for increasing our air power.

There is thus the possibility that after individuals and organizations have constructed workable programs they will continue to use them even when the programs no longer provide their former results. Similarly, psychologists believe that nonadjusted individuals are relatively insensitive to their environment, either rejecting or projecting properties which do not actually exist. Such individuals tend to respond to their environment negatively, and, as a result, they receive a diminished or unproductive return. Pathologies can as easily develop within an organization if there is a series of improper responses to external stimuli: an organization also can be "rewarded" with negative results.

On another level, the behavior of its participants can be

viewed as the internal environment of an organization. Problems constantly arise that affect the maintenance of every organization, and, if all of its units are to be operational and reasonably coordinated, continuity of resources is required. Machines wear out; materials must be purchased; employees quit, are discharged, retire, or die. These resources must be replaced by units that are equally productive so as to ensure the vitality of the organization, and usually this must be accomplished while the organization continues to produce.

Another internal problem relates to the nature of the cooperation between the organizational participants. One reason why employees quit and why stockholders are reluctant to invest additional savings is that both groups are dissatisfied with the rewards of their participation, and this discontent can become so extensive that it jeopardizes the continuity of an organization. Strikes are socially acceptable only because the conditions of cooperative behavior are thought so important that society allows itself to suffer so that good conditions will eventually be assured.

WHO SOLVES THE PROBLEMS?

We have said that a problem solving function must be performed by an organization. However, in the planning of organizational activities, who will actually perform these duties, and how will this function be structured within the organization? Theoretically, all organizational participants could get together and decide, through a discussion mechanism, how every organizational problem should be solved, but, because of the number of problems, this method would be so inefficient that the participants would spend their time arriving at solutions instead of responding to the environment which provides the payoff.

The advantages of specialization clearly extend to problem solving whenever individuals or groups are specially assigned or delegated the responsibility for performing this function. Such a group, which can concentrate on problem solving and become increasingly adept at it, is called the *management subgroup*. Individual ability can be utilized more efficiently if those who have problem solving skills are assigned to the *decision making function*.

MANAGEMENT AS A FORM OF CONTROL

The management subsystem can be viewed as the basic control component of the organization, and, in this context, the functions of management and control become synonymous. Let us briefly consider the elements of control insofar as organizational behavior is concerned.

26

Control can be defined as a self-regulating or homeostatic mechanism for holding a variable within desired limits.[13] The objective of control is to maintain output, which requires the ability to rearrange resources as conditions change;[14] the control mechanism thus regulates or governs the operating parts of the system.

When the control elements have been added to the basic system, the mechanism can be represented as follows:[15]

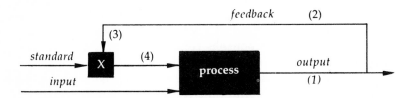

There are four control elements: the output to be measured (1), a sensory device (2) that will measure this output and feed this information back (3) to a control unit, X, which will compare the actual and the expected (or standard) output; if the deviation is too wide, an activating mechanism (4) will change the operating system.[16] The self-regulating feature is that the system continues to operate until the standard and actual outputs are about equal.

Given the foregoing general model, the management system — as the control component of the organization — can be represented as follows:

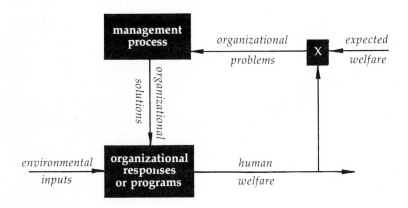

[13] Stafford Beer, *Cybernetics and Management* (New York: John Wiley & Sons, Inc., 1959), pp. 22–23.
[14] Johnson *et al., op. cit.,* pp. 102–103.
[15] David O. Ellis and Fred J. Ludwig, *Systems Philosophy: An Introduction* (Englewood Cliffs, N.J.: Prentice-Hall, Inc., 1962), p. 83.
[16] Johnson *et al., op. cit.,* p. 58.

The organization will respond to given changes in environmental events (or inputs) and will produce a specific amount of welfare for its membership (the output). For particular events and responses, the expected amount of welfare that will be produced is based either on past experience or on previous solutions. The actual and the expected amount of welfare is compared at X, and, if the amounts are unequal, an organizational problem will be triggered and fed into the management process. The management process will formulate a correct solution, which will be fed into the system as input to become part of the set of organizational responses. If the new response is correct in terms of the environmental event, the actual welfare produced will be equal to the expected welfare because the management subsystem contains all the elements needed to control the rest of the organization.

The management segment gives the organization an adaptive and learning capability, and learning capability is the ability to devise new programs for responding to new environmental inputs.[17] The management segment is the organization's self-regulating, homeostatic feature, and, presumably, organizational problems will be fed into the management system until a satisfactory amount of welfare is produced. The organization is a relatively closed system in the sense that problems will continue to rotate until a solution is found.

SEQUENTIAL INTEGRATION OF SUBSYSTEMS

How is the operation of the decision making subsystem integrated with the operation of other organizational subsystems, and how are their efforts coordinated? Observation of the work of organizations shows us that every function is a special activity but that all are usually sequentially integrated.

In the sales function, for example, orders are obtained through sales efforts and are then passed on to the production operation, which produces the specified quantity of goods or services. After production is completed, a shipping or traffic department moves the goods to the customers.

The sales department activity terminated with the production department's receipt of the sales order: where one function stopped, another began; and the work was integrated by means of appropriate communication devices, such as multiple copies of the sales order.

[17] See John G. Truxal, "Concept of Adaptive Control," *Adaptive Control Systems,* Eli Mishkin and Ludwig Braun, Jr. (eds.) (New York: McGraw-Hill Book Company, 1961), pp. 1–19.

28

In a similar way the decision making subsystem is related to the other functions of an organization. The purpose of the decision making subsystem is to produce programs in the form of suitable organizational action, programs which will take the form of policies, procedures, standards, and instructions for the behavior of nondecision-makers under varying conditions. Thus at any given time an inventory of solutions (or programs) will exist, and, given a particular situation, the employee will be expected to draw the proper solution from this inventory. Therefore, if all the programs devised by management are workable and acceptable, management's real job is to revise or construct an inventory of solutions for events that continually recur in the organization's internal and external environments. Once it has done this, management will have completed its tasks, and it will then be the responsibility of the employee to apply these programs correctly.

In short, because it will have formulated applicable solutions for recurring events or sets of circumstances, it is not necessary for management to provide a new solution every time an event arises. For example, if 8:00 A.M. has been designated as a company's starting time, this "event" becomes a daily situation for all employees, and, insofar as they understand and accept this "solution," employees will be at work every morning at eight.

Solutions can be classified by their frequency of use; some are used every day, some only occasionally, and some are never used. For example, management may have decided that the organization should be prepared for fire, war, and earthquakes. Still another event might arise—which management had *not* preprogrammed—that also requires action. Management must then devise new solutions; or, if management sees no need for a change, employees will continue to be guided by the established inventory of procedures and policies. Under the latter alternative, the work of the organization will continue with each operating unit performing its tasks in the usual way.

CHANGING THE PATTERN

When management decides to change the behavioral pattern of its organizational resources it intervenes more actively in the functioning process of an operating unit; and, in such a case, management changes its inventory by devising a solution that is more effective than the present one. Employees will perform a particular duty in the new manner, not in the old. Only after management has implemented the new solution—by having employees learn and apply it—can the relationship between

29

managerial activity and nonmanagerial activity be seen, for it is at this point that the decision making and "nondecision making" functions are connected.

Management of course checks at intervals to see that operating units are functioning in accord with the stock of solutions. Ideally, this inventory of managerial solutions is stored in the memories of the operating employees, as well as in the memories of first-line supervisors, but, on the practical level, operating manuals or files that contain the written policies, procedures, standards, or blueprints are also made available.

An inventory of solutions is accumulated gradually. When a new situation arises, management contrives an effective solution, which is carried out by the employees; then it goes on to the next situation, and thus compiles a stock of solutions. Each solution becomes operational and remains in effect as long as management believes it is the optimum solution.

Some solutions may have been established at the very inception of the business; indeed, an organization may "point with pride" to such policies. For example, a department store may have begun by catering to a certain clientele and may have continued this practice down to the present. A billing procedure might be twenty years old, a hiring procedure fifteen years old, and so forth. Even though such decisions may have been reached fifty (or more) years ago, they remain unchanged and operational because the employees understand and follow them as their behavioral guides. New employees will do the same. The stability and continuity of the organization essentially rests on this repository of past solutions.

However, employees have the problem of selecting the appropriate solution for a particular situation. A set of circumstances will occur, and the employee will review the collection of policies — either from memory or in the company manual — and will select the solution which is applicable to the situation. If all the solutions are numbered according to specific events, the suitable solution can be chosen practically by number. For example, in the event of fire, solution 43 would be selected; if the workload of a production unit expands, solution 93 would be applied; or solution 47 if an employee should quit.

There is no question that selection of the right solution is an act of judgment, but should this act of judgment be included in the duties of the manager? A highly experienced foreman might know all the rules and regulations that apply to his unit of operation, and always be able to respond appropriately, but this activity is not organizational *decision making* insofar as our analysis is concerned; it is *decision-utilization*. The decisions had already been made, and the foreman merely applies them. Needless to say, however, effective decision making will depend upon effective decision utilization.

DECISION MAKING VERSUS DECISION UTILIZATION

There is, as we have indicated, a tendency to confuse decision *making* with decision *using*. However, if the former process is carried out properly, the employee eventually learns all of the operating procedures, because the stock of solutions will have been transmitted from the manager to the employee; and, under these circumstances, there is no longer any need for a foreman to act as a repository of operating solutions. It is therefore important that individuals assigned the activity of decision making fully understand the difference between decision making and decision application.[18]

If a first-line supervisor views his job solely in terms of (1) selecting appropriate solutions for a given situation, (2) instructing an employee in the nature of the solution, or (3) observing the employee to see that he selects the appropriate solution, he is not really performing his managerial job because he is not devoting his time and energy to the formulation of new solutions as they are needed. It is also possible, of course, that he is not prepared to provide a new and needed solution because he simply may not have the capability for solving the problem, being unable to handle a situation for which a solution has not already been constructed.

THE 10-STEP DECISION MAKING PROCESS

Organizational decision making entails the performance, in a sequential pattern, of a series of steps or activities that will produce an effective organizational solution. This sequence can be represented by ten steps — an arbitrary representation — which we shall follow in this text for illustrative purposes. As we have noted, systems analysis is a process of successive breakdowns into smaller subprocesses. How this is done — for example, the number or classifications of breakdowns — is largely at the discretion of the designer. One designer may find it convenient to have five

[18] The difference between decision making (or construction) and decision utilization is sometimes referred to as programmed versus nonprogrammed decision making. See Herbert A. Simon, *The New Science of Management Decision* (New York: Harper & Row, 1960), pp. 4–5.

major decision making processes, while another prefers fifteen. The author has found it convenient to use ten subprocesses, but it must be emphasized that they do not represent fixed "rules" or principles—they merely assist in the design.[19] These steps will be treated in greater detail later, but they are listed here in order to show the distinguishing characteristics of organizational decision making:

1. Organizational objectives must be defined (Chapter 4).
2. Someone must raise the problem of how these goals can be achieved (Chapter 5).
3. The nature of the problem must be investigated (Chapter 5).
4. There should be a search for alternative solutions (Chapter 5).
5. After full evaluation, the best alternative is selected (Chapter 5).
6. Organizational consensus must be achieved (Chapter 6).
7. The solution must be authorized (Chapter 7).
8. The solution must be implemented (Chapter 7).
9. Nondecision-makers must be instructed in the use of the decision (Chapter 7).
10. An audit must be conducted for evaluating the effectiveness of the decision (Chapter 7).

There is no widespread agreement upon which set of activities constitutes the actual decision making process. One reason is that the particular circumstances differ, so that various aspects of a process receive varying emphases. Organizational and individual decision making, for example, have dissimilar characteristics.

We will view decision making as synonymous with problem solving, and a decision will be viewed as an effective response which provides a desired result to a present or possible organizational state or states. Our approach will entail not only the necessity for optimum selection (step 5) but also the effectiveness of the solution (step 10). We will also stress step 3, that part of the process concerned with structuring the problem so that a rational choice of action can be made.

CHARACTERISTICS OF ORGANIZATIONAL DECISION MAKING

In organizational decision making a manager specializes in the class of organizational problems which he works upon—sales,

---

[19] See Chapter 9 for design consequences.

personnel, production, credit, finance, etc. — and specialization requires each manager to have technical competence for working with the problems which may arise in his special area. The sales manager, for example, must know the types of problems that may arise, and their nature and causes: pricing a product, selection of salesmen, consumer motivation, and consumer behavior; and he must also be familiar with the solutions that are applied in his field. However, although each manager needs a particular technical background, the duties each must perform in solving his specialized problems are similar from manager to manager. Devising an effective organizational solution in sales necessitates the same action that is needed for solving production problems.

There are those who assume that, because the nature of organizational problems varies from area to area, the method of problem solving will also vary. For example (according to this assumption), because a personnel problem involves people, it would therefore be handled differently from a problem in product development or research: the handling of psychological problems is assumed to be essentially different from handling problems in physics, electronics, or chemistry. But an examination of the process by which all problems are solved reveals that the same essential steps toward solution are followed, and in the same order.

In the case of product development in the chemical area, the researcher must first determine the problem upon which he will work, then investigate it to ascertain its causal relationships, and then search for and select the solution that will achieve the desired results. Next, he must establish an organizational consensus of the product's feasibility, and have his solution authorized, and then have the solution implemented in terms of the new product's manufacture or sale.

The personnel director must also determine his problem, then define it in terms of its causal relationship, review alternative solutions, select the best solution, and so on, following the same fundamental pattern as the chemist even though different techniques would be required for some of the steps in each decision making process.

When the chemist determines causal relationships he might employ a controlled experiment in a laboratory setting, whereas the personnel director, in the same step, might use the nondirective interview to find out why employees behave as they do. However, on the assumption that an effective organizational solution is desired regardless of the nature of the problem, the problem-solvers will have to perform the same overall activities;

both will proceed through the same steps, and in the same sequence.

THE DIFFERENCE BETWEEN INDIVIDUAL AND ORGANIZATIONAL DECISION MAKING

Organizational decision making, because it is a group phenomenon, differs in important respects from individual decision making; its sharpest focus is upon how a group collectively solves its problems. Managerial action is the most significant part of the former process because it is the *instrumentality* through which the organizational participants solve their problems. It is the organization, not the manager, which must adjust and react appropriately to the environment. It is not the manager who optimizes, it is all the participants of the organization. However, if one concentrates exclusively on the work of the individual manager, he may therefore—erroneously—view organizational decision making as an individual rather than a group process.

Some phases of organizational decision making are *similar* to those of individual decision making: an organization is a single entity, faced with a problem, and a solution must be provided and then acted upon to attain group goals. But organizational decision making is unlike individual decision making in that there is a combination of efforts: the managers select a course of action for the group as a whole, and consensus or agreement is required if the action or solution is to be effectuated.

The extent of agreement that exists at any time can be ascertained by noting the degree to which the employee or nondeciders' actions conform to the manager's solution.

Ideally, nondecision-makers will act in accordance with the solutions of the decision-makers; however, when they do not, the *actual* selection of the solution is made by the employee instead of by the manager, and this, in fact, is how every problem is ultimately solved. For example, if management's stipulated solution is that work will start at 8:00 A.M., and if the employees do not begin work until 8:15 A.M., the actual solution to this problem is 8:15 A.M. A solution that is nonoperational is academic, or *no* solution. Hence, to examine how an organization solves certain problems, we need but observe the behavior of its employees.

It is sometimes assumed that the decision making activities of management relate to the selection of a new line of action, that once this line has been selected a decision has been produced, and that employee conformity comes under another, and distinct, aspect of managerial duties. Employee conformity is not thought to be part of the decision making process because the solutions have already been formulated. We must insist, however, that employee conformity to managerial directions is actually part of the decision making process. To choose or decide the proper mode of behavior for someone else is meaningless if the other party does not accept this choice or decision. And it is the failure or inability to distinguish between organizational and individual decision making that produces this common ambiguity.

We usually assume that when an individual makes a decision that affects his own behavior he will automatically adhere to it, that his selection and action, in a sense, are simultaneous. However, if by decision we mean *solution*, and not merely *selection*, an effective decision (in an organizational context) requires the cooperation of both the decision-makers and the nondecision-makers. Everyone in the organization is involved in the decision making process, at least to the extent of cooperating with the directions of the manager, but the decision-maker can be distinguished from the nondecision-maker in that the former devotes his entire efforts to devising effective solutions while the latter's activities are limited to effectuating the manager's solutions.

Another difference between individual and organizational decision making is in the objectives of the decision. In individual decision making we assume that an individual is attempting to enhance his personal well-being without considering the welfare of others, whereas organizational decision making is concerned with the collective welfare of all organizational participants. Even though certain individuals have been assigned the duty of solving group problems, all organizational participants may be adversely affected if these problems are not solved. Organizational problems are concerned with gaining *organizational* ends.

A further difference between organizational and individual decision making is that an organization usually has more than one decision-maker. Furthermore, the decision making activities of all managers or decision-makers must be coordinated so that their efforts will be optimized. Thus an integrating machinery is necessary for achieving this goal. It is this extension, both in the number and in the specialization of decision-makers, that introduces a new organizational function, managing the managers, and *this* is top management's task.

GROUP DECISION MAKING

The system for solving a group problem may at times be a frustrating experience for the individuals involved. The presence of committees, the need to "sell" one's proposals, and the time expended in obtaining the organization's reaction to a common problem make one yearn for the simplicity and rapidity of individual decision making, of one individual reaching his own decision and acting accordingly. However, if we want the benefits of collective action, we must accept the concomitant system. Nor will the efficiency of group decision making be improved by attempting to structure it along individual lines; decision making systems must be designed in relation to the inherent characteristics of the group.

Another characteristic of organizational decision making is that solutions typically relate to action or behavior, whether physical or mental; those who participate in group activities are going "to do something" to achieve organizational ends. (Problems of a philosophical nature are not particularly germane to an organization.) Group solutions therefore require individuals to change the pattern of their behavior, either to cease a current activity or to engage in a new one; and decision making relates largely to changing the behavioral patterns of individuals or to changing the interaction between them.

EVALUATION OF THE DECISION MAKING FUNCTION

Although each function of the organization has its particular outputs, these functions are meaningful only when they are coordinated to attain the comprehensive goals of the organization. However, when we attempt to evaluate the performance of any one function, we must do so in relation to the activities which have been assigned to it, and this will assure that the individuals who are participating in a given activity correctly carry out their duties. Consequently, the effectiveness of the sales division would be measured largely in terms of the sales it is able to obtain, and the personnel department might be measured according to the cooperativeness of the employees. In similar fashion, decision making should be measured only in terms of its production of effective decisions.

Traditionally, managerial performance was measured only in relation to particular organizational functions: increasing sales would be attributed (for the most part) to the manner in which sales managers were performing their decision making function. If we applied this logic to all organizational activities, we could assume that all employees were functioning properly if an organization or business were receiving adequate profits.

However, some units of the organization may be conducted

inefficiently, which means that profits could be even better; therefore, to get a real measure of departmental efficiency, we must gauge each department by an index that is proper to it. Secondly, if we view the decision making function as a unique entity within the organization, we will measure its performance by the products it turns out, its decisions. One reason for making and stressing this distinction is that when performance is less than adequate, and one wants to establish the cause, it is good management practice to evaluate individuals in terms of their assigned duties so that responsibilities can be better defined.

INTERPRETING THE TASKS OF SUBMANAGEMENT

The tasks of submanagement are often considered from several viewpoints. A common approach is to consider management as performing the subfunctions of planning, organizing, controlling, directing, motivating, and staffing the resources of organization: labor and capital. Our approach, however, designates only one submanagement function: organizational problem solving (which is our way of classifying these activities). Planning requires the definition of an objective, as well as searching for and evaluating alternative means to that objective. Organizing and staffing is the implementation of the selected means. Motivating is the agreement or acceptance by agents that they will effectuate the means. Controlling is the auditing of the activity so as to assure its compliance with the plan.

We should consider submanagement's actions as the integrated substeps of the single function of organizational problem solving, rather than as a series of separate functions. The objective of the managerial function is more easily understood if we first accept its purpose of producing effective organizational decisions, and then we should ask what equivalent activity the individual or group would have to perform to achieve the same result. We can also break the total activity of problem solving into its component subfunctions, then reintegrate them systematically and determine the relationships between them. This approach is similar to the analysis of any job that is performed in an organization; the analyst usually starts with the end purpose and backtracks to find the best way of producing the output. If we postulate a personnel recruiter's job as the acquisition of qualified and cooperative employees for his firm, we can determine the specific steps he should perform to accomplish this end.

If, however, we consider the manager as performing a series of separate subtasks, it is difficult to ascertain an end unit of output that can be backtracked for evaluating the process. And if we say that planning, organizing, and control are really substeps toward the solution of an organizational problem, it means that each substep must be performed for every problem to obtain the desirable end product of an effective solution.

If, as in the first condition, the submanagement position is viewed as a series of distinct operational functions, the manager may not integrate them in a systematic way; he may not go through all the steps necessary for getting an effective solution. If he should view part of his job as planning, and attempt to set about it—either in the absence of a specific problem or without the subsequent steps in the problem solving situation—his efforts will be meaningless.

Another difficulty in thinking of management subfunctions as separate actions is that there is no agreement among authorities about the nature of the subfunctions. One expert may say that staffing is a managerial function while another will say it is not. With such nonconcurrence, the job of management would seem to be somewhat confusing; but if we maintain that the job of management is problem solving, we can sharpen our focus upon its essential aspects.

We can also postulate that problem solving, by and large, is the one and essential task of management because the very environment of the decision-maker is obviously problem-oriented. In the daily operation of his unit, problems are presented for which he must find an effective solution—and in doing this he will have to perform the specific steps of planning, organizing, and control—but his attention will be primarily directed to the problem and its solution. The managerial role is not composed of specific, separate functions in which part of the day is devoted to planning how a unit will operate, another part spent on organizing, another part taken up with control, and so forth. A manager does not function in this manner; he must constantly grapple with problems at hand.

MANAGERIAL QUALIFICATIONS

The final reason for stressing the problem solving aspects of the managerial job is that it permits a better determination of the qualifications an individual should have in order to be able to carry out this duty. Because problem solving is an intellectual task, a potential manager should have analytical skill. And he must be not only highly intelligent, he must also be able to reason effectively, because organizational problems are complex.

Individuals may have analytical skill in solving problems that are not directly related to the organization, such as social or scientific problems, but the individual best suited for the organization is one whose problem solving ability shows a high correlation with the organizational problems of business. Research findings indicate that, on the top management level, problem solving ability is unusually high. Hence, with concentration on this single aspect of the managerial role, the selection and training of managers would be significantly facilitated.

One incidental result of examining subparts as separate entities of the submanagerial job is that the qualities we tend to look for are so numerous that they do not seem to fit together. We say that managers should be able to think clearly, to get along with others, that they should possess leadership traits, initiative, insight, and so on; but the difficulty in stating the *specific* qualifications a manager should have comes from the fact that the essence of the managerial job is not strictly defined. However, if the problem solving aspect is emphasized, and if an individual has this to a high degree, employers might be willing to forgo other desirable traits, which—though they might facilitate one's performance—are not absolutely essential in performing managerial duties.

MANAGEMENT AS AN ENGINEERING SCIENCE

Management, as a field of study, is in a state of flux, and there are many different concepts about the essential nature of this discipline. Indeed, the management—or submanagement—function has been viewed along the entire art-science continuum. Because of this unsettled issue, but without attempting to resolve it, the point of view of this study should be made explicit. The author's view, and the approach taken in this study, is that submanagement lies somewhere between the extremes: it is partially a science and partially an art—or an "engineering science." Although there is a belief that organizational decision making may eventually become a science, there is reason to question this if one keeps in mind the traditional construct of a pure science.

Submanagement is an applied science. Unlike pure science, the objective of submanagement is normative in nature because it is directed toward the achievement of organizational ends; on the other hand, the objective of pure science is to discover new truths.

There are also differences in methodology between pure and applied sciences. Primary emphasis in the pure sciences is directed toward finding causal relationships, and its method attempts to isolate the effect of one variable upon another. To accomplish this it is necessary to hold all variables constant while permitting one variable to change, so as to measure its effect on another. The laboratory, in this context, is the ideal environment because complete control can be achieved.

The endeavor to isolate significant causal relationships led to the development of our academic disciplines. The physical, social, and life sciences specialize in different phenomena, which can be broken down into subseries of areas of investigation. These areas provide the investigator with the opportunity for exploring increasingly narrow phases of action so as to discover more precise relationships between phenomena.

The applied scientist must also deal with causal relationships, but—unlike the pure scientist—his analysis must include all of the situational variables which may affect the outcome with which he is concerned. He does not move toward increased isolation, he attempts to incorporate all possible determinants into his analysis. If a manager is faced with the problem of decreasing sales, he must come to grips with all the possibilities which may be causing this event. Quite obviously, many of these may extend into the traditional disciplines, some of the reasons being psychological, economic, sociological, or physical—and this is of course equally true in the product development area, etc. Hence, in the design of a complex weapons system, one would have to cross and incorporate analyses from many physical disciplines.

In the pure sciences, the phenomenon which is to be analyzed can often be determined by the investigator, and according to his special interest. In the applied sciences, the phenomenon to be worked on is determined by the organizational objectives, and there is the additional task of attempting to exercise some form of control while endeavoring to *change* the variables in order to derive better results. The purpose of an applied science is not the creation of knowledge *per se* but the control of behavioral or physical phenomena as they relate to certain *a priori* welfare objectives.

The pure and the applied sciences are similar, however, in that both require intellectual discipline. Given all the variables in a situation, engineers desire measurable and predictable results; they want to know that predictable results will proceed from certain actions. On the basis of their analyses a fund of usable knowledge is established, or constructed, which can be transmitted to other engineers (who are faced with similar situations), and the latter can take identical actions with the certainty of obtaining the same results. With such knowledge, then, personal opinion does not determine a given situation: results are objective, impersonal, and capable of reproduction. Building a bridge properly does not depend upon personal opinions but upon a specific body of knowledge. The engineer who is knowledgeable in his field can apply this information or he can create new knowledge through systematic analysis.

Engineering is often an art form because the problem with which the engineer is concerned is often unique, and the ingenuity with which he applies his knowledge may depend upon his individual ability. Thus in the construction of a bridge, because all bridges need not have the same requirements or specifications, the engineer must select from his accumulation of knowledge those techniques that will best apply to the project upon which he is working.

At the other end of the continuum, where management is viewed as an art form, its practice and productivity are seen as a function of the talent and creativity of the individual manager. Although rules of the craft may exist, the individual is held to be free in his use of these principles. A mystique generally attaches to the individual, and particularly when he produces incontrovertibly good results. However, he is often unable to explain how he caused these results and unable to transfer this information to others.

According to this latter view, individual talent is the crucial determinant of the effectiveness of the output. Each manager goes about his tasks individually, and his output generally bears his unique characteristic. If submanagement is viewed as an art, each decision becomes the expression or product of an artist. But the growth and maturity of an artist are functions of practice— the painter paints and the musician plays in order to develop his inherent talent. Considerable evidence indicates that the discipline of management is moving away from an art form to an engineering science. Primary emphasis is being placed on technology, rather than on the unique talents of the practitioner, as the source of increased effectiveness.

SUMMARY

A management system is a normative man to man construct whose primary purpose is the production of effective solutions for organizational problems. In order to design this decision system, top management must (1) formulate the general parts of the system, (2) construct a model, and (3) collect and apply data that pertain to the system's operational effectiveness. Systems analysis is a process of subdivision and the establishment of progressively smaller subparts of the system; systems synthesis is a process of regrouping.

Organizations can be regarded as purposeful systems of cooperation among individuals for increasing individual welfare. The problem solving function is needed within organizations because (1) questions arise over how to utilize organizational resources and how to distribute aggregate welfare among members (see Chapter 4, Organizational Objectives) and (2) because organizations must adjust to their environments and new programs of action must be devised.

The management system is integrated with the rest of the organization by providing an inventory of solutions which non-decision-makers will draw upon when corresponding situations take place. Organizational decision making, unlike individual decision making, is a group phenomenon which requires group agreement and adjustment. Management, as a field of study, can be thought of as an engineering science.

QUESTIONS FOR DISCUSSION

1. What are the characteristics of a behavioral system?
2. It is frequently alleged that the invention of social or man to man systems has not kept pace with the invention of machine systems. How do you account for this difference?
3. Is it possible to have nonpurposeful, irrational organizations? Give examples. Would a mob be such an example, or a criminal gang?
4. What are the characteristics of a management system?
5. It has been suggested that the organizational adjustment to environment is a more difficult process than individual adjustment. Give some reasons why this may be so.
6. Although the management subsystem gives the organization an adaptive, self-regulatory capability, is it still possible for an organization to fail? In what manner could such failure be attributed to the control mechanism of the organization?
7. Is it possible for an organization to have no managers? Would a college fraternity be an example? A street gang? If there are no managers, how does the group solve its problems?
8. Where is the inventory of solutions usually stored in an organization?
9. The ultimate test of an organizational solution is whether it increases human welfare, but the solution to a mathematical prob-

lem is the right answer. Contrast these two problem solving situations.

10. What are the differences between an art, a pure science, and applied science?

SUGGESTED READINGS

ECKMAN, DONALD P. (ed.). *Systems: Research and Design.* New York: John Wiley & Sons, Inc., 1961.

GAGNÉ, ROBERT, *et al.* (eds.). *Psychological Principles in System Development.* New York: Holt, Rinehart & Winston, 1962.

GOODE, HARRY H., and MACHOL, ROBERT E. *System Engineering.* New York: McGraw-Hill Book Company, 1957.

HAIMANN, THEO. *Professional Management: Theory and Practice.* Boston: Houghton Mifflin Company, 1962.

HALL, ARTHUR. *A Methodology for Systems Engineering.* Princeton, N.J.: D. Van Nostrand Co., Inc., 1962.

JOHNSON, RICHARD; KAST, FREMONT; and ROSENZWEIG, JAMES. *The Theory and Management of Systems.* New York: McGraw-Hill Book Company, 1963.

YOUNG, STANLEY. "Designing a Behavioral System," *Academy of Management Proceedings, 1963* (pp. 76–83).

PART TWO

AN
ORGANIZATIONAL
DECISION MAKING
MODEL

3

DESIGNING
A MANAGEMENT
SYSTEM

To design a management system, top management must first design a detailed plan of the process by which organizational decisions will be made, stipulating what will be done, who will do it, and where and how it will be accomplished. In addition, the entire decision making procedure must be integrated into a single operating system. As we have noted, systems design construction may be executed by synthesis or by analysis, but the approach we have used is the analytical (or progressive) breakdown of the total system into increasingly smaller subparts. Indeed, as Arthur Hall observes: "A complete diagram of a system, even a simple one, is generally too detailed for direct analysis. The common procedure for analysis is to break down the complete system into individual blocks."[1]

This chapter will thus describe the management system only in terms of the relationships between its subprocesses; in other words, at this initial stage we will try to gain an overview of the total system. An explanation of the system's rationale will follow in Chapters 4 through 7, which will analyze each subprocess by breaking it down into its respective subprocesses. Once this is accomplished, we can decide who will effectuate the system (see Chapter 10, Installation, Operation, and Maintenance of the System). The "when," "how," or "what" decision making tasks that a particular submanager will perform all relate to the component specifications, such as the number of managers required, their capabilities, skills, and training, their degree of

[1] Arthur Hall, *A Methodology for Systems Engineering* (Princeton, N.J.: D. Van Nostrand Co., Inc., 1962), p. 346.

specialization in the system, and so on; but these questions can be answered only after the decision making operation has been blocked out. At this point in our analysis we need only indicate that the basic hardware of the system is comprised of men or of managerial components: the submanagerial group.

Also, to avoid confusion, it should be noted that the model which we will now analyze in detail (in Chapters 3 through 7) is only a suggested design, and that it is utilized for the purposes of (1) indicating the nature of a management system and (2) illustrating the design of a management system. Although the author believes the proposed model is a good one, it is not the only possible design; and the reader should eventually be able to design an alternative model which may more adequately fit certain organizations, or he should be able to incorporate alternative features into his design which may be more effective. The objective of the text, then, is to provide a conceptual framework which the individual can use in systems design.

In the analysis of our model, comparisons will occasionally be drawn between the proposed model and managerial practices that exist in various organizations, and these comparisons should illustrate the capability of the systems approach. Also, given various managerial problems, we should be able to design a managerial subprocess that will effectively cope with them.

Figure 3–1 (pages 48–49) is a schematic that illustrates a total management system and the channels through which each problem will flow. (Step 1, defining organizational objectives, has been omitted for obvious reasons.) The nine subprocesses of the system are numbered at the top of the schematic, as (3) for problem investigation. This is a ten-man management system: three in production, two in sales, and one each in personnel, finance, purchasing, engineering, and production control.

Operations is the set of activities that will be carried out by nondecision-makers in the areas noted, such as production or sales, and these are the areas to which solutions will be applied.

The system is conceptually integrated through an information flow network; if a solution proves unsatisfactory, the problem is fed back to the control unit, which will repeat the process. The system is partially closed.

A management system can be visualized as a work process which manufactures or constructs organizational solutions, and the design of this work process is not unlike that in other organizational subsystems. All organizational problems will flow through a predetermined course, with the manager performing only those problem solving tasks that are assigned to him. This

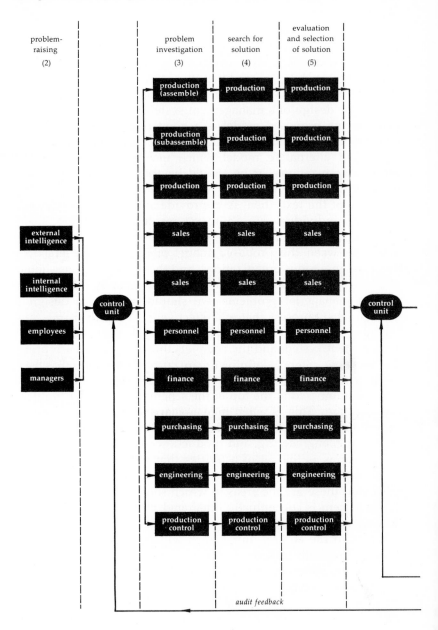

Figure 3-1
A MANAGEMENT SYSTEM
(Step 1, Defining Organizational Objectives, is not shown.)

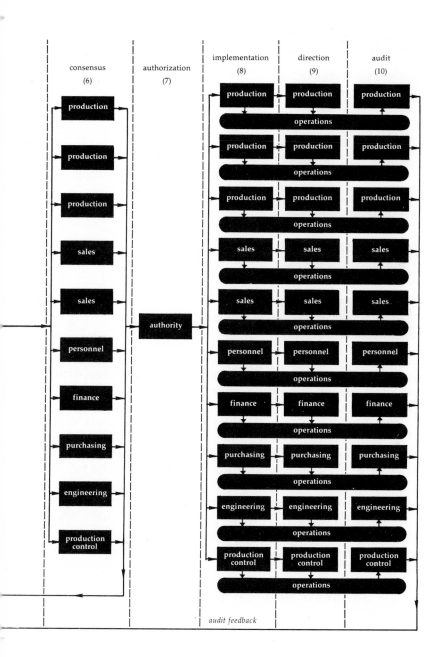

49

Figure 3–2
PROBLEM-RAISING SUBSYSTEM   (Step 2)

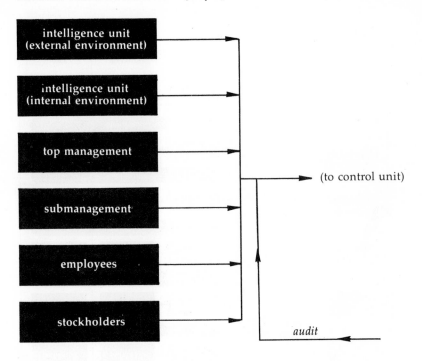

does not mean, however, that every problem will necessarily be solved in exactly the same manner; problems may require distinct treatments. And there need not be a single process; an organization may plan many different processes by which problems will be solved. It is essential, however, that these processes be preplanned, so that once it is decided which process will be used for a given problem that process will actually be followed.

The criteria to be used in evaluating a management system will be explored in greater detail in Chapter 9 (Selecting the Management System); however, it should be kept in mind that when top management initially designs a system the organizational goals it wants to achieve will be the same as the goals for the other subsystems of the organization, such as marketing or production.[2]

PROBLEM-RAISING MACHINERY (STEP 2)

To demonstrate how the system will function, we will briefly describe each subprocess (again, the first step, defining organi-

---

[2] See Chapter 2, The Management System and the Meaning of Organization.

zational objectives, is not shown on the schematic). Step 2 (see Figure 3–2) is problem-raising, which provides the input for the system. Organizational problems can be raised directly by top management, submanagers, employees, and stockholders. Both top and lower management should be able to raise questions; ideally, however, one wants to utilize as many question-sources as possible, which would include the stockholders and employees, for with this large number of problem-contributors a greater involvement in the organization is achieved.

In addition, the organization would establish an intelligence unit, composed of more components, which would be the primary source of problems; and Figure 3–3 indicates the nature of this operation. Data are collected from the internal and external environments, and are classified and arranged; then, in terms of predetermined standards of organizational performance, a comparison is made. If standards are being attained, there is no problem; if deviations are taking place, the nature of the deviation is stated as a problem which must be solved.

The intelligence unit gathers information about specific environments, such as the economy, the government, and so on. Critical external variables are isolated, and crucial publics, such as consumers and suppliers, might be surveyed. A schedule

Figure 3–3
INTELLIGENCE UNIT   (Step 2)

(External and Internal Environment)

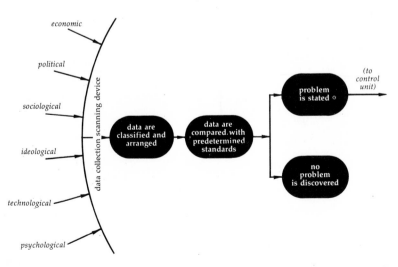

Figure 3–4

PROBLEM-RAISING SOURCES (Step 2)
(Small General Hospital)

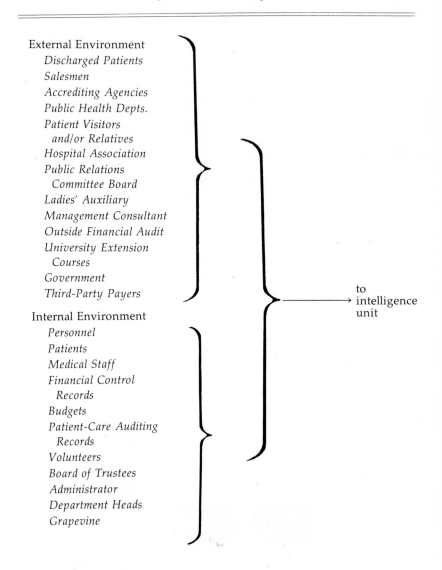

External Environment
   Discharged Patients
   Salesmen
   Accrediting Agencies
   Public Health Depts.
   Patient Visitors
      and/or Relatives
   Hospital Association
   Public Relations
      Committee Board
   Ladies' Auxiliary
   Management Consultant
   Outside Financial Audit
   University Extension
      Courses
   Government
   Third-Party Payers

Internal Environment
   Personnel
   Patients
   Medical Staff
   Financial Control
      Records
   Budgets
   Patient-Care Auditing
      Records
   Volunteers
   Board of Trustees
   Administrator
   Department Heads
   Grapevine

to
intelligence
unit

determines the frequency with which this unit gathers its information; for example, it might be decided to survey consumers semiannually and employees and suppliers annually. Secondary information, from trade associations, the government, banks, and others, would presumably flow in automatically.

The intelligence unit could be centralized so that it is responsible for scanning both the external and internal environments of the organization; or it could be decentralized, and each operating unit would gather information that was critical for its own operation. A mixed unit could also be established which would gather only certain information at a central point, all other data being decentralized. The technological environment, for example, might be surveyed on a decentralized basis.

To illustrate how the problem-raising step can be designed for more than one organization, the following real-world examples should prove helpful. Figure 3–4 refers to a small general hospital and shows the sources for raising problems and gathering information.

Figure 3–5 is the problem-raising schema of a defense manufacturer's structures engineering division.

To facilitate the decision making process, various forms and records must be designed, and this introduces consideration of

Figure 3–5
STRUCTURES ENGINEERING PROBLEM-RAISING (STEP 2)

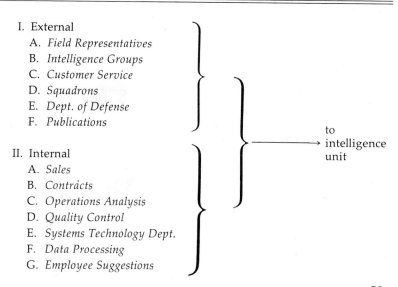

I. External
  A. *Field Representatives*
  B. *Intelligence Groups*
  C. *Customer Service*
  D. *Squadrons*
  E. *Dept. of Defense*
  F. *Publications*

to intelligence unit

II. Internal
  A. *Sales*
  B. *Contracts*
  C. *Operations Analysis*
  D. *Quality Control*
  E. *Systems Technology Dept.*
  F. *Data Processing*
  G. *Employee Suggestions*

the appropriate paper flow. The design of a problem-raising form can be very advantageous because it facilitates the transfer of problems within the organization (see Figure 3–6). It will be noted that this hospital form provides the opportunity for a problem-raiser—identified by name, department, and position—to state his problem, the incidents that surround the problem, the reason he raised the problem, and what he would like to see accomplished. Problem-raising forms can be distributed to all units of operation, to the board of directors, and so on. Individuals would have the form available whenever a problem situation is believed to exist.

The next problem-raising form (Exhibit 3–1, pages 56–57) is used by a large manufacturing firm and it relates primarily to quality control problems. Figure 3–7 (page 58) is a solution requisition, another suggested form.

DECISION MAKING CONTROL UNIT

The need for integrating and coordinating decision making activities has already been discussed, but there is a primary organizational device for accomplishing this goal, which we shall designate the decision making control unit. The responsibility of this unit is to transfer, classify, screen, route, schedule, dispatch or assign, clear, synchronize, coordinate, and follow up on all organizational problems.

The flow chart in Figure 3–8 (see foldout) indicates the nature of this unit and the manner in which it coordinates the problem solving process. Problems raised from all sources are fed into this unit and are screened as legitimate or nonlegitimate problems. Because managerial resources are limited and expensive, a series of screening devices is necessary for ensuring that managers work on problems that have a significant potential organizational payoff; nor should managers have the burden of searching through a vast amount of data or suggested problems before they can determine what they should work upon. The intelligence unit therefore screens data and ascertains problem areas, and the manager avoids the time-consuming task of reviewing reports, records, and bulletins. Various screening devices can be incorporated into the control unit to achieve this result.

For example, when employees and stockholders—and, to an extent, consumers and suppliers—are permitted to raise questions about an organization's operation, some of the questions are insincere or capricious; these are immediately screened out and a form letter is sent to the individuals who raised these

Figure 3-6

A PROBLEM-RAISING FORM

HOSPITAL PROBLEM

I. Statement of the problem:
   (This can be a suggestion,
   complaint, or problem)

DO NOT WRITE IN
THIS SPACE _____

DATE RECD. _____

PROBLEM
ASSIGNED TO

_____

NO. OF
PROBLEM _____

DISPOSITION
OF PROBLEM _____

_____

II. Incidents surrounding the problem:
    (Give facts, names, etc.)

_____

_____

III. Why are you raising this problem
     and what would you like to see
     accomplished?

Your Name _____

Department _____

Position _____

Make out in duplicate. Keep one copy for your record. Drop other copy
in Personnel Office or drop in Mail Office Problem Box.

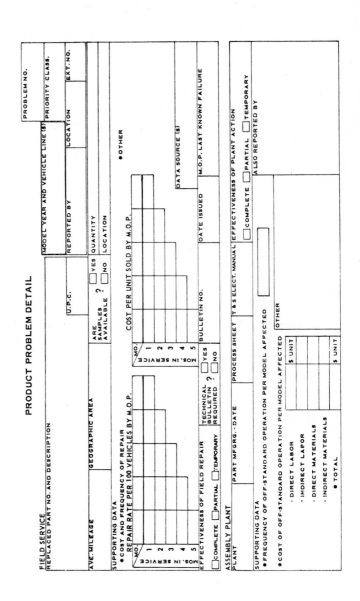

PRODUCT PROBLEM DETAIL

56

ENGINEERING

| ORIGINATING CODE NO. | VEHICLE NO. | VEH. TYPE MILES OR CYCLES | ENG. TRANS. | AXLE OTHER | U.P.C. |

PROB. TRANSMITTED TO DIV. | ACKNOWLEDGED BY DIV. | RESPONSIBLE DESIGN DEPT. | PROJECT ENGINEER | PHONE NO.

DIV. DATE

DETERMINATION OF ACTION (RESOLUTION) | LAYOUT AVAILABILITY | PROBLEM CROSS REFERENCE

ACTUAL SCHEDULED

SERVICES OR PARTS REQUIRED ☐ YES ☐ NO

SCHEDULED PROBLEM? REMARKS:

ACTUAL

	YES	NO	DUP.
DESIGN	☐	☐	☐
ASSEMBLY	☐	☐	☐
VENDOR QUALITY	☐	☐	☐

UPDATE ☐ PROTOTYPE ☐ YES ☐ NO   BUCK ☐ YES ☐ NO   ADVANCED PROJECT REQ'D. ☐ YES ☐ NO   VEHICLE INSTALLATION

PARTS AVAILABILITY		VEHICLE NO.	VEHICLE INSTALLATION				YES	NO	SCHEDULED	ACTUAL
SCHEDULED	ACTUAL		SCHEDULED	ACTUAL	DEV. COMPL. REQUIRED		☐	☐		
					DURAB. COMPL. REQUIRED		☐	☐		
					PART OR SYSTEM		☐	☐		
					SIGN OFF REQUIRED		☐	☐		
					PILOT MOD. EVAL. REQ.		☐	☐		

ACTION	SCHEDULED	ACTUAL	TOOLING TIME (WEEKS)
INITIATE ECR			
ISSUE HOLD-UP			
TOOLING PRINTS			SAMPLE
APP 2906 (DRFT)			PILOT
APP 2906 (C.C.)			PRE-PRODUCTION
REL'D. PRINTS			JOB #1
SAMPLE AVAIL.			NEW/REVISED VEND. CERTF

	YES	NO
RESOLVED IN INITIAL RELEASE	☐	☐
DEV. ISSUED & NO.	☐	☐
ECR REQUIRED	☐	☐

ECR NUMBER

CLASSIFICATION

E.R. NUMBER

	DATE, APP. REQ. TO SUPPORT	SUPPORTS	
		YES	NO
		☐	☐

NEW/REVISED VEND. CERTF ☐ YES ☐ NO

NEW/REVISED DESIGN STANDARD ☐ YES ☐ NO

NEW/REVISED CUST. ACCEPT. SPECIFICATION ☐ YES ☐ NO

CLOSURE SIGN-OFF	DESIGN
PROJECT ENGINEER	DEPARTMENT MANAGER

CLOSURE SIGN-OFF	DEVELOPMENT
PROJECT ENGINEER	DEPARTMENT MANAGER

PROGRESS CODE AND DATE

	A	B	C
1			
2			
3			
4			

COST INFORMATION

	PER UNIT	ANNUAL
PIECE PRICE		
TOOL COST		*
TOTAL		

FACILITY COST

* AT ANNUAL FINANCIAL PLANNING VOLUME

Figure 3-7

SOLUTION REQUISITION FORM (STEP 2)

SOLUTION REQUISITION

To: _____*(control unit)*_____ From: _____*(problem-raiser)*_____

Date: _____ Time: _____

Description of Problem: _____

_____

_____

_____

_____

_____

_____

_____

Emergency ☐   Urgent ☐   Routine ☐

(This section for control-unit use only)

Problem No: *(from log)*   Received: Date _____ Time _____

Inventory File Check: ☐ Solution is on file. Refer to No. _____

☐ Solution is not on file.

Disposition: ☐ Returned to problem-raiser for more information.

☐ Returned to problem-raiser. Cost not justified.

☐ Action initiated. Estimated result date is _____

Assigned Problem To: _____ Date _____

Special Note: _____

_____

- -

Copies of Form: 1) to control unit,
                 2) to control unit,
                 3) at origin.

problems, saying that the firm cannot take action at this time. If a problem is screened and classified as legitimate, the control unit fills out the remaining sections of the problem-raising form, records the time the problem was received, and assigns it a number. A permanent record is maintained for the receipt of each problem and for its eventual disposition. This record assures that no problems are lost, and it precludes duplicating work on the same problem. (Two hypothetical examples are given in Figure 3–9 and Figure 3–10, page 60.)

Problems are then classified as to whether or not solutions already exist, and a complete inventory of solutions and of the situations to which they apply is kept in the control unit. The reason for this is that the problem-raiser may not be completely informed as to organizational procedures or policies that relate to the situation he has noted. If an appropriate operational solution has already been formulated, the control unit will locate it, ascertain if it is being utilized in response to the situation, and will notify the problem-raiser accordingly.

If a situation arises for which a solution has been preprogrammed, but the solution is not being utilized, the control unit decides whether to (1) activate the appropriate program, (2) request authorization to activate, or (3) request additional information about the situation (see Figure 3–8 [6]).

As for the first possibility, let us assume that some predeter-

Figure 3–9

PROBLEM LEDGER

Problem No.	Problem Received from	Date	Sender Acknowl-edged	Date Disposed of	Nature of disposition
3741	Ajax Co.	3/26/65		5/15/65	Devised new solution (No. 5671)
3742	Intelligence	3/26/65		4/11/65	Activated solution No. 374

Figure 3–10

U. S. ARMY AVIATION AND SURFACE MATERIEL COMMAND

DOCUMENT CONTROL REGISTER

Date Received	Case No.	Description of Problem & Document Identification	Solution on File	Date Assigned	Assigned to	Scheduled Completion Date	Date Completed	Remarks

lem-solver, it also knows how much available worktime each problem-solver has. If one problem-solver is overloaded and another has time available, the unit will assign a new problem to the second individual (assuming, of course, he is competent in the area of the assignment). The managerial staff will also have to be increased or decreased, in relation to the problem-input load (a question we will look at more closely in Chapter 10, Installation, Operation, and Maintenance of the System).

SCHEDULING OF PROBLEMS

Given time and experience, the control unit will become increasingly adept at estimating how significant or difficult a problem is. It will also become more skillful in determining the time required for solving problems and thus better able to allocate managerial time for solutions. However, the control unit's judgment of the time required for any problem will always be somewhat arbitrary, and a problem-solver may realize, while working on a problem, that its solution will entail more time than had been estimated. In such a case the problem-solver can request an adjustment of his schedule, and the control unit will respond accordingly. Schedules can therefore be adjusted even while a problem is in the process.

The control unit maintains a control board or master record of the problems being solved, to whom they have been assigned, and their schedule and routing (Figure 3–11, page 64); and it will use this board to follow the progress of each problem, occasionally checking the board to determine if the assigned work sequences for each problem have been finished by the estimated dates. If deadlines are missed, the control unit investigates the cause of difficulty, and it might revamp the schedule or reroute certain problems. Then, too, the problem-solver might meet with hindrances and have to call upon the control unit for additional direction or assistance.

The next action of the control unit—aside from review, rescheduling, and the like—is the actual dispatching of the problem to an assigned problem-solver (Figure 3–8 [14]), perhaps with a copy of the original problem-raising form along with additional information that may have been gathered. Submanagers necessarily accept all problems as their work assignments.

PROBLEM INVESTIGATION (STEP 3)

Upon receipt of a problem, the submanager can begin to investigate its causal aspects. A problem may exist for many reasons:

Figure 3–11

MASTER CONTROL BOARD DATA FOR CONTROL UNIT

Problem No. (Problem-Raising)	Assigned	Date	Problem Investigation		Search for Solutions		Evaluation & Selection of Solution	
			Scheduled Date	Actual Date of Completion	Scheduled Date	Actual Date of Completion	Scheduled Date	Actual Date of Completion
347	Smith	5/27/65	6/1/65		6/5/65		6/15/65	

Consensus		Authorization		Implementation		Direction		Audit	
Scheduled Date	Actual Date of Completion	Scheduled Date	Actual Date of Completion	Scheduled Date	Actual Date of Completion	Scheduled Date	Actual Date of Completion	Scheduled Date	Actual Date of Completion
6/20/65		6/22/65		7/15/65		7/16/65		8/15/65	

1. An earlier solution may not have been followed;
2. There may have been poor implementation;
3. The solution may have been incorrect;
4. No solution may have been provided;
5. The underlying causal factors may have changed; or
6. A new opportunity may exist.

The problem-solver will have to determine why the problem exists so that corrective action can be taken.

The investigation of a problem is illustrated by the flow chart in Figure 3–12 (see foldout). The problem-solver might first check the operating manual to ascertain the nature of the solution (if any) which applies to the situation. Or he might communicate with the problem-raiser to get additional information. Problems that arise from intelligence units or as the result of audits will usually be accompanied by pertinent data, and the submanager should acquire these data. If a solution already exists, he might survey the actual operations and find that the solution is not being utilized, that it is improperly implemented, or that it is ineffective or incorrect.

The submanager must be relatively free to investigate work areas, acquire data from the intelligence unit, and gather new data that he believes are necessary for establishing the reason for a problem's existence. Except for confidential data, it should be a working policy of the system that all operating units will accord full cooperation to submanagers who might be found moving freely throughout the organization collecting data. For example, managers from the engineering department might find it necessary to investigate an activity in the sales department, or the purchasing manager may have to check on some activity in engineering.

Unquestionably, the intelligence unit is a major source of data for both external and internal events, and this unit should have set procedures for retrieving information that is requested by submanagers.

A form can be designed to assist the problem-solver in his analysis of the problem that has been assigned to him — something like that in Figure 3–13 (page 66). Such a form would show the number of the problem and the date it was assigned to the problem-solver. The recording of causal information is primarily for the problem-solver's use, but it might also be helpful later in the decision making process in explaining how the solution was obtained; so this initial record can be doubly meaningful. The use of a particular kind of form could be mandatory or vol-

Figure 3-13

PROBLEM-SOLVER'S INITIAL RECORD (STEP 3)

PROBLEM INVESTIGATION

Problem No. _____   Date Assigned _____

Check Source of Problem

I. Solution No. _____

    1) Not followed
    2) Improperly implemented
    3) Ineffective
       a) Incorrect

II. No Solution

III. Change in Causal Factors

              Internal   External

    1) Technological   ____
    2) Economic   ____
    3) Political   ____
    4) Psychological   ____
    5) Sociological   ____
    6) Ideological   ____

(Supplement this form by attaching written report and graph, and quantify data if possible.)

_____
(Problem Investigator)

Date _____

untary, but if a problem is highly complex we would expect that the keeping of an adequate record would be automatic.

After the submanager has learned the reasons for the difficulty he reports his findings to the control unit. If a solution is not being followed, the control unit notifies the manager who is responsible for the omission, who will take corrective action. If the implementation step is to be carried out again, the appropriate units are notified, and the control unit will reroute, reschedule, and redispatch the problem; and it might have to do this many times before an effective solution is achieved.

If a solution is incorrect, the earlier analysis will be reconsidered to determine whether the error was in the selection of alternatives or whether the underlying causal factors had changed. If no solution exists, the causal factors must again be determined; or a new opportunity also might require causal investigation. If the submanager should uncover another problem area during the course of his investigation, he would also report this to the control unit, and it would be processed like any other raised problem.

Because organizational problems may be interrelated, a dilemma will be created if an investigator is unable to solve a problem until another problem is solved. In such a case the former problem is held in abeyance until the latter solution is obtained. Let us suppose that the engineering, sales, purchasing, and production managers are assigned four separate problems. Independent investigation finds that the four problems have occurred because of a shortage in personnel, and this is reported to the control unit, which routes the information to personnel. Personnel, in turn, reports that the company's salary level in various categories is 20 per cent below the market rates, yet the labor budget will not permit salary increases. The control unit would then turn the problem over to finance, and, once finance has solved this problem, the other problems could also be solved.

As the control unit reviews the location and nature of the problems brought to its attention, it may be able to locate chronically deficient operating areas, and it is then possible for the unit to graph these problems by areas, as in Figure 3–14 (page 68).

Or a group problem might be created. To illustrate, an engineering manager might explore an engineering problem but find that personnel and purchasing subproblems must first be resolved, and he could then request a group solution. An investigator from personnel and one from purchasing would accordingly be assigned to his problem so that, collectively, the three submanagers could work out a solution.

Figure 3-14

PROBLEM INTERRELATEDNESS (STEP 3)
(Prepared by Control Unit)

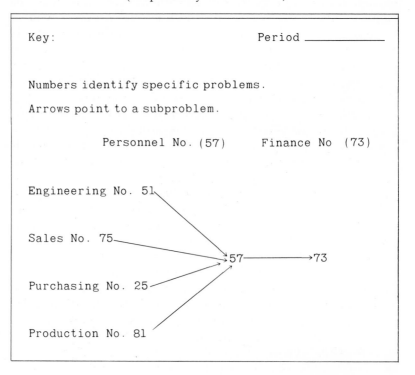

```
Key:                                    Period _____


Numbers identify specific problems.

Arrows point to a subproblem.

              Personnel No. (57)     Finance No (73)


Engineering No. 51

Sales No. 75

                                    57 ──────────→ 73

Purchasing No. 25

Production No. 81
```

ALTERNATIVE SOLUTIONS (STEP 4)

Next in the decision making sequence is the search for alternative solutions. This is probably the least formalized of the ten steps because reliance must be placed on the creative ability of the submanagers. However, the submanager who is assigned to a problem is usually responsible for devising its solution, so he should possess sufficient technical competence or expertise, and he should also be well informed about the latest technological literature.

It is therefore obvious that every organization should maintain adequate library facilities so that its submanagers can keep abreast of developments in their fields. Opportunities should also be made available for submanagers to attend conferences, special university programs, or even in-training courses. In addition to knowing the proven solutions in their areas, submanagers should also be able to create new solutions, and they should be encouraged to experiment and develop along this line. Research and development efforts, for example, should not be restricted solely to the engineering section but should extend throughout the entire organization.

SELECTING THE BEST ALTERNATIVE (STEP 5)

The assigned problem-solver will also evaluate the solutions and select the best alternative. For the organizational purpose of standardizing the calculations of the problem-solver, a solution-comparison form (such as that in Figure 3–15, page 71) might be drawn up. This form requires the problem-solver to calculate the payoff of a proposal in relation to the overall goals of the organization (which in this case was a hospital). More detailed forms can also be designed, such as economic evaluation or summary of analysis sheets (see Figure 3–16, pages 72–73).

If the problem-solver cannot estimate the costs and output of a particular solution, perhaps the engineering, systems, or accounting units can provide assistance. But once the analyst has selected the best available solution, he is also expected to plan how, when, and by whom it will be implemented, directed, and audited. Budgetary adjustments will also be calculated.

CLEARANCE MACHINERY AND ORGANIZATIONAL CONSENSUS (STEP 6)

The next step in the decision making process is clearing those proposals which—directly or indirectly—affect more than one operating unit through all of those units, thus ascertaining the effects such proposals will have upon all of these operations. This function is provided by the control unit. After completion of the fourth and fifth steps of the problem solving procedure—the search for solutions and the evaluation and selection of the best alternative—the total solution is recorded and sent to the control unit. Control then decides which units will be affected by the proposal and which should therefore "react" to it.

Various organizational units can be differently affected by a single solution. A *direct* effect means a solution contains specific suggestions for changes in a specific operation: if the information systems department suggested that all filing be centralized, this proposal directly affects the clerical operations of every unit. Other units would be *indirectly* influenced if proposed changes in the output of a subunit affected either the inputs or the outputs of other units.

For example, the marketing division may have an advertising program solution that is estimated to increase sales by 5 per cent. If we assume that the organization had not been preprogrammed for this change, the production divisions would, without notice, have to increase production by 5 per cent. Additional units could also be involved in the implementation or audit of the solution: the personnel department might have to hire additional employees to carry out the proposal, or the engineering department might have to audit the proposal. A schematic of the clearance and consensus procedure is shown in Figure 3–17, page 74.

After the control unit has decided which units will be affected, it selects those submanagers to whom the proposal should be cleared, schedules their time accordingly, and sets the date by which their reactions should be returned to control. The control unit uses a clearance board (part of the control board or master record) for maintaining a measure of control over the clearance procedure: for recording to whom the solution was next cleared, and when, and when it was returned (Figure 3–18, page 75).

Each unit, after it receives a proposal, calculates the net payoff or the effect a proposal will have upon its particular operation (see Figure 3–17 [2]). Along with the solution, each unit also receives a departmental payoff calculation form (like Figure 3–19, page 76). Other aspects of the proposal, such as its implementation and audit, are also reviewed, and a unit can object to any phase it considers to be impractical. The proposal is also reviewed with employees who would be affected by changes in job content and reward, and their reaction is summarized by an analyst in a supervisory meeting report (Figure 3–20, page 77).

After each unit has completed its calculation of a proposal's payoff to that unit, the calculations are transmitted to the control unit, which composes a total payoff matrix to determine if there will be a net payoff to the total organization (see Figure 3–21, page 78).

Organizational units might desire additional information, or they might believe that serious differences warrant discussion in a face-to-face meeting. Each unit would therefore be given the opportunity to suggest that a meeting be called at which all affected operating units would be represented. The control unit would draw up the agenda for the meeting and arrange the time and place, and the personnel to be present (Figure 3–17 [4]). To assure that participants are prepared for a meeting, the control unit will distribute the agenda in advance. If modifications of the original proposal are indicated as the result of such a meeting, a recalculation of the organizational payoff will then be made.

70

Figure 3 – 15

SOLUTION-COMPARISON FORM

(This is a suggested guide. Make the report as long as you think is necessary.)

No. of Problem _____

Date Assigned _____

I   Compare present and proposed method, policy equipment, etc., in terms of cost reduction.

Present   Proposed

Labor $ _____   Labor $ _____

Material $ _____   Material $ _____

Equipment $ _____   Equipment $ _____

Total $ _____   Total $ _____

Expected Cost Reduction $ _____

Total $ _____

Explain your analysis:

II   Make some comparison in terms of patient care.

Present:

Proposed:

How will patient care be improved?

III   Make comparison in terms of increasing hospital income.

Income produced by present approach $ _____

Expected income produced by proposed approach (explain in detail) $ _____

Recommendations (in detail):

(Signed) _____

71

Figure 3-16

SUMMARY OF ANALYSIS (STEP 5)

I. REQUIRED INVESTMENT

1	Cost of project	$_____	1
2	Disposal value of assets to be retired by project	$_____	2
3	Capital additions required in absence of project	$_____	3
4	Investment released or avoided by project (2 + 3)	$_____	4
5	Net investment required (1 - 4)	$_____	5

II. NEXT-YEAR ADVANTAGE FROM PROJECT

A. Operating Advantage
(Use first year of project operations*)

6 Assumed operating rate of project (hours per year) _____ 6

Effect of Project on Revenue:	Increase	Decrease	
7 From change in quality of products	$_____	$_____	7
8 From change in volume of output	_____	_____	8
9 Total	$_____ A	$_____ B	9

Effect of Project on Operating Costs:			
10 Labor	$_____	$_____	10
11 Material	_____	_____	11
12 Overhead	_____	_____	12
13 Total	$_____ A	$_____ B	13
14 Net increase in revenue (9A - 9B)		$_____	14
15 Net decrease in operating cost (13B -13A)		$_____	15
16 Next-year operating advantage (14 + 15)		$_____	16

B. Nonoperating Advantage
(Use only if there is an entry in Line 4)

17 Next-year capital consumption avoided by project:		17
A Decline of disposal value during the year	$_____	A
B Next-year allocation of capital additions	$_____	B
Total	$_____	

C. Total Advantage

18 Total next-year advantage from project (16 + 17) $_____ 18

72

III. COMPUTATION OF URGENCY RATING

19 Total next-year advantage after income tax (18 - tax) $_____ 19

20 Chart allowance for project (total of column F, below) $_____ ** 20

(Enter Depreciable Assets Only)

Item or Group	Installed Cost of Item or Group A	Estimated Service Life (Years) B	Estimated Terminal Salvage (Per cent of cost) C	Chart Number D	Chart Percentage E	Chart Percentage × Cost (E × A) F
	$					$
					Total	$_____

21 Amount available for return on investment (19 - 20) $_____ 21

22 Urgency rating (21 ÷ 5) · 100 %_____ 22

---

*For projects with a significant break-in period, use performance after break-in.

**Since the chart allowance does not cover future capital additions to project assets, add an annual proration of such additions, if any, to the figure in Line 20.

Figure 3–17

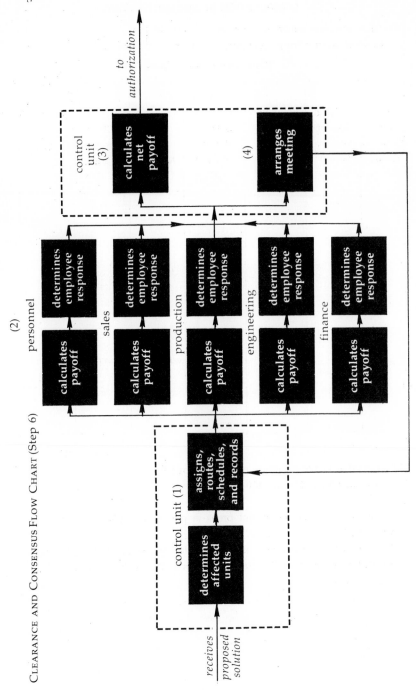

CLEARANCE AND CONSENSUS FLOW CHART (Step 6)

74

Figure 3–18

CLEARANCE BOARD (STEP 6)

Problem and Numbers	Received in Clearance	Cleared to	Returned	Committee Meeting	Transmitted to Authoriza-tion	Comments
Lost Sales Account No. 310	5/9	Decision-Makers B,C,D 5/10	Decision-Makers C,D	Will be required no date yet		D is in disagreement
New Product D1234 No. 318	5/13	Decision-Makers B,C,D 5/14	Not yet			
Changed Package Product No. 325	5/13	Decision-Maker B 5/14				No problems
Advertising Product No. 328	5/17					

Figure 3 – 19

DEPARTMENTAL PAYOFF FORM (STEP 6)

FORM K

Problem No. _____

Cleared to: _____

_____

_____

_____

Not Concerned _____

Calculation of Department Payoff for Considered Alternatives:

Alternative A   Alternative B

Input _____   Input _____

Output _____   Output _____

Payoff _____   Payoff _____

New Alternatives:

Alternative _____

Description of Alternative:

Input _____

Output _____

Payoff _____

Request Consensus Meeting _____

Comments: _____

_____

_____

_____

_____
                                        (signature)

Figure 3 – 20

REPORT OF SUPERVISORY MEETING (STEP 6)

Dept. _____   Date _____

A.   Members present:

B.   Agenda issues discussed:

   1.

   2.

   3.

   4.

   5.

C.   Issues to be referred to employees for comment:

   1.

   2.

   3.

D.   Position of department on issues to report back to department
     head meeting:

Figure 3–21

PAYOFF MATRIX (STEP 6)

	ALTERNATIVE A	ALTERNATIVE B	ALTERNATIVE C	ALTERNATIVE D COUNTER-PROPOSAL BY DEPT. 2	ALTERNATIVE E COUNTER-PROPOSAL BY DEPT. 4
Dept. 1 Payoff	$1,500	$2,000	$2,500	$ 500	-$ 500
Dept. 2 Payoff	800	100	-400	2,000	100
Dept. 3 Payoff	1,000	-200	-100	-4,000	-1,000
Dept. 4 Payoff	-2,000	-800	-1,500	-1,000	2,000
Total Company Payoff	$1,300	$1,100	$500	-$2,500	$600

Figure 3–22

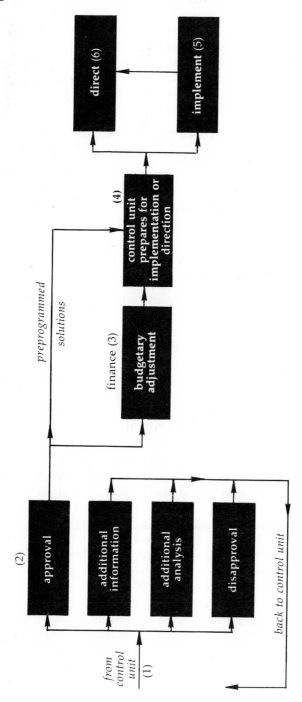

79

It is important to emphasize that a manager who does not agree with a particular solution — or who believes a solution will adversely affect his operation — must be prepared to justify his opposition in concrete terms, for unless he can quantify his objection it will carry little weight. After it has been established that a proposal has an estimated net organizational payoff, and after it has been accepted by the operating personnel, the control unit forwards it for authorization.

THE AUTHORIZATION PROCEDURE (STEP 7)

The design of a decision making process provides for the allocation of individual authority by defining the nature of the decisions an individual can approve. In the ten-man model with which we are concerned (Figure 3–1) — and in addition to managing the entire management system — we have assumed that the top manager will have sufficient time for authorizing all solutions. In larger systems (see pages 87–96) this would not be feasible, and a specific group of submanagers would be assigned this task. However, regardless of a system's size, top management can reserve for itself the proviso that *certain* solutions will always require its approval; for example, solutions in which expenditures exceed $500,000.

Organizational authority is more effectively centralized in the authorization step because the individuals so empowered are able to spend more time in the review and approval of decisions; they may, in fact, be assigned little else to do. And the control unit, of course, is programmed to know which individuals should authorize certain solutions.

The schematic for the authorization step might look like that in Figure 3–22 (page 79). When a solution is ready to be authorized, the control unit checks for the proper person and sends the proposal to that individual (Figure 3–22 [1]). Solutions which cut across lines of authority are directed to the individual who has authority over all of the units affected.

The authorizer will respond in one of four ways: he will (1) approve, (2) disapprove, (3) require additional information, or (4) require further analysis of the problem (Figure 3–22 [2]). If the authorizer is satisfied, he will sign the solution and return it to the control unit, which will send the approved solution to the finance unit for budgetary adjustment (3). After this, control will distribute the solution to the affected groups so that it can be implemented.

If a solution is not authorized it means that, although the analysis was appropriate, additional information is required or that the authorizer wants to examine alternative solutions. There might be solutions in which there is much uncertainty about the possible payoff, and the authorizer might have to make a choice among four or five alternatives. Then too, he might send a solution back for additional refinement before giving it final approval.

However, if the problem solving tasks have been properly performed, authorization is usually a formality. Complete disapproval of a solution is relatively rare because it would indicate gross deficiencies within the decision making process itself.

Authorization, as we have said, involves the approval of monetary or other organizational resources. This means that a solution will be forwarded by the control unit to the finance or accounting department, which will make the appropriate adjustments and set aside funds for implementing the solution. The budgets of operating units are also marked for adjustment after a solution has been implemented. Preprogrammed solutions, that require only authorization, go through the same process but are not required to complete the budgetary or implementation phase.

THE IMPLEMENTATION PROCESS (STEP 8)

The process of implementation is designated in the solution, and individual tasks to be performed in the modification of organizational resources will have been described. The personnel unit, for example, may have to initiate training programs or hire new personnel. Part of any solution, however, is the time estimated for instituting the solution, as well as the cost of implementation.

After a solution is authorized, the control unit instructs various submanagers to begin implementation. It reroutes various phases of the solution among the submanagers and devises the schedule for each. Some aspects might be carried out simultaneously, but others might be executed sequentially; the finance department, for example, might have to negotiate additional credit before the personnel department can hire additional employees.

When the schedule is completed, the control unit dispatches implementation instructions to various submanagers, with the expected completion date (Figure 3–23, page 82). The affected units insert a copy of the solution in their operating manuals, along with the date the solution is to become operational.

THE DIRECTION PROCEDURE (STEP 9)

Some solutions are preprogrammed to cover certain contingencies, and the control unit will activate these programs as we have

Figure 3-23

SOLUTION IMPLEMENTATION ORDER (STEP 8)

To _____   Date _____

Problem No. _____   Solution No. _____

Start of implementation _____

Estimated completion date _____

Comments: _____

_____

_____

(This Section for Implementor's Use)

Date actually started _____   Date completed ____

Personnel to be used _____

_____

_____

Special equipment to be used _____

_____

Cash or working funds needed_____

_____

Sequence of operations _____

_____

Comments _____

(This Section for Use by Audit Only)

Audit dates _____   By   _____

_____   _____

Preparation of form:-   3 copies: 1 copy to implementor
                                     1 copy to audit
                                     1 copy to control

described. This preprogrammed machinery makes it possible not only to plan what the organization will do in the future, it also helps coordinate the intelligence, or sensory, unit and the operating units. When an organization has planned certain adjustments in the event of specific situations in the external environment, the intelligence unit, when it becomes aware of such situations, can notify all affected units that the preprogrammed solutions should be put into effect. (Part of every solution is also a statement of the circumstances under which the solution should be used, and, theoretically, if an organization were preprogrammed for all possible contingencies, it would be completely adaptive. Each operating unit would have a set of solutions. A solution would be changed occasionally, no doubt, but once a new solution was introduced it would be applied as a routine matter.)

A major duty of the submanager who has been assigned the responsibility of directing an operating unit is maintaining the unit's capability for effectuating its designated solutions. Employees quit, retire, or are discharged, and they have to be replaced; machines break down or wear out; materials may be defective; buildings must be maintained; equipment must be serviced or purchased from time to time; materials and supplies must be immediately at hand. Solutions provide the directions for meeting these problems, but someone must be responsible for completing the requisite forms and transferring them to the right units. Thus all maintenance aspects of a unit's operation, for example, will be directed by the maintenance submanager.

Accordingly, if the submanager has a complete knowledge of the operating manual, he will continually verify that employees are following the manual, and he will make any small adjustments that are required. If serious problems arise, he will check the manual for a solution. If no solution seems to fit, he will complete a problem-raising form and send it to the control unit.

It is at this direction step, then, that solutions become behavioral, that they are converted from the manual into action; and it is the supervisor's responsibility to serve as the connecting link between the manual and the employee.

MONITORING MACHINERY
FOR THE AUDIT (STEP 10)

There are three methods for inspecting the effectiveness of a solution. The first method is by determining whether the expected and the actual payoffs are equal, or whether a difference between them falls within an acceptable range (see Figure 3–24, page 84). This comparison might be calculated on a monthly,

Figure 3-24

DECISION AUDIT (STEP 10)

Decision No. 154
Decision-maker: A
Frequency of Audit: Monthly
Date of Audit: May, 1963.

	EXPECTED SOLUTION PAYOFF			AUDIT PAYOFF		
	OUTPUT	INPUT	PAYOFF	OUTPUT	INPUT	PAYOFF
Dept 1	$2,000	$400	$1,600	$1,000	$500	$500
Dept 2	600	100	500	500	100	400
TOTAL COMPANY	$2,600	$500	$2,100	$1,500	$600	$900

Previous Audit: April, 1963
　Specification: Within

Current Audit
　Specification: Output

Trouble: Dept. I Output

Figure 3–25

A HOSPITAL'S BEHAVIORAL AUDIT (STEP 10)

Audit of Policies and Procedures
(To be submitted with Monthly Report)

Name _____

Date _____

Dept. _____

Number of Policy or Procedure	Number of Observations (Describe)	Nature of Violations or Deviations, if any	Actions Taken Concerning Deviations
1. Housekeeping, No. 23 (Floor Polishing)	1. Jan. 23, 11 A.M. observed floor polishing in Main Lobby	1. Performed according to procedure	
2. Housekeeping, No. 27 (Wall Washing)	2. Jan. 15, Administrative Hall	2. Performed according to procedure	
3. Housekeeping, No. 13 (Linen Disposal)	3. 2d Floor West, Jan. 26	3. Performed according to procedure	
4. Housekeeping, No. 23 (Floor Polishing)	4. Jan. 30, Main Lobby	4. Used excessive amount of wax	4. Gave instructions in proper procedure

weekly, or other similar basis. Any large deviations are noted and sent to the control unit in the form of a raised problem.

The second method is by a behavioral check, similar to a preventive maintenance program (see Figure 3–25, page 85). A physical check is made at random times and places to see if the appropriate solution is being carried out, or is proving itself. Here again, deviations become problem inputs for the control unit.

Then, because employees and other problem-solvers also raise problems, the third method of monitoring solutions is by one unit suggesting that another unit is not carrying out a solution properly. This, too, becomes a problem for investigation.

The monitoring step is a feedback or looping operation. Although it is not the only organizational process that inputs problems, it is the organizational segment that evaluates existing programs in terms of proper effectuation.

For the actual mechanics of audit, in the first method of monitoring solution payoff, some system of centralized data processing is essential. For the second method, behavioral checks, one of the problem-solver's responsibilities is to periodically audit all operational solutions, and a schedule is designed that will assure that all solutions are audited. The third method is more or less an *ad hoc* procedure.

The schematized implementation, direction, and audit phases of the decision making process might appear as in Figure 3–26.

THE SIZE OF THE SYSTEM

After the mechanics of the decision making system have been completed, the system's size can be planned. Determination of

Figure 3–26
Implementation, Direction, and Audit (Steps 8, 9, and 10)

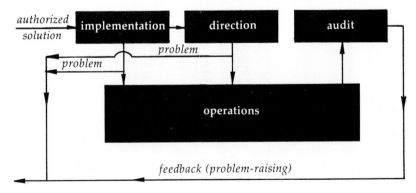

the number of problem-solvers that will be required depends upon how many problems can be expected to arise over a given period and how long it will take to solve the average problem.

Acquiring these data, however, requires operating experience, and, in the absence of such data and experience, we can postulate the required number of problem-solvers on the basis of the number of nonproblem-solvers or employees. If we accept the current figures, we find there is usually one manager for every ten employees, and we will use this ratio to illustrate how the size of a system can be handled. The size-1 schematic (Figure 3–27, page 89) assumes an organization of ten employees, with one manager for performing the decision making tasks.

Suppose we look at a size-2 organization, of 100 employees, for which ten managers would be necessary (Figure 3–28, pages 90–91). How would the problem solving tasks be divided? In a size-2 system it is possible to introduce specialization, according to the classification of problems to be solved. In the organization with only one problem-solver or manager, this individual has to solve every problem, regardless of its nature; but in the second organization a manager can be assigned to finance, to personnel, to purchasing, and so on.

But when *managerial* functions are subdivided, the relative problem load must be considered. Some areas of organizational activity may have more problems than others, and, as a result, require more managers. One also must consider the qualitative aspect of decision making in relation to the importance of any operating area of the organization. Thus if sales or production are the most important functions, a greater number of managers might be assigned to these areas, and perhaps fewer managers to less significant areas.

How is the decision making process designed when organizations are ever-expanding and the number of managers, as a consequence, must also increase? For the most part, this is a matter of merely duplicating the problem solving process for every additional decision-maker. Although managers specialize in the specific organizational problems they work upon, the character of the tasks they do is uniform; all problems of the organization are processed in essentially the same way. Whether a problem is one of production or personnel, the corresponding nine steps are still operational.

If we increase the scale, and consider an organization of 100 managers (Figure 3–29, page 92), there will be increased specialization not only in the problems to be solved but also in the control unit: there will be a control unit for sales, one for production, one for finance, one for engineering, etc. Each unit will perform all the tasks previously noted (scheduling, routing, and the like), but only in relation to the problem solving area for which each is responsible. Thus the sales-decision control unit will classify sales problems according to the kind of problem involved.

This systematic division of problems will follow the same allocation principle that organizations utilize when they make specific people responsible for the effective operation of certain units. Any problem which relates to these units is so designated and is assigned to the man responsible for the unit. Therefore a sales submanager might be responsible for a given sales territory, and the problems which arise in this territory will be assigned to him — if they fall within the range of his problem solving responsibility. Another submanager might be responsible for product design, another for advertising research, another for media allocation, another for export development, and so on.

It should be kept in mind, however, that all problems are first submitted to the master control unit, a single control point which assigns the problems to subcontrol units. A subcontrol unit, in turn, routes and schedules a problem through the problem solving process, and assigns it to its appropriate submanager.

If we further increase the system, to 1,000 managers (size 4), there will have to be three layers of control units, and the work process will look somewhat like Figure 3–30 (page 93). For example, if a problem relates to advertising, master control forwards it to sales control, and sales control forwards it to advertising control, which then processes it through the decision making procedure. If the organization had 1,000 problem-solvers or submanagers, there might be 100 control units on the first level, ten control units on the second level, and one master control unit. The control units thus become linkages when problems are processed through the organization.

If the organization had 1,000,000 employees and 10,000 managers (size 5), there would be four layers of control units (see Figure 3–31, page 94).

The significance of effective control units becomes most apparent when organizations increase in size; whether an organization has 100, 1,000, or 10,000 submanagers, it must successfully meet the major problem of coordinating managerial activities. We have seen that as organizations expand the same processes can be duplicated and augmented with even greater specialization, and that the problem solving activities of submanagers continue to be integrated and coordinated, regardless of the number of managers involved.

Figure 3–27

SIZE-1 MANAGEMENT SYSTEM (One Manager)

| problem-raising (2) | problem investigation (3) | search for solution (4) | solution selection (5) | clearance and consensus (6) | authorization (7) | implementation (8) | direction (9) | audit (10) |

operations

operations

feedback

Figure 3–28

A MANAGEMENT SYSTEM (Ten Managers)
(Step 1, Defining Organizational Objectives, is not shown.)

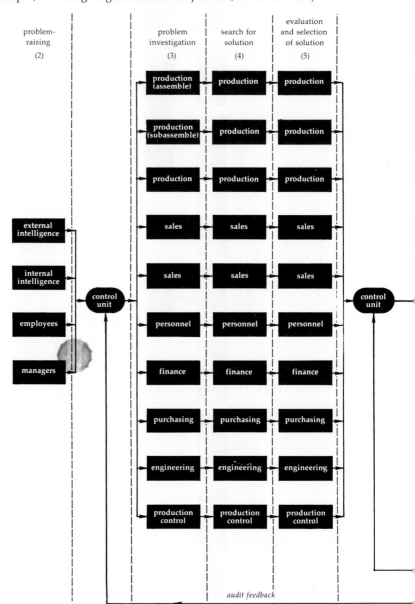

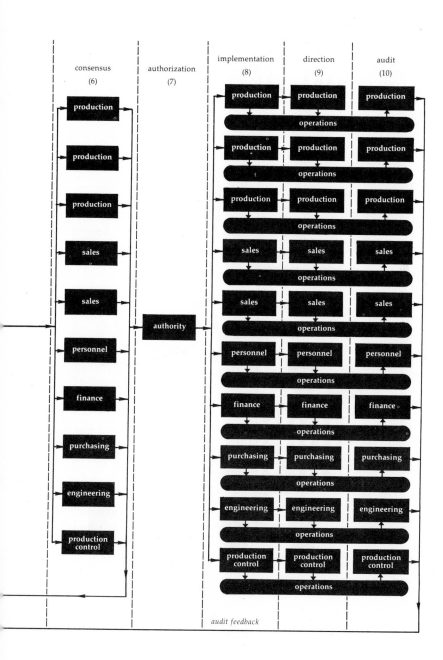

91

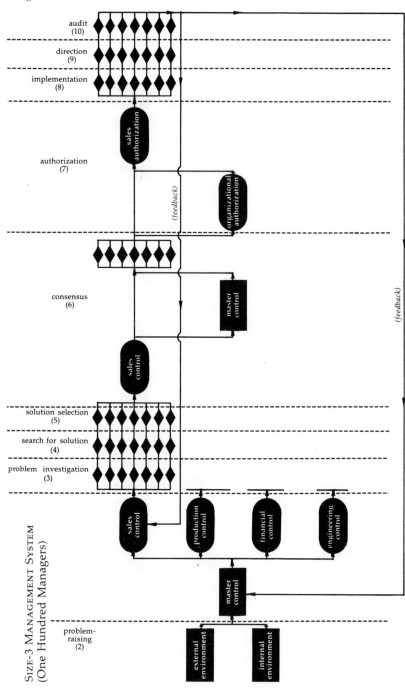

Figure 3–29

audit
(10)

direction
(9)

implementation
(8)

authorization
(7)

sales authorization

organizational authorization

(feedback)

consensus
(6)

master control

sales control

solution selection
(5)

search for solution
(4)

problem investigation
(3)

sales control

production control

financial control

engineering control

master control

problem-raising
(2)

external environment

internal environment

(feedback)

SIZE-3 MANAGEMENT SYSTEM
(One Hundred Managers)

Figure 3–30

SIZE-4 MANAGEMENT SYSTEM
(One Thousand Managers)

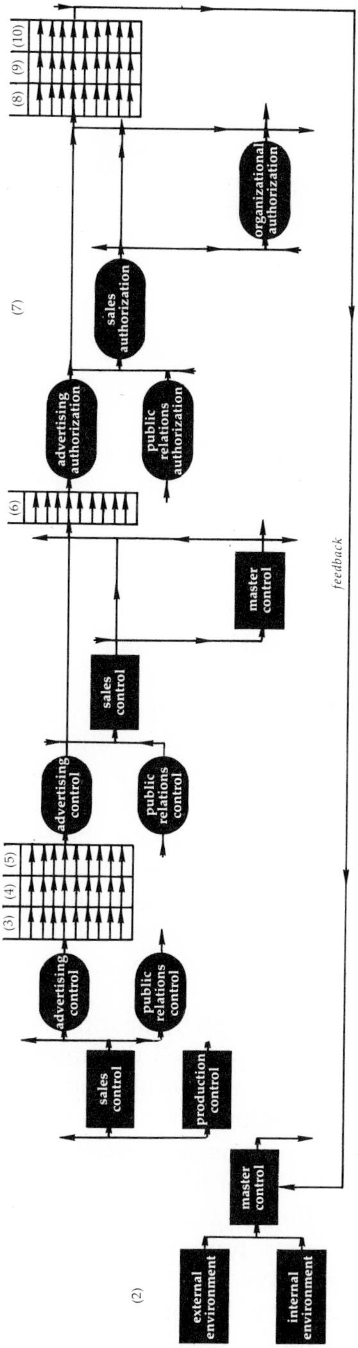

KEY
(2) problem-raising
(3) problem investigation
(4) search for solution
(5) solution selection
(6) consensus
(7) authorization
(8) implementation
(9) direction
(10) audit

93

Figure 3–31

SIZE-5 MANAGEMENT SYSTEM (Ten Thousand Managers)

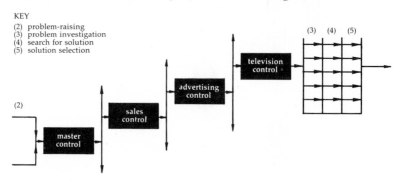

KEY
(2) problem-raising
(3) problem investigation
(4) search for solution
(5) solution selection

In very large organizations, especially those with 1,000 managers or more, the process of securing clearance, consensus, and authorization becomes more complicated. As for clearance in these large organizations, how can one be sure that proposed solutions will clear to the affected units and submanagers?

Let us consider an organization with 1,000 managers. It would have a master control and ten subcontrol units (Figure 3–30). A solution would first go to a subcontrol unit, which would determine whether the solution affected only the units within its jurisdiction or outside units as well. If the solution related to only those operating units within its jurisdiction, it would clear the solution to those units, calculate the payoff matrix, arrange conferences, achieve a consensus, and forward the solution to the individual who could authorize it. If units outside its jurisdiction were affected, it would return the solution to master control, which would clear the solution to the other affected units, which would in turn calculate the payoff matrix of the solution, and so on.

The number of solutions under inter- or intracontrol jurisdiction is important, but it can be assumed that most solutions are within the jurisdiction of subcontrol units and do not have to clear through the master control unit. There is a natural screening process for the number of problems which affect the units in an organization, and the effect of most solutions would be restricted to closely related operating units.

How would the authorization procedure operate in an organization of 1,000 submanagers? We find two levels of authority in the size-4 schematic, and we will assume that the managerial efforts of such an organization have been subdivided along functional lines. There might be 100 managers or problem-solvers in the sales area, but there would be one person who would authorize the solutions which affected that particular unit of operation.

Solutions that were interdependent, as between sales and production, would be authorized on a higher level of the organization. However, these solutions will have been cleared by the master control unit, which would have automatically sent them to this higher authority. All solutions approved by this individual would be binding on all operating units and subauthorizers.

But to assume that ten authorizers are sufficient for an organization of 1,000 managers might be an overly optimistic assumption of human capacity, and the number can easily be adjusted to twenty-five or forty. It is unlikely that more than this would be required if submanagers were correctly performing their decision making tasks.

Authorization, as we have noted, should be the least time-consuming task in the decision making process because it represents only a checkpoint in the process. If 100 submanagers were able to devise 50 solutions per week (a rather high figure[3]) a single authorizer would have a workload of 50 solutions per week (some of which would be review). If the number of authorizers were raised to three, the workload would be reduced to about 16 authorized decisions a week.

Certainly the degree to which the centralization of authority is feasible becomes immediately meaningful, in a well-designed decision making system, when—for 1,000 managers—fewer than forty are required to authorize solutions.

When, in an organization of significant size, problems cut across broad functional lines, and it is felt advantageous to work them out on a face-to-face basis, how can the points of view of the affected units be brought together? Obviously, for the sake of efficiency, we must have some system of representation: instead of assembling all of the submanagers of the affected units, a representative of one or more affected units could present the viewpoint of these units in order to keep discussions manageable. And individuals who have the assigned authority for approving the decisions of a number of operating units could also act as the representative of these units for interdependent problems which involve other authority lines.

If a problem affects only the units within the authorizer's

---

[3] Operating experience in one case indicates that the figure is closer to one decision a week (see Chapter 12, p. 315).

authority, the problem-solvers themselves could convene, present the points of view of their respective units, and resolve the solution in the already-described procedure. They would arrive at an acceptable consensus, then submit their solution to the person who holds authority to authorize it.

However, those problems which reach outside a single authorizer's authority would ultimately have to be approved by the individual whose authority extends over the units affected by the solution. In such cases, these individuals would represent their units when interorganizational problems are discussed. Thus, when such a problem is cleared through the organization, and the solution's payoff is calculated by each unit, they request a meeting of representatives of the affected units, which is arranged by the master control unit.

This system might overburden some representatives, who might not have sufficient time to consider all interorganizational solutions, and additional representatives would then be needed to devote full time to the problems of their constituencies. Screening devices can also be developed to keep face-to-face discussions within reason; for example, only solutions which fall within a set range of expenditures could warrant such a meeting. And, for the most part, one would rely on the payoff matrix as the crucial determinant, rather than upon meetings, to decide if solutions would be forwarded to the authorizer.

SPECIALIZATION OF DECISION MAKING TASKS

If decision making tasks are even further specialized, other benefits will be derived. Until this point in our analysis, specialization has been focused primarily upon the problems to be solved: each submanager has performed all the decision making steps except that of problem-raising and authorization. However, the decision making process can be broken down further if some submanagers concentrate on problem investigation (the search for and the selection of the best solution to a problem) while others implement, direct, and audit the solution. This classification need not be rigid; perhaps each manager might concentrate on only one decision making task. The line-and-staff arrangement, as found in many business firms, is, for the most part, a separation of decision making tasks; staff managers devise solutions, and line managers implement, direct, and audit them. A manager who only directs is similar to many supervisors.

Further specialization can take place if managers concentrate on the utilization of analytical resources for accomplishing

96

specific tasks. For example, in gathering information (which is the third problem solving step) submanagers could employ the services of statisticians, psychologists, economists, psychometrists, and others. In building a quantitative model (in the fourth and fifth steps) mathematicians could assist submanagers, and information retrieval could be centralized in the intelligence unit.

The assignment of separate decision making tasks to submanagers is easily arranged: control units could appoint and schedule each manager accordingly. A personnel problem could be assigned to the personnel department, which would formulate a solution, which could then be authorized by a different submanager; the solution could be implemented by still another manager, utilized by a fourth submanager, and audited by a fifth submanager.

If an organization expands, or contracts, adjustments must be made in the decision making system. Suppose the organization were increasing and new operating units were being added; the decision making aspect of these units would be added to the appropriate control units. For example, if a firm added two units to its plant operation, and this necessitated two additional submanagers, these managers would be attached to the control unit that directed decision making in the production area. If the control unit became too large, it could be subdivided into two control units, and so on. The contraction process would follow the same procedure, but conversely.

SUMMARY

This chapter outlined the total management system. The decision making process was analyzed into ten subprocesses (steps). Of primary concern was the mechanics of connecting these subprocesses, and for that purpose a control unit was suggested that would coordinate all of the decision making activities. This would assure that the output of any one process would become an input into the next process, so that the total system could operate in an integrated manner.

The size of any management system can be increased by adding more decision making channels and more control units. However, large management systems provide increased managerial task specialization.

Having reviewed the system as a totality, we can now analyze it in greater detail, and each of its subprocesses can be further subdivided. The next chapter examines step 1 of the decision making process in detail—defining organizational objectives.

QUESTIONS FOR DISCUSSION

1. What are the characteristics of systems analysis?
2. How does systems analysis (block diagramming) illustrate the interrelatedness of the decision making process?
3. Can you give some examples of a sensory or intelligence apparatus in existing organizations?
4. What are the advantages and disadvantages of having the intelligence unit centralized into a single unit?
5. What would happen if a management system did not have a control unit? If a production system did not have a control unit?
6. Why does the necessity for effective control units increase as organizations become larger?
7. Do you believe it is possible to develop a completely adaptive organization? Explain.
8. In the problem investigation stage, why would individuals sometimes be reluctant to give the problem-solver the requested data?
9. In terms of the system we have described, why is it advantageous to have face-to-face meetings between problem-solvers? Under what circumstances are such meetings disadvantageous?
10. What problems must be considered when an organization has 1,000 — or 10,000 — managers?

SUGGESTED READINGS

BROSS, IRWIN D. *Design for Decision.* New York: The Macmillan Company, 1953.

FLAGLE, CHARLES D.; HUGGINS, WILLIAM H.; and ROY, ROBERT H. (eds.). *Operations Research and Systems Engineering.* Baltimore: The Johns Hopkins Press, 1960.

LE BRETON, PRESTON P., and HENNING, DALE A. *Planning Theory.* Englewood Cliffs, N.J.: Prentice-Hall, Inc., 1961.

MCKEAN, ROLAND N. *Efficiency in Government through Systems Analysis.* New York: John Wiley & Sons, Inc., 1958.

NEUSCHEL, RICHARD F. *Management by System.* New York: McGraw-Hill Book Company, 1960.

REDFIELD, CHARLES E. *Communication in Management.* (rev. ed.). Chicago: University of Chicago Press, 1958.

SIMON, HERBERT A. *The New Science of Management Decision.* New York: Harper & Row, 1960.

4

ORGANIZATIONAL OBJECTIVES

With a broad description of the total operation of a management system behind us, we can analyze its subprocesses in finer detail, and this chapter will examine the first subprocess of our normative decision making process: the defining of organizational goals (step 1).

There are several reasons why organizational goal definition is itself a decision making task. Goals have to be periodically changed as an organization decides to undertake new objectives and to discard others; and, the more rigorously goals are determined and defined, the easier it is to decide upon the means for achieving them. Organizational objectives, then, are the basic criteria for deciding between alternative means. If the objectives are uncertain or ambiguous, a line of action will also be less than clear.

Furthermore, interpersonal controversies may be fomented within an organization because objectives have not been precisely defined, and if the disputants have different ends in mind it is quite impossible for them to agree on means. Also, given only vague objectives, the parties are likely to substitute their own values for those of the organization. It is most difficult to resolve such disputes; and such clashes are "healthy" only insofar as they force managers to define the objectives they are attempting to achieve.

Overall objectives should be defined so that the effectiveness of the present organizational activities can be measured. Although a variety of forceful actions may have been expended, it is nevertheless difficult to measure real effectiveness if the definition of the goals is imprecise. One can justify the perform-ance of almost any action if almost any purpose is as good as another.

Defining organizational goals also follows a psychological rationale; it lends rationality to behavior. Individuals are more secure and effective when they know what they are striving for. If the purpose of their organization is ambiguous, they become frustrated because they have no guides for measuring their achievements; they may even regard their activity as irrational. However, with a set of precise goals before them, an individual and an entire organization will experience a conviction of accom-plishment and a rational satisfaction.

A final reason for goal definition is that if the main purpose of an organization is to maintain and increase the welfare of its members (as we have assumed), the nature of this function must be defined. In this way, organizational behavior becomes more purposeful because each individual realizes that his efforts are directed toward an increase in his own well-being. On the other hand, if an organization's objectives are not specifically related to individual benefaction, the individual will question his group motivation and participation. Defining organizational goals, in short, is largely a matter of determining the attributes or proper-ties of organizational objectives.

ORGANIZATIONAL MEMBERSHIP

Because an organization seeks to maintain and increase the welfare of its membership, we must carefully determine the organization's full membership in defining its goals. A common error is to define goals in terms of only part of the member-ship. For example, the goal of the business organization is fre-quently held to be profit maximizing, or the greatest return on capital investment. Here one is primarily concerned with the capital contributors or the welfare of the stockholders, and the contribution of labor and management is largely ignored.

In the case of a hospital, the goal is often stated as improved patient care, and a similar error is made in that the welfare of the medical staff and the employees is disregarded. This is also true of the Department of Defense, whose objective is assumed to be a more effective defense; but here the personal objectives of the individuals who comprise the armed forces are not considered. This error is again repeated when the objectives of one member-ship group are considered only insofar as they serve to achieve the objectives of another membership group. Value judgments

100

have been made as to which membership goals are most important.

One can say that although profit maximizing on invested capital is the goal of the business organization, the welfare of employees cannot be ignored, for if employees are not reasonably satisfied they will not work effectively to maximize profits. The terms of this logic can be just as easily transposed. One could also say that the objective of the business organization is to optimize the welfare of management and employees, but with the proviso that stockholders will receive a minimum return for the necessary capital they contribute for maximizing the welfare of management and labor. But to define organizational goals in terms of only part of its membership violates the entire rationale of organization. Individuals join organizations to increase their individual well-being, and one cannot expect them to participate effectively in any endeavor in which decisions are made that will minimize their payoffs.

From a decision making point of view, what occurs when a segment of an organizational membership decides that its welfare will take precedence over that of the others? The welfare that is to be maximized will always take priority over that of the other groups, and, in minimizing the welfare of the latter, organizational decisions are made that provide only enough satisfaction for the "minimized" individual to retain membership in the organization; any surplus will always go to the "preferred" membership group.

If employees are not considered members of the business organization, the problem arises — at least from an operational point of view — of getting the employee group to cooperate effectively in maximizing the welfare of a group other than its own.

It has already been suggested that the organization, as a cooperative system, is continually faced with two fundamental problems: (1) how can it create more total welfare? and (2) how is this increased utility to be distributed among the members of the organization? As for the first question, given the business organization, how can the resources of labor and capital be used more effectively so as to increase the output per unit of resource input? If an organization has so many units of capital and labor, and if improved modes of operation can be devised so that each unit produces an increased amount of product for sale, one can assume that revenue will be increased. The second question, the distribution of the increased revenue among the contributors to the organization, means what proportion of the increase will go to the capital and what proportion to the labor contributors.

101

One cannot logically conceive of management and labor as constituting necessary organizational segments for creating increased output—and of then precluding these subgroups from the distribution of that increase. Nor can one separate the functions of production and distribution in considering organizational welfare. Psychologists assert that there is a functional relationship between reward and individual effort, and that—although there are exceptions—the higher the reward, the greater will be the effort. The converse is also true.

Another reason for identifying the constituent groups of the organization and their respective utilities is that, whether or not the welfare of the individual is incorporated into the definition of organizational goals (within the context of the organization), he will nevertheless attempt to optimize his personal well-being. If his welfare is not recognized as a legitimate organizational objective, he has to pursue his objectives covertly, under the guise of increasing the welfare of other membership groups; but when actions are performed in this manner the efficiency of producing the total output can be adversely affected. For example, members of the business organization may seek a promotion, but, because the only stated goal may be increasing dividends, and therefore the only way of getting a promotion is by augmenting the output of their departments, they may attempt to justify a larger operation, ostensibly to increase dividends.

If at the outset one recognizes the personal aspirations of the membership—in this last instance the benefits received from promotion—these goals can probably be achieved more efficiently than by increasing the size of the organization by "empire-building." Unless all the membership groups are identified, the process of creating and distributing welfare may become intermixed, with the end result that the total productivity of the organization may be reduced. When one reviews certain proposals it is sometimes difficult to know if they are really means for achieving organizational ends or if they are other ends in themselves, in a disguised form.

In the main, the business organization has been successful in defining its membership and directing its energies toward the increase of its economic welfare. Some firms have profit-sharing plans while others tacitly recognize the same principle in their salary and dividend policies. It is in the nonprofit and governmental organizations that the greatest welfare discrepancies can be observed; hospital goals, for example, are almost invariably defined only in terms of patient care.

Another peculiar problem in the definition of organizational membership is that one might include nonoperational groups, and then define organizational goals in terms of nonoperational objectives. For example, a business might state its objective as serving the public, the consumer, and the supplier; or a university might claim to serve "the community." Organizational membership should therefore be defined according to the control which can be exercised over its contribution, the permanency of its membership, and the membership's commitment to the organization; but the underlying concept should be that the groups which create organizational output will participate in its distribution.

In a business organization, then, the public, the consumer, and the supplier cannot be described as contributing to organizational output, at least not in the accepted terms of organizational activity. These external groups represent constraints upon the organization. Consumers, and the public in general—insofar as the business organization is concerned—can impose limitations upon how the business organization can increase or achieve its objectives. The organization must operate within its legal limits, and these might be viewed as a community constraint; it must also be cognizant of what its competition is doing, which is a market restraint; and it must be aware of changing consumer taste, another market restraint.

A constraint, however, is not an organizational objective. Although the business organization must be aware of the community at large (its environment), it is not compelled to serve that community; rather, the public imposes certain rules to which the organization must adapt. As will be noted later, the nature of the constraints which an organization faces may determine the extent to which organizational goals can be achieved.

The definition of organizational membership is admittedly somewhat arbitrary; in some instances the consumer is considered part of the membership of the organization, but not in others. The hospital patient is generally considered part of the hospital membership, and his goal of patient care has been the traditional objective of the hospital. In educational systems, students are part of the school membership, and their objective (an education) has also been part of the goal structure of the schools. Perhaps the religious organization is the most striking example of organizational membership, the parishioners being consumers, participants, and revenue contributors in their own institution.

However, in all of these cases—although the members are consumers of the services produced by the various organiza-

103

tions—by and large they fit our definition: they are subject to administrative control; they are more or less permanent members; and their commitment to the organization tends to be complete. Needless to say, no one would consider the purchaser of a box of Tide as a member of the Procter and Gamble organization.

But the membership groups of an organization are not always so completely apparent. In the business organization, stockholders, management, and employees are obviously membership groups, or at least one can easily decide how, cooperatively, these groups can increase their output, and one can arrive at a reasonable arrangement for distributing this output among them. When one views, say, the defense department, however, the same approach becomes awkward. We find that the taxpaying public is a membership group that contributes funds, their individual goals being protection from a foreign aggressor. Another constituent group is the armed services, whose objectives are increased salaries, job security, and so forth. Still another constituent group is the political leadership, which includes Congress and the President, whose objectives might be to win reelection.

If the last three groups are accepted as contributing units of input, our analysis still holds: if units of defense output can be increased—with decreased units of resource input—there would presumably be additional welfare for all constituent groups. The taxpayer would get greater defense per tax dollar, the members of the armed services would receive more personal benefits, and, as a result of all this, the political leaders would be reelected more easily.

THE WELFARE FUNCTION

After the membership of an organization has been established, the welfare of the group can then be defined in terms of its specific benefits: what it is that the individuals expect and actually receive from the organization, the needs that they want satisfied. However, a difficulty arises in defining the welfare function of various membership groups in that this function may be many-sided: individuals seek satisfaction for a multitude of needs.

We have indicated that one of the distinguishing differences between organizations is the nature of the welfare each provides for its membership. Churches offer spiritual satisfaction, business provides economic welfare, the government supplies political welfare, hospitals meet the needs of health, and schools provide educational welfare. These four welfare functions differ in nature, and some can be more readily ascertained than others; economic welfare, for example, is more easily defined than spiritual welfare. And, because an individual may hold memberships in all four of these organizations, his aggregate return will represent the totality of his well-being.

An increased return to the organization must then be converted into individual satisfactions of the membership. If a business organization has a highly profitable year, it must convert some of these profits into dividends for its stockholders and into benefits for its management and employees. In the employee and management sectors, profits can be converted into a variety of forms (such as increased salaries or pensions) but it is always important to determine the form of return which will render the greatest individual satisfaction.

In organizations other than businesses, however, one will not find a precise quantitative measurement of goal achievement. The hospital patient is concerned with medical or surgical care; the student wants a good education; the taxpayer looks for national defense. In each case the objective must be defined. What is good patient care? What is a good education? What is optimum defense?

It may well be that determining the defense budget is one of the most difficult problems with which Congress grapples each year. If we assume that there is a limited amount of money that can be spent on defense in any given year, how should this money be distributed to ensure the best defense? How much for submarines, bombers, missiles, or ground forces? These very difficult decisions are not "impossible" if administrators of the defense establishment and congressional leaders share a clear understanding of what constitutes good defense. In the absence of such understanding, each service could maintain that an increase in its allocation of funds would improve the country's defense posture to a greater extent than increases to the other services.

How, then, does one define *qualitative* objectives? This definition comes essentially from determining the value of the elements in the objective, the properties of the goal. Once a list of the characteristics of an organization's objectives has been established, these properties can be ranked and valued, and a qualitative judgment can then be made in terms of the relative position and importance of each property.

105

COLLEGE EDUCATION AS A QUALITATIVE EXAMPLE

To illustrate the decision-maker's approach to a qualitative definition of organizational goals we will cite the purpose of the university, which is to provide a good college education. The college student should acquire skills, a value system, and an understanding and appreciation of his environment. We can then take the skill area and decide that the student should be able to read comprehendingly, write effectively, think clearly, calculate, analyze, and so on. His value system should include a code of moral values, a knowledge of how our democracy works, and so on. His understanding of his environment could be broken down into its physical, social, and spiritual aspects; and his appreciation might be concentrated on music, art, drama, the novel, and so forth.

In compiling the list of requirements, one could also consider areas of accomplishment which are not usually thought of as part of a college education. Should the skills of shoe repairing, automobile mechanics, or welding be taught? And how about including movies, wrestling matches, and boxing? It is at this point that one must evaluate those properties which, if acquired, will mean that a person is college-educated. And this stage is the most important step in arriving at a qualitative definition of a college education.

The second qualitative aspect in deciding the nature of a college education is ranking the selected properties by their relative importance. Should the acquisition of specific skills — reading, writing, thinking, calculating, and analyzing — be ranked higher than the acquisition of a value system? At this stage one might be able not only to rank the properties but to do so with a quantitative magnitude. We could compare the importance of acquiring physical skills with that of acquiring appreciation of the cultural aspects of contemporary society or its history.

The third step in the qualitative definition of a college education is determining the extent to which a student should acquire any of the properties we have listed. For example, with reference to the quantitative acquisition of reading skills we would want to know the degree to which a student can read and comprehend increasingly complex material, and we therefore have to be able to evaluate the relative complexity of material and to test the comprehension. As a student's reading skills improve, the magnitude of his progress can be measured through periodic testing.

In a similar manner, once it is determined which aspects of his total environment the college student should best understand, we can measure the extent of this achievement. In the area of the physical environment, a student would be tested upon his achievement in physics, chemistry, biology, zoology, and astronomy (if these had been established as the requisite courses), and, over the four-year college span, we could determine his progress in all of these studies. Knowing the extent of the improvement of his understanding, we can then introduce a quantitative measurement into what is essentially a qualitative objective.

Thus, acquisition of an advanced education would be declared as the purpose of a student's attending college. The decision-makers of the university, in turn, would take this objective and give it a precise quantitative and qualitative definition, and a graduate would be expected to have attained commensurate attributes in his four years at college. These attributes would already have been compiled, defined, and weighed in terms of their relative importance and of the degree of achievement expected of the average student in any one of them.

Whether organizational goals have been precisely defined can be measured by the progress in goal achievement. In the case of the university, one can determine, over time, the extent to which college students are acquiring the attributes necessary for achieving the proper objectives. If improvements occur, the degree to which students are obtaining these attributes will be continually increasing. For example, if improvement is technically possible, and if an understanding of one's physical environment is a desirable attribute, each graduating class should have a greater comprehension of its physical environment than did the preceding class. The ability to measure is the ultimate test of precision in defining organizational goals.

MULTIPLE GOALS

Defining objectives in terms of organizational membership encounters the problem of multiple organizational goals. In business organizations the goals are to maximize the economic welfare of stockholders, managers, and employees; but the form of return may be different among these groups in that stockholders receive increased dividends while management and employees derive increased welfare from higher salaries and wages. A university may also have multiple goals of improving the quality of education while increasing the economic and academic welfare of its faculty.

In the multiple-goal situation, management follows the same

principles of definition as in the college education example. Each goal is defined in terms of its properties. These, in turn, are weighed against their relative importance and against the degree of proficiency which must be reached in any single property, with the assumption that the objectives of all membership groups are of equal importance.

A particular difficulty in multiple-goal definition is that an organization may have a multiplicity of specific but noncomplementary objectives in its pursuit of a given goal, and this may reduce the extent to which it can achieve other goals. For example, if we view the nation as an organization, and concentrate on its international objectives, we see that some of its goals are the maintenance of peace, national security, prestige, and influence; however, if national prestige were to be increased by successful aggressions, this goal achievement would clearly preclude the objective of maintaining peace. In this case, rather than having objectives that are additive in nature, we would have a plus and minus matrix. To optimize such a matrix, given all the pluses and minuses, we would still follow a line of action which would yield or attain a net advantage.

To illustrate this approach hypothetically, let us suppose that international objectives can be measured in comparable units, and that one unit of peace equals five units of national prestige. We will further assume that a suggestion has been made that the President meet with a hostile head of state to attempt to reduce world tension. If it were certain, on one hand, that such a meeting would reduce tension and thus promote peace, but would lessen the prestige of the United States, the President's choice would turn on the "quantity" of the expected gain and loss. If the increased units of peace were at least one-fifth of the loss of prestige units, the President would attend the meeting; but if the nation were to lose ten units of prestige and gain only one unit of peace, he would avoid the meeting.

APPROACHES TO QUALITATIVE DEFINITION

A definition of organizational goals is affected by individual judgment because management must still decide on the specific properties of the ends it attempts to achieve. However, it can look to certain guides in making this decision. Reliance on experts is one guide; and, for the properties that constitute a good college education, management can turn to the college professor. To determine the properties of good patient care, management might rely upon physicians; or turn to generals for the definition of a good national defense. It is a logical assumption that professional groups will develop the highest standards in their respective areas; accordingly—and again as an example—professional standards are used to determine if an educational system should be accredited.

Another measurement is market determination. In one form or another, competition exists among organizations for the individual's time, effort, money, and loyalty. Therefore, if an individual selects one organization over another, we can assume that the services which the former organization provides are superior. And therefore if enough individuals fail to receive a satisfactory personal return for their organizational contributions, they will terminate their membership, and the organization will dissolve because it was unable to fulfill its purposes. History shows that many economic, educational, political, social, and religious institutions have disappeared for this reason, and that others have taken their places.

Another qualitative approach is through a consensus of the organizational contributors in which all agree on the specific objectives they are attempting to achieve, an approach that is exemplified by a labor union or a social fraternity. Moreover, the consensus is probably the preferred approach because each individual is able to affect his personal well-being by his individual choice; indeed, individual benevolence is highly personal and variable, and that which is desirable for one individual is sometimes deemed detrimental by another.

Even here, however, all of the noted methods are necessary because the individual is often unable to judge what is in his own best interest. There may be technical reasons, as in national defense or medical care, for relying upon experts; or a student may be too young to make a mature choice. For these and other reasons, it is sometimes unfeasible, or too costly, for an organization to obtain total consensus in a continuing and precise manner.

OPTIMIZING INDIVIDUAL WELFARE

After the welfare function of organizational membership has been defined, the dimensions of increasing that welfare can be examined. The stockholder desires more dividends, management higher salaries, the employee higher wages. Given the external environment of an organization, the extent to which membership welfare will be increased depends on how effectively the resources of the organization are utilized. An organization can distribute to its membership only as much welfare as that membership has produced; managers cannot allot—to the stockholders or employees—that which does not exist. Thus organizational goals, representing the composite of the individual goals, are generally stated as a ratio, or as the greatest output per unit of resource input.

An efficiency concept underlies this dimension. An unvarying intent of organized activity is to get the greatest output per unit of input, which is the same as a search for the optimum utilization of organizational resources. In the business organization we look upon capital as one of the inputs, and the return or the productivity of capital is a measurement of the efficiency of capital's use, given the environment of the organization. Hence, if a particular organization's return on its capital is 20 or 30 per cent per year, contrasted with another organization's return of 5 to 10 per cent, investments are being utilized much more efficiently in the first case, and return is therefore much greater. Labor input can be viewed in much the same way.

This test of efficiency can be applied to all organizations: to private, profit-making organizations, to nonprofit organizations such as universities and hospitals, and to a community organization such as the public school system. To learn the increase in an organization's goal achievement, one must examine the changes in its output and in its resources input. If, in a given hospital, patient care were improving, and the amount of capital and labor devoted to that patient care remained constant, this organization's efficiency would be increasing.

Organizational goals are sometimes appraised along a one-dimensional line rather than as a ratio analysis, a perhaps unrealistic viewpoint because it ignores the fact that the resources of an organization are always limited. Thus if we think of a hospital's goals only in terms of improving patient care, we could assume that in achieving this end there would be no limits on the organizational costs; and that, with no resource limits, the hospital could utilize any number of resources so long as patient care continued to improve. Or, regarding the goals of the defense department solely in terms of improved defense, we could again assume that the costs or resources for achieving this goal are unlimited. This, of course, is not the case; there is a limit to the resources that any organization can expend.

The business organization has traditionally used the efficiency guide in its goal definition, particularly for capital input, but nonprofit and public institutions have not. For example, neither public officials nor the community measure an educational sys-

110

tem by the units of learning acquired per student per educational tax dollar expended; instead, the popular attitude is that better education necessitates increased expenditures. One possible reason for this attitude is that the administrative and operating personnel of these systems lack the incentive to improve their efficiency, perhaps because operational improvements do not generally produce an improved return to the operating personnel. And this may derive from imperfect goal definition, from a disregarded membership, or from inadequate institutional arrangements that do not provide for an increased organizational effectiveness being equitably shared among the organizational membership. Another reason for this may be that because the educational organization provides a public or noneconomic welfare, the efficiency guide is not felt to be as valid or binding.

It may also be that part of the antipathy toward governmental and semiprivate charitable organizations comes from lack of confidence that they *can* use their resources more efficiently. Therefore a first step for these managers might be the redefinition of their objectives, in ratio form, so that they can present data to the public that will substantiate an effective use of the dollar inputs. Insistence upon justifying defense proposals in terms of defense capability output per unit of tax dollar input is a step in the right direction.

Optimizing the utilization of its resources is the specific function and responsibility of management, and management, in performing its decision making function, must continually strive and search for greater efficiency. If there were no need to optimize the use of resources, there would be no need for the managerial function. Effective management of organizational resources therefore results in a greater return to its human resources: capital receives higher dividends; labor and management receive higher wages and salaries; the taxpayer pays lower taxes.

MAINTAINING INDIVIDUAL WELFARE

Since individuals want not only to increase their welfare but also to maintain it over time, an organization must define both its immediate and long-run goals. The achievement of short- or long-run objectives, however, depends largely on the particular means being used. Some programs require considerable implementation time, and the payoff may lie far in the future. For example, a company's research and development division may expend considerable time and money before it produces a profitable product. On the other hand, some improvements are accomplished within a few weeks. A short-run goal usually means a year or less; a long-run goal, five, ten, fifteen, or even twenty years.

As the probability of a program's success decreases, management tends to concentrate on the achievement of goals in the near future—or in a one- to two-year span—and it attempts to work on a step by step basis. And management, although it may hold certain long-term objectives, generally breaks these objectives down into shorter time periods. If these substeps are successful in the near future, management plans the next series of steps, until the ultimate long-run program is reached.

Management retains flexibility when it concentrates on the near future. If events occur which require the modification of a program, it can more easily accomplish this task. For example, management may project a certain organizational size five or ten years in the future, entailing a specific plant or specific capacity, but construction of the plant may proceed on a "piecemeal" basis, affording management the opportunity to review its long-run projections in relation to its actual, developing needs. Management would not construct a plant for meeting a demand that is expected to develop only fifteen years hence.

Another aspect of the welfare maintenance problem is the stability of goal achievement over time. An organization may increase its average return over time, but this return may fluctuate rather widely. For example, over a ten-year period a business may have dramatically increased its return, although in the first two years it may have lost much money, shown a very high net income the next two years, and so on. Despite a high overall return, it seems that people want a stabilized welfare: stockholders want predictable dividends and wage earners want predictable wages.

A variant of stability occurs in welfare consumption when a company postulates a large payoff in long-run goals if the individual is willing to forego immediate benefits. The dangers here, however, are the uncertainty of the future payoff, the cost of immediate denial, and the tendency to become involved in long-run means rather than ends. Under a communistic system, for example, tremendous economic resources may be concentrated upon building an industrial plant, but the project may become an end in itself, and we may find that more steel plants are built so that more steel can be poured to construct even more steel plants. In reality, there is no payoff for the individuals involved.

The twin organizational goals of maintaining and gradually increasing individual welfare must be combined through im-

112

provements over time. With each unit of time, organizational members should find themselves in a better situation than in the past; and the organization should continually improve upon its goal achievement.

If a firm receives a 10 per cent return on capital and pays an average wage of $2 per hour, and if we look for a 10 per cent increase over time, the firm would have to receive an 11 per cent return in the second year and pay a wage rate of $2.20; receive a 12 per cent return in the third year and pay $2.42 per hour; etc. Or, if one would measure a private mental hospital's effectiveness over the long run, he would expect the number of patients who resume their normal roles (per dollar unit expended) to continually increase, as would the wages and salaries of the hospital's personnel.

It is therefore the rate of improvement, over time, that represents the true measurement of organizational welfare and effectiveness.

ENDS AND MEANS

Another problem in the definition of organizational goals is the tendency to confuse organizational means and ends. In the business organization, for example, some economists assert three goals: profit, share of the market, and effective management development. However, it is only the profits — those which are converted into increased benefits for the organizational membership — which can be considered as the end of the organization; the share of the market and management development are only the means for achieving this end. The distinguishing characteristic of organizational goals is that they must represent some form of individual satisfaction; they must be synonymous with individual objectives.

Furthermore, individuals are not necessarily in a better personal position even if their organization has actually won a greater share of the market, although increasing its share of the market may be a means toward this personal end. Maximizing means is nonrational if it turns out that individuals are working toward an end which provides no individual satisfaction. It is therefore apparent that a distinction must always be made between organizational means and ends.

A business organization, to achieve its ultimate goals, must perform certain functions, and each function can be broken into subactivities, such as those of the sales department (or of advertising, product development, customer service, and so on). Each department can also be broken down until we arrive at the job activities of a single individual, and these job activities can then be classified into specific tasks. Each division, department, and individual has its respective outputs, which each attempts to achieve. But these outputs are only the result of *organizational* activities, and they are only the means for attaining organizational goals.

FICTITIOUS OBJECTIVES

Still another problem in defining organizational goals arises from fictitious versus real organizational objectives, as when an organization's stated goals are seldom, or never, utilized. For example, a company may declare that one of its objectives is to increase the public welfare, but there may be no operational attempt to do this, and the decision making process may never utilize this particular goal.

Organizational goals should not be defined on the basis of public relations (and we will not consider this purpose in our context); defining goals should be nothing more than the honest effort by an organization's membership to ascertain what it will attempt to achieve. Once this definition is made, the membership can devote its resources and energy to this particular end. Defining goals, then, is a matter of establishing the nature of the individual welfare which inheres in an organization.

Admittedly, as our analysis has indicated, it may not be easy to select specific objectives that will maximize individual well-being when many individuals are involved in a common enterprise. On the other hand, it is inappropriate for management to sit down and write a list, based upon "opinion," of the goals its organization should pursue. This would seem to have happened in some organizations, if we can judge from their stated or published "credos."

THE APPLICATION OF GOAL DEFINITIONS

Once goals have been defined it is important that they are utilized in the decision making process (how this can be done will be examined in Chapter 5, Devising Organizational Solutions). Whatever the objectives, they must be used by the submanagerial staff to decide between alternative lines of action. If operating goals are hidden, inappropriately applied, not utilized, or varied from manager to manager, the ultimate purpose of the organization may be jeopardized.

Even if goals are not formally defined, they will nevertheless be utilized; every time a decision is made, certain criteria must be used in order to choose from alternative decisions, and these criteria become the real operational goals of the enterprise. If every submanager has the opportunity to decide the organizational objectives for himself each time he makes a decision, he may be using personal rather than organizational objectives; and in such instances the organizational unit is actually operating to optimize the submanager's welfare. Unquestionably, management is a membership group, and its welfare must be enhanced, but it is not the only membership group. Therefore, organizational goals must be rigorously defined and applied.

If organizational goals have not been properly integrated with the decision making process, we can assume that submanagers' decisions will not lead to the enhancement of organizational objectives, and this permits the nondecision-maker, such as the stockholder, to question any decision. Is its purpose directed to the composite goal of all, or only toward the manager's benefit? Confidence in the integrity of the entire decision making process can thus be shaken and withdrawn.

RECORD OF GOAL ACHIEVEMENT

Every organization has a record and a history of goal achievement. Given the objective of the business organization to increase its return over time, a review of these records — principally the income statement — will reveal the extent of these increases (or decreases) and when they occurred.

Is it possible for an organization to reach a state of maximum return, a state in which no improvement is even theoretically possible? Because of the dynamic aspect of the organization's environment and constant technological changes, it is highly doubtful that an organization will ever attain such perfection; but, more realistically, we can visualize a "diminishing" degree of improvement, over time, as an organization *approaches* this unattainable condition. Once again, we will use the business organization as an example.

Over a period of time the return to an organization may increase, but at a decreasing rate; and there may be a point at which one would not expect the organization to achieve more. Such a business may initially have received 10 per cent on its capital investment, and, over a period of time, increased it to 20 or 30 per cent. Theoretically, there would have to be a point at which it becomes highly unlikely that the organization can improve, and this might be the point of 30 or 40 per cent return on investment.

Goal achievement, then, is not conceived in absolute terms; there is no predetermined standard which the organization must achieve, no point at which there is no longer a need to improve its operation. Goal achievement is always dynamic; its measure is its rate of advancement toward a theoretical maximum or perfect state.

After management has defined its overall goals, this definition of achievement remains fixed, or relatively stable, unless the organization undertakes entirely new activities or acquires new membership groups, which necessitates a redefinition of goals.

SUMMARY

The first step in the decision making process is the definition of organizational objectives, which are the criteria used to decide among alternative solutions. Because the organization seeks to maintain and increase the welfare of its membership, the process of definition involves determining (1) the organization's membership and (2) the nature of the members' welfare. Organizations may have multiple goals which are noncomplementary. In such instances, that line of action would be followed which would provide a net advantage to the membership.

In the process of goal determination, management may utilize qualified individuals, market determinants, and the consensus of the organization's members. Individual welfare is a function of the efficiency of resource utilization, and individuals desire not only an increase but the maintenance of their satisfaction or welfare. Thus the true measurement of organizational success is the rate of improvement in individual welfare over time.

Organizational ends and means can be distinguished insofar as ends should always relate to individual satisfaction. Whether defined or not, objectives are the goals that managers actually use as decision criteria in evaluating alternative lines of action.

QUESTIONS FOR DISCUSSION

1. Evaluate the assertion that the objective of the business enterprise is to maximize profits.
2. The corporation can be analyzed from a number of viewpoints: legal, economic, technological, social (a human entity), and politi-

cal. Would the membership and objectives of the corporation vary in relation to each approach? Explain.

3. In evaluating the goals of a society, and depending upon individual values, why is one more likely to conclude that the welfare of a certain group is more important than that of another?

4. Why is it important that the same process be used for producing organizational and individual welfare?

5. The welfare of individuals and groups is difficult to define and measure because it is largely a subjective phenomenon. What economic and political mechanisms can measure individual welfare?

6. Because welfare is difficult to measure, why is it important that our organizational, economic, and political mechanisms provide maximum individual choice?

7. Under what circumstances would it be inadvisable to rely on individual choice as an indicator of welfare?

8. Why do individuals prefer a constant or stable flow of satisfactions?

9. Is it possible for the objectives of an organization to differ from those of the individuals who comprise it? Explain.

10. How can one determine the true or operating objectives of an organization? What is the probability that the operating and the stated objectives will be identical?

SUGGESTED READINGS

BERLE, ADOLF A., JR. *The Twentieth Century Capitalist Revolution.* New York: Harcourt, Brace & World, Inc., 1954.

CHURCHMAN, C. WEST. *Prediction and Optimal Decision.* Englewood Cliffs, N.J.: Prentice-Hall, Inc., 1961.

EELLS, RICHARD, AND WALTON, CLARENCE. *Conceptual Foundations of Business.* Homewood, Ill.: Richard D. Irwin, Inc., 1961.

LINDBLOM, CHARLES E. "The Science of Muddling Through," *Public Administration Review,* 19 (Spring, 1959), 79–88.

MASON, EDWARD S. (ed.). *The Corporation in Modern Society.* Cambridge, Mass.: Harvard University Press, 1960.

5

DEVISING ORGANIZATIONAL SOLUTIONS

Once organizational objectives have been defined, the problem is then how to achieve these goals; and, for that purpose, organizational solutions must be devised. This process of constructing solutions incorporates four subsequent decision making steps:

1. Raising organizational problems (Step 2);
2. Analyzing the problem (Step 3);
3. Searching for solutions (Step 4); and
4. Selecting the best solution (Step 5).

RAISING THE ORGANIZATIONAL PROBLEM (STEP 2)

Raising organizational problems means bringing to the attention of the problem-solvers or submanagers the question of rearranging or modifying an organizational activity so that organizational goals may be attained more effectively. These questions should be thought of as inputs into the decision making process and as the raw material upon which the decision-makers will work.

What is the general nature of an organizational problem, and what events will indicate a problem area? Problem indicators can be classified in two general categories. The first relates to a situation in which the expected payoff from an applied solution is not being achieved. The second is a new environmental state which presents an opportunity to increase one's return.

The sequence of decision making steps will differ in these two situations. When an incorrect solution is utilized, data will have to be obtained to ascertain the reasons, and then the needed corrective action can be investigated. In the second situation, data are collected that reflect the changing external and internal environmental events, and, if it appears that significant changes have occurred which provide greater opportunities for the organization, new programs can be devised to take advantage of these changes.

PROBLEM INDICATORS AS A SCANNING PROCESS

Determining the existence of an organizational problem is an information gathering and sorting process; it is the "perceptual" or "sensory" aspect of an organization and is part of the intelligence unit of an enterprise.[1] As for the first problem category, let us assume it is possible to forecast and categorize environmental states to which an organization will respond with preprogrammed actions. We will also assume that, given the environmental state and the responses, the organization expects to receive a payoff from each response. The intelligence or scanning unit will collect data on the actual solution payoff, and, if the difference between the expected and the actual payoff is too great, this will raise or "trigger" a problem.[2] The scanning data might appear as follows (with an excessive differential recorded for the second state, 767):

Current	Environmental State	Response	Expected Payoff	Actual Payoff	Error or Problem
1.	343	217	$ 15,000	$ 15,500	no problem
2.	767	435	35,000	15,000	problem
3.	134	631	167,000	170,000	no problem

SEARCH FOR OPPORTUNITY

A second broad problem-input category occurs if an environmental state is indicated or forecasted for which the firm has no response, and if a new solution would produce an increment in payoff. Environmental states can be ranked by how favorable their potential payoffs could be. If a firm is the sole seller of a product for which there is great demand, whose price can be increased rapidly, and if there is no possibility of competitors

---

[1] See Chapter 3, Designing a Management System.
[2] See Chapter 7, Effectuating the Decision, for the measurement of the solution payoff.

entering the market, and government restrictions will not be a constraint, the firm is in a highly favorable economic situation if it is also reasonably efficient. On the other hand, an economic state can be unfavorable, with decreasing demand and extensive price competition among many firms, so that even if a firm is highly efficient it could suffer an economic loss.

The capability of an organization is limited because its resources are limited, and it is therefore geared to respond to only a limited number of environmental states. It is obviously uneconomical to provide standby capabilities of men and machines for reacting to all possible environmental situations; a manufacturer of basic steel, for example, cannot maintain idle men and machines on the assumption that an opportunity may arise in the form of a new automobile company.

An enterprise must decide which environmental conditions it will respond to and which it will ignore, and it must, over time, also decide whether it will stop reacting to certain situations and begin reacting to others. Thus it must decide whether to broaden or to reduce its response capability; and it must recognize favorable situations.

OPPORTUNITY IN THE EXTERNAL ENVIRONMENT

New opportunities can arise in either the external or the internal environment of the firm, and, although our distinction between the two is somewhat arbitrary, the external environment (as used in this text) will refer simply to those events that are perceived by the scanning device to occur outside the organization. The emphasis of this chapter will be on the external environment, which represents the major source of new opportunities. Therefore the external environment, and the features that warrant most attention for new opportunities, can be classified into the general areas of economics, politics, technology, ideology, psychology, and sociology.

A changing economic environment means that an organization's customers, competition, or factors (its labor, material, and capital) are—in some manner—changing their behavior. Customer demand for a firm's product or service, for example, may change over time: customers may want more, or less, of the product, or a changed product; they may even cease using a product. Competition is another dynamic aspect of an organization's economic environment, involving competitive changes in price, product, or service. And the factor markets also subject prices and quality to constant changes.

The significance of the economic environment is relatively evident as far as a business organization is concerned: customer behavior continually changes, and a business organization must adapt to these changes. However, the economic environment of other organizations is not so apparent, although it is just as necessary that a public school system be sensitive to changing consumer demand. Increases in income may lead to greater demands for education, and the quality of the desired education may also change; indeed, competitive influences are present even here, as families deliberately move from an "inferior" school district into one that is "better." Nor will voters reelect board of education members who do not provide the services they seek; and teachers, similarly, may refuse to work in a school system that pays low salaries. It is equally important that economic considerations are not ignored in religious organizations: churches have to be built, clergy and teachers hired, and missions continued.

Political affairs is another aspect of an organization's environment. Enacted or proposed legislation may either impose restraints or provide new opportunities. The lowering of tariffs among nations may give businesses an opportunity to enter new foreign markets. Decisions obtained through election results are of course crucial to political organizations, and voters may raise or lower taxes and approve or defeat bond issues, all of which will determine the economic income of all the affected political units — perhaps with the result that new officials will be elected, who are committed to new programs.

International political changes have recently taken on unusual significance, so that it is no longer possible to consider only domestic political changes. Insofar as various business and governmental units are involved with other nations, greater understanding of the political components of these countries is required. Political forces and trends underlie political decisions in both the domestic and the international spheres, which in turn often determine the nature, direction, and magnitude of legislation.

Technology is yet another facet of an organization's environment. Innovation enables changed and improved performance, and we find the results of technological changes in most of our products, materials, equipment, concepts, methods, and systems. Innovations can affect the environment of an organization and can also introduce new ways for pursuing its operations more effectively; thus organizations must be aware of new technologies in order to utilize them fully.

Another environmental factor is ideology, which is concerned

121

with society's value system. On an individual as well as a collective basis, certain behavior and trends are interpreted as good or bad, as having a positive or a negative value. Their stability can be brief or lasting; religious values, for example, are generally stable and persist over long periods of time. And there are the leisure-time vogues and fads: outdoor barbecues in one phase, and water-skiing and surf-boarding in the next. These fads are short-lived.

Organizations also have a psychological environment—and it is important that they also understand how individuals respond to environmental changes. Because an organization communicates with the public—the consumer, the voter, the employee, the investor, the saver—it should know or be able to predict the reactions of each group under various influences, especially when it seeks to modify or direct the behavior of the public.

The sociological environment relates to social structure, role definition, status arrangements, social leadership, inter- and intragroup interaction, and that process of socialization which is concerned with such concepts as attitude, deviance, conformity, aggression, and so forth. Changes in roles, expectations, and status can directly or indirectly affect organizations. The current racial situation has a tremendous impact upon the business, educational, political, and spiritual organizations of our society. And abroad, underdeveloped nations are demanding political independence and self-determination—a major status change and one of the most significant revolutions of our time.

Organizations are vitally concerned with specific aspects of their external environment whenever these aspects are felt to be crucial for success. Religious organizations are fundamentally interested in the ideological aspects of their environment; business is concerned with the economic aspects; our defense area is involved with the political aspects; and charitable organizations are interested in the sociological and economic aspects of their environment. Yet each institution must be made more aware of its total environment because other determinants can also affect its operation. Business, for example, cannot concentrate on the economic environment and ignore the political or sociological areas.

Although the external environment can be broken down into its component factors and analyzed, the organization's environment is really an interdependent, interacting system: ideological changes can create economic and political innovations, which in turn can induce further ideological changes. No single area can be totally isolated from another because an organization is only a small subpart of the total and organic social system. If a business organization wants to understand consumer behavior, it is necessary to collect data on all behavioral subsystems: the technological, political, psychological, sociological, and ideological—as well as the economic.

If information is continually collected and funneled into a central unit, all aspects of the environment can be systematically interrelated and a more realistic view of the actual situation can be obtained. The environment does not break down into neat academic compartments to facilitate its analysis, and therefore, if intelligence efforts are disconnected, biases can develop which overemphasize certain aspects of the environment. The data of the economist should be integrated with those of the political scientist, the psychologist, and the sociologist.

INTERNAL ENVIRONMENT

Organizations also require information about the operational behavior of their resources—about their internal environment— and the dimensions of this behavior are similar to those of the external environment. Although careful attention is directed to the behavioral aspects of the total internal resources—equipment, plant, material, and personnel—personnel is probably the most significant and complex factor.

Organizational action also has its internal economic, political, technological, ideological, psychological, and sociological components. The ideological values and expectations of employees change; and the technology of the organization tends to become more efficient. An organization's internal politics—the nature and amount of influence which individuals or groups are able to exercise—may likewise vary (the informal group or clique, needless to say, is an endemic aspect of every organization). When individuals are moved from job to job within an organization, the nature of their interaction will be modified because of personality factors: some individuals communicate harmoniously with others and some do not. The importance of the economic aspects of the organization, in terms of cost and output, is easily demonstrable, but the impact of the sociological area—roles, status, and expectations—is more difficult to ascertain.

It should also be obvious that changing external events can cause innovations in the internal components of an organization; labor shortages for example will affect the organizational roles of individuals in the corresponding occupations.

THE SCANNING APPARATUS

We have said that in order to be sensitive to changes in its external and internal environments, an organization must have a sensory perception mechanism, an intelligence unit.[3] The function of this unit is similar to that of a radar device; it constantly scans the environments of the organization and registers changes (which constitute the principal source of problem inputs for the management system). For the purpose of our analysis we will assume that such a unit is centralized within the organization and that it possesses the specialists and equipment necessary for executing the following subprocesses:

1. Determining what data to gather;
2. Collecting information;
3. Forecasting environmental events; and
4. Raising problems.

DETERMINING DATA REQUIREMENTS

The first task of the intelligence unit is to determine the data it should collect for deciding whether problems exist. Three classes of data are therefore collected: (1) forecasts of opportunity states, (2) measurements of solution effectiveness, and (3) forecasts of environmental states for which the firm has been preprogrammed.

In categories two and three, managers provide the information which the intelligence unit will scan (which will be examined in Chapter 7, Effectuating the Decision), but, for the first category, the intelligence unit will have to define opportunity states, or simulate the preferred and nonpreferred environmental situations for which there are no programs. The source for this first category of data, we will assume, is the behavioral and informational specialists who constitute the intelligence unit, and who, because of their specialized training, can postulate relatively successful models.

The history of an organization, or that of other organizations, can serve as indicators of the conditions under which the firm or firms have achieved success, and, when these indicators are structured in terms of such environmental factors as economics, politics, technology, etc., the (human) scanning device can search for similar states — as when a retail chain, for example, finds that historically favorable environmental factors have reappeared.

[3] See Chapter 3, Designing the Management System.

These factors might include the percentage of the buying public that receives a particular income or that lives within a particular radius—if these factors have proved to be success-ensuring circumstances. For example, the state department's foreign aid officials may have learned that its program is most successful in countries which have a high literacy rate. The effectiveness of organizations can therefore be surveyed in an attempt to ascertain favorable environmental factors.

Another helpful source of data for opportunity model-building is information on past mistakes; if it is established that certain environmental factors have produced negative results, these factors can be avoided in the future. Thus an organization will learn from its errors as well as its achievements, and it will have a series of models for postulating favorable and unfavorable environmental conditions. As data compilation reveals a trend toward either of these states, an organization will respond appropriately.

DATA COLLECTION

After environmental standards have been established and pre-programmed in keeping with opportunity conditions, the intelligence unit will collect further data in an attempt to forecast the environmental states which will probably occur. These data are usually classified as primary and secondary information. Primary data (or "raw" data or information) will come from an organization's survey of its public, from its customers, suppliers, employees, investors, and competitors—through formal mail-out questionnaires, combinations of questionnaires and interviews, or interviews. (These techniques, however, pose problems of completeness and validity of information.) Secondary information usually consists of published data: government reports, journals, newspapers, trade association publications, and the like (which can pose a problem of sheer volume or quantity). Many organizations therefore maintain private libraries to provide easy access to historical and current information.

DATA SORTING

The flow of data into an organization must be meaningfully arranged in order to facilitate interpretation. For example, when the accounting function examines the internal environment it accumulates data and compiles it into balance, income, and cost statements; as for the external environment, the sales or market research function formulates sales projections; and school reg-

125

istrars similarly project changes in enrollment. Data, it is clear, must be systematized in the form of charts, tables, diagrams, or other symbolic representations, one reason for this being that both external and internal stimuli are discrete occurrences which appear to be random and disconnected. If an employee quits, a machine breaks down, a billing error is made, and two supervisors have a disagreement, and if these events are merely recorded, the implication would be that the environment in which these four events occurred is relatively meaningless.

Certain guides are used in classifying material. First, similar events are *categorized:* in the external environment, all changes in family income can be grouped together, changes in consumer taste placed in another division, relevant political events in still another, and so on. A second guide is *continuity:* data can be arranged along a time or space continuum; and an organization would keep a record of sales, or the number of employees that quit over a certain time period. A third guide is *closure:* incomplete data can be interpolated so that a complete and meaningful pattern of information is provided.

If these guides are followed, events which may otherwise have appeared to be disconnected and insignificant may suggest a definite pattern that can be meaningfully interpreted; and this practice is very necessary in decision making because an organization usually reacts to a relationship between and among events rather than to a single event. Sales policy is not changed because a customer does not purchase an item on a specific day, but if many customers, over a long period of time, no longer purchase this item, the consequent falling sales revenue will emerge as a pattern to which the business organization must respond.

Strong configurations will dominate weaker ones, or those which are incomplete or discontinuous, and a manager will usually turn to the areas of activity which present the clearest figures. However, it is important to note that the clearest pattern need not be the most significant area of reaction, and the manager should not respond to events solely because they are immediate or nonambiguous. The clearest patterns might very often represent unimportant problem areas.

DATA INTERPRETATION

Information, after it has been gathered and organized, must be interpreted to discover if an organizational problem exists, and a screening device will then select any areas that require attention. Coupled with this monitoring device is a trigger mechanism that will alert and activate the organization's problem solving function.

This monitoring device signals the existence of an organizational problem (1) if organizational performance does not meet the expected standard or (2) if new organizational opportunities exist. In considering the first category, we must assume the existence of an internal auditing procedure[4] which collects data in terms of organizational results and performance; any time these data indicate a deviation from the expected norm, the selector will note the deviation and the triggering mechanism will alert the manager to the trouble area. Both the monitoring and the triggering mechanisms can be viewed as a servomechanism of the organizational problem solving function.

A furnace thermostat performs a similar function in monitoring heat standards. When the temperature falls below the set standard, the thermostat triggers the furnace, which emits more heat. Data that relate to organizational performance enter a similar monitoring device, and whenever performance falls below predetermined standards the triggering device automatically refers this fact to the problem solving function for corrective action. The key to interpreting data is therefore a predetermination of appropriate standards for organizational operations. For example, an organization's projected budget for the cost and output of its operating units will provide such a standard. Actual cost data are gathered and compared with expected costs, and a problem is indicated if there is a significant differential.

If opportunity states are discovered for which the organization has no program, the intelligence unit compares its forecasts of what is expected to happen with what the firm would like to see occur in its environment or preestablished opportunity situations. If these situations are equal, or are predicted to be equal (within the time required for the firm to respond), another problem is triggered. This is essentially an intelligence unit's comparison of forecasts with the inventory of ranked environmental models.

Let us suppose that a firm which manufactures television sets has no present capability for servicing the European Common Market, but let us further suppose that it has formulated an opportunity environmental model which indicates the minimum requirements for achieving success in this market. If the intelligence unit predicts that the prerequisite conditions will exist in five years, this prediction or forecast would trigger a problem

[4] See Chapter 7 for a discussion of the audit procedure.

of how to supply this market. Ideally, the firm would enter the market when it met the minimum requirements.

In the determination of opportunity models and in subsequent forecasts, considerable freedom must be granted the specialists in the intelligence unit. They should be permitted to search for random opportunity situations — as in our Common Market example — because some preferred opportunity states will have a random characteristic, such as technological innovations in television sets. Organizations also can have preprogrammed responses for changed situations; in these cases all characteristics of the situation are recognized, and the only required action is implementation of the programmed policy.

Falling sales might be used to exemplify a preprogrammed response. If it becomes necessary for a firm to constrict its operations because of a falling sales volume, it may have already prepared a program for doing this most efficiently. Thus, whatever the amount of the sales volume drop, a program for that condition could be put into effect. If sales dropped 10 per cent, a specific program would be automatically effectuated; and still another program would be used if sales dropped 20 per cent. On the other hand, increases in sales would also have specific and related programs. An entirely new program situation occurs if a firm has not devised its responses, and a program must then be planned by the problem solving machinery.

Even with preprogrammed responses, an organization may require considerable time for adapting to changes in its external determinants. If a forecast could be made of the nature of these determinants, the organization could begin to adjust even before their occurrence, and before these events could have a negative effect.

We see, then, that isolated problem situations are described and forwarded to the control unit, which sends them to the appropriate problem-solver. In the management system we have outlined, the scanning and problem-raising processes are separated from the problem solving function so that information can be filtered out and so that only the problem areas themselves will be brought to the attention of the problem-solvers.

It is neither essential nor practical for comprehensive information about organizational operations, even in condensed form, to flow into the problem solving function of an organization. If operations have been properly formulated, most information will be only confirmative, and there is little reason for inundating submanagers with nonessential data. If a problem-solver must search through columns of figures and through charts, graphs, and reports to ascertain the existence of a problem, he may never have time to provide a solution.

ORGANIZATIONAL INSENSITIVITY

Organizations, unlike individuals, are not born with a sensory apparatus, yet "sensory" devices must be developed because of an organization's dependence upon its external and internal stimuli. Every organization has had one or more executives who were closely attuned to their environment, and who helped the organization respond and successfully adapt to it through appropriate actions. However, if an organization becomes unaware of its environmental changes, keeping its policies and practices "intact," these policies may someday prove to be outmoded. By way of illustration, Henry Ford insisted upon manufacturing only one model (the Model T), and only in black. Other car manufacturers began to change their models every three or four years, and, as a result, the Ford Company—which had initially provided the public with what it wanted through highly successful policies—lost its automobile leadership after fifteen years because its original policy had become outmoded and ineffective.

Many actual information-gathering devices, which should continuously and systematically cite changing events, are not as developed as they could be. Indeed, some organizations have extremely primitive information-gathering devices, and some have none at all; still others have mechanisms for gathering internal data but none for external data. Or, if an organization gathers external data, it may be only for specific problems, where only limited information is needed: when a new product is put on the market, or *after* school bond issues have been defeated. Such makeshift expedients are hardly continuous, systematic, or comprehensive.

Information collection, of course, can be costly, but by and large it is better to have an overabundance of intelligence data than not enough. Moreover, although information that is regularly received tends to be repetitious and not always pertinent, because environmental factors tend to be stable, it is also true that major events—favorable and unfavorable—do not occur on a daily basis. Therefore, the advantages of continual collection heavily outweigh the disadvantages: an organization can react only to situations it has definite knowledge of, and the sooner it reacts the better off it will be.

An interesting aspect of individual information gathering is the way in which our senses continually provide more information than is essential for the performance of a task at hand. Even though he is swimming, let us say, a person is instantly aware of lightning or of a heavy wind, and he can then respond appropriately. The analogy with organizations is clear and apt.

ORGANIZATIONAL MYOPIA

Although many business organizations concentrate on accumulating economic information, they sometimes neglect the political, psychological, and sociological areas; they seldom have consultants who can explain these aspects of their environment. The Underwood organization, for example, is one of the few which makes political projections, in much the same way that economic projections are made. It is as though organizations chronically suffer from political myopia. Business concentrates almost exclusively on economic information, and hospitals on technological data, and political parties on voter behavior, so that when events occur that are outside the scope of their collected information — which could nevertheless significantly affect their operations — managements are often unprepared. It seems it would be well worth the effort for organizations to develop a sophisticated process for amassing political information, but only recently have even large business organizations hired full-time economists for collecting and interpreting information, and it is therefore not surprising that even fewer organizations have staff political scientists, psychologists, or sociologists doing work similar to that of the economists. Or, too often, organizations rely upon untrained individuals for such study, interpretations, and projections.

Internal data collection is usually more effective than the collection of data on the external environment, but this is as we would expect since the former is usually the product of a long and orderly process. Even before the development of our modern equipment, business firms kept detailed books, records, and other forms which were periodically submitted and interpreted by the decision making center. School systems still keep detailed records of students, grades, attendance, the student-teacher ratio, and the scores on achievement, personality, and intelligence tests. Defense units maintain precise records of costs, inventories, and operations; and religious institutions know the number of their parishioners, their financial income, and the weekly church attendance.

Decision-makers, with their ready access to accurate information, are more acutely attuned to their internal environment;

however, as a result of this awareness, submanagers may over-react to comparatively minor internal changes in their environ-ment simply because they *are* more aware of them, and they may not respond adequately to major changes in their external envi-ronment. This imbalanced reaction occurs because they are rela-tively isolated from external circumstances, which again indicates that the sensory apparatus must be designed and incorporated into the total operation as an important component of the adap-tive capability of an organization.

PROBLEM INVESTIGATION AND DIAGNOSIS (STEP 3)

The third step in the decision making process is analyzing the reason why predetermined objectives are not being achieved, and this is the first task which must be performed by the indi-vidual to whom a problem is assigned. Put another way, it means that we must isolate the nature of the negative factors that are hindering goal achievement before we devise the techniques that will cope with these determinants. The internal sensory appara-tus of the organization may indicate a trouble area—for example, profits might be declining—but corrective action cannot be taken until the specific causal factors, within or external to the organi-zation, are isolated.

Problem diagnosis, for the most part, is an investigatory process, a search for clues; and three general reasons offer a good basis for investigation:

1. The initial plan of action might have been inappropriate.
2. The plan of action might have been suitable but improperly executed.
3. Events in either the external or the internal environment might have changed so drastically that current programs no longer apply.

Because the search for causal factors also involves the process of elimination, a line of investigation can be started in any one of these three areas in order to isolate the critical factor or factors. Given a negative result, for example, the investigator might backtrack to see how the activity had been executed. In this kind of investigation, employee behavior can be compared with the initial plan, and if behavioral deviations are found which would produce the negative results, the cause will have been quickly isolated.

However, if it is found that the plan had been properly exe-cuted and that nondecision-makers had performed their duties as had been predetermined, the plan itself could be examined. Since a plan is a solution to a problem, and since it requires the execution of tasks according to specifications, the *manner* in which the plan was devised is important. This second form of investigation, then, is a search for errors that may have been committed while the solution was being reached.

If this second type of investigation fails to reveal the negative causes, the third possibility is to examine any changes that may have taken place in either the external or internal environments of the organization.

Because organizational solutions are based on an expectation that certain events will occur, problems arise when these events do not take place, or when unpredictable events occur instead. For example, a business organization may be confronted with a falling sales volume, but if the initial sales program had been good, and properly planned and executed, the difficulty may have emanated from a change in the organization's environment, which is the third area for problem investigation. The technique is first to ascertain the changes that have occurred, and next to determine those changes that produced the present results. A long list of possibilities might be compiled; the falling sales volume might reflect a change in consumer preference, a decline in consumer income, age changes in the population, population shifts, political changes, specific activities of competitors, and so forth. Such a list would obviously have to be refined.

Many techniques can be used to detect the crucial and negative factor, but each technique would attempt to hold constant all of the possible determinants and vary them one at a time in order to determine the effect that changes in one independent variable have upon the dependent variable—which in this case is sales.

At this point we shall consider only the general process of detection, leaving the specific techniques for examination in Chapter 8 (Decision Making Technology). There are two general investigative approaches, the deductive and the inductive. The deductive approach is largely one of model application, in which a general model is designed which includes the mathematical, statistical, historical, and physical workings of various phenomena. When data from an existing situation are adapted to the model, deviations will indicate the changes in the determinants. The inductive process, on the other hand, starts with the existing situation and seeks to isolate specific cause-and-effect relationships. A combination of the deductive and inductive methods can also be used, but in all cases the effort is to establish the relationship between the changes within the organization (particularly as they affect organizational objectives) and the changes in the organization's environment.

Certain external factors will be more crucial than others. For instance, if it were established that when national income falls 2 per cent sales in a given company will fall 10 per cent, the organization knows that a 5 to 1 relationship exists, and it can then plan its operations in keeping with changes in national income. In the usual situation, as it affects a particular organizational suboperation (for instance, marketing), there is a multiple causal relationship between external changes and successful (marketing) efforts.

For the most part, the same approach applies in considering the internal environment of the organization. A plan of action is based on the assumption that the internal resources will behave in a certain predictable manner; if any internal resource unit does not so behave, the deviation will denote a change in the internal environment of the organization and its specific causes will have to be isolated.

The behavioral sciences provide a broad framework or guide for determining the possible causes of a negative condition. Because these sciences are primarily concerned with causal relationships, they often provide clues for investigation, thereby saving an organization the time and expense of exploring each possibility. When behavioral models are used, reference is first made to the general and then to the particular factors. Or, if we reconsider the falling sales volume example, the causal factors are checked at the outset. The economic, psychological, sociological, and other sciences all have behavioral models which may apply to a troublesome situation. In the economic area, increased competition has various effects upon sales; in the sociological area, models of attitude, status, influence, and social mobility will show the effects of consumer taste; and psychologists' work on motivation can provide clues for changes in consumer choice.

CAUSAL SYMPTOMS

When an organization investigates the causes that produce certain results it is sometimes impossible to isolate a pure cause-and-effect relationship, or one in which a predictable quantitative change will occur in organizational results because of a minute quantitative change in the value of a determinant. At best, one may gain only a few insights into the possible causes while never precisely isolating the actual cause.

These clues can therefore be called the symptoms of the cause, and an analyst can make a judgment of what the symptoms indicate and then deduce the cause. An investigator who has had considerable experience, and who really understands the specific symptoms, might be reasonably certain of the underlying causal factor, frequently without any further investigation.

By serving as clues which require follow-up, symptoms may also be helpful in indicating areas for investigation. For example, there may be fifty possible reasons why a firm's sales volume is declining, but it may be neither feasible nor efficient to investigate all of them. However, given the negative results, one would study the "standard" clues, and these might reveal the area in which further investigation is warranted.

If, in a firm's collection of data, a relationship emerges that appears to fit the general models of the behavioral sciences, insight will be gained into the operative causal factors. For example, if the economists' general marketing model shows that the number of firms in an industry has been increasing but that the demand has been relatively inelastic, then, even though price decreases have occurred, we would conclude that sales decreases are a natural consequence. A socio-psychological model that relates social attitudes to increases in individual income would show that, under these circumstances, individuals tend to emulate those whom they consider to be their social superiors. Social attitudes produce a social hierarchy, so that if beer is associated with the "plebeian" group and Scotch with the "upper class," beer producers are faced with the problem of an inverse relationship when individual income rises.

A common investigative error is the attempt to determine critical causal factors without the use of extensive analysis. Consequently, an excessive employee turnover may be attributed to economic factors, such as low wages, but the critical validity of this attribution may never have been conclusively established.

Another error is sole reliance upon personal experience in directing investigations. Because experience is limited, and often biased, investigators might tend to work with oversimplified models. Therefore, each organization should provide a library in which all pertinent behavioral literature can be found and thoroughly reviewed. Such facilities will help the investigators acquire additional background information and thus present more realistic and impartial findings.

The second problem category, the search for opportunity, presents a somewhat different problem in evaluating factors which affect organizational success. Because the intelligence unit has presumably forecast the favorable environmental events, there is no need to diagnose these environmental factors, and one can move immediately to the construction of a solution. However, if the problem-solver is not completely satisfied with the forecast, he may want to confirm it by performing additional analyses. And, if there is a good basis for his dissatisfaction, the control unit can schedule his work accordingly.

FINDING AN ORGANIZATIONAL SOLUTION (STEP 4)

An organizational solution is a reaction (to internal or external stimuli) which attempts to bring about maximum goal achievement; it always expresses itself in an active form. Given a problem situation, the solution will be the action or measures that cope with it, and the reaction will be carried out by the resources of the organization—by its equipment, machines, employees, and material, whatever is necessary for executing the action. It is not enough that the factors creating the difficulty are isolated; corrective action must be prescribed and applied.

There are many terms that describe the various actions of an organization: policies, procedures, methods, standards, plans, blueprints, systems of operation; and such terms can be categorized into an organization's programs or responses. Policies will probably mean the preprogrammed reactions a firm will undertake coincident with certain eventualities. A procedure, method, or system might designate the manner in which an action will be performed.

Policies, then, would indicate a required action or series of actions, while *procedures* specify their performance by specific organizational units, whether a group, a subgroup, or an individual. *Standards* become the qualitative and quantitative measures of performance and results. Policies, procedures, and standards therefore comprise the *total plan* of action or reaction. And *plans,* we should point out, usually have a time dimension; they can be devised for present or future situations. Immediate plans are the lines of action necessary to respond to current events; projected plans are the lines of action to be used if certain events occur in the future.

In searching for an appropriate solution one must inquire if it will adequately cope with the negative determinant. If it is found that the falling sales volume is caused by a lack of consumer information, the firm might consider an increase in advertising. However, if it is found that the fall-off is due to lowered consumer income, an increase in the advertising budget will obviously have a rather limited effect on rebuilding the sales volume.

The search for appropriate solutions or reactions will be guided, then, by the causal factors. By and large, there are four reaction patterns that can be utilized in negative situations:

1. The cause can be eliminated.
2. The characteristics of the cause can be changed.
3. An improved adaptation can be sought.
4. The situation can be abandoned.

An example of the first reaction, eliminating the causal factor, is replacement of an employee who performs his job inadequately with an employee who will perform the job properly.

The second reaction, changing the characteristics of the negative factor, implies changing the properties, direction, or magnitude of the cause. An example is an advertising campaign that is designed to alter consumer preference in response to a firm's learning that its falling sales volume is caused by a shift in consumer preference.

To illustrate another change in the direction of the causal factor, suppose it were found that the sales volume was falling nationally because of decreasing consumer incomes. An organization such as the National Chamber of Commerce, using political means, might attempt to have the government act to increase consumer income through reduced taxation. In this instance, the attempt is to reverse the downward direction of consumer income and, in addition, to alter the magnitude or the rate at which the factor changes.

The third approach to a negative situation is to adapt more effectively to its causes if little can be done to alter them. Adaptation occurs when a firm, convinced that the factors causing reduced sales are not amenable to any modification by the organization, reduces its costs so as to minimize its losses.

The fourth reaction pattern to a negative event, leaving the situation, occurs if a retailer moves out of an area because his customers are also moving out.

(Of course, because the individual or the organization may be responding to a variety of factors, an actual approach might include all four reaction patterns.)

Where does one look for a solution? It can usually be assumed that—somewhere—there is a body of knowledge that indicates how most situations should be met. The search for an appropriate solution is really a search for the technical knowledge of how to do something, and we can usually assume that other organizations have experienced similar situations and devised suitable reactions. Consequently, the search for a solution consists of a review of the available fund of knowledge and selection of the solution which best fits a particular problem.

Voluminous literature is published in professional and non-professional journals and books; firms sometimes publicize their success with certain policies; unpublished organizational material is often available as informal information; or an organization can contact several others to ascertain how a problem situation has been handled. Frequently, of course, the situations are somewhat unique, so that solutions devised by other organizations must be modified if they are to be used in other applications.

However, after a review of the available knowledge a firm may still be confronted by a situation for which there is no appropriate solution; the causal factors may have been isolated but correctives are not available. The firm must then devise a new solution. This is a highly creative process which adds to the store of knowledge. Scientific efforts to project man to the moon provide a good example of the basic issues involved. The necessary space technology for accomplishing this project is not yet fully developed, and much of the project is based only upon research and laboratory findings. It is therefore apparent that this process — and others as well — involves experimentation and utilization of existent knowledge for devising new forms of action.

A similar activity is carried out in many organizations through research and development programs that are directed toward the discovery of new products or to an improvement in the manufacture of existing ones. However, much of this effort has been directed to the physical and life sciences, and the applied socio-behavioral sciences have been explored to a much lesser extent. It is the exceptional educational system that has a research and development department that devotes its efforts toward improved learning techniques. Even in such important areas as national economic policy, the federal government does not have a research and development agency that can provide Congress and the President with solutions to specific problems. Many firms carry on extensive sales programs but do little research to develop improved techniques. Organizations cannot adapt or adopt an action that does not exist; organizations are usually limited to utilizing knowledge that already exists.

By way of summary, then, an organization should have a library for preserving its knowledge or it should provide ready accessibility to other inventories of information. An organization should also be able to retrieve its technology and apply it to any relevant situation with which it is faced. (The importance of these abilities and resources cannot be overstated.) Decision-makers, another source of information, can accumulate further information with which to confront problem situations. However, because organizational operations are becoming increasingly complex and because the technology of many operations is rapidly expanding, the amount of knowledge in any one executive mind is always far less than the total, necessary knowledge. That is why an organization must utilize all sources of information in an ultra-efficient manner.

SELECTING THE BEST SOLUTION (STEP 5)

Because the search for solutions may produce many good solutions, the next step in the decision making process is to select the best of these. Because the goals of the organization have already been defined, the only selection criterion is the amount of the organizational payoff. But how is the payoff—moreover, the greatest payoff—to be calculated?

We have said that payoff is the difference between the input and the output of an action, and we will use the following data to illustrate a sales information problem:

	Annual Output	Annual Input	Payoff	Efficiency
Present Action	$100,000	$10,000	$ 90,000	10 to 1
Proposed Action 1	150,000	10,000	140,000	15 to 1
Proposed Action 2	75,000	25,000	50,000	3 to 1
Proposed Action 3	100,000	25,000	75,000	4 to 1
Proposed Action 4	50,000	10,000	40,000	5 to 1

The output is the revenue attributed to an action as estimated by the sales information program, and the input is the cost of each action. The difference between the output and the input of each proposal is its payoff. Once this data is available, the payoff of each proposed action is compared with the payoff of the present action; for instance, the difference between the payoff of the present action and of proposed action 1 is $50,000. If there is a fixed ratio between the increase of sales and the increase of profits of 10 to 1—that is, if for every $10 increase in sales, profits increase by $1—the addition to profits resulting from proposed action 1 will be $5,000. After a review of all four proposed actions, we would choose proposal 1. (The figures in the last column represent how much output will result from each unit of resource input, or in other words, the *efficiency* of the action.)

Because many operating programs may be devoted to a single output (such as sales), the output of a given subaction would represent only part of the total. However, if all other actions remain the same, variability in one action will change the total output. (The problems in attributing specific outputs to specific solutions are reviewed in the discussion on auditing solutions in Chapter 7.)

The first estimate that must be made is the output of any given solution or action. For example, if one reason why sales are not increasing is the lack of customer information, various techniques for communicating information might be considered, including advertising and the hiring of more salesmen. Each technique will disclose a certain quantity and quality of information, and each will mean a different customer reaction in terms of their purchases. Each alternative must be accompanied by an estimate of the sales it will produce, or the output of each solution. The same measurement of output will apply to other operational areas, such as production, control, personnel, or purchasing.

Where does one obtain the data for the results of any action? A prediction requires past experience, and the data of other firms may be available, but it might also be necessary to test a number of solutions in order to determine their outputs. In a laboratory situation, pilot studies can be conducted for such testing with the investigator attempting simulation on a smaller scale; and, with this laboratory model, the problem-solver would enact various solutions and then measure his results. For example, if an educational system seeks to evaluate various teaching techniques, it can duplicate a representative classroom situation and can run experiments prior to their adoption for systemwide use. Wage incentive and other techniques can be tested in the same way.

Here again, books, brochures, and professional articles which relate to determinants or suggested solutions can offer vital information on the effectiveness of specific solutions, and allied organizations and investigators who had been confronted by similar situations may have published the results of their corrective actions. If a manager has had considerable experience in using a particular approach, his opinion of its application and effects is another instrument for obtaining historical data. However, the number of times a manager has actually applied that action would be highly significant for its predictive value.

The dilemma a manager frequently faces is that he is unable to predict with certainty the output of particular alternatives. He may search the literature and study the particular determinants, but he may find no data for measuring the effectiveness of the alternatives he may have before him.

One reason why a manager will be unable to predict the results of alternative actions is the lack of precise historical data. In many areas of organizational activity no effort has been made to measure the efficiency of actions according to the specific environmental determinants. A body of opinion may hold that certain actions are more advantageous than others, but nothing more than this; there may be no substantiated information. For example, it is usually assumed that a student derives the best educational results if the teacher-student ratio is small, but has this belief been tested and substantiated? And what of the relationship between the student-teacher ratio and educational output?

Another reason for nebulous predictions is that the causal situation may be interdependent, not discrete, and a multiple solution must apply to all of the causes simultaneously. Employee (or other) productivity may be low because of three or four interconnected reasons, and the attempt to cope with only one of them would have no practical effect. The problem of school drop-outs may be caused by such related determinants as low income, little motivation, few job opportunities, and a lack of parental interest. If the wrong solution or an inappropriate action is selected for an organizational problem, the negative situation will persist.

Calculating the input, which is the next step in estimating the payoff, relates to the amount of organizational resources that are needed for performing a postulated action; one line of action might very well require more money, personnel, space, or equipment than another. Organizational resources or inputs can usually be calculated on a cost basis, in terms of unit cost, which means that after a manager has outlined a particular organizational action he will have to be very realistic in estimating the amount and the cost of the organizational resources needed to effectuate the program.

For example, a production operation might require 200 hours of labor, at an average cost of $2 per hour, and the total labor input cost would therefore be $400. In the matter of the student-teacher ratio, the greatest unit of output per unit of input should be the goal. If we assume that the educational output increases at a decreasing rate, and that the cost increases at an accelerating rate, the ratio could be shown this way:

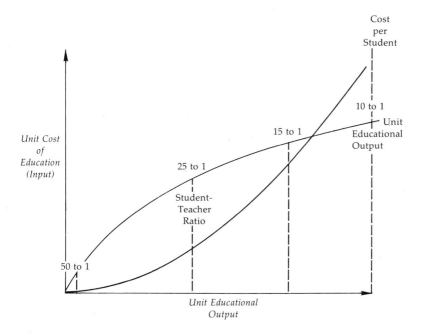

The optimum ratio would be 25 to 1—or the point at which you have the highest unit of educational output per unit of educational input.

If the payoff of an improvement in a suboperation has no effect on any other suboperation, the extent to which this improvement helps increase total goal achievement will depend on the importance of the particular suboperation for goal achievement. But any ability to increase the output while at the same time decreasing costs will always enhance the residual or differential, which means improved goal achievement.

PREDICTABILITY

Inability to predict with certainty the inputs or the outcome of various actions introduces an element of risk in the decision making process: either specific actions will not produce the expected results, or the results will not be reliable. But if the decision-maker knows the amount of uncertainty in his predictions, the risk factor can be reduced. In a situation where the results of an action are completely predictable, however, the problem-solver can be sure that his initial estimate of the consequences was accurate.

At this stage there can be only an estimate of what the input-output payoff for any alternative might be. In estimating the likelihood of success for a postulated action, various data can offer probable results—25 per cent, 50 per cent, and so forth. For example, if it were estimated that a given budgetary increase in advertising would result in a $5,000 increase in sales and that the probability of this increase were 50 per cent, the average output in sales revenue resulting from such an increase in the budget would be $2,500.

One should also try to calculate the probabilities of the input; that is, how costly the effort to achieve a given line of action will be, or the degree to which organizational resources must be utilized.

In cases where there is little basis for prediction it may be possible to deduce the limits of an action's output in terms of the worst and the best possible results; and a prediction of these extremes might be enough to warrant action.

If the problem-solver cannot predict the output of a solution he might still be able to acquire precise data on a solution's input or cost. If the cost is relatively low, the plan can still be undertaken because, in terms of the risk, the loss would be tolerable. However, as the cost of solutions increases, the necessity for having increasingly precise output data becomes more urgent; it becomes worthwhile to test solutions before large organizational resources are committed. However, the cost of acquiring data must also be determined, as well as the cost of the experiments which are designed to reduce the risk. Thus data collection becomes an input for selecting alternatives.

The effectiveness of all solutions is ultimately measured against the expected payoff. If the deviation is too great, a problem will be triggered, and the rotation of this problem through the management system will lead to an increasing accumulation of information, which should reduce the uncertainty of predicting solution results. The actual solution operation is itself an information supplier. Thus uncertainty is reduced not only through the ability to forecast valid results but also through the ability to react quickly when the expected results are not forthcoming. Predicting future events with complete certainty will probably never be possible; however, the more adaptable an organization is, the less costly the problem of risk.

The problem-solver may have a series of alternatives which do not provide any information on the probability of a solution's success. How, then, can he make a choice? At the very least there should be rough estimates of output and input, but if there are not, a systematic choice simply cannot be made. In the absence of this information, where there are only suggested lines of action as the basis for choice, the determining factor will be the subjective preferences of the problem-solver. There is always the possibility in nonsystematic problem solving that when the problem-solver is confronted with a situation which requires action, he will turn to almost any available line of action and *hope* that it will solve the problem. However, action or change *per se* can never guarantee an improvement.

Another aspect of selection, and one which is also subjective in nature, is the degree of risk an organization is willing to tolerate. A certain alternative may show a high payoff, but the probability of a successful solution may be 1 to 5. Because someone must eventually assume the responsibility for selecting a line of action, the executive decision-maker's willingness or unwillingness to tolerate a high risk will determine the final selection.

Still another aspect of uncertainty is related to a basic dilemma: if an organization faces a situation which is critical, or which endangers its very survival, it might select solutions with extremely high risks in the hope that they will produce very high payoffs. However, if the problem is not critical, there can be little reason for carrying out a solution whose payoff probability is exceedingly low.

FEASIBILITY

The feasibility or workability of a solution is an obvious consideration. Frequently, in terms of technology, personnel, equipment, and costs, the requirements of a solution preclude its use because the organization simply does not have the resources or cannot acquire them in time. Some solutions, for these reasons, are unworkable in a particular organization's situation and must therefore be rejected.

HEURISTIC SOLUTIONS

Before selecting the best solution to a problem, an analyst should have at least two alternatives—although he will want as many alternative solutions as possible because of the greater likelihood for achieving a bigger payoff. But the present action always represents one possible action, and as long as an improvement

143

toward goal achievement can be made, an additional alternative that offers improvement over the existing state is of course acceptable. This procedure is usually referred to as *satisficing* behavior. *Optimizing* behavior, on the other hand, assumes that the decision-maker knows all the available alternatives and can predict their payoffs with reasonable certainty.

Then, too, it may sometimes be too difficult or costly to search for and evaluate all possible alternatives. Moreover, in a relatively dynamic situation, because external and internal determinants change and because organizations must respond rapidly to these changes, there may not be enough time for an exhaustive search and analysis of all possibilities. Therefore, even though there may be a theoretically ideal or optimum solution to a problem, a problem-solver may not always discover it, selecting instead a suboptimal solution. Indeed, organizational solutions are usually of a suboptimal nature, and only rarely can we assume that an ideal or unimprovable solution has been achieved. From the dynamic point of view, however, we must be content that, with sufficient effort over time, an organization will move through a series of improvements and will approach the optimum or maximum state. (The decision making process proposed in our study—because of its informational constraints—is essentially satisficing.)

GENERAL-PURPOSE AND SPECIAL-PURPOSE PROGRAMS

Solutions can be classified as general- or special-purpose programs. The former is an appropriate organizational response to a range of changes in one or many determinants of an organization's internal or external environment; the latter is a response to a discrete change in that environment. For example, adjustment of the production function to changes in sales revenue might be posed as a problem, and a general-purpose solution could be applied to every change in sales revenue over a period of time, but a special-purpose solution would apply only to a specific change in sales revenue, such as a 5 per cent increase or decrease. One should always attempt to develop a general-purpose program so as to economize the efforts that are involved in problem solving.

General-purpose programs, however, may be effective only within a certain range of change, and only for certain determinants. Consequently, in designing such programs one must postulate their "perimeter" or range of application; if that range is exceeded by the requirements of an actual situation, another

144

general-purpose program will have to be created. For example, given a 40 per cent increase in sales revenue, a particular program would be used to adjust the production function to meet this increase, but above the 40 per cent figure another program would probably have to be applied.

A combination of general-purpose programs should therefore be provided for responding to all feasible ranges in the variables which affect an organization, and these general-purpose programs may consist of sets of discrete organizational responses which have been preprogrammed for the changes. The reason for this is that it is very difficult for organizational behavior to respond continuously under frequent or major changes in stimuli. Even though the internal and external variables may change in a more or less continuous pattern, an organization's response will tend to be discrete.

Let us again use the example of a rising sales revenue. If the increase is seen as a rising curve over time, a general-purpose program would indicate, at specific points on the curve, that certain responses are required for the adjustment of the production facilities. If, in a given period, sales have increased 5 per cent, the reaction might be to consider new lines of production; if the increase had been 10 per cent, new lines of production would have been started; if it had been 20 per cent, perhaps a new plant would have been constructed. Each of these responses would have been discrete, but all of them could have been incorporated into a single general-purpose program that indicated all possible responses to the relationship between a rising or falling sales revenue and the production function.

General-purpose programs should be realistically devised in terms of possible subsequent changes in either the internal or external environment. One should concentrate on the changes that seem most likely to occur—or on those negative changes which, if they took place, could be ruinous (such as fire or war). The latter developments, although they may never occur, are critical for the survival of an organization, and preprogrammed responses must therefore be formulated.

OVER-RESPONSIVENESS

There is always the danger that solutions will be too narrowly conceived and that they will be directed toward a single incident—and an incident which may be merely indicative of a chronic situation. Or the incident may be only one of many similar events which have occurred, and which will occur in the future.

Therefore a solution should be devised that will cope with all related incidents.

For example, an employee may threaten to quit his job if he does not receive a salary increase, and the organization is confronted with a double problem: what should it do about this particular employee, and how should it respond to similar incidents in the future? (The second question is the more vital because its solution will be applicable to other situations of this kind.) The organization will have to decide if a salary adjustment should be made for the particular employee, and then it will adopt a long-run salary adjustment program designed to prevent an excessive turnover of employees. This assumes, of course, that there had been no such program or that it had been operating imperfectly.

Under pressure of time, however, a decision-maker may have repeatedly solved a problem without ever devising a single, long-run solution for its recurrences. A general rule for problem solving, therefore, is that a problem should never be solved twice—to do so is merely "fire-fighting": the solution will be ineffective, the problem solving effort will be dissipated, and managerial time will be used uneconomically. "Fire-fighting"—the habitual practice of rapidly improvised methods—may occur because the problem-solver does not properly process his problems; he may concentrate only on an immediate situation, disregarding past events and probable future repetitions, and his performance in immediate situations may frequently be quite incidental to the development of an effective long-run solution. Moreover, if the problem-solver must achieve immediate short-run results, and if he is given multiple problems, he may be constrained to devise a discrete solution for each incident as it arises. Paradoxically, perhaps, the manager is so busy solving a problem "once" that he does not have time to solve the same problem "twice"; so busy solving immediate problems that he cannot effectively apply their solutions on a long-run recurrent basis; so busy manning the fire hose that he cannot devise a fire prevention program.

But let us reconsider the employee who threatens to quit unless he receives a salary increase. If this problem must be solved every time an employee requests an increase, a new solution is needed for each request, and if, in an organization of 500 employees, each asks for a raise once a year, then 500 such solutions are required annually. Although one long-run solution might require double or triple the time for devising a single short-run or temporary solution, if 500 single solutions are involved, the expenditure of managerial time for providing immediate solutions results in an extremely inverse ratio.

Of course, immediate solutions are required in some situations, or sufficient time may simply not be available for developing an *effective* long-run solution. In such cases it may be that two variant solutions—one for the immediate problem and one for the long-run situation—are required, the temporary solution providing only more or less makeshift efficiency until a permanent solution can be devised.

Once a temporary solution has been devised, however, the decision making process should work on the long-run solution rather than turn to other immediate situations (which is the usual tendency). Moreover, when an incident arises which requires a solution, one function of the problem solving process should be to consider whether this incident can be expected to arise in the future. If it is likely that troublesome incidents will occur repeatedly, the design of their permanent solution should take precedence over other existing problems. If the decision-makers lack time for such a task, managerial inefficiency or understaffing may be indicated. In any case, the attempt of one individual to solve a multitude of problems in a short period of time will not resolve a long-run situation.

SUMMARY

Step 2 in the decision making process is the raising of organizational problems, and these problems may arise because of an incorrect solution or because of new opportunity states. A scanning apparatus is required for collecting information, forecasting environmental events, and raising problems. The third step involves isolating the determinants of unfavorable situations.

Finding an organizational solution (step 4) is a search for organizational responses that will produce more effective results in terms of the isolated determinants. The four reaction patterns to a negative situation are: (1) elimination of the negative cause, (2) changing the characteristics of the cause, (3) seeking an improved adaptation, and (4) abandoning the situation.

Selecting the best solution (step 5) involves estimating the payoff for each suggested alternative response (output minus input) and selecting the response with the highest payoff. If this cannot be accomplished with certainty, it may still be possible to estimate the degree of risk involved. Whenever the available information is limited, the decision making process is fundamentally a satisficing process.

QUESTIONS FOR DISCUSSION

1. In terms of increasing organizational payoff, which choice do you believe is more significant: selecting the appropriate environment to which to respond, or selecting the correct response?
2. Does an organizational problem exist if a manager is dissatisfied with an organizational situation? Explain.
3. It has been said that when an organizational problem arises, it is usually better to do something rather than nothing. Evaluate this statement.
4. Is it feasible to preprogram an organization for every contingency? Explain.
5. Distinguish between individual and social values. What is the function of ideology in maintaining the continuity of society?
6. What kind of solution is required when it has been ascertained that a problem is caused by several environmental determinants?
7. What is the difference between the symptom of a cause and the cause itself?
8. In a problem situation there is a tendency to suggest solutions without a thorough investigation of the causes. How do you explain this tendency?
9. When the problem-solver finds no ready solution to his problem and selects the solution he believes is most appropriate, what effect will such action have on the estimated payoff? Some problems, such as cancer, have no solution at this time; give some organizational examples of similar, unsolvable problems.
10. Explain how an effective feedback device tends to reduce risks in problem solving.

SUGGESTED READINGS

CAMPBELL, NORMAN R. *Foundations of Experimental Science*. New York: Dover Publications, Inc., 1957.

CHERRY, COLIN. *On Human Communication*. Cambridge, Mass.: M.I.T. Press, 1957.

FELLER, WILLIAM. *Introduction to Probability Theory and Its Application*, vol. 1 (2d ed.). New York: John Wiley & Sons, Inc., 1957.

KEMENY, JOHN G.; SCHLEIFER, ARTHUR; SNELL, J. LAURIE; and THOMPSON, GERALD L. *Finite Mathematics with Business Applications*. Englewood Cliffs, N.J.: Prentice-Hall, Inc., 1962.

MILLER, DAVID W., and STARR, MARTIN K. *Executive Decisions and Operations Research*. Englewood Cliffs, N.J.: Prentice-Hall, Inc., 1960.

TORGERSON, WARREN S. *Theory and Method of Scaling*. New York: John Wiley & Sons, Inc., 1958.

WASSERMAN, PAUL, and SILANDER, FRED S. *Decision-Making: An Annotated Bibliography*. Ithaca, N.Y.: Cornell University Press, 1958.

6

ORGANIZATIONAL CONSENSUS

Organizational consensus, step 6 in the decision making process, is organizational agreement upon a solution which has been developed for an organizational problem, whatever its nature. Two internal groups must accept the decision: other managers, whose units of operation may be affected, and the nondecision-makers, who will execute the solution. The first group, the managers, is also concerned with the problem of suboptimization, and this is the problem which we will first consider.

SUBOPTIMIZATION

Up to this point the problem solving process has been viewed largely in terms of the steps an individual performs in solving a problem, but in actual organizational problem solving many problem-solvers usually work simultaneously on different problems. How, then, is organizational problem solving (which must be executed by many individuals) to be coordinated so that satisfactory organizational results will be achieved? And how can the organization prevent individual problem-solvers from devising solutions which are contradictory, or which will work at cross-purposes with the solutions developed by other problem-solvers? Before we consider the solution of this crucial problem, it will help if we review the nature of the suboptimization dilemma in closer detail.

It is, in fact, the division of labor in organizational decision making that creates the problem of suboptimization. Because problem solving and the subsequent implementation of the solutions is usually done by the subunits of the organization, the possibility arises that solutions, while beneficial to the originating unit, may adversely affect other operating units, possibly even negating the benefits of the change. Furthermore, the outputs of operating units are frequently contradictory; if an organizational unit pursues only its own payoff, without considering that of other units, the total consequences may be undesirable. All this should lend emphasis to our earlier observation that operations within organizations are interdependent, and that a change in one area may affect other areas as well.

In an interdependent organization the output of one unit may be the input for the next operating unit. Thus if a unit attempts to maximize its payoff, and introduces changes which will affect not only its payoff but also its output, the input into the next unit will be changed and will affect the payoff and the output of that unit. A change in one unit, then, may produce various outputs for other units, which may be either beneficial or detrimental.

The common credit-sales controversy is an example of this. One objective of the credit department is to maintain a low ratio of bad debts while the objective of the sales department is to increase sales volume. The sales department therefore tends to deemphasize the credit risk factor whereas the credit department—more cautious, and seeking high credit standards—emphasizes this factor. If the credit department is autonomous, or at least free to determine the organization's credit standards, it may reject many potential customers, thereby reducing the sales volume. The bad debt ratio may be extremely low because of these high standards, but the benefits so derived may be more than offset by losses in sales.

Similar situations can exist between the personnel and the industrial engineering departments, for one objective of the former department is the maintenance of harmonious employee relations, which includes relations with the union. To maintain high employee morale, the personnel department might be more ready than the engineering department to accede to employee or union demands for altered work practices. Or, because an objective of the engineering department is to minimize labor costs, employees might find certain engineering-inspired changes in work practices and employee benefits undesirable.

As each unit pursues its respective payoff, competitions or conflicts may arise, with each unit attempting to shift certain inefficiencies of operation to other units in order to maximize its payoff. Referring to our examples, we will recall that the sales department, seeking a high sales volume, would place the burden

150

of poor credit risks on the credit department; and that the engineering department sought lower labor costs, and employee antagonism resulted, which was referred to the personnel department.

As a department pursues such tactics, another department may counter by introducing "protective" changes, or it may refuse to cooperate with the changes suggested by other units. Such emotional and attitudinal consequences as in-group – out-group dilemmas may result, and hostilities may be exhibited – or waged – between two departments. These situations are very frustrating for managers of subunits, who must attempt to maximize the efficiency of their particular units, and who know their endeavors are being thwarted by managers in other units.

Under the bureaucratic decision making system, these disputes might move up the organizational ladder to be resolved by higher management, but various "bottlenecks" might impede such solutions. Top managers may not have enough time to cope with these difficulties, and, as a result, the disputes may remain chronic, or they may intensify. If such contention permeates an organization, rather than working together to increase organizational payoff, units may seek to undo the efforts of others. Indeed, such an attitude is not unusual – or such an outcome so extreme – inasmuch as members of operating units generally view their individual welfare in terms of the success of the subunit to which they belong; and this may be equally true for decision-makers and nondecision-makers. Salesmen, however, who are not a part of the decision making phase of sales, usually realize that their welfare is conditioned by the success of the entire sales function.

This unproductive competition is actually furthered when individual managers are awarded salary increases (or the like) on the basis of their subunit's achievement. The consequent interference by managers to curtail another's goal achievement has a direct effect on individual aspirations, and cooperation is difficult to achieve under these conditions because it may mean forgoing personal organizational benefits which will fall to a "competing" co-manager.

Another outcome of suboptimization is a limitation of the rate of change in organizational operations. If individual managers are able to oppose changes, the number of solutions that is finally agreed upon may be very limited indeed. Staff managers, moreover, have traditionally faced opposition from line managers, who are reluctant to accept staff suggestions.

In considering an organizational improvement, one must of

course calculate the net organizational payoff rather than the payoff to a subunit, but how can the total organizational effect be determined? And how can each subunit know how contemplated changes will affect its operations? Each subunit must know the change being considered if it is to ascertain the effect upon its particular operation. If we can assume that a decision-maker is an expert in his area of operation, he will be able to make such a judgment, and, knowing the proposed change, the subunits must calculate its effect in terms of the output, input, and payoff of the particular unit.

For example, if a credit department proposes to tighten credit standards and the sales department is made aware of this proposal, the sales department—believing this change will have a direct effect upon its operation—will have to calculate the proposal's effect; and both the credit and the sales departments will have to convert the effect of this change into expected profits for the organization. The credit department, with rather rigid credit standards, would presumably reduce losses on debts and thereby increase organizational profits by that amount; or it could reduce the amount of capital tied up in accounts receivable or notes which the company must discount. The sales department would calculate the effect of the tightened credit standards on sales volume, and, if we assume that the sales volume would be reduced, this reduction would be interpreted in its effect upon organizational profits.

Thus, for a proposal of which all affected operational units are aware, each unit can calculate the effect upon its operations; and a review of these calculations will indicate the total net payoff for the organization. If a positive net payoff is indicated, the solution will be accepted. In our case of credit tightening, if the credit benefits overcompensate resulting losses in the sales area, the organization will accept the credit department's proposal.

The computations of a proposal's effect upon departmental operations and its total net payoff might appear as shown below. We will assume that department 1 suggests change A, and that the figures for 1, 2, 3, and 4 are the calculated departmental payoffs for each department.

	Departments				Total Net Payoff
	1	2	3	4	
Change A ...	$5,000	− $2,000	$1,000	− $3,000	$1,000

The consequences of the change will be that two subunits (2 and 4) will function in a less optimum manner, but economy will be

152

achieved in another unit (3), as well as in the unit suggesting the change (1).

To take another example, if a sales department wants to maintain or ensure a certain sales volume, the production department may have to turn out more costly units; that is, the cost of production will be higher than the present selling price. At other times the production department may be unable to utilize the full efficiency of the plant because of lowered sales requirements.

To calculate the total net organizational effect of any change, the control unit will clear and receive a feedback from all affected units, then calculate the total payoff, making it possible for each unit to participate in the total decision before its implementation. In the absence of such machinery, subunits have little alternative but to initiate changes without considering the operations of other subunits.

The control unit can also be used when one subunit seeks a specific change in the operation of another subunit. In some instances, as we have noted, the operations of several subunits are complementary, and a change in one necessitates changes in the other. A subunit may also find that there is nothing wrong with its operation, but that its output might be measurably improved if other subunits changed certain aspects of their operations. All units of operation, then, serve as mutual constraints upon each other.

When the initiative for change originates outside the affected unit, or when a manager believes that another unit's operation can be improved and that the result will benefit his own unit as well, there should be provisions for consideration of these suggestions by the affected units. Internal improvement initiation is a vital part of the problem-raising machinery.

Even though a total calculation is made of the effect of a decision upon an organization, it may sometimes be necessary to modify the initial decision in order to accommodate other operating units. Such suggested modifications can in turn increase the aggregate return. Returning to our earlier example of change A, in which departments 2 and 4 calculated a (negative) departmental payoff of −$2,000 and −$3,000, respectively, department 4 may suggest a modification in change A that will reduce its negative payoff from −$3,000 to −$1,000 and thereby increase the total organizational payoff to $3,000.

It is only when all decision-makers are brought together, through the control machinery, that a fully acceptable solution can be worked out. The initial solution may therefore not be the final solution; as it clears through the organization, any number of modifications may be made. The criterion will always be the total organizational welfare.

EMPLOYEE ACCEPTANCE

Not only must submanagers agree among themselves before any proposal is accepted, nondecision-makers, who execute the solution, must also accept it. Because the new solution will probably replace and improve an existing method of operation, it will usually require nondecision-makers to change their behavioral patterns, to eliminate a task they usually perform and to incorporate a new practice. A new behavioral pattern will emerge, and this may require learning new skills, or retraining, or it may necessitate greater physical, mental, or psychological effort. Moreover, nondecision-makers are usually reluctant to change their mode of work; present work patterns are comfortable and routinized, and pose no threat to an individual's image of his ability to perform; he is psychologically secure. And, with a change, he may fear some loss of organizational benefits.

Because individuals resist change, why should securing agreement with nondecision-makers be a necessary step in the decision making process? In the final analysis, an organizational solution is the only line of action which the nondecision-makers actually take; it is the final response to the situation for which the new action was devised. Even if this ultimate action is inconsistent with the action specified by the submanagers, the *real* decision is the one actually executed by the nondecision-makers. In other words, if the new solution is not executed, or not carried out as specified, it is not an effective decision; and therefore the terms "organizational decision," "solution," and "line of action" are almost synonymous.

THE PROBLEM OF ORGANIZATIONAL CHANGE

A universal problem faced by management in organizational innovation is overcoming opposition to organizational change by nondecision-makers. Although everyone in an organization may offer lip service to the belief that progress is inherent and desirable, considerable resistance nevertheless takes place at the moment of actual innovation.

Opposition to change is usually covert—but no less crippling for that—in delaying, blunting, and sometimes completely negating suggested improvements. There is rarely an expression of direct or complete opposition when a directive is announced by

154

management, but when management subsequently checks upon the directive's progress it will often find delays, excuses, misunderstandings, fault-finding, allegations of lack of time or personnel, etc. The stratagems of covert opposition to organizational change are wide-ranging: from merely ignoring instructions, to slowdowns or deliberate obstructions.

Unions publicly profess the principle of change, but, by means of the labor agreement, arbitration, or the strike, they frequently attempt to maintain the status quo if they believe it is to their advantage. And, although their tactics may differ, non-union personnel have been equally "successful." Behavioral research study of organizations reveals a complex net of cliques and factions, called the "informal organization," which operates to negate changes, and very often with much success. These cliques and factions permeate most organizations.

When the opposition to change is widespread and well organized (either formally or informally), the introduction of a new system or line of action is a frustrating, exhausting experience for any executive. Furthermore, as a consequence of a protracted struggle to implement a change, executives become more cautious and amenable, and may eventually be forced to accept the status quo. Or, as its enthusiasm wanes, management may reach informal understandings with employees on the degree to which a change will be implemented. The end result of all this may be that the nature and extent of organizational changes are severely limited.

In many instances, therefore, organizations do not attempt to exploit available technologies, but this does not necessarily mean that management has been ineffective or indifferent to organizational innovations. It may not have taken advantage of potential opportunities because of "built-in" resistance and obstructions. However, in all cases, the real question is not whether organizations should or should not innovate, but whether their rate of innovation will be rapid enough to maximize organizational objectives.

Management has used three methods for meeting the problem of employee resistance to change. First, it has emphasized the need for effective communication and persuasion in introducing changes, providing employees clear and cogent reasons for the innovations (on the assumption that if an innovation is understood it will be accepted). Second, it has provided for limited employee participation in planning various changes. Third, whenever practicable, it has attempted to alleviate the negative aspects of the change, such as unemployment. In short, proposed organizational innovations are (or should be) planned and publicized as early as possible, and are introduced in a manner that will safeguard job security (which may include transfers, temporarily discontinued hiring, and so on).

Although evidence indicates that, when all three approaches are followed, change is more acceptable, there is no evidence that these procedures alone will create an ideal organizational climate in which individuals will "enthusiastically" seek and accept change. The underlying reason why individuals oppose organizational change is that, in many instances, they receive no increase in their well-being, and in some cases organizational benefits are lost. The motivation for a willingness to accept change is an expectation that, as a consequence, the individual will be in a more favorable state than at present. If this expectation is not validated there is little reason for compliance. Again, when changes occur, individuals must readjust, which is essentially a learning process; and psychological research indicates that learning is most likely to take place under certain conditions: the individual must be rewarded positively for acquiring a new pattern of behavior (which reinforces the new pattern), then successive actions and rewards will facilitate this behavior, and learning is thereby accomplished.

If the rewards or the circumstances under which learning takes place are negative, effective learning is unlikely; an individual will instead devote his energy to avoiding a potential penalty and to maintaining his present reward system. If enough constraints are introduced into the situation, and if the individual is unable to avoid the penalty, he can be forced to learn, but at a slower rate than through a positive reward system.

Therefore, when a change is proposed to a group, each member asks himself if it will be individually beneficial. If the change has negative consequences, the group will formulate opposition to its implementation so that existing benefits will not be jeopardized.

It is not true, however, that individuals are opposed to change *per se;* they oppose only those changes which have—or are perceived to have—a negative effect upon their welfare. (Salary increases can be considered as organizational changes, and one finds little opposition here.) If an individual believes a proposed change will bring deleterious personal results, it is only rational for him to oppose its implementation.

Generally, there is little real incentive for an individual to accept organizational changes because of the tendency to define goals in terms of only one participating segment (as noted in Chapter 4). If business believes that management's first or only

156

obligation is to maximize profits for stockholders, its basic reason for introducing change must be to accomplish this purpose. Management then uses innovation to increase the differential between the firm's total revenue and its total costs, to augment profits by decreasing the factor unit costs, be they labor or capital. Management constantly searches for new approaches by which the factors of production—capital, labor, and materials—will be utilized more effectively in producing a greater profit.

When organizational objectives are defined in this manner, an almost impossible dilemma in organizational change is created. On one hand, management approaches the individual and asks him to cooperate in effectuating its desired changes, but, on the other hand, it offers him no benefits—because the consequent profits have been committed to the stockholder. The individual is asked, with no positive incentive for himself, to cooperate in making a more efficient organization, and, because his rewards have been precluded, the individual's reaction to the change is negative. It is therefore possible that, over time, as this reaction is reinforced, rigid oppositional attitudes will emerge even to changes that are not negative.

If a verbal question of rewards is raised, the usual managerial response is that "If the organization prospers, the individual will prosper," or "Efficient operations are necessary to maintain jobs." Commitments of precisely how an individual will benefit, and when, and to what extent, are untendered; or, at best, the individual receives vague statements that signify very little.

Nor is there much incentive for an individual to accept organizational changes when the processes of creating and distributing organizational welfare have been made separate and distinct. This is, essentially, another aspect of the failure to offer positive rewards for participation in increased productivity. In most organizations, where the reward system is largely economic—as in business, government, and education—the rewards received by individuals are based on factors that are completely divorced from their contributions to the total organizational goal achievement. The reward factors are, instead, based on labor market conditions or an equitable rate structure. The result of all this is that individuals and groups within the organization pursue their economic goals separately, and sometimes in opposition to the organizational processes for creating an increased economic return.

In part, this separation of organizational efforts and rewards derives from management's dual concept of the individual's economic role. Its reward system views the individual as a seller of labor: if a firm wants to retain an employee's services, it must pay the market's going labor rates; and adjustments in the return to the individual will reflect only changes in these rates. (Other criteria are also used in this connection; the cost of living, for example.)

The other employee role, from management's point of view, is a producer of economic goods and services, an individual with a proprietary interest in the firm. He is thought of as a partner in a joint enterprise, as one who should be concerned with the economic well-being of the firm, with its efficiency and its profitableness.

The reason for this dual concept is easily explained. The firm must pay the going rate to obtain labor services, and, since wages and salaries are more or less determined in the marketplace, management's profits can be increased only if its organizational participants are cooperative and highly productive.

This dualism, however, is a convenient rationalization by management. Either the employee is a seller of labor or he is a partner in the common undertaking; he cannot be both.

If the employee is only a seller of labor, then, in terms of the reward system, the firm's productivity is a matter of indifference to the employee: it need be financially capable of paying only his salary or wages. In a situation of full employment, with alternate job opportunities, even this financial capability may not be very significant: if a firm cannot meet competing rates, the employee can readily sell his labor to a firm that can and will pay more. Or, if he is reasonably cooperative, he may retain his job; and if, through a union or an informal organization, he can limit management's ability to discharge him, he need only produce a minimum amount to assure continuation of his wages.

The employee cannot logically be considered, even in management's view, a partner in a common enterprise because a partner must participate directly in increased returns to the enterprise. Since his rewards are based on comparative market rates, and not on the return to the enterprise, the employee, in effect, remains a seller of labor; and he opposes innovation if it might eliminate his job or other benefits, and if it offers him no positive reward.

Attempts have been made to resolve this dilemma of the dual role. Incentive plans have been introduced which reward the employee on the basis of his output; the greater his efforts, the higher his reward. However, much of the traditionally difficult physical work of organizations has now been taken over by machines, and it is now widely recognized that increased productivity is largely a function of how rapidly organizations incorporate new technologies.

Another approach is the profit-sharing plan; but it is almost impossible for an individual in a large organization to see a relationship between his efforts and his return; he tends to view the return as a delayed wage payment. Nor do profit-sharing plans provide the incentive machinery that is necessary for the acceptance of rapid innovation.

The managers responsible for introducing changes — staff, supervisors, and middle managers — have no positive tools for promoting the acceptance of change by nondecision-makers, so great emphasis has been placed on persuasive techniques. But a manager will not be successful with these devices because individuals will not accept change on the basis of human relations skills, good conference techniques, or the ability to verbalize; they change when they are provided with concrete rewards.

Submanagers frequently rely upon negative incentives, punitive in nature, if they do not obtain cooperation. But, because of labor unions, informal cliques, labor market conditions, and personnel policies that can lead to organized employee opposition, the effectiveness of negative incentives is doubtful. Furthermore, the cost of applying them may outweigh the value of the enforced cooperation.

Regardless of any particular reward system, however, there is a basic mutuality of interest among all organizational participants. In the business organization, stockholders, managers, and employees know that they must pursue their individual objectives collectively; but the missing element seems to be a specific organizational machinery which will coordinate not only individual goals but also the mutual goals of the entire organization — machinery that would also gear the motivating or reward system to the acceptance of organizational change. There has been a growing recognition of this problem, and several companies have formulated plans that incorporate such a concept. Lincoln Electric, Kaiser Steel, and American Motors have organizational mechanisms for distributing "shares" in improved effectiveness.

A SUGGESTED APPROACH

The remainder of this chapter will suggest how the production and distribution functions can be effectively coupled, and it will advance the same fundamental elements that are contained in the distributive mechanisms mentioned above (as well as the Scanlon Plan). As with the total management system, alternative

159

subprocesses can also be considered for resolving the dilemma of employee motivation, and our approach will show how motivational aspects can be incorporated into the management system. First of all, the employee should be accepted as a full partner in the enterprise and his return should be based—in part—on his contribution to the enterprise.

When an organizational solution is devised, its expected net payoff is known; that is, if everyone cooperates as planned, a certain amount of additional revenue will be earned. The distribution of this increment can then be calculated for the factors who will participate.

Let us now suppose that an engineering department suggests a production process modification that will result in a cost savings of $10,000 per year, which we will consider the gross return from this innovation. But the change may entail expenditures for new equipment, the cost of the innovation, so that subtraction of this cost will yield the net remuneration per year or the net amount available to the participating factors. We will say that the net amount is $9,000, but, because of the financial risk involved in any change (there is no absolute assurance that the actual remuneration will equal the estimated payoff), management may decide that the firm should receive 30 per cent of the net remuneration, or $3,000, which will leave $6,000 annually for the organizational participants, including the managers. If sixty individuals are involved, and if the $6,000 is divided equally, each employee will receive $100 per year for his participation in bringing this change about.

Thus, whenever management approaches an organizational unit for a modification of its function, management's plan should incorporate and specify these same two factors:

1. The innovations the individuals are expected to make;
2. The positive rewards the participants will receive for producing the change.

For the employee, the reward will represent a more desirable state, a goal to be sought, but a goal that can be achieved only by following through on the suggested innovation. It is clearly in the individual's self-interest to endorse and implement the change.

If the change should produce less than the planned amount, the parties will readjust the distribution accordingly (payoff is allotted only after it has been earned). Cost controls, in either case, must be accurately quantified so that the distribution for a given change can be isolated in a given period.

A dual wage and salary system is part of this approach: indi-

160

viduals would receive regular salaries, and, in addition, prorated returns from relevant organizational changes. The latter returns could be distributed semiannually or annually, or allotted as a bonus. And if a firm wishes to reduce its financial risk, its base wages or salaries might be relatively small (compared with other firms) while its bonuses would be relatively large, depending upon how rapidly the efficiency of the factors had improved.

It would of course be ideal if organizational changes resulted in the increase of everyone's economic welfare, but this is not always possible; changes will also eliminate jobs or skills. Therefore, because the burden of change might not be equally apportioned, part of the return on improvement would be funded for alleviating resultant problems (such as unemployment). These funds could be expended for severance pay, retraining programs, or however they were needed.

If negative factors are present — a recession, changes in consumer demand, or the like — a firm's economic environment might preclude individual gain. Under such circumstances, however, the suggested approach would still be operational but it would be directed toward minimizing losses rather than maximizing increased returns. Moreover, when a firm faces adverse conditions, the need for internal flexibility is even more pressing.

The extent of a firm's ability to meet the economic needs of its participants depends in great part upon the flexibility of its production factors: capital assets, management, and labor. Unemployment, declining sales, and falling dividend payments reflect an inability of the plant factors to adjust effectively to the internal and external pressures upon the firm, but the proposed approach merges the objectives of the organization and the individual and makes them identical.

ADVANTAGES

Many real advantages accrue to organizations which share net increases of income on the basis of increased productivity. Inasmuch as profits are the return on investment, this approach produces greater profits than the nonsharing approach; and increased return to the factors of production (which are integrated in a complex process) depends upon whether a factor (be it labor or investment) is utilized more efficiently — or is able to increase its output per unit of input.

If employees, managers, and stockholders are to prosper, then, they must do so through mutual, cooperative effort, and these efforts must be effectively integrated. If one sector refuses to work with another, both will suffer. If stockholders purchase improved machines or materials, but employees do not use them correctly, the total output—of labor and capital—is not likely to increase. Conversely, labor cannot increase its productivity without improved machines and materials.

Given the constraints of the marketplace, there are only two approaches that factors of production can use to raise their incomes: to increase productivity, or to increase the individual's share from the return to the enterprise. The suggested method for deriving increased return is to make a larger "pie" (the first approach) rather than to increase the size of the shares from that proverbial pastry (the second approach). Labor cannot significantly augment its wages or salaries by receiving an increased proportion of organizational revenue (at the expense of stockholder dividends); neither can management reasonably expect to increase dividends by cutting salaries and increasing workloads: if either party attempts to increase its share too aggressively, the other party will eventually withdraw its cooperation. Employees would leave for other jobs, stockholders would invest elsewhere, and the firm would ultimately fail.

In short, to increase the return to all factors of production, the emphasis must be upon producing more effectively, and the essential determinant of increased revenue for all factors is the rate of organizational change: the more rapidly innovations are introduced, the greater will be the return. This then suggests that if an organization's efficiency increases rapidly enough, return to the stockholders (even if they share in the increase) will be greater than if the total efficiency is less and their share of return is greater. If management attempts to gain the total increased productivity return, it will really reduce productivity and will therefore receive less return for the capital investment sector.

Of course, it can be argued that employees are paid to carry out the directives of management and that there is no need for them to share in the income from increased productivity (an assertion often made in defining the role of employees), but the argument, as a matter of operational fact, is rather unrealistic. Employees, individually or concertedly, can delay or make ineffective those organizational changes they conceive as undesirable. Consequently, if participants share directly in the increases of organizational productivity, the labor segment will be motivated to increase its organizational efficiency to such an extent that the return to investment will be greater than the "loss" involved in the distribution process.

Economic theorists usually assume that, in a perfect competitive labor market, employees automatically receive the value of any increase in their productivity. However, under the imperfections of the *actual* labor market, this does not occur. There is good reason as well as much evidence for believing that gross inefficiencies exist in many organizations because of the absence or inadequacy of the motivating factors for innovation.

Because many organizations have not designed machinery for considering not only how to increase organizational welfare but also how to distribute it, the problem of innovation has, in a sense, been polarized. Within the organization, management tends to emphasize the problem of more effective production, but individual employees concentrate upon distribution, their personal derivation from the change. This polarization is best illustrated in the controversy over automation: management maintains that unions oppose automation and thereby impede progress and increased productivity while unions accuse management of ignoring human values and the unemployment consequences of automation; and both parties are correct, to an extent. Unions sometimes nullify desirable increases in factor productivity, or ignore the problem of using the factors more effectively; but managements ignore the problem of a distributive return for increased productivity. And so each believes the other is being unreasonable.

Apparently, in their collective bargaining, management and unions have confused the two aspects of organizational innovation and are unable to distinguish between the similarities and the differences of their economic interests. It is of mutual interest to increase output per man-hour, yet the two economic interests differ over how the rewards of that output will be apportioned. However, the more rapidly they can increase output per man-hour, the less difficult will be the problem of dividing and distributing rewards, because, in absolute terms, both parties will be in better circumstances.

There is, of course, a difference between an absolute and a relative increase. Although stockholders may receive a smaller share of the increase than labor when output increases rapidly, their *absolute* return on invested capital may still be increasing rapidly. For example, over a period of time stockholders may receive only 10 per cent of the return from increased productivity, but they may receive a 30 or 40 per cent return each year on their invested capital. The important consideration, however, is not which organizational segment obtains the larger *relative* return from productivity increases but the production of an *absolute* increase over time. If employees each year are able to increase their wages or salaries by 10 or 20 per cent, the *amount* that stockholders receive is perhaps not relevant so long as they do gain over the long run. Therefore, if the efficiency of output takes place very quickly, all interests will be benefited.

There are several guides for apportioning rewards and for assigning or setting priorities. The return to capital, in relation to the market return for the kind of risk involved, must be considered first. If stockholders are currently receiving 10 per cent on similar investments, then from any increase in productivity an amount at least equal to this 10 per cent would first be withdrawn. Then, if a "by-product" of this increased productivity is unemployment (to be avoided as far as possible), the organization should be sufficiently flexible that it has sufficient funds for assisting these displaced individuals (for severance pay, training programs to acquire new skills, or the like). The remaining money would then be distributed to everyone who had participated in the increased productivity.

The greatest difficulty in every organizational innovation is determining the organizational factors which have produced the new output. The engineering department, for example, may suggest certain changes, which line management authorizes and for which it commits funds; and employees then implement the changes. After the net income of the increased productivity has been achieved, the question is which segment of that return did each organizational factor contribute? What should the engineering department, the line management, the stockholders (whose funds were used), and the employees receive, all of whom helped bring about the changes?

If solutions, as often happens, cut across several units, the personnel department can participate in working out an appropriate payoff distribution for all affected individuals.

Rigid rules cannot be applied; sharing in increased productivity should be decided by internal negotiations among the organizational units. However, because some gain will be available for all, there should be sufficient incentives for working out an equitable system of distribution.

By way of summary, it is only when an individual receives an immediate remuneration that positive attitudes can be formed within an enterprise for pursuit of a continuous program of organizational innovation. As we have stressed, if the individuals actually responsible for performing the new and necessary activities are excluded from sharing in the net gains of innovation, economic growth will be thwarted. And again, if it is assumed that remunerative increases in productivity will or should go only to stockholders, other individuals have little incentive for increasing productivity; economic change, in this context, will have a negative connotation and will therefore be opposed.

THE NONPROFIT ORGANIZATION

The public or private nonprofit organization presents rather special motivational problems. When we considered the private for-profit organization we found that its efficiency could be increased and that the resulting increased return could be distributed among all the participants. A similar distribution, however, does not yet appear to be feasible in nonprofit organizations because they have no machinery for allocating the returns of increased productivity to their operating personnel.

A board of education, for example, compiles a yearly budget for a school's cost of operation. If improved effectiveness occurs during that year—if the amount of education increases per student—more students are educated per budget dollar or an equal number receives the same quality of education at a lower cost; there is a budgetary surplus which is transferred from the budget of the operating units to the general fund of the board of education for use in the next academic year. Or, if the system's purchasing agent operates more efficiently, this savings is also so returned.

The operating personnel therefore realize that little is personally gained by budgetary efficiency, and that the only way of increasing their personal return is by increasing salaries, which means a higher budget and higher taxes. The taxpayer, usually uninformed about the amount of education he is purchasing, is reluctant to pay higher taxes. It is therefore easy to see that, as a result of all this, public and private nonprofit organizations may be financially deprived.

If the parties, a school system and its taxpayers, could agree upon a measurable educational unit of output per unit of input, an improvement in this ratio could be shared among the operating participants. The taxpayer would then receive more education per tax dollar and the operating personnel would receive higher salaries; in the long run, everyone would receive a positive gain. The present dilemma, however, is compounded of inadequate goal definition and poor communications between the affected parties (particularly with the taxpayer and the exchange value of his tax dollar). When budget surpluses accrue, it is doubtful that these funds should automatically revert to the taxing authorities; but the public relations responsibility clearly rests with the managers of these organizations: the members of the boards of education and the superintendents of schools.

The profit-making organization has an advantage over the nonprofit-making organization in that it can determine (or at least measure) its output, its gross revenue, its input, and its unit costs. Improved effectiveness will emerge as a revenue that can be apportioned among the parties. But the same approach for both profit-making and nonprofit-making organizations is not at all impossible; it requires only that nonprofit organizations improve their ability to measure organizational achievement.

The public organizations, particularly elected officials, should make every effort to interpret the tax dollar's exchange value for the taxpaying electorate, and the electorate can then move intelligently to increase or decrease its tax burden. For example, if it could be shown that a higher tax would permit a greater unit of educational output per tax dollar input, it could be shown that it is in the taxpayer's interest to approve or accept the higher tax. Such information, however, is not usually presented or elucidated when elected officials appeal for added revenue. Moreover, a considerable body of evidence indicates that public organizations do not operate as efficiently as they might, that they are underfinanced, and that the taxpayer is disturbed by the amount of taxes he presently pays.

SECURING AGREEMENT

At the stage of our proposed decision making process that calls for the agreement of the nondecision-makers, each individual is informed of his new duties and of the return he should expect for performing his stipulated tasks. This means that, along with the distribution formula, the data for a solution and its payoff are presented to those who will participate in executing the new solution. This information is best imparted by representation; that is, submanagers are assigned from various operating units to act as the representatives of these units. (It is neither efficient or necessary for all of the participants to convene and work out the various arrangements.)

The proposals to be discussed could be reproduced and distributed to the representatives of the affected units before the meeting. Each representative would then present the proposed solution to his employees in terms of what each is expected to do and of what his return will be. The decision-makers, of course, will have worked out a solution that will provide the greatest total payoff to the organization; however, if a major deficiency in the initial proposal had been overlooked by the problem-solver but is uncovered by an employee, the correct data would be fed back to the problem-solver so that the solution could be revised.

The aspects of a solution that are usually discussed with non-decision-making personnel pertain to the implementing procedure, the specific training that is needed, and the work changes that may have to be made. If the group then accepts the distribution plan, no further discussion is necessary; but if the distribution is believed to be inequitable in some respect, the representatives of the units would have to reconvene in committee and achieve a new consensus. A time limit is then imposed by which a final agreement must be reached; and the final agreement will be in writing (see Chapter 7, Effectuating the Decision).

Because economic interest is the basic motivation in organizational participation, a distribution of money has been assumed as the reward for increased productivity, but there are sometimes other employee objectives. In such cases the monetary return for increased productivity can be converted into the particular satisfactions requested by the group, depending upon the payoff arrangements the organizational participants believe will be most meaningful to them. For example, if a group desires an air-conditioned office, its bonus fund could be so allocated; or the participants might vote in favor of a pension plan, or a longer vacation.

Once agreement upon the new solution has been reached with the nondecision-makers, written understandings are distributed to the organizational participants which specify individual duties and the associated personal returns or considerations.

Reaching an agreement can be thought of as a system of internal organizational negotiations, as a market mechanism which attempts to determine — through an exchange transaction — the economic value of the work or contribution of an individual or group. The cooperation engendered by this transaction can be based on the market concept that all cooperative efforts posit the possibility of individual gain by means of the exchange. The system proposed in this study also eliminates reliance upon coercive techniques for gaining cooperation (which this writer believes is costly and ineffective). A system of organizational negotiations takes full advantage of positive motivation and it minimizes negative methods.

Occasions may arise — after negotiations have been completed — when a unit's representative will object to a solution and will refuse to implement it. (Although all units must agree to a change if everyone is to benefit, operations are interdependent, and the refusal of one unit to accept a solution can jeopardize the gain of the other units.) At such a point, representatives of the other units may then resort to coercive bargaining to enforce acceptance of the proposal, or another unit may have to perform the work of the dissenting unit. If the dissenting unit is intransigent to every proposal, its members may have to be replaced. (A negative device is justified in such an instance because a few individuals should not be able, or permitted, to deny a potential gain to a larger group—and to deny a total organizational achievement as well.) Once individuals have entered into an agreement there should be an organizational mechanism that can ensure compliance; and, if there are violations, penalties should be assessed. Material breach could mean that an individual will be discharged from the organization.

The crucial aspect of every agreement is the matter of performance. If two or more individuals agree to carry out certain actions at certain times, performance or violation of the agreement can be easily verified. In the usual commercial situation this breach of contract makes the violator liable to the other party, so that he can be taken to court, sued, and penalized. At the minimum, a person who violates an agreement is required to sustain the losses incurred by the other party. In an organizational context, however, it is difficult to establish such a judicial procedure, yet the principles are essentially the same.

However, an issue even more fundamental is at stake. Contracts are based on good faith, and, unless organizational participants can trust each other when they enter into a contract, there is little hope for cooperative effort, which must always assume that each individual will fulfill his agreements. This basic integrity is fundamental to every market system. All organizational participants, freely entering into arrangements that all deem beneficial, are equally bound to honesty and integrity.

PARTICIPATION VERSUS AUTHORITATIVE MANAGEMENT

The procedure that we have suggested and described can be categorized as *participation management.* The organizational solution is determined by management, then communicated to the nondecision-maker, whose acceptance is sought—and must be obtained—for operational enactment. The organization is now assured that its decision will actually be carried out, but a certain permissiveness inheres in the decision process in that employees can question the proposal or suggest modifications. Such questions also serve as a preoperational check of a solution's validity because employees are aware of the practical operation. Opposition to a proposal is also provided for.

This suggested plan is not extraordinarily time-consuming since employees must always be informed, sooner or later, of any decision that involves a change in their duties. But in the decision making process it is important that they be informed before a new operation is authorized (the next step of the process). Once a solution is authorized it will be executed: authorization "finalizes" the decision.

However, if a submanager should authorize a decision before he secures a consensus, he may experience opposition from other managers and employees (often hidden and indirect) when the decision is implemented. A power struggle may ensue because a manager may feel that his authority has been challenged, and he may be unable to compromise or backtrack without losing face. Therefore, great difficulty can be experienced through neglecting to achieve organizational consensus, and much time and effort can be wasted. (Because this can be a serious and persistent problem, it will be considered later in more detail.) The importance of obtaining consensus before the authorization—if cooperative behavior is to ensue—cannot be overemphasized.

SUMMARY

Organizational consensus is the obtaining of agreement from submanagers and employees upon a suggested solution. Submanagerial agreement is necessary for avoiding the problem of suboptimization which occurs when individual managers pursue their own lines of action, disregarding the impact this will have on other operating units. Also, by having a proposed solution cleared to the managers of other operating units (by the control unit), its *total* organizational payoff can be calculated.

Employee agreement (which also should be obtained before a solution is authorized) can be achieved by incorporating the changed task performance and the expected increment (or reward) in the initial proposal.

QUESTIONS FOR DISCUSSION

1. In the absence of a control unit, how can the efforts of the managerial staff be coordinated?
2. If effective devices are not present for integrating the work of the managerial staff, why will each manager concern himself only with the operation of his particular unit?

169

3. Although determining the organizational payoff of solutions will delay solution implementation, why should this be preferred to permitting each manager to execute decisions without clearance?
4. An organizational payoff may provide that certain organizational units can operate at less than full-efficiency states. How can this be justified? Is it advisable for all units of an organization to attempt to operate at full efficiency?
5. Although investors and employees are not legal partners, they are economic and technical partners. What is the difference in these partnerships?
6. Why do individuals resist organizational change?
7. A marketplace permits buyers and sellers to come together and negotiate terms of exchange. Can the organization be viewed as a marketplace in which the manager is a buyer and the employee is a seller of labor? Explain.
8. Why does opposition to organizational change tend to be covert rather than open?
9. Why cannot management use economic coercion in introducing organizational changes—or merely discharge all employees who do not immediately and correctly follow instructions?
10. Is management in any way obliged to pay the lowest possible wages and salaries and to insist that employees work as hard as possible? Explain.

SUGGESTED READINGS

CARTWRIGHT, DORWIN, AND ZANDER, ALVIN (eds.). *Group Dynamics: Research and Theory.* New York: Harper & Row, 1953.

COCH, LESTER, AND FRENCH, JOHN R. "Overcoming Resistance to Change," *Human Relations,* 1 (1948), 512–532.

GINGZERG, ELI (ed.). *What Makes an Executive?* New York: Columbia University Press, 1955.

LANGSNER, ADOLPH, and ZOLLITSCH, HERBERT. *Wage and Salary Administration.* Cincinnati: South Western Publishing Co., 1961.

LESIEUR, FREDERICK G. (ed.). *The Scanlon Plan: A Frontier in Labor-Management Cooperation.* Cambridge, Mass.: M.I.T. Press, 1958.

McGREGOR, DOUGLAS. *The Human Side of Enterprise.* New York: McGraw-Hill Book Company, 1960.

STRAUSS, GEORGE, and SAYLES, LEONARD. *Personnel: The Human Problems of Management.* Englewood Cliffs, N.J.: Prentice-Hall, Inc., 1960.

SUTERMEISTER, ROBERT A. *People and Productivity.* New York: McGraw-Hill Book Company, 1963.

WALKER, CHARLES R. *Toward the Automatic Factory.* New Haven: Yale University Press, 1957.

WHYTE, WILLIAM F. *Money and Motivation.* New York: Harper & Row, 1955.

YODER, DALE. *Personnel Management and Industrial Relations* (5th ed.). Englewood Cliffs, N.J.: Prentice-Hall, Inc., 1962.

7

EFFECTUATING THE DECISION

After a solution has been obtained and its implementors have agreed to perform it, it must be authorized for execution. Effectuation, which covers the last four steps of our normative decision making process, includes the *authorization* (step 7), *implementation* (step 8), *direction* (step 9), and *audit* (step 10) of a solution. This chapter will treat all four of these organizational decision making steps.

AUTHORIZATION (STEP 7)

Authorization is the approval of an organizational solution by the individual or individuals who have, or who have been assigned, this legal right. It is a necessary step in the decision making process because only certain individuals have, or have been delegated, the responsibility for deciding how the resources of an organization will be used. Moreover, they are legally responsible and accountable for this act.

An organizational decision may involve the use or the exchange of property, which only the legal owner or the agent of the owner can approve. For example, in solutions which involve the purchase of equipment, incurring debt, or entering into contracts with other parties, someone must assume these legal responsibilities. A contract, to be fully binding, must be signed; therefore, so that reasonable control will be exercised over the uses of property, most organizations restrict such control or authority to only a few qualified individuals. Furthermore, because the owners of property are interested in an adequate re-

171

turn, the question of uncertainty or risk arises in connection with the uses to which that property will be put. Here again, competent individuals must be responsible for these risks.

DELEGATION OF AUTHORITY

Delegation of authority means that the owners of property have assigned, to a legally appointed agent, the right of deciding how their property or organizational resources are to be used. An agent, in turn, can apply his decisions only in an area that is within the scope of the authority granted by the owners. The owners can limit his authority, or they can define it very broadly. Consequently, an agent can be assigned to exercise his "best judgment" in handling a stated amount of property, or his authority can be curtailed—let us say—to making purchases of only $100 or less.

When the decision making machinery is designed it is therefore necessary to designate individuals who will have the right or power to approve all, or only certain, solutions. In our normative model, given a ten-manager system, only one manager would authorize solutions.[1] Upon completion of the consensus step, a solution is sent by the control unit to this manager. When systems increase in size, a similar increase will be required in the number of authorizers, and these will come from the submanagerial staff.

Some authorizers may do nothing more than check and authorize solutions. In large systems, top management can always reserve the right to authorize certain solutions, for example, those that involve a specific level of costs. In other instances, the board of directors may be the authorizers. In these situations, where the authority of all authorizers is defined, the control units (which would have this information) will route solutions to the proper authority points.

There is sometimes confusion as to what rights have actually been assigned to an individual, and it is often assumed that individuals who have been delegated authority have thereby been assigned the responsibility for executing all the relevant problem solving steps. This, however, is not always the case, nor should it be. Solving an organizational problem may involve ten distinct steps, but only one step is needed for its authorization or approval. Nonauthorized personnel can perform the other nine decision making steps and still act within the legal requirements

[1]See Chapter 3, Designing a Management System.

172

pertaining to organizations, or an organizational problem can be solved by an outside consultant, or by employees or staff; however, unless these individuals have the legal right to determine how the organization's property will be used, they cannot authorize these solutions.

If the decision making process has been properly designed, all organizational decisions should be satisfactory; in other words, the authorization step is essentially a formality because the best use of organizational property will already have been determined in the previous steps. All that should now be required is the appropriate signature or assent.

However, individuals with authority to decide how the property of the organization should be utilized should not be considered as automatic representatives of the decision making machinery. Such an assumption could, in fact, preclude the design of more effective problem solving procedures. In some decision making systems both the assignment of problem solving duties and their authorization are carried out by the same individuals, a design that is characteristic of the bureaucratic system, particularly the straight-line-of-command variety. There are, at least in theory, many different decision making systems.

The difference between the problem solving machinery and the authorization structure of the organization is, for the most part, implicitly recognized. We can find examples of the development of line-and-staff relationships in which staff personnel will raise and investigate problems and recommend various lines of action to properly authorized line personnel. The staff personnel carry out the major part of the problem solving activity with the understanding that they cannot authorize their suggested recommendations; then the appropriate line official, who has this authority, receives these staff recommendations, considers them, and authorizes them with his signature if he approves them.

After they are approved, these lines of action will be effectuated by other staff officials or by submanagers who did not have the delegated right to authorize the solution. In such cases, a review of the processes which the organization went through to solve a problem often shows that the only step which involved the person who had the right to authorize was the authorization step itself; the other steps of the decision making process were carried out by others.

There is an advantage in having certain managers primarily assigned to the authorization step: tighter organizational control can be exercised because fewer individuals are required to authorize solutions. Instead of also performing other steps in the decision making process, these managers are freed to authorize more decisions, and, as a second result, fewer authorizers are needed.

Unfortunately the distinction between the assignment of decision making duties and the delegation of authority has not always been explicitly drawn in the typical organization. As a result, considerable controversy between line managers and staff officials frequently ensues. Top management may not have designated the individuals who are to perform particular decision making tasks nor the individual responsible for the authorization step. Confusion therefore arises in many organizations when decision making tasks and organizational rights are intermixed. Staff officials may believe they have properly performed their assigned activities in constructing an organizational solution, and that they are then frustrated by line officials' claims of organizational authority to accept and implement the decision making tasks (or to reject the solution).

Delegated authority, however, should not be viewed as the right to accept or reject organizational solutions: any solution which provides a net payoff should be accepted automatically, regardless of the authority allocation within the organization. Although the authority step is part of the decision making process because of various legal requirements, organizational authority may not always be essential in the decision making process. A social or recreational group, for example, might have a rather elaborate decision making process, but, if the use of property is not involved, an authorization step would not be needed.

ORGANIZATIONAL EFFECT OF AUTHORIZATION

In terms of our proposed decision making process itself—and aside from the legal requirements of the organization—a solution's authorization indicates that a specific problem has been resolved and that no further suggestions or modifications will be considered unless the circumstances should change (a solution can always be reconsidered for sufficient reasons). Prior to its authorization, however, a solution is only suggestive because it is still subject to change or modification; various alternatives are being weighed and evaluated; the reactions of various individuals are being sought: the solution is still in the "discussion stage."

But it is the authorization step that helps the participants recognize the difference between solutions that are under consideration and those which have been finalized. Thus a commu-

174

nications function is also served when a solution is authorized; individuals in the organization can distinguish between official and tentative decisions.

Official decisions must be followed and upheld; but "unofficial decisions" are merely suggestions that have been made by non-authorized personnel—by various individuals suggesting various ways of how activities might be carried out—so it is frequently difficult to know which is the appropriate action to follow. Only if the official solution is clear can it be definitely known which activities are authorized and required and which are only suggestions.

Once the solution to a particular problem is authorized, the organization considers it final and binding, and the second phase of effectuation begins. The organization is then committed to the solution's implementation.

Because recipients of verbal instructions may be unable to distinguish between orders and suggestions, authorized solutions should always be in writing and have the appropriate signatures. Nondecision-makers should be required to follow only those actions which have been systematically recorded in the operating manual of their unit. Unofficial decisions have no legitimacy; they are not binding and should be ignored.

If a solution is to replace or amend a standing solution, this intent must be clearly indicated in the new solution, and the original decision should be removed from the manual. If all solutions are not systematically recorded, it may be difficult or even impossible to avoid personnel clashes—or even the repetition of discontinued procedures.

IMPLEMENTATION (STEP 8)

Implementation is the effectuation of an authorized decision, the conversion of a solution from an intellectual concept into organizational behavior. Until now the solution has been little more than an idea, or a plan on paper, but now, with its application, the behavior of organizational resources must be modified to conform with the plan.

The implementation of a solution might involve the purchase of new machines, the hiring of additional personnel, expansion of the physical plant, or the training of existing personnel; therefore, the solution should also stipulate how the decision is to be effectuated: the duties that must be performed by certain individuals, when they must be performed, etc. If new equipment

175

must be purchased, who will be responsible? If new personnel is to be hired or if present personnel must be trained, how will this function be accomplished?

For example, suppose an organization decides its employees should receive a physical examination once a year at company expense. The implementation plan might look as follows:

IMPLEMENTATION OF YEARLY PHYSICAL EXAMINATION

1. The Personnel Department shall recruit, interview, and recommend to the controller a qualified physician who will participate in this program (as has been outlined). Two weeks allowed.

2. The Legal Department shall draw up an appropriate contract which shall be signed between the controller and the selected physician. One day.

3. The Purchasing Department, with the advice of the physician, shall purchase the necessary supplies and/or equipment, as stipulated in the medical routines. Two weeks.

4. The Engineering Department shall make a new layout for the dispensary. One week.

5. The Maintenance Department shall receive plans from Engineering for any structural changes, including new electrical outlets, and carry them out. Two weeks. It will also install equipment upon arrival. It will receive dates of shipment from Purchasing Department. (Requires three days' notice.)

6. The Personnel Department shall allocate a personnel clerk to schedule, notify, and maintain records of medical examinations, acting upon the advice of the physician for the design of the necessary printed forms. Purchasing Department will purchase an appropriate file and handle the printing. Two weeks. Training of personnel clerk: two days.

7. Total time for implementation: eight weeks.

8. Operational date: June 1.

The problems involved in an implementation process are not always fully realized, and, as a result, new solutions are often introduced without adequate organizational preparation. Sub-

176

managers, once they have devised and authorized a solution, may believe that the work of the decision making process has been completed; yet, unless the implementation step is thoroughly planned, confusion and frustration may result when attempts are made to input the solution into the organization. In the implementation step, existing organizational routines may often have to be changed.

The learning of new routines, if it is to be both rapid and successful, should take place in an accepting, encouraging environment; unfortunately, however, the learning process is not always suitably structured in the decision making process of many organizations. It is sometimes unplanned, hurried, or even headlong, and is sometimes combined with other demands on the affected individuals. In some firms a supervisor may expect his employees to perform a new procedure almost automatically, after one very brief lecture. When he later realizes that the new procedure has not become operational, he may have to repeat his instructions, and he may do this with much impatience and with ill-tempered admonitions. However, individuals who are under pressure or threats—or under an anxious supervisor who is pressured to meet deadlines—find it more difficult to learn. In fact, a negative reaction pattern may be induced, and employees may rebel by consciously or unconsciously thwarting or delaying the learning process. The attempt to hasten what should be a natural process can produce the opposite effect inasmuch as learning can be fostered, whatever one's ability and motivation, only at a reasonable pace.

The cost of organizational implementations fall into two classifications: (1) disruption of other work routines and (2) costs of relearning. We will first consider the costs of the disruption.

Solutions, of course, because they are introduced into an ongoing organization, disrupt the usual routine of organizational activities, so it is at the implementation step that continuity of output and improved effectiveness—the twin goals of an organization—tend to conflict. An improved solution obviously means that current routines must be changed, and these routines are the activities which comprise the production process.

The ambivalence of disruption becomes more real when we look at the line-and-staff differences that exist in many organizations, with staff managers emphasizing change and improvement and line managers stressing stability and continuity. Each group may therefore have difficulty in understanding the other because of their differences in objectives. Line managers, for example, may seem conservative to staff officials because of their fear that changes may adversely affect the continuity of operation, their primary concern.

Then, as organizational units adjust to a new solution, their former effectiveness in executing their regular activities may decrease, a cost which should be included in the original estimate of a solution's total cost. Production lines may have to be stopped as new equipment is introduced; older employees may have to adjust their work patterns; desks may have to be rearranged and walls taken out; and so on. A routine is an adjustment or a natural rhythm of work in which individuals find themselves comfortable — and often quite efficient — and the above are only a few examples of possible disruptions of the everyday work routine.

The extent of disruption, or the cost of introducing a change, should of course be minimized. Some changes can be made during periods when organizational activities are at a relatively low level. Organizational training can be conducted during similar periods. It might also be possible to rearrange production lines at a time when they are not being used for their regular activities. And some organizations are naturally "endowed" with slack periods which are readily usable for retraining; for example, the armed services. However, in most organizations regular routines must be performed while the new activities are being introduced; both must proceed almost simultaneously, and this introduces the second cost factor: relearning during the implementation step.

Most organizations direct their primary attention to "getting out the work," and work schedules, consequently, seldom include adjustment time for learning new routines. For the most part, time away from actual job performance is considered lost time, which is sometimes a shortsighted view that will only increase the cost of implementation. Management, reluctant to take individuals off their jobs for training, further handicaps an individual's learning of new work habits by having him perform his regular tasks more or less at the same time.

If an organization requires change, suitable time should be scheduled and set aside: perhaps one hour of learning experience in the individual's eight-hour day. This means that work could be halted at regular times to instruct employees in new procedures. For example, because of the rapid innovations in the medical sciences, it is not unusual for hospitals to schedule formal training sessions for nurses during part of the regular work week. Staffing schedules are designed accordingly, so that the hospital can operate continuously.

178

IMPLEMENTATION SCHEDULES

In order to estimate the cost of changeover and determine operational dates, an implementation schedule will estimate the time required for the solution to be introduced and become operational ("operational" meaning that the organizational activities are being carried out in a manner consistent with the solution and that the affected units are meeting the established standards of performance). This requires an estimate of the time it will take for each operation to make the necessary adjustments.

For example, if new equipment is to be purchased and installed and if present personnel are to be retrained—or, for that matter, if new personnel are to be hired—the expected time for accomplishing each task should be calculated. Furthermore, some solutions must be introduced sequentially; that is, one phase of the solution must be accomplished before the next phase can be undertaken. There could thus be a series of subcompletion dates, one for each phase of the solution, the control unit of the organization being notified of each subcompletion so that it can activate the next phase.

The control unit will be responsible for assuring that all segments of a solution are properly introduced, but it may not always be able to estimate exactly how long it will take to introduce a new program. The control unit must therefore be given a certain amount of discretion in determining the completion date because the time sequence may have to be readjusted to meet unexpected problems. Once this schedule is delineated, the cost of introducing the solution can be estimated and added to the initial cost of the solution, further refining the net value of its incorporation into operations.

Most solutions become immediately operational because of the unexceptional situations for which they were designed; these are usually routine procedures in which certain activities are regularly repeated. Because sales orders are continually received, a new billing procedure, for example, would go into effect at once. On the other hand, although a program for a merger might occur only occasionally, and at an indefinite time in the future, an organization would still want to utilize the program if and when it was needed.

The customary approach in planning implementation has been to simulate the real situation and to "run through" the program in order to practice its operation. A series of drills might be conducted to facilitate remembering specific activities. An example of extensive preparation is the Strategic Air Command's continual training in complex programs everyone hopes need never be executed.

For programs which will not become immediately operational, some judgment must be made of the extent of organizational preparedness. Fire is a classic example of this situation. An organization can prepare an action program for its units in case of a fire, but this program obviously cannot become operational until an actual fire takes place. Such factors as the risk involved if the organization is not prepared and the extent to which operating units should be trained have to be considered along with the cost of the actual preparation.

Paper programs can provide answers, even in the absence of intensive preparations, by informing individuals of the duties they should execute when the need arises. The written specifications of employee tasks under certain conditions may often be sufficient for the execution of future programs.

DIRECTION (STEP 9)

The ninth step in the decision process, direction, is an organizational unit's application of the appropriate solution when a preprogrammed event arises. Just as an individual has a sensory apparatus which makes him aware of the events occurring around him, and, upon certain stimuli, makes him classify their nature, select a suitable response, and perform the required action, an operating unit is designed so that it will perform essentially the same process. The unit must have a sensory apparatus which perceives and understands external stimuli, and it then acts upon its environment.

Each organizational unit is expected to carry out a series of prescribed activities or programs, which are the designated solutions or responses to specific events, every time these events occur. For example, the same procedure is repeated every time a sales order is received: receipt of the sales order is the event and the billing procedure is the prepared response to the event. Consequently, every unit of an organization should have an inventory of operating programs that will cover every expected situation.

Direction is therefore determined by two functions: (1) recognition of situations or events, and (2) selection of the appropriate responses. Part of every organizational solution will include an explanation of the circumstances to which it should be applied, and this explanation should be sufficiently clear so that the program can easily be associated with the event. Ideally, the nonde-

180

cision-makers will carry out the direction, and, if the implementation step is properly executed, the nondecision-makers will have learned to recognize the conditions under which specific programs should be utilized.

When uniform reaction is expected of a group, there must be an explicit agreement on the stimuli to which the group will respond, and the submanager who is attached to a unit might be required to perform this particular task. He must exhibit sensitivity to the changes in his unit's environment and be able to select, from the inventory of prescribed responses, the response appropriate to the situation, and then communicate this information to the members of the unit. However, if the full nature of a situation is relatively obvious, it might be possible for the whole unit to accomplish this in a routine way. The primary factor, in either event, is the notification of a programmed change; it is then assumed that the unit and the responsible personnel know all of the programs and will respond accordingly.

Theoretically, because habitual organizational behavior becomes more productive and efficient, the inventory of programs could be retained in the minds and work habits of the employees. Thus, given any situation, it can be expected that the employees would react — either as a group or individually — according to plan. If an organization were completely preprogrammed, if no new situations or events arose, and if the organization maintained its payoff, hardly any management would be required. Nondecision-making individuals would respond and adjust to all events, and the organization would function in an absolutely predictable manner.

However, not all programs are continuous, and memories are often short and imperfect; it is therefore best to prepare a written inventory or operating manual that contains all of the written programs for every unit. If necessary, a person can turn to his fully indexed manual and immediately find the appropriate reaction.

We have so far been considering individual or specific organizational units, but direction, as part of the decision making process, can be applied to an organization as a whole. When changes take place in the external environment — or are external for a particular operating unit — the needed program must still be selected and executed. Let us now examine the mechanics of such a total-organization adjustment.

Organizations are typically composed of small work units, or of groups of face-to-face individuals; and their environments are

Figure 7–1
ORGANIZATIONAL "NERVOUS SYSTEM"

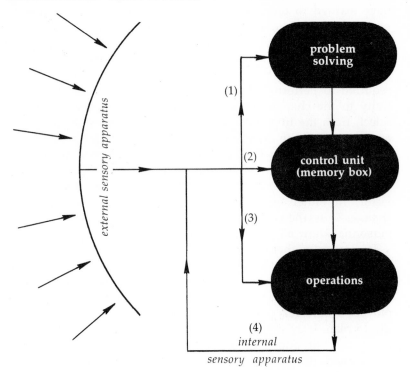

restricted to what the individuals can observe taking place around them, which can be quite limited. Therefore most units have little idea of what is happening outside the organization or even in other parts of the organization, and operational correlation therefore requires an organizational "nervous system" which will keep units sensitized to occurrences outside their immediate environment so as to ensure an integrated behavior. This is largely a communications function.

Figure 7–1 is a schematic representation of such an operation. It can be seen that the flow of data is from the sensory apparatus to the problem-solver, who devises a new program and places this program in the solution inventory, which can be considered the organization's "memory box." The new program is then implemented in the operations of the organization. (This same pattern, of course, will also be followed in situations involving the internal environment.)

Other reaction patterns are also conducted by this system, including a classification of events for which the organization is

182

already programmed but which require adjustment by certain subunits of the total organization. These messages flow from the sensory apparatus to the external-internal centralized control unit (or memory box), which selects the correct program, which, in turn, is communicated to the appropriate operations. Upon receipt of the program the operating unit will make the necessary adjustments.

The Figure 7–2 flow chart illustrates this operation in more detail. In addition to a control unit for each operating unit (which can direct interactivities within the unit), a centralized memory or control unit is necessary for adjusting internal operations among all units of the organization.

If we consider the external environment in connection with preprogrammed action, we would expect most external messages to emanate from the sensory or intelligence unit. Assume now that the organization has been preprogrammed to adjust to a falling sales volume: when sales reach a critical point, this information is picked up by the data processing center and the message flows to the control unit, where the appropriate program is selected and communicated to operations. Moreover, each operating unit can communicate with a centralized memory device if it faces a situation with which it is unable to cope. If operation 3 is overloaded, and, as a result, creating a bottleneck in the work-flow situation from operations 1 through 5, it would notify the control unit, which would adjust operations and relieve the overload.

Rarely do operations proceed exactly as planned; and too often do unforeseen difficulties occur. For example, if an organization has a program for acquiring qualified personnel over a certain period of time, and if the personnel department is unable to fulfill this program (assuming that these situations had been preprogrammed), the personnel department would notify the

Figure 7–2
CENTRALIZED INTERNAL DIRECTION

(cu = control unit)

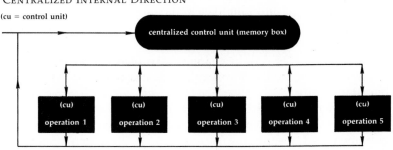

affected unit about the situation so that the unit would apply the program appropriate for the problem. A set of programs would also evolve for unpredicted, isolated events, and this repository or inventory of programs would attempt to provide for various contingencies. Internally, there would always be a rational response to events as they happened, controlled by the control unit. Of course, when events occur for which there is no program, this problem must be channeled to the problem solving unit.

Although an organization can be preprogrammed to react to most events, certain programs may be so important that they must be specially authorized before any organizational adjustments can be made. Such a solution would carry a notation that it must be authorized by a specific person every time it is used. This program, after it was selected, would flow to the individual who has the authority to trigger it. Acquisition of another firm would be an example of such a program, or the choice of location for a new plant. Because a major program involves great risk, a most careful rechecking should ascertain that all of the precipitating events were actually occurring.

Under a variety of changing events, several operational programs might be simultaneously triggered if the operating unit were called upon to perform different operations; a clearance check is therefore needed to make certain that this does not happen in a unit. Priority criteria must be established that will select the program that should be carried out first.

A distinction should be made between the implementation step and that phase of the direction step which involves changing the routines of operations. The implementation step installs a new routine, which has not yet been performed; in the direction step we can assume that the organizational participants know the routine and can quickly shift to it, even if it is not presently being utilized. For example, an accounting department may have to change to a different routine every December in closing a firm's books, and, although this may be done annually, everyone in the accounting unit will have to be notified; department stores must likewise adjust for Christmas shopping and then for the after-Christmas sales. When programs are stored so they can be quickly utilized as certain changes take place in the external or internal environments, an organization has achieved very valuable adaptability.

Another major classification of reaction patterns is the routine or daily events to which operating units are currently programmed and responding (see Figure 7–3). When operations

184

are interdependent, these actions are connected by the use of appropriate forms and records which serve as messages from one unit to another. Messages flow directly from the sensory apparatus to operations, so there is no need for special sensory data to clear through the control unit or units. On the individual level, this behavior is performed almost without thinking, like driving a car. A sales order, classified as the sensory input, proceeds from sales to billing to production, and the operations are immediately programmed to handle the order. Or, as another example of this internal operation, an operating unit would notify the personnel department that an employee has quit, whereupon personnel would recruit and hire a replacement.

Organizations are not automatically endowed with highly developed "nervous systems"; these must be designed and built. Even then, a serious shortcoming of these systems is their lack of a memory unit for storing programs for use when the need arises. Many highly developed routines are perfectly adequate as long as no new events appear, but, when new events occur, individual

Figure 7–3
REACTION PATTERN FOR ROUTINE EVENTS

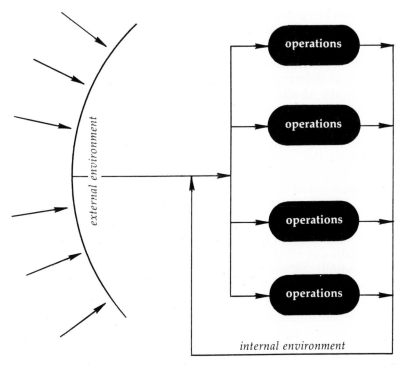

units may begin to improvise, and this can disrupt not only the work of other units but the equilibrium of an entire organization. Once established routines have been broken, the old programs may still be followed (regardless of circumstances) merely because no substitute plans had been made by the organization.

A positive approach to such a situation is exemplified by the armed forces. A complex series of battle plans or tactics may be developed which is dependent upon the moves of a potential enemy. In the actual combat situation, given the actions of the opponents, the various tactics or strategies can be called upon rather rapidly. Although the enemy might make a completely unpredicted move, which necessitates the formulation of new plans, the more preprogrammed the forces are the more swiftly they can respond.

AUDIT (STEP 10)

After a solution becomes operational it should be periodically monitored to ensure that it is being followed and that the organization is receiving its predicted payoff. Nondecision-makers may deviate from a given solution (even though they have agreed to follow it), but the audit will uncover this so that corrective action can be taken. The audit of solutions will also indicate if the internal and external variables are remaining stable. (It will be recalled that an organizational solution is a response to certain changes in either the external or internal environments, and one method of determining if the environments have changed is to evaluate the effectiveness of a given solution. If the solution is not producing its predicted payoff, the circumstances upon which it was posited may have altered.)

At any rate, the results of a given solution can be measured by comparing the actual results of a decision with its estimated results, by comparing the actual course of action with the stipulated course, and by comparing a decision's actual input, output, and payoff with its estimated input, output, and payoff. The actual behavior of organizational participants can be directly observed in relation to the expected behavior, and deviations can be noted.

All actions are assumed to produce a certain output, be it a product, service, or state of affairs, and the relationship between the estimated and the actual output can be measured. If, for example, an organizational solution had been estimated to produce a certain sales volume, the actual volume would be compared with the estimated volume to establish the solution's effectiveness. The expected input can also be compared with the actual input or costs, and excessive costs will indicate a solution deficiency (these data are usually the easiest to collect). Finally, of course, a solution's estimated and actual payoff can be compared.

Data for determining the effectiveness of a solution can usually be found in an organization's operating figures, and the data processing center can design procedures for isolating the pertinent data. With an adequate internal cost system, it should be possible to determine the input of any organizational solution. Organizational solutions which have measurable outputs in terms of financial units also can be readily ascertained. Thus, with both input and output data, payoff data can be calculated. However, some solutions will not be amenable to quantitative or financial evaluation, so a physical check is necessary for observing actual behavior.

A significant factor, of course, is the cost of the audit. Obviously, one would not monitor a solution if the audit cost would be greater than the solution's payoff. Ideally, the check should indicate the true situation without excessive cost, and the standard to be used will depend upon the measurability of the solution and the collectibility of data. One may have to use only that aspect of a decision which can be most easily checked. In a nursing procedure, for example, performance may have to be observed because neither the output nor the payoff can be quantitatively determined; or a solution for increasing employee morale might not be measurable in rigorous, quantitative terms. Therefore, changes in employee productivity might be measured instead, on the assumption that there is a direct relationship between changes in morale and productivity.

Fundamentally, the monitoring device must be determined by the subject to be measured. For example, the testing of students has been the traditional measure for educational efforts, but measuring the density of steel requires highly precise electronic mechanisms. If an appropriate measure of a solution's output or input cannot be devised, some questions must attend the use of the solution, for only by accurate measurement can it be established if an organization is receiving a worthwhile return for its efforts.

The problem-solver must, as part of his solution, provide the mechanics of its measurement, and this may require unique measuring devices that are geared to the particular action of the solution. Measurement of customer satisfaction, for example, will necessitate a mechanism different from that used to test the quality of a television picture tube. A by-product of providing such a device is that it encourages the problem-solver to define his inputs and outputs precisely. If a solution's payoff cannot be measured effectively, it can be fairly asked if its variables were precisely determined during the problem's analysis.

BUDGETARY ADJUSTMENTS

Measuring the effectiveness of specific solutions requires a somewhat different approach when we consider the process of budgeting organizational units. (A solution usually requires a change in the budget of an affected unit.) Budgets usually incorporate two sets of data: the expected output and input of organizational units, and the data can be expressed in physical and financial terms. A plant's budget will include data on either a monthly or yearly basis, and it will also include the number of items of a given quality that the plant is expected to produce (the output), along with a given amount of labor, material, and overhead (the input).

During the budget period, however, solutions are being implemented which could significantly change the unit budgets in terms of output, input, or payoff. Therefore, if the budget is to be used as a monitoring device, its adjustments should be made part of the decision making process. If, for example, the budget of an operating unit had been $10,000 a month, and a solution provided that its estimated output would remain the same but that its costs would be reduced by 10 per cent, from the time this solution became operational the budget of the unit would be reduced to $9,000 per month.

Some decisions will affect more than one budgetary unit and will result in greater efficiency for certain units and in less efficiency for others. Unit budgets should be adjusted accordingly, so that part of the savings that accrue from the increased efficiency of one unit is transferred to others as compensation for the efficiency loss they sustained in carrying out a solution. Suppose it were decided that the payoff would be increased if an organization marketed five additional products, but that the resultant increase in sales volume (with a greater payoff per unit of sales cost) necessitated higher production costs because of shorter runs, additional setup time, and the like. At the time that such a solution was made, the budgets of both the sales and production departments should have been readjusted: the costs of the production department adjusted upward and those of the sales (or marketing) department adjusted downward.

188

The budgeting mechanism can thus be viewed as a transaction device for transferring funds among operating units of an organization, each being financially self-contained and each having its own budget. Decisions, particularly those which affect more than one budgetary unit, would be based on the exchange rate or price between these units in the attempt to achieve a greater payoff for the aggregate operation.

If an organization shares increases in net payoff with its participants, the budget can also be used as an account for any surplus. In a business organization this is already done for the stockholder by providing reserves for depreciation and by a surplus account for paying dividends. Similar accounts can also be established for the managerial and employee sectors, with a depreciation account for retraining or severance pay and a surplus account for bonus payments. It can be assumed that effective decision making will increase payoff per unit of organization and will also provide unit surpluses for bonus payments to the contributors of organizational effort. In order to apply the motivational process outlined earlier, a flexible budget is essential.

Admittedly, budgetary adjustments will be partly based upon estimated changes in costs. If decisions are faulty and have to be made again, the budget would have to be readjusted. However, when budgets are regulated by operating decisions it is quickly determined if units are performing properly, since budget overspending indicates a violation in executing planned decisions. A unit's costs would be geared to the assigned output for each decision, and, because a unit might execute several decisions, these costs would be cumulative. Actual costs that are higher than the estimated costs would suggest that one or more decisions had utilized greater organizational resources than had been stipulated.

Exceeding the budget provides only a gross measurement of compliance or efficiency because it cannot show which solution had not been effectuated. However, if decisions are properly classified, other measuring devices might ascertain the faulty decision, and a check of all operating decisions might locate the difficulty at once. From a cost point of view, if the operating units remain within their budget it can be assumed that organizational solutions are being implemented according to plan.

The budget, it should be kept in mind, is only one of many monitoring devices that can be used. In a hospital situation, for example, the budgetary device is not as significant because the organizational goal is patient care: regardless of the cost of nursing care, one would still make physical checks of procedures to

189

be certain they were consistent with good patient care. But this could be equally true in the business area when the quality of the product is an overriding consideration.

Adjustment of the budget with each decision gives it a dynamic instead of the static characteristic it seems to have in many organizations, which prepare an annual or fixed projected budget for each unit's expected annual costs and output (to which each unit is expected to adhere). A flexible budget is not pegged to a definite time period, but certain outputs and costs are projected for all operating units and checks are later made against these.

A static budget, as we have implied, does not relate well to the decision making process. Because decisions are made for an entire organization, costs may be transferred — sometimes unknowingly — between certain operating units, which, from a budget viewpoint, would misrepresent these units as operating inefficiently. If the budget is to be employed as a control device for measuring internal effectiveness, it must be adjusted to planned internal changes; otherwise, various units or their submanagers might be criticized for situations which are not of their making.

Nor does a static budget take into account the dynamic nature of the external and internal environments of an organization. It is very difficult to forecast the total environmental state of an organization and then determine its total output and costs. Nevertheless, in many organizations managerial performance is evaluated by reference to fixed budgetary standards for particular operating units rather than on the basis of the value of solution output. We have not reviewed the budgetary device in great detail, but we can say that a static budget is probably not as effective as a dynamic budget.

In summary, the audit is the last step in the decision making process. If difficulties are found with any solutions, they are treated as new problems and are fed back into the decision making process (which can be considered a closed managerial system through which problems flow). Faulty solutions are repeatedly input until an effective operating solution is evolved. The decision making system is self-adjusting and should operate in a relatively routine manner. The audit is a looping step from operating units to the management system.

It was noted in Chapter 3 that part of the intelligence unit's operation could be independent audits of solution effectiveness. Because all solutions are numbered and because the mechanics of measurement are provided, a schedule of solution audits can be formulated. Trained individuals could serve as internal solution auditors—an activity not unlike the financial audits conducted by certified public accounting firms on the financial condition of an enterprise. The intelligence unit, rather than the problem-solver, is better able to perform an impersonal audit.

CONTENT OF AN ORGANIZATIONAL SOLUTION

We have said that all organizational solutions should be authorized and issued in written form. Figure 7–4 (page 192) is an example of such a solution's appearance after it has gone through the decision making system.

The number of this solution is *Personnel Procedure No. 21*. It will be noted that this procedure is also a revision of an earlier procedure, and is therefore labelled *Amendment A*. The analyst is the individual who devised the solution, in this case the personnel director. Number *316* denotes the number assigned to the problem, and *7237* is the number of the file that contains the supporting data and worksheets.·

Section A specifies the circumstances for applying the solution. Section B is the actual solution (and here we are concerned with what is to be done, who is to do it, how it is to be done, and so on), which describes a line of action which can be mental or physical: it can involve men, machines, materials, etc.

Section C contains the procedure's expected output, input, and payoff. This output is the reduced selection time required to hire an employee; the input is the reduced size and cost of maintaining the "flying squad" of employees who fill in for those who have quit, been discharged, or retired. (In this example, the costs of checking references by mail or by phone was found to be approximately equal.) The payoff is the amount of the reduction in cost.

Section D, which could be made part of every decision, shows the expected distribution of the savings from the increased efficiency, the accounts which will receive the $120 increased monthly payoff. Because there is a fixed ratio division in this case, 50 per cent of the distribution goes to the organization and the other half goes to the personnel department.

Section E shows the budgetary adjustment at the time the decision was made, which here relates only to the personnel department. The explanation for how this calculation was made is that, on a monthly basis, it would have cost $620 to maintain a "flying squad"; however, under the new procedure, it will cost only $500. The monthly budget of the personnel department will

Figure 7-4

HOSPITAL POLICIES AND PROCEDURES FORM

PERSONNEL PROCEDURE NO. 21
PERSONNEL SELECTION: AMENDMENT A
ANALYST: FRED JONES, PERSONNEL DIRECTOR

PROBLEM NO. 316, FILE NO. 7237

A. Application
   1. The following procedure shall be used for check-
      ing the references of employee applicants.

B. Reference Check Procedure
   1. Information concerning reference check shall
      be gathered by phone, by hiring clerk.

C. Expected Payoff
   1. Output: Selection time reduced 2 days per em-
      ployee.
   2. Input: Cost of Flying Squad reduced $120 per
      month.
   3. Payoff: $120 per month.

D. Distribution of Expected Surplus
   1. Hospital capital account increased $60 per
      month.
   2. Employee in personnel department, surplus ac-
      count increased $60 per month.

E. Budgetary Adjustment
   1. Personnel budget reduced $120 per month.

F. Implementation
   1. Mr. Smith (Purchasing) shall order additional
      phone installed; to be placed on selection
      clerk's desk. Completion date: June 27, 1965.
   2. Mr. Jones shall train hiring clerk in use of
      phone to collect data concerning references.
      Completion date: June 28, 1965.
   3. New hiring schedule effective July 1, 1965.

G. Audit
   1. Monthly budgetary audit of Flying Squad, by
      Accounting Department.
   2. Physical audit.
   3. Quarterly statistical audit on average hiring
      time; by Mr. Jones (Personnel).

H. This subprocedure replaces Subprocedure No. 7
   (collecting data by mail) in Personnel Hiring
   Procedure No. 21. Effective January 16, 1960.

I. Authorized June 15, 1965.

          Thomas White, Hospital Administrator

be reduced by $120, and the calculations for this procedure will be made part of the record.

Section F details the implementation of the decision: the who, when, where, and how of its introduction into the organization (the date it is to become operational is very important). In this instance the personnel director is primarily responsible for implementation; moreover, because the procedure means that new selection techniques are needed, the present personnel will have to be retrained during a specified training period.

The next part of the decision, section G, specifies the audit; it tells who will monitor the results in terms of output, input, payoff, and budget. Because the payoff was calculated at $120 per month, the monitor will compare this with the actual results. If there is a notable discrepancy, the monitor will suggest that the problem be solved again, or that disciplinary action be taken, or whatever action seems to be indicated.

Section H identifies the solution that the new policy replaces. To avoid possible confusion, and to keep the records current, the rescinded solution would be removed from the unit's operating manual, usually on the date when the new solution is expected to become operational.

Because of the accumulations of written decisions, an index is used to facilitate locating the appropriate decision and action, and a classification system is required for every operating unit (or each unit has its own operating manual). A system of cross-indexing further facilitates the location of solutions, and there might be a set of production solutions, sales solutions, personnel solutions, credit solutions, etc. (our hospital example used a personnel system).

No matter what kind of classification is used, it should be complete and clear, so that whenever individuals are confronted with an unfamiliar situation they can easily refer to their manual for the action required. Of course, problems or situations that are not covered in the manual will be processed through the decision making process as new problems which require a solution.

It is not necessary that the manual of each operating unit contain every solution an organization develops. Most solutions will relate to specific operations: production solutions will be found in the production manual and sales solutions in the sales manual. However, a total or comprehensive index for all operating solutions and for all organizational units is necessary for other purposes, especially for the various control units. But, whenever a problem arises, the initial response at any level should be to refer to the operating manual for the programmed solution.

Written organizational solutions are the output for the decision making process and they are the record of its work. This record makes up the operating manuals, which are also used for checking the consistency of actual operations against their solutions. The manuals can also be used as a job-training device for new personnel.

Some solutions must be kept confidential, and only a few individuals will have access to them; therefore their storage and communication will be specially handled. For the most part, however, solutions will be widely distributed.

STANDARD UNITS OF OUTPUT

The output unit of the management system, as we have said, is a written solution that has a particular informational content. All problem-solvers, in fact, are required to produce solutions that, as necessary components, include the conditions under which they will be used, the time and manner in which they will be used, the implementors, their specific tasks, and so on.

It is important that an organizational solution have these predetermined characteristics because the value of a system is ultimately determined by its output. If the unit of output is undefined, the value of the output or the effectiveness of the process cannot be ascertained. And, unless the nature of a system's output is predetermined, a process cannot be designed to produce a desired output. Finally, a uniform unit of output is a standard of measurement for work performance, and the efforts of submanagers can be quickly reviewed in terms of the product of their work.

If the content of an organizational decision is left to the discretion of each manager, and because each may have a different concept of the components of an organizational solution, there can be as many different outputs as there are managers. Moreover, one manager may believe that a solution should not be written, another may not concern himself with the expected payoff, and so on. Differing outputs imply different decision making processes, and the range of the value of output will vary accordingly.

SUMMARY

Authorization (step 7) is largely a formality, but it is necessary for meeting the legal requirements of property utilization. Moreover, because it requires the formal approval of special personnel,

194

authorization also indicates that a decision has been reached to which all organizational participants are committed.

Implementation (step 8) involves converting a paper plan into an operating reality. This can include the purchase of new equipment, the training of personnel, etc.

Direction (step 9) affects solution utilization. Given a dynamic internal and external environment, the sensory mechanism must recognize changes and select appropriate solutions—and see that they are utilized. Organizational recognition and response represent the communications network or "nervous system" segment of an organization.

The audit (step 10) considers the valuation of solutions. Expected and actual solution payoffs are compared, and, if significant differences exist, problems are triggered and fed back into the decision making process. A solution should include a determination of how its effectiveness will be measured, and there should be a reluctance to accept any solution that is immeasurable.

QUESTIONS FOR DISCUSSION

1. It is sometimes stated that authority and responsibility should always be equal. What does this concept mean in a legal context? In an economic context? In a technological context?
2. Is the authorization step required in designing a management system for a nonprofit organization? Explain.
3. Why is the authorization process sometimes confused with the decision making process?
4. What is the difference between the implementation and the direction of a solution?
5. Why is the implementation step frequently ignored as part of the decision making process?
6. It is sometimes asserted that the learning of new work skills and routines is solely the responsibility of the individual worker. Does this attitude serve the best interests of a firm? At what point does the responsibility of the firm end?
7. Organizational operations are integrated by an internal sensory apparatus. Give examples of how this apparatus functions.
8. It has been asserted that considerable information must be readily available if an organization is to have adaptability. Evaluate this statement.
9. What control mechanisms are necessary for distinguishing between environmental events an organization (1) is currently responding to, (2) can respond to but is not doing so, and (3) has no program to cover?
10. What is the significance of the feedback mechanism?

SUGGESTED READINGS

ASHBY, W. ROSS. *An Introduction to Cybernetics.* New York: John Wiley & Sons, Inc., 1956.

BURLINGAME, JOHN F. "Information Technology and Decentralization," *Harvard Business Review,* 39 (November-December, 1961), 121–126.

DRUCKER, PETER F. *The Practice of Management.* New York: Harper & Row, 1954.

FISCH, GERALD G. "Line-Staff is Obsolete," *Harvard Business Review,* 39 (September-October, 1961), 67–79.

FORRESTER, JAY W. *Industrial Dynamics.* Cambridge, Mass.: M.I.T. Press, 1961.

GALLAGHER, JAMES D. *Management Information Systems and the Computer.* New York: American Management Association, Inc., 1961.

8

DECISION MAKING TECHNOLOGY

The design of a decision making system must take into account the distinction between its process and its techniques. *Process* relates to the performance of a systematic sequence of operations for producing an organizational solution (the proposed ten-step sequence of a decision making system has already been discussed). *Technique,* as we will define it, relates to the method, or mode of performance, or the manner in which each operation is accomplished. Linear programming, cost accounting, and simulation are examples of techniques.

In the manufacture of a product it is first decided through what operations the material will flow: perhaps cutting, polishing, and assembly; and then the specific tools for each operation are considered: saws, scissors, or choppers for the cutting operation.

Similarly, one stage of the problem solving process is isolating the causes of a problem, and a variety of techniques is available to suggest cause-and-effect relationships. Should a controlled laboratory experiment or a regression analysis be used? These and other techniques that will be discussed or mentioned in this chapter are the tools of the problem-solver, and they constitute the decision making technology.

Given a problem input, one can always assume that there is a "best way" in which problems can be solved, that there is a set of techniques—or combination of sets—that will produce the best solution, or a solution at least as good as that which would be produced by any other set or combination. When an automobile production system is designed, a variety of machine tools is available to the designer, but he must select the tools that will optimize the organizational objectives of production. If an automatic stamping tool will form automobile doors at a cost of $1 per door, while a hand tool would jump the cost to $50 per door, the stamping tool would obviously be selected. Similarly, top management must incorporate into its system the problem solving technology which will produce the best organizational payoff. Once such a technology is established, submanagers will be expected to apply the stipulated tools.

One clear guide in determining a system's technology is that the technology should be geared to the work to be performed, not to the technical capabilities of the managerial staff. In other words, the experience its middle managerial staff has had in utilizing the tools top management selects should not affect top management nor deter it from selecting the best available tools. If middle managers are inadequately trained, development programs should be instituted.

How does top management actually incorporate a technology into the decision system so as to secure effective performance? First, it reviews the available techniques; second, it determines the stage in the decision making process at which techniques can be applied to advantage; third, it determines the circumstances in which the selected techniques should be used.

REVIEWING AVAILABLE TECHNIQUES

Review of the decision making technology entails searching through the literature, ascertaining the techniques which other organizations find useful, and sometimes experimenting with — or developing — new techniques. Once the review is accomplished, a fairly complete list of techniques will emerge, and, at this initial stage, top management will eliminate those which clearly would not fit into its decision making process.

DETERMINING THE STAGE FOR TOOL UTILIZATION

Top management next reviews the characteristics of the listed tools to determine the stage in the decision process at which they can be applied effectively. Some techniques would be restricted to the performance of only one task while other tools would perform several operations.

For example, the statistical tool of correlation establishes the degree of relationship between or among variables,[1] and is also

[1] Murray R. Spiegel, *Outline of Theory and Problems of Statistics* (New York: Schaum Co., 1962), p. 241.

198

valuable in the causal determination of organizational problems. If the sales volume unexpectedly deviates from its predicted value, and it is uncertain which of many variables is causing the deviation, correlation might suggest the significant causal factor.

After top management had determined the stage for using a particular technique, the following list of techniques[2] might be compiled:

1. Definition of Organizational Objectives
   a) Welfare, utility, benefit, or value measurement theory
2. Raising the Problem
   a) Sampling theory
   b) Reliability analysis
3. Isolating Determinants
   a) Partial correlation
   b) Multiple correlation
   c) Regression analysis
   d) Factor analysis
   e) Model building:
      1. physical
      2. abstract
      3. mathematical
      4. statistical
   f) Controlled laboratory experiments
   g) Historical analysis
   h) Personal estimation
   i) Logical deduction
4. Search for Solutions
   a) Search theory
   b) Heuristics
   c) Information theory
   d) Linear programming
   e) Nonlinear programming

   f) Dynamic programming
   g) Simulation
5. Selection of Best Solution
   a) Cost accounting
   b) Linear programming
   c) Simulation
   d) Heuristics
   e) Nonlinear optimizing
   f) Dynamic programming
   g) Invention
   h) Probability theory
   i) Sampling theory
6. Consensus
   a) Group dynamics
   b) Information theory
7. Authorization
   a) Theory of risk
8. Implementation
   a) Critical path
9. Direction
   a) Cybernetics
   b) Servo theory
   c) Sampling theory
10. Auditing
   a) Sampling theory
   b) Reliability
   c) Servo theory
   d) Information theory

SELECTING THE TECHNIQUES

After the tools to be used at each stage of the decision making process have been selected, and assuming that all submanagers are knowledgeable in the application of each technique, what

[2] A detailed account of the characteristics of all these techniques would fall outside the scope of this analysis.

guides would be utilized in selecting a set (or sets) of techniques, given any problem input? The list of various techniques shows that different combinations of instruments can be applied for any input.

For example, twenty-five techniques that could be utilized in solving a problem could, theoretically, be grouped into many combinations. It is, however, highly desirable to have a system which incorporates considerable technological diversity because the problem input will also be diverse; but, to achieve the most effective solution, those specific tools must be selected which are best adaptable to a particular problem. Having a problem in the second stage of the decision making process, the problem-solver might want to know whether it is better to apply sampling theory or to apply reliability analysis; and, in the third operation, if he should use partial correlation, multiple correlation, regression analysis, factor analysis, or personal estimation. Perhaps no two problems will be exactly alike, and each will require special treatment, but the incorporation of variety into the decision making process does not obviate the requirement that the process be predetermined.

Given a particular problem input, and many combinations or sets of available techniques, which techniques can be expected to produce the best results? There are six guides for choice: (1) feasibility, (2) cost, (3) output, (4) reliability, (5) stability, and (6) balance. After the nature of these guides has been discussed, the strategies which might be followed in their application will be briefly noted.

(1) FEASIBILITY

In general, decision making tools are operational only when certain conditions exist, and various limitations can restrict their use. For example, one wants a sample size of at least thirty if a correlation analysis is used; and Professor Gerald Thompson has noted a limitation in the use of the critical path:

> *A simple mathematical algorithm has been derived (critical path). However, the algorithm assumes that there are sufficient resources to do all the jobs as they are laid out in the schedule. If there are limitations on the amounts of various resources, such as labor skills, or machine types, then the simple answer given (bi-critical path) no longer holds.*[3]

[3] Gerald Thompson, "Some Approaches to the Solutions of Large-Scale Combinatorial Problems" (paper presented at Ford Foundation Seminar of Mathematics Applied to Business, University of Kansas, 1963), p. 7.

Functions must be linear if linear programming is to be used. For simulation to be an effective implement, the model with which one is working must reasonably reflect the reality one is attempting to understand and/or control. Irwin Bross made the following observations on the shortcomings of model applications:

> The use of models also has some drawbacks. The model is subject to the usual dangers inherent in abstraction. A mathematically feasible model may require gross oversimplifications. There is no guarantee that an investment of time and effort in constructing the model will pay dividends in the form of satisfactory prediction. No process, however, can provide such a guarantee.
>
> The symbolic language is also subject to limitations. It may be beyond the ability of a mathematician to manipulate the symbolic language so as to obtain useful results. In such cases it may be more efficient to use direct methods. In gambling-game problems, such as the game of solitaire, it may be easier to play a large number of solitaire games and determine the probabilities by the Direct System than to embark on a mathematical analysis of the probabilities.[4]

If a preliminary evaluation of the problem indicates that the conditions necessary for the effective use of specific techniques are not present, these tools should not be considered. In addition, constraints may be indicated which will affect the feasibility of applying various tools. There may, for example, be a stipulation as to the time a solution is required; and, if a solution is needed in one or two weeks, this precludes the utilization of techniques that require more time.

Another serious constraint might be the limitation of trained personnel. It was noted that, regardless of the decision making technology incorporated into its system, an organization is expected to staff the system with personnel who have the skills required for solving problems in the manner stipulated (this will be explored later in the chapter). However, there may at times be "shortages" in the required skills.

Some techniques, of course, are highly sophisticated, and if personnel trained in these techniques is lacking, the mode of analysis would be temporarily restricted to the skills of the available staff. Skill differentials among staff members in the extent of their training or facility in the use of certain techniques will

---

[4] Irwin D. Bross, *Design for Decision* (New York: The Macmillan Company, 1953), p. 171.

require top management to determine not only what techniques to utilize but also what personnel have the requisite technical skills to work on a given problem.

A final constraint may be (at least temporarily) that the decision making system has an excessive number of problems to solve, and management might therefore have to turn to implements which will conserve managerial time.

(2) COST

Cost is the second guide for choosing techniques, and here the rule is that the cost of deriving a solution should always be less than the value of the output resulting from a particular mix of techniques. To obtain this estimate, one must of course have a conception of both the cost and the output of instruments. Even though it may be difficult to make such an estimate with any precision, reasonable ranges can be established.

To determine the total cost of applying an analytical device, one should consider the time, the cost of personnel, and the hardware costs (the computer time that is typically expended whenever the tool is employed). The hourly rate of personnel and computer time is not difficult to establish, but the total time for a particular technique could vary considerably, depending upon such factors as the availability of data and the number of variables. The cost of data collection is a major cost factor in problem solving. If data collection involves interviews with potential customers in the marketing area, and if a rather large amount of special data is expected, it can be very costly.

Further, utilizing a technique such as systems simulation (for building a statistical, mathematical model of a phase of an organization's operation) might involve several years' work and much managerial time. The use of such devices unquestionably costs more than an intuitive managerial decision (selection of a solution based upon a manager's experience, opinion, or "feel" of the situation), and the latter method is unlikely to consume an excessive amount of managerial time.

(3) OUTPUT

The third guide for choosing a technique lies in estimating the output of any tool. If, by selecting a particular strategy, the end result—the organizational solution—will produce a greater payoff, the necessary tool or set of techniques would obviously be desired. Although some tools will yield reasonably good organizational solutions, there may be others that will produce optimum solutions. And, where the solution to a given problem has a very high potential payoff, one would be willing to use more costly, precise analytical tools and to collect a large amount of data. For example, if a firm which markets many different toys employs a comparatively expensive strategy to assist its selection of a toy that would significantly increase sales, these techniques would be justified because of the potentially high payoff.

Also, if one were working with problems whose solutions involve large organizational expenditures, small improvements in the preciseness of results might engender significant gains to the organization. If a firm were now spending $50 million a year on advertising, it might be beneficial to use expensive problem solving devices to ascertain whether the same advertising effectiveness could be achieved for $49 million.

In general, however, one may be satisfied with approximate optimal solutions because, to achieve greater accuracy, the costs of the necessary techniques may rise faster than any benefits they could produce. And if considerable effort is required to achieve only a slight improvement in the value of a solution, the value of the tool (except under special circumstances) would be almost negligible. Obviously, in such instances one would not risk major managerial costs for only minor solutions.

(4) RELIABILITY

The fourth factor to consider in selecting a decision making strategy is the level of reliability that can be attained—or how much error in a particular solution is tolerable. In formulating a solution one would like to know not only the estimated payoff but also how reliable that estimate is—or its expected range of error. To illustrate, a manager might suggest a solution with an estimated payoff of $50,000, plus or minus $10,000.

Some tools are highly reliable and the problem-solver can then be reasonably certain that the values of the estimated and actual solutions will prove almost identical.

When reliability is known, uncertainty or risk in solution selection is reduced, and an authorizer may even accept a solution with less payoff if it provides greater reliability. As a general example, a statistical model may have high reliability if it can predict with considerable accuracy—given certain changes in the values of the instrumental variables—what the effect on dependent variables will be.

When an intuitive approach is used, reliability can seldom be determined in advance of a solution's results because it is very difficult to apply tests to solutions that are informally or unsystematically derived. Although a solution may initially appear to have considerable merit, it may actually produce results that are significantly different from expectations. The problem-solver who uses an intuitive approach cannot be sure, within a predictable range, that his expected payoff will actually result. Generally, when one is evaluating great potential gain or loss, the best approach is to select techniques that will provide the highest reliability in terms of both expected and actual payoffs.

(5) STABILITY

The fifth guide to consider in tool selection is the length of time a solution will be used, its stability. If it will be frequently employed, over a relatively long period of time, a rigorous standard will be required. If a new billing procedure is being formulated which will be used daily, and which will be in effect for five years, great care would be exercised in its construction.

One aspect of solution stability is that the structural relationships between the external determinants may be constantly changing, thereby requiring continual solution modification.[5] Under these conditions a highly refined product may not be needed; time-consuming techniques cannot be used effectively if determinants change very rapidly. By the time a rigorous solution is designed, the situation for which it was intended may have altered, rendering the solution useless. Therefore, when a situation is highly dynamic, one may have to be satisfied with gross approximations.

(6) BALANCE

The final criterion for the selection of techniques is that balance should be maintained between the decision making tools, and reasonable balance necessitates the use of mutually consistent tools between the decision making stages. The construction of a decision must always be viewed in its totality: what will the consequences be as the problem flows through the *entire* decision making process? Nor will the quality of a decision be better than the validity of the least productive decision making step. For

---

[5] The value of the exogenous variables may change but the structural relationship between such variables or coefficients may remain constant. Thus the above problem of solution instability would not necessarily arise, and the model would continue to be useful.

example, one would not put into practice a primitive data collection device in the problem-raising step and follow this with a complex regression analysis. If one knows there will be difficulty measuring the effectiveness of a given solution (the audit step) in a certain area of the organization, such as public relations, one would be most reluctant to construct a sophisticated mathematical model in the third and fourth stages of the decision making process.

Professor Wainright Martin had an interesting experience with this last facet of the decision making process.[6] An organization gave him the problem of determining how often maintenance should be performed on its electrical transformation system. (At the time of this assignment, the organization was performing detailed maintenance every four months.) Dr. Martin collected considerable data and then constructed a mathematical function for both the cost and the output of the system's maintenance work. His analysis concluded that, rather than every four months, equally good maintenance could be discharged every three or four years, without adverse effects and with considerable savings to the organization.

He subsequently learned that there had been great difficulty in the utilization of his recommendations because, if they had been followed, significant layoffs in the maintenance area would have resulted. Because one of the tacit objectives of this organization had been to maintain the level of employment, a discrepancy existed between the definition of organizational objectives in the first step and the sequential operations of the decision making process. In this case—although the second, third, and fourth steps of the decision making process were operating in a rigorous manner—the first step, a value analysis (or the determination of organizational goals) had been inadequately performed. Dr. Martin had been told that the objective of the organization was to minimize its costs; however, he subsequently learned that this was not the case, after his recommendations had been submitted.

Professor Russell L. Ackoff makes a similar observation:

One of the things OR [operations research] has learned about putting results to work is having a considerable effect on its methods. Solutions are generally carried out by personnel whose mathematical sophistication is less than desirable. Consequently, if the OR team wants to assure use of its recommended

[6] E. Wainright Martin, lecturer at Indiana University, related this experience at the Ford Foundation Seminar of Mathematics Applied to Business, at the University of Kansas, 1963.

decision-rules, it must simplify the rules handed over to execu-
tives and operating personnel. In many cases this means the team
must either translate elegant solutions into approximations
that are easy to use or sidestep the elegance and move directly
to a quick-and-dirty decision-rule. Operations research is learn-
ing that an approximation that is used may be a great deal
better than an exact solution that is not.

In some problems the urgency attached to obtaining a solu-
tion, or the limitation of resources, may also require direct
movement to quick-and-dirty solutions. In many cases such
'solutions' need not deviate from the optimum (in the purist's
sense) by too much. It is OR's job to see that as little sacrifice
of effectiveness is made as is possible.

Operations research has learned another general lesson from
its involvement with implementation of results. A solution must
be 'spelled out' in the language of those who will use it. In the
process of translation and operation the OR team almost always
finds aspects of the situation which it had not taken into account,
aspects for which adjustments in the proposed solution are usu-
ally required.

There is a long distance between a recommendation and a
successful application. Operations research is developing a
healthy respect for the difficulty of covering that distance.[7]

After the organization acquires some experience in utilizing
various tools to solve specific problems, the characteristics of
these problems will become identifiable and this itself will facilitate the selection of tools. Problems can be classified to enable
more exact selections of effective techniques. An attribute of one
class of problems may be that it has multiple states and requires
multiple-stage solutions, and dynamic programming has been
consistently useful in solving this problem. Or a regression
analysis might have been effective in solving problems that
involved the manipulation of controlled variables to affect un-
controlled variables. Incoming problems can also be classified
into queuing, allocation, or inventory problems.

Some record, then, should be maintained to indicate which
techniques were used to solve a classification of problems. On
the basis of this compiled experience, one can then evaluate
successes and failures and predict whether specific techniques
will be successful in solving similar problems.

[7] Russell L. Ackoff, "The Development of Operations Research as a Science,"
Scientific Decision-Making in Business, Abraham Shuchman (ed.) (New York:
Holt, Rinehart & Winston, Inc., 1963), pp. 59–60.

TOOL SELECTION STRATEGY[8]

Given our six guides for selecting a set of tools, one is then faced with the problem of how the guides shall be applied, or what strategy shall be followed. How shall the tools be integrated or weighed? Should one always pick the lowest-cost set of tools, or those which will give the highest reliability?

In all likelihood, "trade-offs" will have to be made between suggested guides; that is, in order to gain greater reliability one will have to accept higher costs of solution construction. It would seem, however, that the criteria of feasibility and balance would have to be met before any consideration of the other four criteria because the first two act as constraints upon the others. Given feasibility and balance, a judgment would have to be applied to trade-offs of the other four guides.

Unquestionably, many aspects would be weighed in making such exchanges; and some have already been indicated, such as the nature and significance of the problem to be worked on, the availability of data, the problem solving load of managers, the amount of risk that the organization will or can tolerate, and the constraints that are present. Furthermore, these relative weights might change as a solution emerges. For example, low-cost tools may be selected at the outset, but the significance of the problem may increase later and then reliability criteria may be critical. It would thus seem that no one strategy for weighing and integrating the suggested guides will be universally applicable.

MECHANICS OF TOOL SELECTION

Who will decide how and when an organizational problem is to be solved? There are three possibilities: the control unit could decide, the individual manager could decide, or both the control unit and the manager could decide.

In the first approach a new problem is sent to the control unit, which decides upon the set of tools to be used at each stage in the decision making process (using the guides discussed), and which routes the problem accordingly. The submanager would receive not only an assignment of problems and an expected completion time, but a list of the techniques to be utilized as well. His assignment sheet might look like that in Figure 8–1. However, the choice of tools could be left to the discretion of the individual to whom the problem has been assigned.

[8] The author is indebted to Professor G. D. Hanrahan of St. Louis University for his observations on tool selection strategy.

Figure 8–1

PROBLEM ASSIGNMENT

Problem No.____   Date Raised ____   Date Assigned ____

Schedule and Route_____

Decision Steps	Estimated Time	Decision Techniques
2	2 months	Regression Analysis
3	1 month	Heuristics
4	3 months	Simulation: Statistical Model
7	2 weeks	Probability Theory
8	2 weeks	Critical Path
9	2 months	Provide Servo–Controls
10	1 month	Sampling Theory
	10 months Total	

A listing of techniques by the control unit may be insufficient for planning and controlling this aspect of the decision making system, and one might desire a specific outline in the form of a research design. This design could be submitted either by the control unit, or the submanager, or via their mutual efforts. After the nature of the problem had been reviewed, this research design would include not only the proper techniques but also the relevant variables, their definitions, the data sources, the likelihood of obtaining data, significant tests, and other information.

If a research design were required, it might be more efficient to assign the problem to a submanager, who would draw up the design and submit it to the control unit. The control unit could then approve the design, deduce the schedule, and route the problem, all based on the design. To have the control unit itself design the problem solving strategy might in some cases be an unreasonable burden.

In his formulation of a research design, the submanager should be required to justify his selection of a decision making strategy in relation to the guides discussed earlier. He would stipulate the feasibility, cost, output, reliability, stability, and balance in his design. The control unit could then evaluate the manager's design on the basis of these criteria and suggest any needed changes.

208

The middle manager may have difficulty in applying all of the suggested criteria; for example, he may be unable to determine if he has reasonable balance, and sometimes he may be unable to utilize all of the criteria because he may not be able to estimate potential output. Even with a detailed research design, the manager may still encounter obstacles during the actual problem solving process. Data which were thought to be available may be lacking, or in a nonusable form; techniques may prove to be unfeasible, and so on.

It is only after enough data have been collected and alternative solutions have been examined that the best solution will begin to emerge, and this may require continual changes in the technical mix. One method of treating this aspect of the decision making process is to apply a multiple problem-solving strategy. A feedback device would be used during the problem solving process. If a manager found that certain techniques were ineffective, he could turn to alternative tools and could notify the control unit so that it could reschedule his work.

The merit of permitting the problem-solver to select his own tools, with the approval of the control unit, is that the individual problem-solver will be familiar with the problems that arise in his organizational area and with the availability and quality of data. If the problem-solver is knowledgeable in the use of various decision making techniques (and also knows their limitations), he is in the best position to decide which strategy to discharge. If the control unit has sole jurisdiction over the selection of techniques, it may assign inappropriate tools to a manager because it is not fully familiar with that manager's area.

Conversely, when the manager is given sole discretion over the particular tools to be used there is the possibility that he may use, or even overuse, the same devices, tending to adjust the problem to the techniques that he knows or prefers rather than adapting the tools to the problem at hand. The danger is that the manager may alter problems that do not lend themselves to solutions by the tools he knows, or he may suboptimize in his use of tools; that is, he may employ inappropriate techniques because he is most familiar with these. If the manager is unacquainted with statistical or mathematical techniques, he may rely almost wholly on his personal experience or intuitive judgment in solving a problem. If he repeatedly uses the same techniques, the situation may become like that which Irwin Bross describes:

There is another very grave danger in the use of models. After a scientist plays for a long time with a given model he may become

attached to it, just as a child may become, in the course of time,
very attached to a doll (which is also a model). A child may
become so devoted to the doll that she insists that her doll is a
real baby, and some scientists become so devoted to their model
(especially if it is a brain child) that they will insist that this
model is the real world.[9]

There is danger, then, that the elegance of problem solving can become an end in itself, a display of virtuosity by the problem-solver: a problem may be subjected to an excessive amount of data collection; or mathematical or statistical models may be created of the most precise order; or lengthy manipulations of these models may ensue in a search for the optimum solution. Yet the contribution of all this to solutions or organizational objectives may be minimal, and comparatively primitive techniques might have produced a better result.

There will always be a measure of competition among managers over who does the most effective job, but this competition should be based on the goals the organization is endeavoring to achieve and not on the skills or knowledge of the problem-solver. Competition can also be manifested in subgroups of managers who allege that the organization will obtain the best results by utilizing that set of skills which they have acquired, and who may denigrate the approach of other groups of managers. For example, statistically oriented managers may ridicule managers who are qualitatively oriented.

However, it is most unlikely that one set of techniques will always be demonstrably superior to all others—although some tools have advantages over others in certain situations and can be used more effectively in those applications. Therefore the question is not really one of good or bad techniques; it is which techniques can be used most efficiently under particular circumstances.

It would seem that by far the best approach is to have middle managers formulate their research designs and submit them to the control unit for approval, then top management can make sure that the appropriate decision making tools will be employed. Whenever possible, tool specialists should be placed in the control unit: persons, for example, who have considerable operations research experience. These specialists can then review the research designs and can suggest advisable changes; and they can knowledgeably approve or refuse a design. Managers who are unable to construct research designs, or who consistently pro-

[9] Bross, *op. cit.*, pp. 171–172.

pose the same techniques—or who have avoided the use of more sophisticated tools—might require additional training, or replacement.

From time to time top management should sample not only the submitted solutions but also the research designs so as to establish how the solutions are being derived. In this way it will know that the control unit and the submanagers are selecting techniques on the basis of the criteria that top management had specified. When top management stipulates the circumstances under which specific tools shall be used, along with the mechanics of tool selection (research design, sampling of designs, and control unit approval), it can efficiently control its decision making technology and assure that the most effective solution payoffs will be produced. If such planning is absent, it is questionable that top management can exercise the necessary control.

THE MANAGER AS A TECHNICIAN

Once the techniques that will be incorporated into the decision making system have been established, the submanager may have to acquire the requisite skills and capability for using these tools;[10] indeed, the very knowledge and ability for using the selected analytical devices can be considered as the manager's "tool kit." How accomplished or skillful a manager is will of course depend upon the range of tools he is able to use and his proficiency in using them. As a practitioner, the manager must muster a considerable body of knowledge.

The incorporation of a set of defined techniques into the decision making process facilitates the selection and training of managers, and one is then better able to distinguish between a qualified and a nonqualified prospect. Consequently, if top management decides that in order to construct solutions properly a manager must be facile in the use of systems simulation or regression analysis, and if a managerial applicant is unfamiliar with these tools, the applicant would not be qualified for the position. Furthermore, if a manager is not knowledgeable in a specific device, he would be expected to acquire further education to overcome this deficiency.

TECHNOLOGICAL CHANGE

There is every reason for believing that new decision making techniques will be invented and that new applications will be

[10] See Chapter 10, Installation, Operation, and Maintenance of the System.

found for those which now exist. An interesting example of this development in the history of operations research development was noted by Professor Shuchman:

> The first use of organized Operations Research appears to have developed during the "Battle of Britain" in 1941. . . .
>
> As a result of the work of these scientists [on the use of radar], it has been estimated that British power in air defense during the "Battle of Britain" increased tenfold. This was so astounding a success that the military proceeded to organize additional teams of scientists to study other problems of weapon use, tactics, and strategy. . . .
>
> The achievements . . . did not go unnoticed on this side of the Atlantic. Consequently, when the United States entered the War in December 1941, our military quickly emulated the British and organized Operations Research teams. . . . Operations Research has become a permanent and important part of our military apparatus.
>
> After the war, many of the scientists who had participated in military Operations Research returned to peace time activities with the conviction that the method and techniques which they had used to improve military operations could be used with equal success to improve business operations. . . .
>
> . . . Today, an estimated 5 per cent of the nation's business organizations either have their own Operations Research department, employ outside Operations Research consultants, or use a combination of both. Even more significantly, 60 of the nation's 100 largest firms . . . now have Operations Research departments. The discipline is slowly coming of age as a management tool and as it matures it will undoubtedly come into ever wider use in American business.[11]

Furthermore, equipment is being continuously developed to assist in a more efficient utilization of these tools. Professor Gerald Thompson has said:

> The computer was originally developed to solve problems of numerical analysis such as differential equations, partial differential equations, integrals, etc. . . . it has been used for such widely diverse problems as . . . choosing investment portfolios, simulating business operations, and so on.[12]

As these developments occur it is essential that top management be aware of recent, emerging instruments so that it can substitute

[11] Abraham Shuchman (ed.), *Scientific Decision-Making in Business* (New York: Holt, Rinehart & Winston, Inc., 1963), pp. 2–6.
[12] Thompson, op. cit., p. 24.

212

new techniques for older ones. It should also continuously review the literature to help note the new techniques.

Top management decides whether or not to install an innovation in its decision making system in the same manner that it decides to install any other change in its organization. The nature of the technique is reviewed; its relative advantages and disadvantages are weighed against those of the current technique; and the determinant is whether the innovation will significantly increase solution payoff. Before commitment to a suggested innovation, experimentation might have to be conducted; and a series of problems would be solved by both the existing and the proposed techniques.

The results of the suggested techniques could be simulated by formulating a solution to a given problem with different tools. The decision would be selected on the basis of accepted techniques, and, with these results as a guide, the traditional techniques would be compared with the new to see if the new techniques offer advantages over the old. Or, if this method is not feasible, one may have to experiment with the new technique on selected problems. If one then finds that the new technique produces a better solution, it can be incorporated into the decision making system by adding it to the inventory of tools.

An organization's need to invent and develop new decision making techniques becomes apparent when it is found that some problems cannot be solved effectively with the existing technology. (Even a highly developed technology may not be applicable to all problems, and the tendency then is to rely on the intuitive approach.) Top management should direct researchers to turn their attention to these problems and search for effective techniques for handling them.

An organization may even acquire personnel for the specific purpose of conducting research and development in the decision making technology. These efforts might be directed toward an evaluation of the analytical devices found in the physical or behavioral sciences, and experiments might be conducted to determine if these devices might be effectively applied in an organizational context. New developments in mathematics, statistics, economics, and other fields might also have significant potentials for an organization.

Another source of improvement is the managers themselves. Because a manager, through his creative ability, devises new techniques, these innovated tools also can be incorporated into the decision making system. Thus one source of improvement is merely the differential in managerial performance.

Planned decision making facilitates the rapid installation of new techniques into the decision making process. With the systematic evaluation of new implements, with a tool selection control mechanism, and with training programs for instructing managers in newly selected techniques, new tools can quickly be put into operation as they are required. But if the choice of tools is left to the discretion of the manager, the only other way of introducing new technology might be to encourage the staff to use the latest tools, and certainly this is a dubious course that has little assurance of positive results.

An organizational lag, in fact, seems to exist in the area of managerial technology. A relatively sophisticated set of tools has been developing rather rapidly, but the application has lagged considerably behind this development, and, for the most part, managers continue to use intuitive, primitive tools. Top management, however, cannot leave the choice of techniques to an individual manager and expect its organization to take full advantage of the developing technologies.

MANAGEMENT AS A DYNAMIC PROFESSION

Because management is an applied field, much like engineering or medicine, it strives to improve its technology. Despite all of the present processes and techniques, and on the basis of historical experience, improvements and change have been inherent attributes of the profession. It is therefore unlikely that final or ultimate management truths, of universal application, will ever evolve.

How technological change affects the individual manager is a recent problem which has not received enough attention; such analysis has chiefly been restricted to the blue-collar, skilled, semiskilled, or unskilled worker, where one was concerned with technological unemployment, retraining, job opportunities for the untrained, resistance to technological change, and so forth. But it now appears that similar problems exist on the managerial level. Herbert Simon has suggested that in twenty years it may be feasible to program computers to perform much of the managerial work of middle and lower managers in many organizations:

The electronic computer is bringing about, with unexpected speed, a high level of automation in the routine, programmed decision making and data processing that was formerly the province of clerks.

The area of programmed decision making is being rapidly extended as we find ways to apply the tools of operations research to types of decisions that have up to now been regarded as judgmental—particularly, but not exclusively, middle-management decisions in the area of manufacturing and warehousing.[13]

And:

With operations research and electronic data processing we have acquired the technical capacity to automate programmed decision making and to bring into the programmed area some important classes of decisions that were formerly unprogrammed. . . .

Even management people, long accustomed to reassuring their blue-collar and clerical workers on these points, reveal exactly the same anxieties when the talk turns to the automation of decision making.[14]

Will such a development result in the extensive unemployment of the middle manager? Professor Simon does not think so; however, he believes that the nature of the managerial job, particularly in the middle and lower levels, will change from that of making programmed decisions to making nonprogrammed decisions. He observes:

The important point is that the task of middle managers today is very much taken up with pace setting, with work pushing, and with expediting. As the automation and rationalization of the decision making process progress, these aspects of the managerial job are likely to recede in importance.[15]

If the decision making process should evolve as Professor Simon suggests, it would seem, on the whole, that such a development would be highly beneficial to the organization. It would mean that managers would spend less time on decision utilization or programmed decisions (the application of solutions which have already been made) and more time on the construction of new solutions (nonprogrammed decisions). The end result would be a significant increase in solution output.

However, technological change may require that the manager receive additional training throughout his career. This may

[13] Herbert A. Simon, *The New Science of Management Decision* (New York: Harper & Row, 1960), p. 20.
[14] *Ibid.*, pp. 35, 36.
[15] *Ibid.*, p. 48.

become necessary because the computer may be assigned some of his tasks and he may be required to perform other tasks, or because new decision making techniques may be introduced into the organization which he will be expected to apply. As these new instruments are developed, time and training facilities will have to be provided for the manager. These facilities can be instituted into a firm's management development program or they can be incorporated into university-extension management programs.

It appears that the managerial job of the future will necessitate the application of quantitative and behavioral tools by management, and most quantitative methods cannot be acquired on the job: linear programming or regression analysis, for example, require classroom instruction. As a growing, explicit body of knowledge and techniques emerges, the manager of the future will not be qualified until he has completed a prescribed sequence of intensive instruction.

SUMMARY

The incorporation of the appropriate decision making tools in the system design necessitates top management's review of available techniques and their allocation of these tools to the proper decision making subprocesses.

Guides for tool selection are: (1) feasibility, (2) cost, (3) output, (4) reliability, (5) stability, and (6) balance. The manager should be required to formulate a research design that will indicate the tools he will use and the reasons why he will use them. Because managerial technology is constantly changing, training programs should be established for maintaining high managerial proficiency.

QUESTIONS FOR DISCUSSION

1. What are some of the essential similarities between physical, behavioral, and conceptual tools?
2. It is frequently noted that ours is the age of technology and that we are confronted with a technological explosion. Explain the nature and implications of this phenomenon.
3. The concept of technology is usually associated with machines, but is there also a technology in which man is the primary actor? Give examples of technology in the political world or sports area which are essentially man to man systems.
4. The guides for tool selection—feasibility, reliability, and the others—can be combined in a number of ways, according to the

relative emphasis that is given to each criterion. Devise various combinations, such as one which uses a least-cost guide, and describe the consequences.

5. Select any management tool and discuss its feasibility. Under what circumstances would it be useful? Or detrimental?

6. What difficulties would be encountered in attempting to estimate the average cost of various management tools? Give an example.

7. What type of trade-off could be considered between the cost of achieving a good solution and its desired reliability?

8. What are some of the disadvantages of the intuitive approach as compared with more rigorous statistical and mathematical techniques?

9. When decision process and techniques are not integrated into a single system there is a danger that the criterion of balance in the use of techniques will not be observed. Explain.

10. Why is it more desirable that tools be selected in terms of problem input rather than in terms of the tool-competence of the manager?

SUGGESTED READINGS

Ackoff, Russell L. (ed.). *Progress in Operations Research*. New York: John Wiley & Sons, Inc., 1961.

Churchman, C. West; Ackoff, Russell L.; and Arnoff, E. Leonard. *Introduction to Operations Research*. New York: John Wiley & Sons, Inc., 1957.

McCloskey, Joseph F., and Trefethen, Florence N. (eds.). *Operations Research for Management*, vol. 1. Baltimore: The Johns Hopkins Press, 1954.

Miller, David W., and Starr, Martin K. *Executive Decisions and Operations Research*. Englewood Cliffs, N.J.: Prentice-Hall, Inc., 1960.

Shuchman, Abraham (ed.). *Scientific Decision-Making in Business*. New York: Holt, Rinehart & Winston, Inc., 1963.

Starr, Martin K. *Production Management: Systems and Synthesis*. Englewood Cliffs, N.J.: Prentice-Hall, Inc., 1964.

PART THREE

ADMINISTERING A PLANNED SYSTEM

9

SELECTING
THE MANAGEMENT
SYSTEM

After top management has completed the designing phase it will probably be confronted with a choice between two or more organizational problem solving models. This choice might be necessary because (1) several alternatives may have been developed in the design process, and because (2) improvement of an existent system may be the objective. While the original system was being planned, the process and technology for utilizing it may not have been conclusively decided upon, or several models could have been formulated which incorporated alternative possibilities.

The components of a management system can be rearranged in numerous combinations. The sequence of steps may vary, with authorization either preceding or following consensus; models may be considered with or without employee participation; and each submanager may be permitted to select his own decision making techniques, or it may be that the control unit will review all decision making strategies. To assure the construction of a good prototype, top management may deliberately develop several possibilities so as to provide a wider range of choice. It may also seek to prevent the screening out of potentially productive models during the designing process before serious evaluation has been made of them.

The most probable situation, however, is that top management is dissatisfied with its present model and wants to improve it. On the assumption that no system is perfect, management constantly strives to increase the value of its system, replacing the system in use if it finds a better, and feasible, alternative. With every management process under review, top management more or less constantly evaluates its present system and compares it with proposed improvements. These evaluations and comparisons, of course, can involve many major and minor variations.

How can top management choose the best problem solving model, given the pertinent data of its organization? Essentially, the selective criteria it uses will be very similar to those set forth in Chapter 8 for evaluating a system's technology. Whether one reviews the components of a system — with its specific techniques and processes — or the system as a totality, similar criteria are applied: measurability, feasibility, reliability, payoff, and stability. Therefore, this chapter will study the application of these criteria in the selection of a total management system.

MEASURING SYSTEM PERFORMANCE

To apply the suggested criteria, top management must collect data that will provide realistic estimates for a model's performance. Two parts of a system can be measured for arriving at such estimates: the product and/or the process.

The *product* is the output of an activity, whereas the *process* is the activity or series of responses which will ultimately produce (or contribute to) a system's product. When *process* is used, one can infer the system's product; for example, in measuring the proficiency of a scientist one might look at his skill in identifying problems, collecting evidence, and analyzing data.[1] The *product* of a management system is the total organizational solution payoff per year; it is the value added to profits as a result of managerial effort.

The table on page 222 illustrates how a model would be selected on the basis of these combined measurements. Under *criteria* are the guides to be employed in selecting a model; under *measurement* are the parts of the system to be measured (its process and product); and under *estimates* are the estimated performances of models A and B.

Quantitative and qualitative data must be used in making the estimation. Reliability, stability, and payoff lend themselves to quantitative measurement while feasibility and measurability must be measured in qualitative terms. Quantitative estimates

[1] Robert Glaser and David J. Klaus, "Proficiency Measurement: Assessing Human Performance," *Psychological Principles in System Development*, Robert Gagné *et al.* (eds.) (New York: Holt, Rinehart & Winston, Inc., 1962), pp. 450–451.

COMPARISON OF MODELS

Criteria	Measurement	Estimates A	Estimates B
Measurability	Product		
	Process	1	2
Reliability	Product	±7%	±3%
	Process	1	2
Stability	Product	10%	5%
	Process	1	2
Payoff	Product	$2 million/yr.	$3 million/yr.
	Process	$1 million/yr.	$2 million/yr.
Feasibility	Product		
	Process	2	1

determine the extent of difference between models; qualitative estimates establish the better model but cannot ascertain the degree of difference.

Model B ranks higher than model A in measurability, reliability, stability, and payoff, but lower in feasibility. In quantitative terms, model B has an estimated $3 million per year payoff, with a reliability or error rate of ±3 per cent. Model A's estimated output is $2 million per year and its reliability rate is ±7 per cent. Model B would be preferred over model A.[2]

How can top management acquire the data necessary for making a reasonable estimate of how well a suggested model will perform? Let us assume that management is considering two alternatives: the first is its present model and the other model is a suggested improvement. We will further assume that the present model is measurable, insofar as top management already has the data on its performance,[3] and that the measurement of the suggested model may require simulation because the organization has had no operating experience with it.

Simulation pilot studies could be conducted. It is not difficult to select small suboperations in an organization, to set up several

[2] For an explanation and application of the suggested selection criteria, see pp. 225–233.
[3] See Chapter 11, Control of the System, for the measurement of ongoing systems.

management models in miniature, and to collect data on their performance. In a large organization, different decision making models can be instituted in two or three plants, and, to the extent that each plant represents the characteristics of the whole organization, data so collected might be sufficiently representative for making a valid choice. (Pilot studies are also fairly common for testing other operations; in marketing, for example, sample cities are selected to evaluate advertising programs for new products, and firms often build small pilot plants for testing new production processes.)

One might even be able to find representative suboperations within an organization that reflect a model under consideration, particularly if an overall, uniform, and integrated decision making system has not been installed. Managers may employ different techniques and their respective performances may provide a standard of measurement. Or models might be simulated in a laboratory setting, and management teams might be formed to solve identical organizational problems in accordance with the requirements of the alternative system. Assume, in this case, that the best possible answers to the problem inputs had already been predetermined and that the simulated behavior had been reasonably realistic. Such data, if they can be inexpensively collected, can be very valuable. This "gaming" approach has also proved to be an excellent technique in management training.

It may then be possible, given enough data from pilot studies or from actual operating results, to develop a mathematical and/or statistical model that will simulate any suggested changes in the system. The data which this fairly complex management model requires include valid values of various parameters of the system, such as the number of problems which the system can handle, the average processing time, its error rate, payoff in relation to the processes and techniques, and several others. Unquestionably, such a model would be of great value, but simulation techniques are useful only when they realistically reflect the ongoing decision making system of one of the alternative models or the context in which the system would be instituted.

Another approach to the acquisition of data is to install the model system on a trial basis, with the understanding that it might eventually be accepted, rejected, or modified (which is also the basis upon which simulation is used[4]). Actual operating experience would be the ultimate test of a model's validity.

[4] See Chapter 11, Control of the System.

Although both the product and the process measurements can be used to evaluate alternative models, it is sometimes impossible, impractical, or undesirable to measure a system's performance quantitatively in terms of its product. Instead, one would have to infer the superior model after having compared their processes. The use of the product measurement might be precluded when the output of one or more models is not measurable, when it becomes apparent that there is no need to simulate, when simulation is not feasible, or when simulation does not produce valid data.

In the first instance, most organizations do not measure the product of the ongoing management system by systematically collecting performance data of the decision making model in terms of the input, output, and payoff for each decision. As a practical matter, however, top management may have to choose between its current system—for which there are no decision making payoff data—and another system which—although it incorporates product measurement devices—has not been tested in an actual operating context. Top management can only evaluate the processes of both systems.

If a system is highly complex, it may be impossible or impractical to acquire valid output data, as in large-scale economic and political systems. Economic systems can be so intricate that it is impossible to construct a detailed and exact model of how the total system operates; so one must generalize about the nature of economic processes and attempt to deduce the best system from these abstractions. Political systems are similarly evaluated, in terms of their respective processes, for the same reason. Is the legislative or decision making process open to public scrutiny; and does it provide for open committee hearings, consider many alternatives, and allow for amendments prior to its vote or decision? If it provides these essential features, we merely conclude that it is a "good" government; political systems are rarely compared in terms of their product, or the total number of decisions produced per year, or the extent to which different systems increase the general welfare.

How, then, can organizational performance be measured in terms of process? In comparing two or more models which incorporate action sets within their design, we would have to infer which set is best in relation to their respective selection criteria; and management systems must therefore be constructed in operational or action terms. One must specify the nature of the input and the output, and, even more importantly, the sequence of task performance on the inputs. On the basis of such data, the models can be ranked by their expected performance—perhaps to the extent of generating sufficient confidence for installing the superior model in the organization so that the actual product can be established. On the basis of operating experience, the validity of the inference will be learned.

SELECTING THE MODEL

Now, with the ability to make reasonable estimates of performance, we will study the application of the criteria of measurability, feasibility, payoff, reliability, and stability in selecting a model.

Measurability is a system's ability to evaluate its own performance, either quantitatively or qualitatively. Ideally, the machinery of the system will indicate the payoff, inputs, and outputs; and this would require that the unit of input and output be defined in the design. The payoff is the value added per decision, and a system should be able to indicate the number, value, and cost of all these organizational solutions, which necessitates the incorporation of measuring devices into the decision making system.[5] The extensiveness of a measurement process depends, in part, on the amount of control which must be exercised in its operation.

The preliminary appraisal of alternative models should discover each system's ability to measure its performance. If it cannot measure its performance, a system's desirability (or undesirability) cannot be established because it can never be known if it is performing as designed, nor can its particular excellencies or deficiencies be known. The effective selection of improvements can be accomplished only if the performance of the present system has been measured; then, as changes are introduced, the differentials can be determined.

When models are measurable, the superior system can be inferred from the specific measuring devices used in each. Does one model more effectively measure single outputs of the system? Can it tell how efficiently a problem is being solved in the construction of the solution? Does the model stipulate its tasks in a clear, complete, and integrated manner, so that reasonable inferences can be drawn? (Of course, if a model is vague or incomplete it cannot be measured.) Models in operational flow chart form should be presented so that they show a total view of the

---

[5] See Chapter 7, Effectuating the Decision, for examples of measuring apparatus.

system, and inferences can then be readily drawn from the processes.

The distinction must now be made between measuring the effectiveness of a system and the effectiveness of the managers who operate it; however, whatever system is ultimately selected, managerial performance must be measured in relation to that system.[6] Unfortunately, there is a tendency to regard managerial and system performance as synonymous, but if (in our context) managers do not function properly it is either because of inadequate training or poor selection. (In practice, however, estimated and actual system performance will differ because of managerial performance and not because of a deficiency in the design of the system.[7])

Feasibility is another criterion for comparing alternative decision making models, for one must be reasonably certain that the selected model will operate as planned. A model must therefore be "realistic": it must be capable of being installed, of achieving the expected payoff, and of performing its task requirements within the environment of the system. Although some models seem to be highly desirable, their requirements place their execution beyond the range of human capability (the familiar dilemma of theory and practice), and unrealistic schemata break down under implementation. In this connection, an organization may continue to operate with a truly unrealistic system only because its submanagers have informally improvised more realistic procedures, ignoring the system's formal requirements with the result that the planned system is nonoperational.[8]

Unrealistic models may require skills that managers either do not have or cannot readily acquire. They may provide insufficient time for task performance, or they may ignore constraints in the external and/or internal environment; they may also (unknowingly) call for contradictory task requirements. If a model entails filling managerial positions with charismatic leaders, we must conclude that such a model is unrealistic because of the rarity of such persons — even apart from the difficulty of defining charismatic qualities. It is equally unrealistic to specify that

---

[6] See the Maintenance of the System section in Chapter 10.

[7] This is only one possible reason; see Chapter 11, Control of the System, for other reasons.

[8] For a discussion of how actual operating management activities may differ from model postulates because of this factor of unreality, see Leonard Sayles, *Individualism and Big Business* (New York: McGraw-Hill Book Company, 1963), pp. 19–25.

managers be so eloquent that they will be able to persuade non-managers to carry out instructions with enthusiasm. It would also be absurd to require that submanagers never consider their own self-interests but only the objectives of the organization.

It is also unrealistic for a model to require that responsibility and authority always be combined. Because of the dynamics of organizational change and the interdependency of organizational operations, which could result in a continual intervention by superordinate managers in the work of submanagers, it becomes most difficult to fulfill this requirement in practice.

An example of an external constraint is the collective bargaining process, which directly or indirectly affects the decision making process. If collective bargaining factors are ignored, some aspects of a model will not be operational.[9] Another constraint is the time it takes to implement a model: if an organization faces a set of serious management problems, and requires a system almost immediately, models which necessitate long-term implementation would of course be precluded.

Top management may also impose constraints upon itself. If it takes the position that none of its present managers will be dismissed as the result of changes in its decision making system, a model must be selected which is consistent with the skills and qualifications of these managers.

Another consideration is whether the required actions of a model follow logically or whether a certain action precludes a consecutive, planned action. If, for example, a model should provide that discipline for violation of a solution will be exercised in the audit step—before employee acceptance of that solution—this provision might lead not only to employee rejection of the system but also to ineffective employee controls. On the basis of pilot studies or process reviews, then, top management can determine if a model has undesirable nonoperational characteristics, and the model can be modified (or rejected) if any are discovered.

The ultimate criterion for the selection of a model is, of course, the organizational *payoff,* and, because top management endeavors to optimize organizational objectives, it will select the decision making model whose expected payoff is greatest. In making this evaluation the designer will estimate both the number of decisions and their average added value in terms of organizational objectives. The model which produces the largest number

[9] See Chapter 13, Interorganizational Cooperation, for a review of collective bargaining as a decision making process.

of solutions, with the highest average value per solution, should provide the greatest output.

Models are compared so that an estimate can be made of which will produce the highest number of solutions. For such comparison we need reasonable data on the number of problems to be raised (the input) and on the average time required for solutions. One model might take twice as long as another to solve problems although each has the same number of managers for handling the same quantity of problems. The number of solutions will also be limited by any restrictions placed on the number of problems that can be introduced into the system. Time data will show simply the average time elapsed from the date problems were introduced to the date when their solutions become operational.

When the decision making processes of two alternative models are evaluated, all other factors being equal, the model that provides the more logical sequence of operations and the more adequate controls (in which there is no backtracking, bottlenecks, or loss of problems in transit) will provide the faster process and will produce more solutions at lower costs. For example, a model with an estimated annual problem intake of 400 and an average problem solving time of six months would obviously be preferred to a model whose capacity is only 50 and whose average solution time is two years.

The average added value per decision can also be estimated from data on the increment in value for each decision produced. Both the number and values of all decisions would be aggregated to obtain the average value per decision (added value being the increase in payoff brought about by a new solution). The output of a system can be calculated from the total decisions and the average added value of each solution. If one model produces 1,000 decisions, whose average added value is $1,000, the system's output is $1 million. Another model, which produces only 500 decisions in the same time but whose average added value is $5,000, would have increased the total output by $2.5 million. Therefore, the total decisions and their average added value are critical in the evaluation of a model. Decision making models or systems can produce rapid solutions, but if decision-makers are not able to make good analyses, the average value per decision will be diminished. Incorrect solutions could even result in a negative payoff.

When the estimated value of decisions is reviewed in relation to a process, models are compared to decide which would most likely produce correct solutions, and it is here that the exclusion of stages and techniques can become quite critical. If a design

228

does not have a consensus step, suboptimization may result. If a provision is not made to utilize regression analysis, it may not be possible to derive organizational solutions that will affect specific external determinants. Without the audit step, the effectiveness of solutions cannot be determined, etc. And although two models might include a solution audit step, in one model this might mean reliance upon the middle manager's personal observations while in the other it might entail independent audits.

When the average cost for solutions is estimated, the average time to construct a solution is multiplied by its cost in man-hours, computer time, and so forth. If construction of the average solution requires 100 hours of managerial time, if the average managerial man-hour cost is $7.50, if computer time averages $50 per solution, and if the overhead is $200 per solution, the average cost per solution would be $1,000. The average solution cost subtracted from the average output per solution yields the net payoff per solution. If one uses the figures of an average added output value of $3,000 per solution and an average cost of $1,000, the net payoff per solution is $2,000. Thus, if 1,000 solutions are produced per year, the value of this model would be $2 million.

One difficulty in calculating cost figures per solution construction is that managerial man-hours may also be spent in organizational functions (in solution application, for example) rather than exclusively in solution construction. It is therefore sometimes necessary to distinguish between managerial man-hours devoted to problem solving activities and those devoted to other activities, which may or may not be specified. However a manager's time is actually assigned, the cost of his hours spent in decision making activities should be charged to those assigned decision activities, and the cost of whatever time is spent in activities other than solution construction should be apportioned to solutions rather than to the cost of reaching solutions. Hence, if a purchasing manager devotes 50 per cent of his time to purchasing, these costs should be attributed to the purchasing procedure under which he is working.

The fourth criterion in model selection is *reliability*: the extent to which it can be expected that an actual operation will reflect the estimated performance of the initial design—or the extent to which deviations from planned patterns of behavior can be expected to occur. All decision making models will specify a standard of behavior for the problem-solvers or managers; however, it is unlikely that any model will work so perfectly that actual operations will conform exactly to the predicted pattern.

At the outset, when a model is still assumed to be the best available, some deviations could result in a lower-than-calculated payoff. Such deviations could also indicate less-than-optimum behavioral patterns and could therefore produce undesirable results. On the other hand, other deviations could result in improved and better-than-predicted results.

Thus when several models are being considered, every effort should be made to determine the degree to which actual behavior may deviate from planned behavior. One should also try to compute the degree to which actual payoff will vary from estimated payoff. These considerations attempt to determine the error or reliability rate because errors will almost inevitably occur in solution construction, and, given any decision, it is unlikely that the expected and the actual payoff will be identical. A reliability estimate of 4 per cent (or ±2 per cent) obviously denotes a much more acceptable range than 20 per cent.

Error in management systems is probably not normally distributed: one cannot assume that an actual solution payoff will deviate as much on the positive side as on the negative side—that for every decision which produces $1,000 less than was expected, another decision will produce $1,000 more than was expected. The more probable situation is that errors will be distributed in a skewed, or irregular, fashion on the negative side—that is to say, the less reliable the system, the greater the negative variance between the expected and actual payoffs.

Assume a model A that produces an estimated $2 million added payoff per year and a model B that produces an added $1 million. Model A might be found to be less reliable than model B when the error rate of the system is determined, and, if this is so, it could just as easily produce a $2 million deficit. Model B, on the other hand, could be much more reliable, and might deviate only from $750,000 to $1 million per year. Top management might very well select model B although its estimated output is lower.

Because individuals are subject to forgetfulness, mistakes in perception, and miscalculations, human components introduce errors into any man to man system. In addition, the selection, training, and motivation of middle managers is an imperfect science, so that some will not have the level of skills or knowledge which a system requires. During the design process, if these areas of potential error are considered, control devices can be built into the system as detection devices which will catch and correct any deviations from the expected managerial behavior.[10]

[10] See Chapter 11, Control of the System, for examples.

230

When, in process evaluation, a system is planned as completely as possible, the opportunity for random, unintended behavior is reduced. A critical review of the control devices for coping with potential errors will differentiate the extent of their reliability in various systems. The controls in a reliable system will detect and respond to errors made during the process of solution construction, will discriminate as to the nature of the errors, and will correct them rapidly. Standby apparatus can also be alerted if components fail to operate, and independent detectors can double check against possible failures.

The last criterion in the selection of a decision model is its estimated *stability*, a system's ability to adjust to both external and internal events or changes and still maintain the expected payoff.

The stability of a system can be measured by its degree of oscillation, its deviation from the norm, and its required time for returning a system to its normal output or steady state. The product of a system will tend to oscillate below its expected norm as the system adjusts, as the following graph indicates.

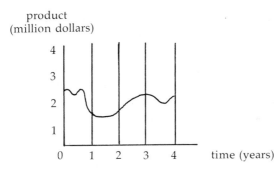

The accepted performance of this plotted system is $2.5 million per year. At the end of the first year an event occurred which caused the product to fall by approximately $1 million. Yet the system adjusted to this event in slightly less than two years. (Some oscillation will always occur in a system because of minor environmental variations.)

For assurance of a stable system, events must be accurately predicted, and the system must be provided with mechanisms that will minimize fluctuations.[11] An inflexible system will be unable to adjust to changes in its environment, and, if its payoff is adversely affected, submanagers may have to improvise in-

[11] See Chapter 10, Installation, Operation, and Maintenance of the System.

formal administrative procedures, in effect, abandoning the model.

Changes in personnel are some events that should be expected. As managers move in and out of a system, will the system be able to staff or replace itself with the requisite qualified personnel? Does the system have a self-improvement capability? As decision making technologies improve, can the system incorporate these changes rapidly?[12]

Changes in the size of an organization will also affect its system as the number and complexity of operations alters its load. Organizations increase in size because of mergers or because of increasing demand for their services, and it is important that a decision making system have the adaptability for coping with such changes. Organizations can have serious problems in this area. Firms may merge, but it may take a considerable amount of time before management is able to function with reasonable efficiency. Although it might seem that a legal merger of two or more firms results in a consolidation, in one large organization, the fact is that two or more managerial groups often continue to operate as though the original organizations still exist.

Furthermore, when organizations grow very swiftly, there will often be a lag in the growth and capability of the managerial systems. As a result, a managerial staff can become overburdened and organizational operations can exhibit gross inefficiencies. The inability of a management system to adjust may then serve as a constraint on both an organization's operations and further growth. In some cases, however, although the demand for the services of an organization diminishes and the size of other subsystems is lessened, the size of the managerial staff may remain constant, and the cost of maintaining an excessive managerial staff can become a serious handicap for the entire organization. Indeed, Parkinson's law could be at work here, insofar as managers might be creating work to justify their positions.

Given these various possibilities of change, is there an apparatus that can ensure a desirable state of stability—and can corrective decision making adjuncts be added to an existent system without disrupting the entire model? Whatever the increases in its problem input load, a model that has an effective scheduling and routing mechanism, which avoids bottlenecks and queuing problems, will provide a great measure of stability because such a system can continue to operate efficiently under these conditions. This mechanism can also be added to an existent system.

[12] This problem was discussed in Chapter 8, Decision Making Technology.

Rigidities, on the other hand, can be woven into a model in the form of precise relationships among managers, in which everyone's authority and responsibility is minutely defined. If such a system is to be adjusted to handle an increased number of problems, all managerial jobs may first have to be redefined and new jobs established, with a considerable loss of time before the relationships among managers can be reestablished. A submanagerial staff may offer strong resistance to these changes and disruptions, and top management may be reluctant to undertake really extensive changes. This can compound the difficulty, while the system becomes increasingly unstable.

If, in evaluating two or more models, top management knows the nature of the changing inputs that will be introduced into the system (some of which have already been mentioned), it will have to ascertain that internal procedures have been provided for modifying the system so that it can cope with these inputs. In addition, it will have to consider the time it will take to make the adjustment and the extent of the disruption that will be involved. And, if the design has no adjustment apparatus, top management must be exceedingly cautious in its acceptance of changes.

In summary, the selection of a model will still depend upon the personal judgment of top management. However, if the criteria and measuring devices herein suggested are applied, top managers will have a much firmer basis for making its selection; and, when the model is installed in the organization, top management can have greater confidence in expecting—and receiving—proper performance.

EVALUATING THE PRESENT SYSTEM

Although top management may not be contemplating changes in its existent system, it may still want to determine if any submanagement problems exist or whether improvements should be considered. The same criteria can be applied here. It would appraise only one model on an investigative basis, and meaningful deficiencies in the reliability or stability of its present system would be a stimulus in searching for improvements. Top management could take a random sample of decisions and evaluate them. It could acquire a descriptive history of how these decisions were constructed by establishing the processes the decisions went through, the techniques that were used, the time that was consumed, the personnel that were involved, and, finally, it could determine the quality of the decisions in terms of the value that had been added to organizational objectives. The investigators could examine the solutions of a single manager or a random sample of solutions from a large group of managers. (All this would also help determine the present system's effectiveness of operation.)

After such an investigation, the resulting descriptive model could be subjected to the standard criteria, a judgment could be made of the ongoing system, and it could then be decided whether model changes should be contemplated.

PRINCIPLES AS A GUIDE TO SELECTION

Another guide in the choice of a management system is the principles approach. Because there are several disadvantages in this criterion, it has not been recommended, but because it nevertheless represents a major approach, it will be briefly explored.

In the principles approach a normative or ideal management system is posited that incorporates a set of "good management principles"; and, insofar as a proposed management model conforms to the ideal, it is acceptable. However, this approach is based on the sheer assumption of a direct cause-and-effect relationship between good principles in a management system and good organizational results. In other words, if a model includes "limited span of control," "short lines of command," "reporting to only one superior," "equality of authority and responsibility," etc., the belief is that organizational performance will be positive, and, if these principles are violated, the results will be negative. This assumption is founded largely on the operating experience and observations of practitioners.

One great disadvantage of the principles approach is that the ideal model—supposedly a composite of all these principles—has never been systematically validated. There is little rigorous, empirical evidence to support the assumption of the relationship between "good principles" and organizational performance, and management systems should not be designed and instituted on the basis of mere opinion. Unsystematized organizations, of course, may be highly successful, and some practitioners may attribute this to a principles design, but the causes of success will probably be found elsewhere.

A second disadvantage in this approach is that the efficacy of principles is difficult to measure, a difficulty which Fremont Shull has commented upon as follows:

> *Traditional management prescriptions appear particularly vulnerable to criticism from the standpoint of prediction. At least*

234

two major weaknesses are apparent. First, the traditionalist may have become so enamored with his preconceived schema that unprejudiced observation and measurement are impeded. Second, published dogma may have imparted to the practitioner a "way of life" to which he feels he should conform, and, whether or not he does, he rationalizes or conceals his actual behavior and aims. To such a degree, reality is not represented in the model and its predictive capacity is destroyed. To this extent, then, prescription becomes a set of moralistic bromides or clichés.[13]

Dr. Shull further observes that:

Many conventional models are incapable of describing or predicting various actualities of individual and organizational behavior. Consider, for example, the utility of the traditional framework in forecasting an individual's promotion because of low performance in his present assignment; or predict the personal and organizational energies dissipated in political maneuvering among members of a hierarchy.[14]

The inability to predict behavior from a set of principles follows from the fact that such propositions are really only organizational states or characteristics. To measure the performance of a system one must measure the product, or process, or both. Although principles represent the attributes of a system, and although one can determine if such attributes are present or absent, they cannot provide a basis for performance measurement.

One should — if this approach were valid — be able to establish the precise relationship between attributes and performance, and that the presence or absence of certain attributes will produce a certain performance. The mere fact that certain characteristics are present does not ascertain ·a relationship; another standard of measurement is required to do this. Assertions that managerial performance will improve if the manager uses judgment, initiative, and leadership, or if he is sensitive, kind, and considerate of other viewpoints (although true), add very little in terms of design or in the ability to evaluate system performance. Nor can such assertions measure behavior or its results.

[13] Fremont A. Shull, Jr., "Administrative Models and Organization Research," *Selected Readings in Management,* Fremont A. Shull, Jr., and André L. Delbecq (eds.) (2d series; Homewood, Ill.: Richard D. Irwin, Inc., 1962), p. 57. This article, in modified form, appeared in the *Academy of Management Journal,* 5 (August, 1962), 124–138.

[14] *Ibid.,* p. 53.

Product and process, on the other hand, lend themselves to measurement. If a system is supposed to produce a product, it can be evaluated in terms of the expected and the actual product. As for process, given alternative sets of behavioral patterns, one can infer—deductively or inductively—the set which will lead to the desired product. Process is observable, and because of this we can distinguish between behavioral patterns.

Another measurement difficulty is that the statement of principles is frequently ambiguous. Does a "limited span of control" mean that one person should never supervise the work of more than six individuals? What is the meaning of "supervise"?

However, the most serious shortcoming of the principles approach as a selection device is the absence of rules that are independent of the system. System selection, we would emphasize, depends on the application of independent criteria, such as measurability and payoff. We cannot select a system on the basis of its characteristics, for, without criteria, there is no way we can evaluate it, and the result is circular reasoning. The ideal model must be tested in terms of its stability, feasibility, etc. If at the outset, we *theorize* upon the characteristics of the ideal model, operating models based on this ideal will be no more valid than the ideal. Not until an ideal model is *tested* can we determine how "ideal" it really is.

It has been suggested, for example, that linear programming should be included as a technique of the system. Linear programming would then become an attribute of a system and one might differentiate systems between those that have linear programming and those that do not. However, one could not conclude that the former system is good merely because it includes this technique. Neither can it be said that a model is good because authority and responsibility are equal. Only when it is proved that the measurability, feasibility, reliability, stability, and payoff of a system are improved by equality of authority and responsibility (etc.) can one conclude that "principles" are significant.

We do not mean that these same principles have no *value*, even in the design of systems, but it must be proved that the *performance* of the management system will be enhanced before any attribute is incorporated. Principles, of themselves, are not effective for selecting a management system.

THE "MANAGEMENT JUNGLE"

Management literature has proposed alternative management systems, and there is a wealth of material on how the manage-

236

ment function should be performed, in all of its aspects, but there is almost as much controversy over which approach or technique is superior.

Professor Paul J. Gordon has observed that "far too much of the recent literature on administrative theories has been dedicated to scuffling over which of several schemes of classification of a complex terrain might be better."[15]

Lyndall F. Urwick noted the same phenomenon when he observed: " 'Inky warfare' is both an occupational disease and the favorite hobby of some professors. Through practice they become extremely skilled at the gentle art of verbal in-fighting."[16]

That there is a combat, both Professor Koontz[17] and Professor Suojanen are agreed. Professor Suojanen has said that "today it is almost impossible to find two people who share more than a very general agreement as to what should be included, and what excluded, in the definition and study of management theory. Disagreement and controversy have almost reached the point where any theoretical light that has been generated has been overwhelmed by emotional heat."[18]

Whatever management approach might be used by the practitioner or by the theorist, if agreement could be reached on a common set of effective criteria, the various techniques, processes, and approaches might be better evaluated. This would not only do much to reduce the present controversy, it would also help produce a set of *optimum* operational techniques and processes.

Unfortunately, system selection criteria have usually represented only the personal opinions of the practitioner or the academician, and not always with good results. Again, although there is no concurrence upon which management approach is correct, we believe it should be possible at least to agree upon criteria for evaluating the different approaches, and we submit the criteria we have previously advanced—payoff, measurability, feasibility, reliability, and stability—for serious consideration. At the very least, it is certainly reasonable to assert that management's behavior should lead to optimization of the organizational

[15] Paul J. Gordon, "Transcend the Current Debate on Administrative Theory," *Academy of Management Journal*, 6 (December, 1963), 290.

[16] Lyndall F. Urwick, "Management in Perspective," *Academy of Management Journal*, 6 (December, 1963), 316.

[17] Harold Koontz, "The Management Theory Jungle," *Academy of Management Journal*, 4 (December, 1961), 175.

[18] Waino W. Suojanen, "Management Theory: Functional and Evolutionary," *Academy of Management Journal*, 6 (March, 1963), 7.

payoff, for, as Professor Gordon has observed: "One system is better or worse than another only because it has more use in achieving the purposes intended."[19]

Any proposal that would change managerial behavior should ultimately strive to increase payoff. Thus, whether one is evaluating an ongoing management system, or a single model, or reviewing suggested improvements in some phase of a system, this criterion would always be operational.

Also, if a reliable body of technical knowledge on managerial performance is to develop, it is necessary that both the behavior and the results of managers be measured against agreed upon criteria. And it is only through the acceptance of common measuring criteria (whether they are used deductively or inductively) that personal opinion can be removed from the important area of decision making and that differences over the best management practices can be resolved.

SUMMARY

From a number of alternative management models, top management must select the system which is best for its organization, and the estimated performance of each model can be based upon data relating to its payoff or process. These data can be acquired by simulating the proposed models.

The (suggested) criteria that should be applied in selecting the best model are *payoff, measurability, feasibility, reliability,* and *stability.* The principles criterion (does the model incorporate "good" principles of management?) was not recommended because it tends to involve circular reasoning.

QUESTIONS FOR DISCUSSION

1. Under what circumstances will top management be faced with the necessity of choosing among alternative decision making models?
2. Would you consider the domestic political decision making system fundamentally different from the totalitarian system? Explain.
3. Is the performance of a student typically evaluated in terms of the product or of the process? How would one infer a student's product by reviewing his learning process?
4. Why is it important to simulate system performance? Is it possible to deduce model performance from a paper proposal or blueprint?
5. What is the ultimate test of system performance? What does this suggest about the follow-up process in model construction?

[19] Gordon, *op. cit.,* p. 290.

6. What are the essential differences between the criteria of reliability and feasibility?
7. Why is it easier to evaluate the estimated performance of management models if their processes are represented in flow chart form?
8. How would you evaluate the performance of an ongoing, existing organization? What procedures would you employ?
9. Explain why circular reasoning occurs when the principles approach is used to evaluate a management system.
10. Why is the use of personal value judgments questionable in the evaluation of various management approaches and techniques?

SUGGESTED READINGS

CHAPPLE, ELLIOT D. *The Measurement of Management*. New York: The Macmillan Company, 1961.

DAVIS, ROBERT H., and BEHAN, RICHARD A. "Evaluating System Performance in Simulated Environments," *Psychological Principles in System Development*, Robert Gagné *et al.* (eds.). New York: Holt, Rinehart & Winston, 1962 (pp. 477–515).

GLASER, ROBERT, and KLAUS, DAVID J. "Proficiency Measurement: Assessing Human Performance," *Psychological Principles in System Development*, Robert Gagné *et al.* (eds.). New York: Holt, Rinehart & Winston, 1962 (pp. 419–474).

GORDON, PAUL J. "Transcend the Current Debate on Administrative Theory," *Academy of Management Journal*, 6 (December, 1963), 290–302.

KOONTZ, HAROLD. "The Management Theory Jungle," *Academy of Management Journal*, 4 (December, 1961), 174–188.

SHULL, FREMONT A., JR. "Administrative Models and Organization Research," *Selected Readings in Management*, Fremont A. Shull, Jr., and André L. Delbecq (eds.). 2d series; Homewood, Ill.: Richard D. Irwin, Inc., 1962 (pp. 47–58).

SUOJANEN, WAINO W. "Management Theory: Functional and Evolutionary," *Academy of Management Journal*, 6 (March, 1963), 7–17.

10

INSTALLATION, OPERATION,
AND MAINTENANCE
OF THE SYSTEM

After top management has selected the best model for its management system, it must install the system into the organization and make it operational, converting a paper plan into an operating reality. This also means, of course, that the submanagerial staff will be expected to alter its decision making activities so as to conform with the requirements of the new system.

Two main questions or considerations should be kept in mind when the new decision making machinery is installed: (1) How shall the existing managerial staff be encouraged to accept the system? and (2) How shall the new system be installed? (The amount of disruption the system will cause in the ongoing decision making process should also be determined and provided for.)

ACCEPTANCE OF THE SYSTEM

To facilitate both the installation and the operation of the new system it is important for the managerial staff to adopt a positive willingness to make the system work. Perhaps the best way of approaching this subject is by considering some of the reasons why resistance or opposition may occur and the means by which both can be overcome.

Submanagers may oppose the innovation through fear that they may lose their individual organizational benefits; therefore the managerial staff must be assured that, as individuals, they will be in a better position under the new plan because the system will represent a *net gain* for them. Systems vary in their intrinsic and extrinsic satisfactions, but it can be assumed that a manager will prefer the approach that furnishes him the greatest benefits. For the moment—although the individual managerial benefits derived from a planned system will be explored a little later[1]—we will simply assume that most managers will find themselves in a better situation and that, before the installation of the system, managers should be assured their welfare will be increased.[2]

A second reason for managerial reluctance in adapting to a different process is merely the inherent human repugnance to change and uncertainty. To the extent that managers have adjusted to their earlier system, they have established a routine, but, because change frequently introduces unknown elements in the work environment, anxiety is often created. To alleviate this concern—and to do this before the new system is implemented— the submanagers should receive information about the plan's expected operation. If possible, they should even participate in the new design and be allowed to offer suggestions or changes both before and after the system's effectuation (although it is understood that the major responsibility for the design will rest with top management).

If top management unilaterally imposes decision making innovations upon the submanagerial group, changes of which the group has been totally unaware, it should not be surprised if the response or conformity is less than enthusiastic; top management would then have created the opposition that it should sedulously seek to avoid. However, if lower management participates in the design stage, it will become familiar with the plan and will have a better knowledge of what its duties will be when the system is finally installed; it will also become better aware of the system's potential benefits. Another reason for submanagerial participation is the almost inevitable reaction that the new plan, at least in part, is "their" system. Moreover, submanagers can often suggest excellent modifications for improving a system's operation, and these would be forwarded for top management's evaluation and decision for incorporation into the system.[3]

Another cause for a middle manager's concern is his fear that he may not be able to meet the new minimum performance requirements because, in all likelihood, higher standards will mean increased demands upon the staff. Top management

[1] Pages 259–260.
[2] For exceptions, see pp. 242–244.
[3] It should be noted that the criteria for accepting improvements are the same as those discussed in Chapter 9, Selecting the Management System.

should therefore make a tenure commitment to its submanagers that they will not be discharged if they cannot meet the changed performance specifications. Moreover, although a permanent training capability must be developed, special training may also be necessary during the installation stage, and this feature could be expected to offer hope and assurance while actually raising the performance of deficient managers. Then, once the system becomes operational and staffing needs arise, the organization would attempt to select managers who hold the requisite qualifications.

Furthermore, if top management should commit itself to a policy of upgrading all potentially capable middle managers, these individuals would require additional training. But because such a policy would entail the acquisition of basic quantitative skills and behavioral knowledge (on the university level), and because many managers would be involved, consideration would have to be given to instituting a training program. This program—if adopted—could be conducted by the organization's personnel who are already skilled in the activity, and personnel in organizational planning or management development would be trained first, so that they in turn could train other managers. Formal classes could be held, a curriculum would be formulated, instructors would be selected to teach the material, and submanagers would be assigned to attend designated classes that would be of help to them.

(Despite the amount and the quality of training that would be offered, some managers may still lack the basic abilities for performing adequately in the new system, and they might have to be transferred to jobs which require less responsibility [if management had decided not to dismiss anyone].)

If middle managers believe the new system will not need the same number of managers (fearing the plan will be "too efficient" or will produce a greater output with less staff), the issue of job security will appear. However, it would be most unlikely that a managerial staff would have to be reduced since the problem solving output can be expected to increase; it is quite possible that additional managers will have to be hired.

Still another problem is the psychological adjustment of a manager. In a bureaucratic setting, the decision making function is usually centralized in a few individuals, and, either formally or informally, submanagers are usually encouraged to be passive and dependent, to receive and give instructions, and to follow the rules and regulations that have been handed down. Chris Argyris has observed:

242

If the principles of formal organization are used as ideally defined, then the employees will tend to work in an environment where (1) they are provided minimal control over their work-a-day world, (2) they are expected to be passive, dependent, subordinate, (3) they are expected to have a short-time perspective, (4) they are induced to perfect and value the frequent use of a few superficial abilities, and (5) they are expected to produce under conditions leading to psychological failure.[4]

The introduction of a planned system requires a measure of independence and initiative which some individuals may have difficulty supplying. Dependent personalities, for example, would have difficulty in accepting responsibility for solving problems; they will prefer that others perform this task so that they will not have to take the consequences for poor decisions.

However, in a highly centralized situation, in which middle managers are given little opportunity for exercising autonomy in solution formulation, passive behavior can also be an organizational affectation which individuals use to keep their jobs. Given a real chance, many middle managers will eagerly accept decision making responsibilities that had previously been denied them. Individuals who are *actually* dependent personalities may then have to be transferred to other positions.

In any event, middle managers who have been accustomed to going to higher management with every problem (in the expectation that they will be told what to do) would no longer be encouraged to behave in this fashion. Although such a tendency may continue after the planned system begins to operate, part of the training program would be that top managerial personnel will not only refuse requests for ready solutions but will encourage middle managers to work out their organizational problems independently. Through such consistent behavior, middle managers will realize that top management is fully committed to the changes it has instituted.

A further reason for managers' reluctance to accept a new system is the belief that their share of organizational benefits may be adversely affected. Managers who do well in one system may not be equally proficient in another. Thus, while there may be a net increase in benefits for all managers, some will do better than others in promotions, salary increases, and the like—just as

---

[4] Chris Argyris, "The Individual and Organization: Some Problems of Mutual Adjustment," *Administrative Science Quarterly* (June, 1957), 18.

managers who had developed a set of skills that worked successfully in the old system had been rewarded accordingly.

There is little question, then, that the installation of a new
management system is a technological change which will raise
problems of adjustment for its operators. In essence, however,
change on the managerial level is no different from change in the
other operating parts of an organization.

If the new system provides the managerial staff a net increase
in organizational benefits, if managers have had an opportunity
to participate in the system's design before its installation, and if
training facilities are provided, there is little reason to believe
that the managerial staff will not readily accept the new design.
Once the process is understood, considerable effort can be expected to make it operational.

In a relatively large organization, as we have noted, some
personnel will be reluctant to accept the changes because of a lack
of basic abilities, personality difficulties, or dissatisfactions with
the new reward arrangement. But top management's primary
concern should be whether the new system will increase the
achievement of the organizational objectives, and the newly
formed machinery should increase not only the benefits of the
stockholders, the employees, and top management, but also those
of the submanagement group. Total organizational payoff obviously takes precedence over the benefits for any individual.

The nonmanagerial, or employee, sector must also be prepared
for the installation of the system. Employees should be informed
of the nature of the system—particularly in relation to their
expected roles—and they should be told about the individual
benefits they can expect to derive from it. The extent of employee
participation will depend, of course, upon the particular design,
but if employees are to be informed of proposed solutions in the
consensus step, and given an opportunity to comment upon
them, the operation of this mechanism will have to be explained.
Other parts should also be explained, such as the raising of
problems and especially employees' participation in the payoff
that will be distributed because of the results of the improved
operations. If it becomes apparent that some of the new features
will benefit the employee sector, it is most probable that these
nonmanagers will willingly accept the system.

As for employee responsibility, it is important that all employees understand the consequences when the system's procedures
are not followed. They must understand how organizational
authority will be exercised and they must be cautioned to follow
only those decisions that have been properly constructed within

the context of the system. This means, in effect, that authority will now reside in the decision making system and not in any individual. If a decision is improperly made, the employee need not (nor should he) conform to it.

The board of directors or trustees will also have to accept the new management system before it can be installed. The board would be given an opportunity to review the system and submit suggestions and modifications. The system would not be unchangeable, and whenever the board believes that modifications would improve it, these changes can be incorporated. Because the board of directors will be primarily interested in total organizational performance, the review of all proposed changes should stress how the design under consideration will augment the organizational results.

Of course, the new management system will also facilitate the work of the board of directors, which is concerned with controlling the managerial staff, and a review of the system should stress how much easier it will be to locate and correct operating units that are not meeting the board's performance requirements. Since the board must shoulder responsibility for the successful operation of the organization as a whole, it will be especially interested in seeing that submanagers carry out their decision making tasks.

The board of directors, under the charter of the organization, will have to approve certain decisions, such as new stock issues. To meet this situation, a triggering device could be built into the system which will forward the appropriate solutions for the board's approval. This device would be placed in the control unit.

INSTALLATION OF THE SYSTEM

After the new program has been explained, the next step is the installation of the system. Two approaches can be adopted here: the total system can be implemented at once, or it can be installed sequentially.

If the total system is to be installed in one operation, a detailed outline of the operation should be presented to the managerial staff which specifies each manager's position and the tasks he is expected to accomplish. If the plan is to be established sequentially, it can be done in several ways. Various operating units might install the system separately: sales may be revamped first, then production, then personnel. Another approach is sequential introduction of the "machinery": the control unit could be introduced first, the intelligence unit second, and so on. Or top management could select the aspects of the current decision making system that present the most serious problems and introduce the machinery to cope with these areas in the proper sequence. If suboptimization is a major problem, the consensus apparatus may be the first piece of machinery introduced.

Several factors would be weighed to determine the best approach, and one of these factors is the adjustment of the submanagers. There would be merit in making this change at one time because submanagers would then know what is expected of them and could begin to adapt sooner. If the changes were introduced sequentially, managers would be forced to undergo a series of learning experiences, which, on the individual level, could be even more disruptive. Or, if the total system were installed at once, some parts would become operational quickly and present no difficulty, and energy could be directed toward correcting problems in other areas.

If the organization is large, the plan might have to be put in piecemeal because of the great difficulty of retraining managers; the introduction of the entire mechanism into an organization of two or three thousand managers would exceed the staff's ability to assist all managers simultaneously.

New tasks are usually learned more quickly if each component is mastered separately. After a person has become adept in one step—for example, if he can perform the consensus step well—he can then proceed to the next phase. But if a manager is expected to learn too many tasks at one time he may be unable to understand them properly. He might thus be overwhelmed and therefore anxious about his ability to cope with the entire system and achieve the performance standards that had been set by top management. All this, of course, would argue for sequential introduction.

Another reason for considering a sequential approach is that the system's subprocesses can be tested, corrected, and modified before the installation of the next operation. However effective an original design may be, its installation and operation will reveal minor imperfections that necessitate "debugging." The sequential approach affords opportunities for doing this.

Top management should postulate a schedule of the time it will take to install the system, the date by which it should be operational, and the date by which decision making performance should meet the expected standards. It is only reasonable to assume that considerable time will be involved, and so, at the outset, an approximate schedule should be established that allows enough lead time to cope with unexpected difficulties that may arise when the mechanism is actually installed. The lack of a fairly tight schedule will only delay the system's benefits. There is even a possibility that the total system may not be installed.

A certain measure of disruption must be expected in the present ongoing system as one method is phased out and another is introduced. Even though the mechanism being replaced is less effective than the new one, it nevertheless produces decisions. One must therefore minimize the decrease in decision output while the system is being changed. However, the amount of disruption can actually be quite minimal, particularly if no planned process is being replaced. (An unplanned situation is internally disruptive in itself, so a planned approach will begin to reduce this disequilibrium immediately.)

OPERATION OF THE SYSTEM

After the system has been installed, top management must exercise individual responsibility in the system's daily operation, although its actual participation will be quite limited because a system is largely self-effectuating.[5] Individual top managers may directly supervise various operational portions of the system; for example, the marketing vice-president would supervise the segment concerned with formulating marketing solutions.

Top management may also reserve the authorization step for itself, or at least the authorization of solutions that incur a large cost. It could also raise organizational problems and feed them into the system, as would middle management. Further, top management may want to construct specific solutions, or have its immediate staff do this.[6] And submanagers, particularly in the control unit, may have occasional questions that require counseling.

CAPACITY OF THE MANAGEMENT SYSTEM

An important aspect of operating the system is the necessity for a day by day adjustment of capacity to changes in the amount and nature of problem input. System capacity relates to the size and ability of a system to cope with the nature and number of problems that it must solve. If, for example, the system is too small in terms of its problem input, a backlog of problems will result. Although a forecast will have been made of the system's total

---

[5] See Chapter 3, Designing a Management System.
[6] Apart from the middle managerial staff, a personal staff may be assigned to top managerial personnel to assist them in their duties.

manpower needs, and although submanagers will be acquired accordingly, variations in the type of problem input can necessitate frequent adjustments of the system. Because in maintaining the decision making capacity of their segments top managers must have complete and current data, and therefore full access to the system, decision making channels will be modified to cope with variations in problem input.

In part, the capacity of a system is a function of the time it takes to perform each of the decision making steps. In a planned system that requires ten suboperations for constructing a certain solution, the time component of each of these operations will vary. In a particular situation the consensus step may require as much managerial time as all other steps combined, and the only way the speed of the entire line can be increased is by reducing the time expended on the slowest step, which represents a bottleneck in the system. There is then a backlog or queue of problems waiting to go through this operating step. When such constraints appear, it is necessary to investigate the operation of the system at that point and to attempt to modify it so that problems can be processed faster.

Top management can use three devices in coping with this problem. A storage facility can be provided that will hold problems until they can be worked upon, or the control unit can hold problems in an active inventory. The second method is to speed the operation at this particular stage by redesigning the bottleneck operation. The third approach is to provide more channels at that step or to build more capability into the system.

The problem of balancing the process operating time between suboperations is always present. Ideally, the capacity of each decision making stage, or the number of channels, would be such that the time required at each stage would be equal. If it is found that the implementation step uses the greatest amount of time, more managers may have to be assigned to operate this step (additional personnel can usually achieve this balance). If consensus takes five times as long as any other step, five times as much managerial time should be scheduled for consensus.

Because the performance rate of suboperations may vary, the top manager may have to reassign managers, from time to time, to different parts of the operation. The problem of overload exists in every system, and, unless a time balance is maintained between operations, increasing the rate of one operation will not increase the total output. The critical problem is the slowest suboperation. It makes little sense to substitute the computer for men at the auditing step if the implementation step consumes the greatest amount of time; that is, if the computer cuts the audit solution time in half, but there is no comparable implementation improvement, the result is merely a longer queue at the implementation step, and the time required per solution remains the same.

Providing adequate capacity also implies the ability to reassign additional personnel, given changes in the nature of the problem input. Over a year's time, for example, the marketing area's number of problem inputs that relate to advertising may decrease while those concerning market research may increase. The control unit can schedule its maximum assignment capacity, but beyond this point extra personnel will be needed. If there are several control units in the marketing area, the vice-president (let us say) could reassign management personnel from one unit to another. Requests for such adjustments would be initiated by the control unit, but they would be authorized and executed only by top management. Top management would be continually aware of the state of the decision making system and would allocate personnel in whatever way was necessary to assure balance between input and output.

MAINTENANCE OF THE SYSTEM (MANAGERIAL DEVELOPMENT)

After the system is installed and operational, it must, of course, be maintained, which is essentially a staffing problem. Managers leave or retire, are promoted, or transferred, and additional personnel must be added. The maintenance of the management system is usually referred to as management development, and it relates to the selection, training, placement, promotion, and motivation of qualified managers. In order to maintain the system, then, qualified managers must constantly be supplied, and its operation is jeopardized if its staff is untrained, unqualified, or understaffed. Although the personnel department will usually man the system, top management will determine the procedures and policy by which this will be accomplished.

A system is no better than the personnel who comprise it. If the design is optimum and if the submanagers are motivated and qualified to execute it, the organization will get its best results. If the design is good, but the submanagers are either unmotivated or unqualified, this limitation will be a constraint on the system's effectiveness, and, in actual practice, it will operate at the middle level of managerial capability. This is equally true of design; if the managers are qualified and motivated but the apparatus is poorly planned, the design will be a constraint upon the managers' effectiveness. Each part of the system, the design and participants, should supplement and complement the other.

MANPOWER REQUIREMENTS

To ensure an adequate supply of problem-solvers there must be an estimate of future staffing requirements, and there must also be sufficient lead time for selecting and preparing these managers for their roles. The problem solving load and the managerial replacement or turnover rate will determine the number of managers required.

As for problem-solvers, the required number can be ascertained by dividing the number of problems to be solved by the average amount of managerial time a solution takes. Assume a situation in which, on the average, 500 managerial hours are needed to solve a problem — or one manager can average four problem solutions per year. If such an organization has twenty managers, it can solve 80 problems a year. Or, if it is estimated that 120 problems will have to be solved yearly, the firm will have to acquire an additional ten managers.

Therefore, to determine managerial manpower needs, the expected number of problems to be solved and the average time required to solve each problem should be known, which necessitates a forecast of the problem input. Some of the factors to be considered in making such a projection are the size of the organization, the dynamism of the organization's environment, the nature of the input channels, and the economies of scale. Adjustment of the management system to changes in the size of the organization and to the nature of the input channels has already been discussed,[7] which leaves the organization's environment and economies of scale to be considered.

The more rapidly the environment changes, the greater the number of problems that will be presented to an organization; and organizational problems are a function of organizational adjustment. If a firm is part of an industry that is subject to rapid technological changes or rapid shifts in consumer tastes, these changes could present conditions for which the organization is unprepared and which require many rapid solutions. On the other hand, if an organization is part of a stable environment and has been able to formulate a set of effective responses which can be utilized repeatedly, it may face a gradually diminishing prob-

[7] See Chapter 7, Effectuating the Decision.

lem solving load, which reduces its need for managers. An economic guide in managerial hiring is that managers are added to a system until the added revenue produced by the last-hired manager is equal to the cost of hiring him. Top management would receive relevant data as this point is approached and as solutions are audited.

The forecast of managerial manpower needs would consider not only the problem solving load to be handled but also the normal attrition rate. Managers who retire or resign will have to be replaced; but retirements can be estimated from the ages recorded in the managerial personnel files, and, with operating experience, the number or rate of resignations can also be gauged.

The problem backlog in the control unit or units is another source of information for the number of managers required. If the managerial staff is operating at full capacity, incoming problems will have to be stored in the problem backlog. If this backlog or queue increases over time, additional managers must be hired to handle the augmented load.

An overstaffing problem can also be inferred from the schedule: a staff that is underutilized has available managerial time and a shortage of problems demanding solution; accordingly, fewer managers are needed. In the initial operation of a management system, data for projecting manpower needs may be inadequate and reliance may have to be placed on the problem backlog.

As one redesigns the problem-raising mechanism (the problem input source of the system), and assuming that this mechanism acquires all unsolved problems, it may well be that many unsolved problems pending under the previous management system will be added into the new system, so that there may be an unusually large backlog at the outset. Top management should therefore take a long-term view of this phenomenon; it should not add a large group of new managers but should, instead, gradually reduce the backlog with the approximate number of managers needed for coping with its normal problem workload. Whatever kind of management system an organization has, a managerial manpower projection, based on its turnover rate and estimated workload, will have to be made, and this projection can be prepared by a small staff attached to top management. The total number of managers should be changed only when manpower projections indicate a long-run increase or decrease in need which appears to be a relatively permanent trend. An organization may also face short-run fluctuations which impose temporary overloads or underloads on its total system, but impermanent overload problems can be subcontracted to consultants who know the system's operation and who will follow its procedures.

Consultants can also be used when certain problem solving skills are otherwise unavailable, which is a frequent occurrence in small organizations which find it too costly to hire full-time personnel with highly specialized managerial skills. For example, a small firm may find that it is advisable to hire an outside consultant (from a university or a management consulting firm) to construct a statistical or mathematical model for its production function. Indeed, sophisticated levels of decision making need not be restricted only to large organizations; top managers in smaller firms should be aware of all the specialized techniques and they should not be reluctant to obtain or use them.

When an organization has a period of insufficient work for its managerial staff, managers who are not being fully utilized can undergo short-term training sessions to upgrade their basic skills, to review new techniques in decision making, or to perfect the skills they already have. (Or they could be temporarily assigned to the performance of other duties.)

As was mentioned earlier in this chapter, extra capacity can be built into a system upon its introduction. If it is estimated that three months will be needed to solve a problem, and staffing requirements are based upon this figure, it may be advisable to add another month to provide for temporary overloads and for possible mistakes in the estimate. Extra capacity also relieves pressures on an overloaded system—those which originate outside the organization, from customers or the government, and those which result from employees. If employees must wait a long time to have their problems solved, they can become frustrated or disappointed in the managerial staff.

In short, top management should avoid pressure on its decision-makers that could lead to errors in calculations. Extra capacity provides this relief, and it gives greater stability to a management system in that it is one method of contending with a fluctuating workload input (the harried, overworked executive is indicative of an unstable system). At the same time, top management should strive to avoid underutilizing its submanagers and its system.

There is good reason to believe that optimum system efficiency will be achieved if there is a reasonable forecast of long-run managerial manpower needs, along with proper scheduling, daily adjustments, subcontracting, and a provision for extra capacity.

SELECTION OF MANAGERS

The managerial selection process entails job analysis, recruitment, screening, training, assignment, and promotion of managers. The first step in the selection process, job analysis, involves the preparation of job descriptions and specifications. A job description is a list of the decision making tasks to be performed and the techniques which a manager is expected to utilize. This list will be derived from the decision making system, and it will represent a further reduction of the process in terms of each operating component, which is the middle manager.

Specialization, in a relatively large system, will exist not only in terms of the nature of the problems to be worked on, such as marketing or personnel problems, but also in terms of the decision making process. Some managers may be placed in the control unit; others may spend much of their time in authorizing solutions; still others may be placed in the intelligence unit and spend most of their time in auditing solutions. The amount of work in the subprocesses will determine not only the number of managers required for each process but also the job content for each manager.

A minimum level of competence is also part of a job description: how well must each task be performed? Time allocations would also be made for various tasks; for example, a manager might spend most of his time in decision utilization and much less time in the construction of new decisions.

Job specifications, or the minimum qualifications an individual must have for performing a job, can be deduced from the job descriptions. These specifications will detail the skills, aptitudes, education, and personal characteristics needed for the various jobs. The more explicitly a decision making system is designed, the easier it will be to determine these specifications, and, in turn, to select qualified managers.

In an unplanned system — because the tasks which a manager will perform are unknown — it is impossible to describe the qualifications an individual should have; therefore, to "compensate" for the lack of planning, an attempt is made to hire managers who are paragons of excellence. Or, put another way, in an unstructured setting — in which future events and situations cannot be predicted — managerial selection is based upon obtaining personnel whose range of capability will guarantee effective handling of any contingency; managers must embody the best qualities of insight, understanding, impartiality, enthusiasm, integrity, etc. However, from a selection point of view, it is difficult to define these personality traits and to know the degree in which alternative applicants possess them.

When the decision making system is precise, the qualities needed by a successful manager are well defined because the tasks he will perform have been defined; and the organization can more easily determine whether an applicant has the requisite background or the potential to be so trained. Because the emphasis is upon problem solving, the manager or potential manager will usually be above average in intelligence. Indeed, the intelligence quotient may be the critical indicator for managerial capability because, given high intelligence, potential managers will be educable and motivated by the challenge of new and complex problems.

A college education would be a prerequisite for a managerial job; specific knowledge and skill is required, and much of this can be acquired in college. For example, after a decision making system has been reviewed, the college courses that are most beneficial can be ascertained. To calculate a decision's pay-off, a knowledge of cost accounting techniques is imperative. A system may also require mathematical and statistical techniques for problem solutions, and therefore an applicant should have acquired such capability in his academic work. It is also desirable that an applicant have some knowledge of the operation in which he seeks to be placed: if he is being hired to solve marketing problems, he should be familiar with the marketing operation, etc. An understanding of behavioral backgrounds, acquired through such courses as economics and psychology, can be valuable in working with environmental variables. Problem solving and knowledge of techniques is also highly useful background. Finally, in terms of earlier job experience (if any), did the applicant work on problems, or utilize specific techniques for solution, and how successful or proficient was he?

After job specifications have been established, potential managers can be recruited, screened, trained, and assigned. Recruitment sources, of course, can be external to the firm, such as colleges or private placement bureaus; or nonmanagers can be recruited within the firm. Opportunity should be provided for individuals to rise in an organization, and nonmanagers should be encouraged to acquire the qualifications for a managerial job; they should not only be informed of job qualifications but should also be counseled in the means for acquiring such positions. If an individual has the potential for performing a managerial job but lacks the education, firms can help overcome this handicap by offering financial assistance for additional training.

254

Screening devices are reasonably predictive or accurate in evaluating a potential manager; his background can be investigated, tests can be given, and the individual can be carefully interviewed. His experience and education will be reviewed; and perhaps he will be able to furnish samples of organizational solutions he has produced. Tests can be given to measure his intelligence quotient and skills, and he may be given actual problems to solve in order to demonstrate his specific skills; he might even be asked to formulate a research design for a problem's solution. An interview will then test an applicant's communication skills.

The emphasis, as we have said, will be placed upon the required decision making skills, but this does not preclude consideration of an individual's character traits, such as truthfulness or reliability. Although it may be difficult to establish possession of these character traits, this aspect of selection would be applied to all employees, not only the managers.

Because managers may be moved from one area of a system to another, their selection should consider not only their capability for performing a specific job but also their potential. For example, an "over qualified" individual might be hired with the understanding that after he has acquired knowledge and training in the system he will be moved to a more responsible decision making position. Job specifications may therefore require qualifications of a greater magnitude than are actually needed for the specific job being considered.

A firm can evaluate the effectiveness of its selection process by the decision output of its managers, and the information that has been acquired through the selection process can often be correlated with high- and low-output managers. The characteristics of the potentially productive problem-solver might then be isolated more clearly, and these data could serve as a new predictive device for the personnel department. Because top management will have direct responsibility for the work of submanagers, it should (when possible) have the power of final approval of recommended personnel.

A new manager, once selected, must be trained; and an orientation program could explain a system's mechanics and philosophy in some detail. The steps in the process and the techniques to be utilized could be set forth; and, once a trainee has a good idea of the nature of the process, the system could be simulated. Trainees could be given previously solved problems and assigned to work on them, and their solution constructions would be compared with those which are operational. Errors, misunderstandings, and the like would be correlated throughout this process.

After a new manager has been placed on the job and assigned problems, he will require close supervision and should be expected to submit his total analysis either to his superior or to a training manager, who would review his results and rectify any irregularities. This probationary, on-the-job training period would continue until the supervisor believes the new manager is adequately experienced and skilled to assume responsibility for his work. (If a supervisor is provided to direct the activities of managerial trainees, he would naturally have to be a decision making specialist who thoroughly understands the system and its tools.)

Further training may be indicated if, upon review of the operating system, top management finds deficiencies among the managers. The managerial force might then be called together to review the manner in which top management wants the system to operate. Because top management will review the operation regularly, and will incorporate improvements as needed, the training of managerial personnel would be a more or less continual process. Therefore, in an organization which has a large number of managers, it is advisable to establish a teaching staff of permanent or semipermanent personnel.

THE MANAGER AS A PROFESSIONAL

Increased research and study in the design and operation of decision making systems will lead to a more professional attitude toward management. The basic characteristic of any profession, be it medicine or engineering, is a long period of formal education and training, and the manager of the future will be expected to master a complex body of knowledge and a technical set of tools. This knowledge can be incorporated into the curriculum of colleges and universities, and many such institutions have already begun to do this.

In a highly specialized society—if we can predict what lies ahead for the job-seeking manager—it would seem that (1) educational prerequisites will become increasingly stringent, (2) longer educational programs will be necessary, (3) greater specialization will take place at the graduate level, and (4) greater uniformity will develop in school curriculums.

Although most of the current managers are college trained, there is little agreement on the kind of education which will best prepare the manager, or even on how meaningful managerial education is. Today's operating managers have, in fact, highly differing educational backgrounds; however, as a valid body of knowledge and techniques emerges, this variability will be reduced. Less reliance will be placed on experience and inherent talents because neither completely provides for the acquisition of the necessary managerial qualifications. The day when a manager on the shop floor could apply "common sense" is drawing to a close, and the opportunity to work up from the ranks — without a managerial education — will become exceedingly more restricted. The concept that a man can manage without formal training is becoming more and more untenable.

Managers will be expected to be acquainted with more tools and to possess more knowledge, and this expectation will demand a longer course of education, which will include not only undergraduate work but a graduate program as well. Professional specialization will be introduced on the graduate level. As managers seek to become expert, in either the profit or the nonprofit organization, they will want to specialize in statistical or mathematical techniques, or to concentrate on a specific organizational function, such as personnel or marketing.

Universities should develop greater uniformity in curriculums because the preparation they can offer is necessarily standard or generalized. Universities will also be subject to more professional scrutiny as a closer relationship develops with organizations. A student-manager residency may be established as part of a manager's formal training, and students may actually be placed in organizations and given problems to solve.[8] Organizations, on the other hand, should realize that many universities conduct valuable research and development in new decision processes, techniques, and applications. The history of operations research and the invention of the computer are impressive products of these institutions. Indeed, increasing "professionalization" is accompanied by a growing realization in top managements that they will be unable to staff their management systems if the universities do not provide the requisite formal training.

MANAGERIAL PROMOTIONS

Let us assume that a firm will hold to a policy of internal selection, that individuals will be promoted within a management

---

[8] This approach is already being developed; e.g., the doctorate offered by St. Louis University in Health Organization Research. This program provides not only for a one-year residency but also for summer placement in an organization for participation in research-team solutions of organizational problems.

system. This line of promotion, however, should be different from that in a pyramidal structure because advancements in the former will be based upon the degree of decision making responsibility that inheres in a certain position. An individual might move from a position which utilizes decisions to one that constructs new decisions, then to a control unit, and then to a position that authorizes solutions; the ultimate promotion would be to the position of top management. This progression would mean not only greater decision making responsibility but greater decision making capability as well. Thus, an examination of the tasks to be performed in the decision making process shows that the degree of competence needed for utilizing decisions is less than that needed for constructing new solutions. When new solutions are devised, analytical ability is called into action.

Individuals who are placed in the control unit must have the analytical ability to construct new solutions and also be able to operate the management system. They will approve the decision making strategy to be employed (frequently in the absence of meaningful data) and they will be working in even less-structured situations than managers who construct only new solutions. An individual who is responsible for authorizing solutions represents a major control and checking device on the entire system within the scope of his authority. But a top manager has the greatest amount of responsibility, and his function demands the greatest measure of competence in the decision making area because he is responsible for the total system.

An index of managerial competence can be formulated by analogy with other professional groups, which might have four or more categories, such as *junior, intermediate, senior,* and *supervisor.* A junior manager would have the least responsibility and would be in a learning situation; an intermediate manager would be in the group which is responsible for solution construction; a senior manager would be assigned to the control units; and a supervisor would be an authorizer. (Top management would be a qualitatively different managerial classification.) Each group would have a salary differential.

As for the promotion criteria that top management would utilize, Karl Deutsch and William Madow have discussed the possibility of promoting managers according to a "wisdom-based" criterion, a group's record for correct decisions, which is based upon the following assumptions:

1. There are n clearly identifiable managers whose decision making records can be compared.

258

2. The decision to promote will be based on *n* clearly distinguished decisions.
3. These decisions are independent of each other.
4. There is a clear criterion for distinguishing "correct" from "incorrect" decisions so that the decision making performance of each candidate can be clearly established.[9]

And Wainright Martin and Ira Horowitz have concluded that:

> *All men are not equally able decision-makers, and there are very few of us who have never made what subsequently proved to be an incorrect decision. Management cannot hope to have an organization composed of individuals who are always right. The more reasonable goal is an organization which is managed by individuals who are more likely to be right, on any given decision, than other individuals who might be making the decisions which they are responsible for.*[10]

Although past decision making performance is certainly a critical indicator of a manager's future performance, if there is a measure of specialization in the management process for decision difficulty, factors other than past performance will have to be reviewed for promotion purposes. Top management must still make the judgment of an individual's ability to perform new and more difficult decision making tasks because an individual may successfully construct new solutions but be unable to work effectively in a control unit.

MANAGERIAL MOTIVATION

The organization must motivate the manager to perform at his highest capability—or at least to meet a system's minimal performance standards. This can be accomplished by the provision of benefits. Because managerial motivation will be explored in greater detail in the next chapter, our present discussion will be confined to a brief review of extrinsic satisfactions, particularly those of a monetary nature.

Part of a firm's salary policy should be to pay the going market rates to acquire managerial competence, and this rate should be

---

[9] Karl W. Deutsch and William G. Madow, "A Note on the Appearance of Wisdom in Large Bureaucratic Organizations," *Behavioral Science*, 6 (January, 1961), 72–73.

[10] E. Wainright Martin, Jr., and Ira Horowitz, "A Note on the Effect of Statistical Contamination on the Selection of Management" (mimeographed article, Indiana University, 1963), p. 12.

considered the base salary for a particular job (market surveys can reveal the salaries that other firms are paying for comparable jobs with the same specifications). In addition, however, an organization can establish an incentive or bonus system whereby managers receive a part of the value added by each decision.

For example, it may be decided that the managerial staff will receive 10 per cent of any actual increments that result from the solutions it has constructed. (It may be recalled from our discussion of the consensus step [Chapter 6] that the organization can decide how increments will be distributed among the participants, and submanagement is one of the participating groups in this distribution.) The incentive or bonus arrangement could be applied on an individual and/or group managerial basis, but, because many solutions will be constructed by more than one manager, in all likelihood the arrangement would be a group incentive, with a declining payment to the manager. In the first year of a solution's operation the managers might receive 10 per cent of its value, in the second year 6 per cent, and in the third year 3 per cent.

A bonus system will encourage a manager to construct as many solutions as time permits—and the best that he can devise—because his bonus will be based on the actual (as distinct from the expected) value of the solutions. If he constructs a wrong solution, the firm will presumably receive a negative payoff, and the manager will receive nothing. As with many incentive or bonus arrangements, however, the amount received can vary for reasons other than individual effort: under adverse economic conditions, total incentive payments may go down. And differentials between managers can be considerable: one manager may be assigned a problem whose solution will render an organizational payoff which is relatively minimal whereas another may be assigned a problem which has a very large payoff. Thus, although there can be limitations or inequities in a bonus arrangement, this possibility should be weighed against the probable consequence of providing no bonus at all, and inequities can be partially compensated for by a provision for a group incentive.

Negative incentives, in the form of withdrawal of organizational benefits, must also be provided to maintain minimum performance standards. If, over time, a manager indicates little improvement because of a lack of ability or motivation, top management cannot permit him to remain in a sensitive management position; some action—in the form of transfer, demotion, or discharge—must be taken. Positive and negative incentives must be applied and maintained to achieve the maximum managerial motivation. When a manager performs well, he must be rewarded; when his work is deficient, he must be made to face negative consequences.

SUMMARY

Installation of a management system involves acceptance of the new system by the existing submanagerial staff, and this can be gained by permitting the staff to participate in its design, by providing for net increases in the distribution of organizational benefits, and by the appropriate training facilities. The installation should be made sequentially, or in a piecemeal (but rational and nondisruptive) fashion.

Operation of a system requires that sufficient capacity be provided for handling the problem solving load of the organization. Capacity can be increased by adding more channels, by speeding up problem solving time, or by storing incoming problems.

The maintenance of a system (usually referred to as management development), relates to the selection, training, placement, promotion, and motivation of qualified managers.

QUESTIONS FOR DISCUSSION

1. Why might managers be reluctant to accept a new system? How can such opposition be overcome?
2. Why is there reason to believe that a management system will be more effective if submanagers participate in its design?
3. Why do some managers prefer the "bureaucratic" system to a more systematic approach?
4. If, with a planned system, managers will be used more efficiently, why are additional managers sometimes required?
5. Why is a board of directors concerned with the nature of the management system?
6. If a planned management system is introduced into a bureaucratic organization, why would we expect the disruption to be minimal?
7. Is there a possibility that top management may have an excessive workload even with a planned system? How would you solve such a problem?
8. What would be the consequences if a management system is unable to adjust quickly to variations in the magnitude of the problem input?
9. How can estimates be made of the dynamism of an organization's environment?
10. If a job is unstructured, why is it likely that its job specifications will be ambiguous?

SUGGESTED READINGS

Bennett, Willard E. *Manager Selection, Education and Training.* New York: McGraw-Hill Book Company, 1959.

Houston, George C. *Manager Development: Principles and Perspectives.* Homewood, Ill.: Richard D. Irwin, Inc., 1961.

Jennings, Eugene E. *An Anatomy of Leadership.* New York: Harper & Row, 1960.

Mahoney, Thomas A.; Jerdee, Thomas H.; and Nash, Allan. *Identification of Management Potential.* Dubuque, Ia.: William C. Brown Company, Publishers, 1961.

Newcomer, Mabel. *The Big Business Executive.* New York: Columbia University Press, 1955.

Yoder, Dale. *Personnel Management and Industrial Relations* (5th ed.). Englewood Cliffs, N.J.: Prentice-Hall, Inc., 1962 (chapter 19).

262

11

CONTROL
OF THE SYSTEM

After a management system has become operational top management must see that it operates as planned, and this can be accomplished by the use of appropriate control mechanisms. Professor Richard Johnson has observed that "the objective of control is to maintain output which will satisfy system requirements,"[1] which, in our context, is the total expected increment in organizational welfare (per year) that is attributable to submanagerial effort. Controls are necessary because of the various events that can affect a system's operation and payoff: managers will make mistakes in solution construction (or they may attempt to circumvent the system altogether); problem input loads will vary; new decision technologies will emerge; and management personnel will change.

A control mechanism must be formulated in order to provide system adaptability. As the environment changes, sensory devices will detect these occurrences, notify the activating center or centers, and indicate the proper responses for achieving the purpose of the system. This chapter will be concerned with the formulation of such a control apparatus.

Two control mechanisms are necessary: the first will regulate nonmanagement subsystems (such as marketing) and the second will control the management subsystem. The regulation of nonmanagement subsystems must assure that solutions are produced which will improve the performance of these subsystems. Control of the management subsystem must permit top management

[1] Richard Johnson, Fremont Kast, and James Rosenzweig, *The Theory and Management of Systems* (New York: McGraw-Hill Book Company, 1963), p. 70.

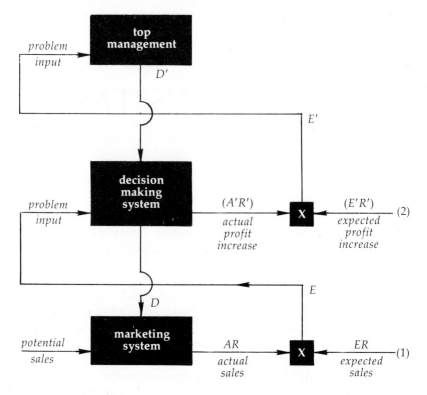

Figure 11–1

SCHEMATIC REPRESENTATION OF THE NONMANAGEMENT
AND MANAGEMENT CONTROL FUNCTION

to govern its work in terms of the design, installation, and maintenance of the total management system in order to improve submanagerial output. Figure 11–1 illustrates the function of the two mechanisms.

Control mechanism 1 represents a marketing subsystem; and actual operating results in sales (AR) are compared with the expected sales (ER) at X. If there is a differential or error (E), a problem is input into the decision making system, which will devise a new operation (D) that will be incorporated intó the marketing system. The process will continue until $AR \cong ER$ (until AR is approximately equal to ER).

The same operation occurs in control mechanism 2, although the inputs and outputs are different. $A'R'$ is the actual organizational payoff from solution construction; $E'R'$ is the expected payoff; and E' is the error differential, or the problems relating to the operation of the decision making system. These problems are

264

fed into the top management sector of the organization, which makes the appropriate adjustment in the subsystem (D') until the actual and expected decision making payoffs are approximately equal ($A'R' \cong E'R'$).

Each control apparatus has four elements: (1) performance standards, (2) sensory devices for signalling actual behavior, (3) a measuring unit for comparing actual and expected performance, and (4) actuation or correction devices. The part that each element plays in the control apparatus will now be considered.

CONTROLLING THE QUALITY AND QUANTITY OF DECISIONS

Control mechanism 1 (in Figure 11–1) is concerned with the proper construction of each decision (managerial quality control) and the appropriate number of decisions produced (managerial production control). This mechanism (described in more detail in Chapter 3) can also be interpreted in terms of control theory, or in terms of how the four elements of control can be built into the management system.

Figure 11–2 (page 266) presents a broad view of the quality control program. It furnishes a series of inspection points, coupled with feedbacks, so that decision making errors can be detected and returned to the problem-solver for correction. Because of the errors that can be made in the construction of a solution, points 1, 2, and 3 enable an error to be rectified before a solution is applied.

What functions do the four control elements perform so as to secure the highest quality for each decision? Performance standards, the first element, is part of the plan of the management system. Robert Miller has observed: "To the extent that task requirements are specified completely according to the operational universe of task inputs and outputs and their time relationships, we have at hand complete performance criteria."[2]

Performance standards must be verified at each inspection point. When problems are raised, they are screened by the control unit to ensure that only those of merit will be considered. And a complete solution requires exact data: worksheets must indicate solution calculations, and the initial research design must stipulate which techniques will be employed. At the consensus and authorization steps a solution must produce an ex-

---

[2] Robert B. Miller, "Task Description and Analysis," *Psychological Principles in System Development*, Robert Gagné *et al.* (eds.) (New York: Holt, Rinehart & Winston, Inc., 1962), pp. 216–217.

Figure 11–2

QUALITY CONTROL MECHANISM WITH FOUR INSPECTION POINTS OR CONTROL ELEMENTS

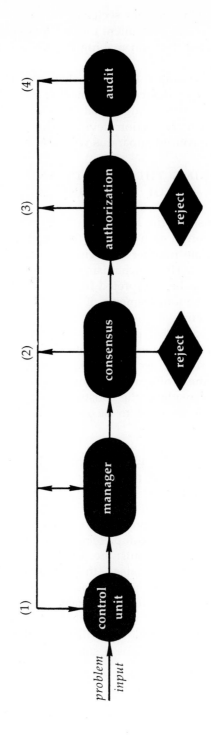

pected net payoff in organizational objectives. However, at the last inspection point, the audit indicates the expected payoff, which is the standard for comparison.

The second control mechanism or element, the sensory devices, reflects the actual performance of the problem-solver, and this is designated by his recorded analysis and solution. The actual and the expected performances are then compared for error, which is the third control element.

At the first point of inspection, the control unit determines if a solution meets the established requirements in form and content (it must tell when it will be employed, under what conditions, its payoff, the implementation plan, and so forth). The control unit also reviews a solution for clarity: if it is stated ambiguously, better explanations will be demanded; if its terminology is highly technical, or not meaningful to everyone who must implement it, it will have to be restated in less complex terms.

Because, at the outset, a control unit may have approved the decision making techniques to be used, the analysis will be reviewed to confirm their proper employment. If questions or shortcomings are noted, the solution will be returned to the problem-solver for a more complete analysis. The control unit will question aspects of the analysis which appear dubious, it will indicate the places where additional work is needed, and it will suggest the process by which the problem-solver might proceed (perhaps by exploring an alternative technique). All of this is correction, the fourth element in control.

Each of the subsequent inspection points in Figure 11–2 has the same four elements and operates largely in the same manner. At the second point in the inspection process, the consensus step, a solution is cleared to others in the organization, who consider its feasibility or challenge its analysis. If necessary, a solution can be sent back to the analyst for appropriate changes or further explanations.

The third inspection point is authorization. The authorizer has the authority to examine the analysis for acceptability, and he can instruct the problem-solver about further work which might be indicated. For example, if the risk is considerable, the authorizer can request development of a more reliable solution.

The last and probably the most important inspection point is the audit. After a solution has become operational, a comparison is made between its expected and actual values; discrepancy will trigger a new problem, which is reassigned to the problem-solver. The problem-solver will then reconstruct his solution in order to achieve equality between the two values.

267

As for the question of production control, the scheduled or required number of solutions (the output) will be maintained by the control unit, which sets a time limit for each solution and investigates missed deadlines. The control unit must route problems so that the full capacity of the staff will be utilized.

(Another important aspect of a submanagement system is that it serves as a control device for a total organization by providing the organization with its adaptive capability. The management system detects environmental changes and provides the correct organizational responses so that the total membership's welfare is maintained and/or increased.)

CONTROLLING THE MANAGEMENT SYSTEM

Control mechanism 2 relates to the control of the total management system and provides a feedback to top management on its own performance. It is able to determine if the decision making system is operating as had been anticipated, if any difficulties have been encountered in the system's installation, and if the system is being effectively maintained.

The feedback in control mechanism 1 was directed toward the endeavors of each manager to be certain that he was conforming to the standards established for and within the system. However, solution deficiencies can result not only from errors by submanagers but also from those of top managers. Submanagers might follow the prescribed procedures and still not produce in accordance with the expected standards because of some failing of top management: various aspects of the decision making machinery may prove to be unfeasible; estimates of payoff may require adjustment; or training programs may be insufficient.

Control mechanism 2, as shown in Figure 11–3, reveals two possible approaches. In model A, information about the product of the system is gathered and compared against the standard or desired output; if discrepancies exist, the system is modified. In model B the same process occurs, except that information is collected about the operation of the system rather than its output; if variances exist in this area, the system is also modified. With this background, we can proceed to discuss the nature of each of the four elements in this control apparatus.

PERFORMANCE STANDARDS

The performance standards, the first control element of the management system, is the expected total-solution payoff; and this

268

Figure 11–3 (A and B)

DETAIL OF FIGURE 11–1 MANAGEMENT CONTROL FUNCTION SCHEMATIC

model A

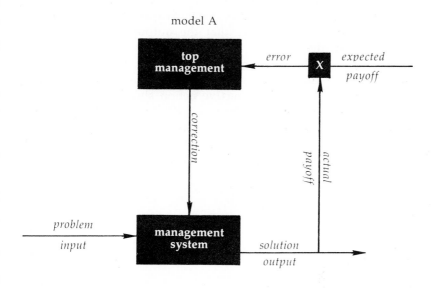

model B

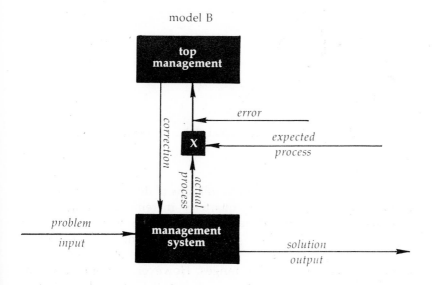

amount was derived when the model was selected. (Chapter 9 mentioned a model which was expected to produce 500 decisions per year; the expected added value per decision was $20,000, and the system's anticipated output was $10 million per year.) In actual practice it is unlikely that the output of a system will exactly equal the expected output. Variations occur; therefore, when it establishes performance standards, top management must consider how much variation or fluctuation is acceptable and the point at which corrective action should be taken. The acceptability range of variability for a $10-million system, let us say, is ±5 per cent, or $1 million dollars per year. On a quarterly basis of $2.5 million dollars, the payoff could have a variation of ±$250,000. The following graph illustrates this range.

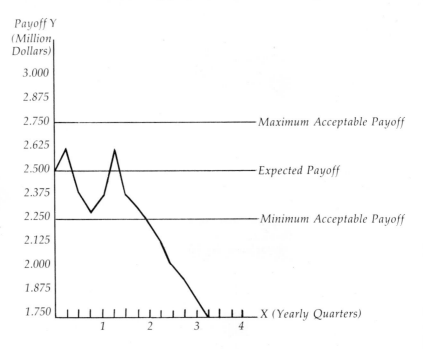

The Y axis measures payoff in millions of dollars and the X axis denotes operating time in quarterly increments. Because the expected quarterly payoff is $2.5 million, the acceptable minimum payoff is $2.25 million and the expected maximum payoff is $2.75 million. Therefore, for the first two years of the operation, payoff fell within agreeable ranges. However, at the end of the second year, payoff fell below an acceptable figure, which clearly indicates to top management that there are faults in the system.

270

Top management will also be concerned if a system performs significantly *better* than had been expected. Because the fundamental purpose of control is to ensure that a specified output is maintained, top management can be confident that it is doing this only if its system performs as expected. Significant deviations indicate that components of the management mechanism are not functioning as intended and will have to be adjusted — which in the latter case might be merely a matter of increasing the expected payoff because the original estimate was too low.

SENSORY DEVICES

The second element of control, the sensory apparatus, perceives how well a system is operating and issues a series of reports to top management. Top management, which might conduct a product review on a monthly basis, would receive information on the quantity of solutions produced and on their costs, outputs, and payoffs. These data would be compared with the expected quantity, cost, output, and payoff, and the differential would be noted (see Figure 11–4, page 272).

The internal intelligence unit, which has the responsibility for ascertaining total organizational performance, would collect data on the performance of the problem solving subsystem. Data on the quantity of solutions would come from the control units, which maintain a record of the problems raised, assigned, produced, or placed in a backlog. The intelligence unit can then determine the cost of solutions by calculating (from the production schedule) the managerial time expended in solution construction and the average managerial hourly rate. Value added (or output) would be derived from audits, which the intelligence unit would conduct in determining the effectiveness of the operating solutions. Payoff would be the differential between the output and the cost, and totals could be easily calculated.

Top management is also interested in the solutions that are being processed through the system; for example, in the number of solutions that are returned for additional work or that are rejected at inspection points. A form such as that in Figure 11–5 (page 273) will give these general data, with the left column listing the various points of inspection, the middle column indicating the number of decisions which proved to be acceptable at these points, and the right column totaling the unacceptable decisions at the inspection points.

In addition, top management might need a more detailed record of individual decision making performance in order to

271

Figure 11–4

MONTHLY MANAGEMENT SYSTEM SUMMARY
(PRODUCT REVIEW)

Month _____

	Product Review	Expected No.	Differential
1. Total Problems Assigned			
2. Total Solutions Produced			
3. Backlog			
4. Average Cost per Solution			
5. Expected Average Cost per Solution			
6. Cost Differential			
7. Average Added Value per Solution Produced			
8. Expected Added Value per Solution			
9. Differential			
10. Actual Payoff per Decision			
11. Expected Payoff per Decision			
12. Payoff Differential			
13. Total Added Payoff			
14. Expected Total Added Payoff			
15. Differential			

Figure 11–5

MANAGEMENT SYSTEM SUMMARY (PROCESS REVIEW)

Point of Inspection	1. Number Acceptable	2. Number Unacceptable
1. Control		
2. Consensus		
3. Authorization		
4. Audit		

locate problem areas more readily. Figure 11–4, which is similar to an income statement, would reveal only gross tendencies, but Figure 11–6, another sensory device, would supply rather detailed information on individual managerial performance.

Top management may also want to receive a general progress report of how problems are being handled, which could be provided in the form of Figure 11–7 (page 274). Whether data were supplied in the form of Figures 11–6 or 11–7 (or both), managerial performance would be adequately reported on an individual level.

Top management must also have a precise analysis of the areas of organizational operations in which profits have increased as a result of new solutions; and Figure 11–8 (see p. 274) shows how these data might be presented. Decision *671*, in this example, instead of producing a $2,000 reduction in costs, produced a $3,000 reduction; and the production area produced $18,000 worth of profits in this quarter. If an organization uses a budgetary adjustment device (see Chapter 6), budgetary figures at the beginning and at the end of quarterly periods can be compared, which would also indicate increased profits.

Figure 11-6

MANAGERIAL OUTPUT PERFORMANCE

1	2	3	4	5	6	7	8
Manager	Problems Assigned	Problems Completed	Problems in Process	Estimated Value per Decision	Actual Average Value per Decision	Differential per Decision	Comments by Control Unit

273

Figure 11-7

PROBLEM PROGRESS REPORT (BY CONTROL UNIT)

1	2	3	4	5	6	7	8
Manager	Prob-lem As-signed	Schedule	Con-trol	Con-sensus	Authori-zation	First Audit	Com-ments
Jones, S.	357	Delayed 2 weeks	OK	Modi-fied	OK	Esti-mated (1,000) Actual (800)	

Ultimately, top management is interested in the operating results of the entire organization, and changes in total operating profits will reflect not only the consequences of new solutions but changes in environmental states. It is important to be able to distinguish between these two conditions. Even with the best of managers and a well-designed system, total organizational payoff may not always increase; in a severe recession, for example, total profits will go down. However, apart from the introduction of new solutions into the organization under changing environmental conditions, solutions are taken from the solution inven-

Figure 11-8

QUARTERLY ANALYSIS OF PROFIT INCREASES EFFECTED BY NEW SOLUTIONS

1	2	3	4	5	6	7
Area of Opera-tion	New Deci-sions (Num-ber)	Expected Results of New Decisions (Cost Reduc-tions)	Actual Results	Operations Costs (Beginning)	Operations Costs (Ending)	Comments
Produc-tion	373 433 671	$ 5,000 10,000 2,000	$ 5,000 10,000 3,000	$375,000	$357,000	Decision 671 produced $1,000 more than expected
	Total	$17,000	$18,000			

Figure 11 – 9

ENVIRONMENTAL STIMULUS-RESPONSE REACTION

1	2	3	4	5	6	7
Previous State	Previous Solution	Previous Payoff	Present State	Present Solution	Present Payoff	Differen-tial
433	433	$10,000	257	257	$ 5,000	$ 5,000
677	677	20,000	344	344	10,000	10,000

tory to achieve an effective organizational response; but some states will demand different responses to secure different total organization results.

Figure 11 – 9 capsulizes this stimulus-response reaction. Columns 1, 2, and 3 indicate that, in an earlier period, environmental states 433 and 677 were present. Solutions 433 and 677, the established solutions for these states, produced profits of $10,000 and $20,000, respectively. However, in the present period, previous condition 433 changed to 257, and condition 677 changed to condition 344. These changes necessitated the utilization of different solutions, 257 and 344, which reduced total profits by $15,000 (column 7).

The payoff of the submanagement system represents the increment in total organizational payoff, given the environmental states. Changes in total organizational payoff and managerial payoff would be identical only if the environmental states remained constant, a condition represented by Figure 11 – 10. In this situation the states remained the same; however, new so-

Figure 11 – 10

PAYOFF CHANGES UNDER CONSTANT
ENVIRONMENTAL STATES

1	2	3	4	5	6
State	Old Decision Number	Payoff	New Decision Number	Payoff	Differen-tial
79	79	$10,000	79a	$20,000	$10,000
85	85	5,000	85a	10,000	5,000

lutions were introduced. Solution 79*a* was substituted for 79, and 85*a* was substituted for 85, which resulted in a total increase in payoff of $10,000 and $5,000, respectively.

It must further be decided which top managers will receive reports on decision making results. In a large organization with 1,000 submanagers, the president will obviously be unable to review in any great detail the performance of each submanager. Therefore, because specialization must exist on even the highest management level, top managers will be responsible only for certain decision making areas and will receive only the results which relate to those areas.

On the other hand, it can be assumed that top management — either in committee as a whole, or in subcommittees — will evaluate the total system performance; and so they will receive aggregate data about the system in the form of Figures 11–4 or 11–5. Top managers would secure information about individual performance from forms similar to Figures 11–6 and 11–7.

COMPARISON OF ACTUAL AND EXPECTED PERFORMANCE

Top management can, as we have indicated, serve as a measuring unit for comparing actual and expected results in order to determine the nature of any difficulties that may be present (the third element of control), but unacceptable results may have to exist for a period of time before corrective action can be taken. (Top management can refer to the Figure 11–5 data [the Process Review] to determine which decisions are unacceptable at particular times.) A decision making unit may even achieve unacceptable results for one month, but, in a subsequent month, perform beyond the standard; however, if a unit falls below its standard for two or more months, action should be taken.

Regardless of the range of decision quality and time deadlines, if an intelligence unit (which collects data about decision making performance) learns that a decision making unit has fallen outside the range it must notify top management. Such deviations are used as a flagging device; even though top management receives total information on decision making performance, its immediate attention should be drawn to the trouble areas.

SOURCES OF SYSTEM BREAKDOWN

Before corrective action can be taken, a determination must be made of why a difficulty exists, and deficiencies can derive from several sources. They can emanate from the original design, or from the system's installation, operation, maintenance, or control. When the plan of the system is at fault, qualitative indices can make this known to top management. For example, submanagers may request that a section of the plan be modified because they are having difficulty with it in its present form; or the control units' reviews of solutions in their qualitative reports may mark consistent errors by submanagers at particular points in the system (perhaps by using the form in Figure 11–6).

If many solutions are being returned to problem-solvers (as the form in Figure 11–5 might show) because of errors in calculations prior to solution implementation, it could be that aspects of the system are not feasible. Or a review of the payoff of individual solutions (using the form in Figure 11–7) might reveal that certain types of problems are difficult to solve, which might be symptomatic of an incorrect tool mix and indicate that greater caution should be exerted by the control unit in its approval of research designs. Some suboperations continually show poor results (the form in Figure 11–8 might show this), which may be a manifestation of environmental factors that require other problem solving techniques; or it may indicate that lower standards of expected payoff should be fixed.

These indices, however, are generally not of sufficient precision to locate or define the exact nature of the fault; a detailed examination of the content of actual solutions may have to be made to ascertain the error. Top management should then begin at the end of the decision making process, with the audit of these solutions, and backtrack through the process, checking out each step as it reviews the solutions. Redesign will be needed when top management finds, at any point in the system, that submanagers are following the stipulated procedures but still receiving poor results. However, 'to justify a redesign, this condition should be fairly widespread throughout the system and all of the mistakes should be identical.

Another trouble source could be in the process by which the system was installed, and this would be demonstrated when areas of the organization, on either an individual or departmental basis, are not performing as well as others (Figure 11–8). These departments are most often those which have recently expanded, or contracted, or been newly created; top management may have introduced modifications in the processes or techniques of the system and then find that the submanagers are not coping with the changes (Figure 11–5). When an installation problem is disclosed, additional training is in order for the submanager.

If the fault lies with the maintenance of the system, the information provided for by Figure 11–6 will supply a detailed summary of each manager's continuing performance. Unquestionably, significant proficiency differentials will exist among managers; some will be more capable and skilled than others, so that the value of their output will be proportionately greater. Proficiency measurements would probably reflect a continuum of skill from zero to optimum performance — at the same time providing information about individual managerial ability and denoting the available inventory of decision making skills.[3]

Minimum performance standards must be established for all managers. In terms of actual performance, however, the value of some managerial decisions may be two or three times above this minimum standard. Performance below this standard would be unacceptable.

There are usually three reasons why a middle manager does not perform properly: (1) faulty selection, (2) poor training, or (3) insufficient motivation.

If a manager has been selected improperly, he will probably not be capable of performing the tasks required by the system. The data of particular concern in this connection are the relationships between the estimated and the actual value of his decisions. Consistently large differentials are often symptomatic of the absence of basic qualifications;[4] and consistent return of an individual's decisions at the control, consensus, authorization, or audit steps also indicates a poorly selected manager (Figure 11–5): the total performance would be faulty whether it was measured on an absolute or an interpersonal basis. If such a manager is given additional training, and his errors continue, the evidence is conclusive that he should not have been selected.

However, if a manager has a mixed record, which might indicate poor training, additional training can be beneficial. It may be that only part of his decisions are imperfect, and the control unit may notice that the problem-solver is unfamiliar with certain tools, or unable to structure environmental variables. Investigation and counseling by top management should suggest the manager's training needs.

The third reason why a manager may not meet performance requirements is that he is insufficiently motivated, which is usually manifested by a general lack of effort. Also symptomatic of this condition are missed deadlines or a record of mixed deci-

[3] Robert Glaser and David J. Klaus, "Proficiency Measurement: Assessing Human Performance," *Psychological Principles in System Development*, Robert Gagné *et al.* (eds.) (New York: Holt, Rinehart & Winston, Inc., 1962), pp. 421–422.
[4] See Figure 11–6, columns 5, 6, and 7.

sion quality. Such a manager's performance may have been acceptable, until suddenly, inexplicably, he fails to meet minimum requirements. He may object to some of the directions by the control unit; he may demonstrate an unwillingness to learn, or to accept counseling or instructions from top management; yet his personnel records may prove that he has the required experience, intellectual capacity, and training.

The conclusion that a manager is not properly motivated is a qualitative judgment, to an extent; and the control unit can assist top management by a review of its experiences with the manager in question. It should be recalled (from Figures 11–6 and 11–7) that the control unit has an opportunity to record its comments on the disposition of every decision; it will therefore have noted the manager's cooperativeness or other meaningful behavioral aspects as they relate to decision making.

An interesting aspect of the motivational problem arises when a manager bypasses the problem solving system to reach a decision. Even though the organization has an explicit decision making system, it is still possible that a manager will make decisions as he chooses and will effectively avoid the decision making system that has been stipulated by top management. For example, a manager may continue to give verbal instructions to nonmanagers, or to change operations at will, which present control difficulties. The measuring tools that have been reviewed may not detect this behavior. (As long as a manager performs *within* the system, deviation from expected norms will be revealed directly at the inspection points or indirectly by the summary reports. If a manager's work is excessively delayed, this will appear on the schedules; if his steps are improperly performed, this will be noted at the inspection points or in the auditing of solutions.)

But how can deviant behavior be detected when new decisions do not enter the management system—when verbal decisions have been issued with no written record? The manager, on his own initiative, has ignored the entire management system to run his own operation; he is reluctant to follow instructions, or he does not want to subject his decisions to review, or he may lack confidence in his ability and fear the consequences of a review of his decisions. The problem is not insurmountable and there are many ways by which such behavior comes to the attention of top management.

When employees thoroughly understand the conditions under which they are obliged to perform their tasks—when they know that they should not follow unauthorized decisions—they will refuse to follow a manager's instructions which bypass the decision system. Furthermore, if employees are given an opportunity to raise problems they can indicate that the manager has exercised pressure on them to conform to his wishes. The very act of raising a problem brings to the attention of the control unit deviant managerial behavior which may also be indicated by deviations in operations. Budgetary figures also reflect differentials which are not accounted for by recorded decisions (Figures 11–9 and 11–10). Finally, independent behavioral audits of operations will discover if employees are performing duties at the instructions of a manager—tasks for which there are no written solutions or records and which are performed in avoidance of the management system.

The extent to which a manager can ignore the system will therefore be limited. He is required to work on all problems assigned to him by the control unit, and a record is made of these assignments. His time is also scheduled, and if he does not use it properly he will miss the decision deadlines.

An excessive backlog of problems (Figure 11–4) can mean that the managerial staff is not increasing rapidly enough. This would be the case especially if the number of solutions produced differed significantly from the expected number. However, it may take a while to gather experience and sufficient historical data to develop realistic performance standards. There may in the past have been little information about decision making performance, and under a new system, although reasonably good deductions can be made of expected performance, some time must elapse before the actual performance can be ascertained.

In the interim there may have to be reliance on an interpersonal comparison of managers to indicate how well the system is operating. In such a case, an initial performance standard, based on the average payoff per manager, could be calculated. However, interpersonal comparisons must be used with caution because individual output is not entirely a function of managerial skills; certain environmental factors may be at work that produce variability in managerial output.

Variability also comes about because of the degree of complexity that is often introduced in arriving at a solution. Some managers may attempt relatively sophisticated decision making techniques, which may not always produce better solutions; other managers may take a more conservative course, and use less complex techniques, but obtain better results. If techniques are too highly specialized, the manager (in the short run) may achieve poor results. Of course, the reverse can also occur.

280

The measurement of managerial performance will also be affected by whether a solution construction has been an individual or a team effort. If many individuals had a part in the construction, team measurements will be applied and regular proficiency measurements can be used. However, when various aspects of solution construction and utilization are investigated, and if some actions have not been properly performed, it must be established which member of the team is responsible for the difficulty. Top management may find that standards have been set incorrectly. If the average initial expected payoff per decision consistently differs from the average payoff that managers are actually producing, top management may have to readjust the standards of the system to a more realistic level. The sensory apparatus of the control system may not have detected a true reflection of managerial performance, or the data may have been incomplete or untrue. If the actual operating results are compared with the expected budgetary results and found to be highly inconsistent, it may well be that the data collection of managerial performance is defective (Figures 11 – 9 and 11 – 10).

ACTUATION

Actuation, the fourth element of the control mechanism, involves the taking of corrective action to eliminate indicated system defectiveness in order that the expected and actual system payoffs will be equal. We have seen that the fault may be found in the design, installation, operation, maintenance, or control of the total system. If the deficiency rests in the design itself, top management will generally follow the same approach in revamping the system as was pursued in establishing it (Chapters 2 – 10).

In its redesign of the system, top management may find that the duties of submanagers have not been clearly defined, or that middle managers may not know what to do in various situations and at certain steps in the decision making process, or that problem situations may arise which require a more complex treatment than has been stipulated in the system. Submanagerial tasks may have to be rewritten. Additional options may have to be introduced at the consensus step. A more thorough search for decision making tools may have to be made in order to cope with problem inputs that have proved intractable to solution by current methods.

If it is discovered that submanagers require a more precise statement of an organization's changing external environment, top management would have to revamp the intelligence unit.

More data would have to be collected with greater frequency, and a more rigorous classification would have to be made of economic, political, and other factors. The data collection process may itself require other techniques for signaling significant changes in the environment.

In actuality, the design of the management system should continually evolve since it can be assumed that top management will never be able to formulate a perfect system. Imperfections will arise over time, and management will continually refashion parts of the system. Through such a process, then, the plan will be made increasingly efficient because it will be capable of solving a wider range of problems with better accuracy. Furthermore, the gross differential between the total expected and total actual payoff should decrease over time.

A faulty system installation will require additional training or consultation with the submanagers on its operation. Minor modifications might be in order. Top management is responsible for the system's daily operation, and, apart from checking channel capacity and manpower supplies, control units should be monitored to ensure proper routing, scheduling, checking, and reviewing of the operations of their problem solving channels. Procedures in the control unit may have to be redesigned, or individuals in these units retrained, and so forth.

The fault may relate to the maintenance of the system. For example, if it is found that a manager does not have the basic capability his position demands, he may have to be transferred from the management system. If this condition is widespread, the selection criteria should be reviewed very critically. And, as we have already noted, the personnel department should continually attempt to correlate decision making results and managerial characteristics in order to improve the selection process.

If the problem is one of training, top management can counsel the individual managers by pointing out their errors and by reinstructing them in the proper performance of their tasks. Or the managers can be trained again. If the top manager finds that the problem involves motivation — if a manager's past performance has been satisfactory but his present performance has drastically fallen — further investigation may be necessary to ascertain whether the dissatisfaction is of a personal or organizational nature.

If it is a personal problem, the difficulty may be psychological, or domestic, or the like. Personal problems are difficult individual situations and the top manager can do little to correct them. However, an organization might provide such facilities as clinical assistance, a leave of absence, or a temporary transfer to a less responsible position—arrangements that would give a manager the time to work out his personal problems so that he will soon be able to devote his full attention to his job.

It is also possible that managerial dissatisfaction can arise from organizational causes. It might be the disappointment felt by a manager who was not promoted, or the belief that the control unit has assigned too many problems, or that pressure has been too intense, or that solutions have been excessively modified during consensus, etc.

If a manager is only temporarily aggrieved, top management should review the "rules of the game" with him and every attempt should be made to clarify possible misunderstandings. If a middle manager dislikes the way the system operates, he should be reminded that he is free to submit proposals for its modification.

A submanager who willfully bypasses the decision making system is a disciplinary case. He should first be warned; but if he persists in doing this he may have to be discharged. If a manager deliberately ignores the system, this is even more serious. After top management has designed what it believes is an optimum management system, a manager who knowingly refuses to adhere to it should be subjected to disciplinary action. The management system should be viewed as a set of company rules and regulations for the behavior of managers, and persistent violations should lead to discharge.

Revision of the control mechanism could entail the reexamination of reports, more rapid data collection, the employment of new accounting devices for measuring solution payoffs more effectively, or the adjustment of performance standards.

In fact, once a system is installed top management will devote most of its effort to redesigning, maintaining, and controlling it. Data will constantly flow to top management, some of which will indicate trouble areas, and top management will respond in a way that will improve total system performance. The control apparatus will function as a closed system in which errors become problem inputs into the top management sector of the organization, and they will be regularly detected and recycled by the control mechanism until the system meets the expected standards. Over time, with top management continually working on the system, improvement in its performance should occur. Although an optimum system may require much time, reasonably good feedback will guarantee that continual progress will be made.

EVALUATION OF THE CONTROL MECHANISMS

Control mechanisms 1 and 2 (see Figure 11–1) will provide significant improvements over the approach currently used by many organizations for controlling their management operations. They can be evaluated initially in terms of how they incorporate those attributes that are generally assumed to meet effective control apparatus requirements, but, in the long run, top management will adjust them in their proper relation to system performance.

First of all, the suggested mechanisms have all the necessary components of a control system: performance standards, data collection (sensory devices), performance comparison, and actuation. Secondly, the system is largely directed toward measuring and correcting controllable behavior. Performance standards are not directed towards events which may affect organizational performance that is outside the control of top or middle management; they are instead directed at submanagerial behavior, which can be corrected, or at top management's functions, which they can remedy themselves.

One of the dangers in setting up a control mechanism is that the measuring devices may be "contaminated." Robert Glaser and David Klaus point out that contamination arises when performance data are affected by other parts or components of the system, one; two, it may test factors that are not germane to performance; three, a halo effect may be present; four, performance standards may promote undesirable response sets in the individual; five, when the behavior to be measured is poorly specified and a superior must make some judgment as to a subordinate's effectiveness, a judgmental bias may enter into the superior's rating and a differential performance rating may result because of the likes and dislikes of the superior. In other words, a measuring instrument should truly measure what it is that you want measured.[5]

Another desirable characteristic of the suggested control instrumentality is that it is homeostatic or self-regulating (a homeostat is a control device for holding a variable between desired limits by a self-regulating mechanism[6]). Generally, errors in a system are self-correcting, and considerable feedback exists in mechanism 1 before and after the solution is made. The solution

---

[5] Glaser and Klaus, *op. cit.*, pp. 441–442.
[6] Stafford Beer, *Cybernetics and Management* (New York: John Wiley & Sons, 1959), pp. 22–28.

is reviewed at a series of checkpoints, and, if it is unacceptable, it will be sent back to the problem-solver for reevaluation. This will be fairly automatic and will prevent· the problem-solver from making serious errors. Moreover, an effective intelligence unit will pick up factors which will guide the problem-solver in reaching appropriate adjustments in his operations via new solutions. Not only do loops exist within the submanagement system itself, and between the submanagement system and the operating systems, but also between the organization and its environment; and all will have self-correcting features.

Another desirable feature of the suggested control mechanism is its rapidity, which permits the built-in feedback to remedy serious errors before they are made: solutions will be corrected while they are in the process of being constructed. One thereby avoids the dilemma of waiting for solutions to be effectuated and for their operating results to be evaluated before it can be known that solution mistakes had been made at the outset.

The control mechanism is also capable of handling many different deficiencies in the system, and it can be geared to those difficulties that can be expected to arise. As Stafford Beer observes, in order for the system to be adaptive, one, a good deal of information has to exist in the circuitry; two, a high level of variety must exist in its planning centers; and three, a rapid motor response must be present.[7]

An attempt was made in this analysis to predict the possible error source in a submanager's construction of a solution, and distinct responses have been programmed into the system to deal with each type of error. Research design provides proper tool selection, consensus prevents suboptimization, and so on. Moreover, responses are automatic; given an error identification, there is a predetermined corrective response that the submanager should follow.

The same condition exists for mechanism 2. It is recognized that top management can make mistakes in performing any of its responsibilities; however, although the mechanism is only partially automatic, errors will still be located and a reasonable range of responses will be given.

In many management control mechanisms, given the same number of errors that can be made, there may be only a few response corrections, and this might mean the continuation of error. For example, although an organization will usually discharge a manager if his performance appears inadequate, and

[7] *Ibid.*, p. 111.

although this response may be appropriate if he willfully refuses to carry out instructions, it is difficult to know if this response will significantly improve decision tool selection and utilization by other managers. And, of course, discharge will not remedy most of the errors that arise in a management system.

Another worthy feature of a control system would be that data are not too costly to collect, but in the proposed control system it would be difficult to draw a cost conclusion. If one is to achieve a worthwhile measure of control, a great deal of information is necessary; yet it would be hoped that this information could be gathered easily and inexpensively.

This control system is also valuable because it should not consume very much top managerial time. It is self-effectuating, and top management will not have to constantly supervise or direct submanagers.

CONTROL FROM THE SUBMANAGERIAL VIEWPOINT

The control mechanism should prove highly acceptable to submanagers because it is essentially noncoercive. The mechanism of self-regulation enables the problem-solver to correct himself while he devises a solution, thereby eliminating top management's intervention in his problem solving activities and reducing management's pressure upon the middle manager. Submanagers will not be confronted with the problem of close, daily, personal supervision of their activities by their superiors.

While a solution is being constructed, it is reviewed and corrected by other submanagers who are *not* in a position to reward or punish the problem-solver. He, in large measure, will be on his own. Moreover, if the reward system is geared to the value of the solutions produced, self-correcting devices will be of assistance to the submanager in that he will gain higher rewards from a better solution.

The system is impersonal because only objective performance criteria are applied. Top management, in reviewing submanagerial performance, does not have to consider intangible personality characteristics, such as "judgment," "cooperation," or "initiative" (evaluations in which the personal biases of top management can become a significant factor). The system is also uniform in that the standards are used for all submanagers. Managerial performance, moreover, is measured only in terms of personal effort, and a manager is not held accountable or penalized for events over which he has no effective control; that is, if environmental events adversely affect the output of a particular

286

operation. The demands made upon the manager are of an expected and stipulated behavior, and a clear understanding of managerial duties is established prior to any evaluation. The statement that "if the manager had been more capable he would have intuitively known what to do" is unjustified.

The establishment of explicit performance standards and tasks should result in greater submanagerial freedom because the only pressure to comply would be applied to stipulated duties and to nothing more. The personal attitudes, biases, and mannerisms of top management would no longer be critical guides for the conduct of the middle manager. This problem is quite important, and will be treated in Chapter 14 (Individualism Within the Organization).

Professor Beer has observed that the "concept of control is naive, primitive, and ridden with an almost retributive idea of causality."[8] Management control is indeed often thought of as the ability of one man personally to affect the behavior of another, as synonymous with the exercise of personal power: the greater the power of the top manager, the more must submanagers follow his directives. But these features can be avoided if the control mechanism is properly established; otherwise, submanagerial abuse, of a subtle or a gross nature, can all too frequently become a reality.

SUMMARY

Proper solution construction is ensured by a series of inspection points in the management system. The control unit assures the production of the appropriate number of solutions.

Any top managerial errors in the administration of the management system are detected by meaningful data collection and related to the expected performance of the system. These data are analyzed, and, once the cause of the error has been determined, corrective action can be taken.

QUESTIONS FOR DISCUSSION

1. What are the four elements of a control mechanism? Identify these in a self-regulating central heating process.
2. What is the significance of feedback in providing for a self-adaptive system?
3. Why would you expect more effective control if top management

---

[8] *Ibid.*, p. 21.

limited its efforts to the control of the management system rather than to the control of the total operation?

4. How can it be determined that the point of overinspection is being reached?

5. Why may it be unfair or unsound to evaluate a manager solely in terms of the operation he is managing?

6. Control theory is based on the assumption that errors will usually occur in the operation of a system. Could one be more optimistic and assume that managers will not generally make mistakes? What problems might arise if this assumption is followed?

7. Could one deliberately create an unstable situation for management by setting higher managerial performance standards? Under what circumstances would this be advisable?

8. Why is it important to formulate expected performance standards at the outset, even if these are of questionable validity?

9. What problems may arise in the attempt to distinguish between a solution that derives from changes in environmental states and a new solution construction?

10. In terms of organizational payoff, what problems arise when the nature of the control mechanism is highly personal—when one person, at his own discretion, has the power to influence the behavior of another?

SUGGESTED READINGS

Beer, Stafford. *Cybernetics and Management.* New York: John Wiley & Sons, Inc., 1959.

Bonini, Charles P.; Jaedicke, Robert K.; and Wagner, Harvey M. (eds.). *Management Controls: New Directions in Basic Research.* New York: McGraw-Hill Book Company, 1964.

Malcolm, G. Donald; Rowe, Aloe; and McConnell, Larimer. *Management Control Systems.* New York: John Wiley & Sons, Inc., 1960.

Roberts, Edward B. "Industrial Dynamics and the Design of Management Control Systems," *Management Technology,* 3 (December, 1963 [100–118]).

Shillinglaw, Gordon. *Cost Accounting: Analysis and Control.* Homewood, Ill.: Richard D. Irwin, Inc., 1961.

Wiener, Norbert. *The Human Use of Human Beings: Cybernetics and Society* (2d ed.). Garden City, N.Y.: Doubleday & Company, Inc., 1954.

PART FOUR

INTRA- AND INTER-
ORGANIZATIONAL
DESIGNS,
AND INDIVIDUALISM
WITHIN
ORGANIZATIONS

12

A HOSPITAL
CASE STUDY[1]

After a top manager has become convinced of the advantages of planned decision making he is ready to install such a system into his organization, and it is at this point that he becomes personally involved in daily interactions with colleagues, submanagers, and employees. He will meet and work with them to revise the existent organizational setting; but what, on an interpersonal level, will be the nature of this endeavor? To explore this question, this chapter will detail a four-and-one-half-year participation in the design and installation of an actual decision making system for a 250-bed general hospital. We believe that such a history will be helpful to any innovator by providing a close look at what he can anticipate in another situation and by enabling him to formulate certain responses in advance.

Our analyses of top management's subfunctions have heretofore been treated abstractly and separately; in a real situation, however, these functions tend to be intermixed: the steps of design, installation, and the rest are carried out more or less simultaneously. Our chronicle will further illustrate that the top management process is a continuing process; that individuals work with one aspect of the management system, then with another, and the system gradually evolves. In a real situation it is most unlikely that the top manager will be able to develop a complete operating system with a single, initial effort.

---

[1] The author participated in the design and installation of the hospital's system and has been able to review it on a continuing basis. The author is indebted to the *Academy of Management Journal* for permission to publish some of the material in this chapter which originally appeared in his article, "Designing the Management System" (July, 1964).

THE ORIGINAL SETTING

Let us first review the hospital's administrative process at the time the system was initiated. The new administrator, who had recently assumed this top management position, had no experience as a hospital administrator but had received a master's degree in hospital administration, and had earlier served in a supervisory capacity in other hospitals for seven years. The hospital under consideration is a short-stay general hospital which provides both medical and surgical facilities. It has five hundred employees, and is one of approximately seventy hospitals in a large metropolitan area. It is relatively old, having been in existence more than sixty years.

The decision making process under the previous administrator followed the traditional bureaucratic pattern, the hospital having been divided into nursing, pharmacy, housekeeping, and other departments; some of these, depending on their size, were subdivided into smaller units. For example, the nursing department was divided into nursing education and nursing service; and nursing service, in turn, was divided into surgical services, central services, and other subunits. Each department head was delegated administrative authority and was held responsible for his department's operation. This authority, however, was restricted in several ways: each department head had to receive the administrator's approval for purchases of any capital item that cost more than fifty dollars, and for all salary adjustments for departmental personnel.

A standard cost budget had been determined along departmental lines, and the administrator and department heads received monthly reports on the cost of labor and material expended in each department, along with the production units for each. Production units were based on the service rendered by each department: the dietetic department was measured by the number of meals served; the nursing department by the number of patients processed, according to surgical, pediatric, obstetric, and other such classifications; the laundry department by pounds of laundry; and so on.

The administrative personnel were paid the going rates for their particular classifications; they had been carefully selected; and they were encouraged to attend professional institutes or classes so as to be fully familiar with the changes that might occur in their areas of responsibility. These personnel should be assumed to have been as capable as those in the other hospitals in the city.

Under the previous administrator, most of the departmental operations (apart from capital expenditures) had been left to the individual heads. Each devised the rules, procedures, and policies for his department, and directly supervised employee activity; and each had the right to hire or fire, and to recommend salary adjustments or to change work content. Each was also responsible for staffing his department.

The previous administrator's attention had centered upon plant improvements because it was this top manager's responsibility to approve all capital expenditures. It was also in this area that the greatest pressure was exerted by department heads; and the requests by middle managers for additional equipment or space, or for renovation, usually exceeded the capital expenditures budget. The hospital's age, which caused serious maintenance problems, combined with the administrator's personal interest in plant innovation, to put additional emphasis upon these expenditures.

To keep informed of the hospital's total operations, including the departmental production reports, the administrator maintained "open-door" and "making-the-rounds" control devices. Under the first device, the medical staff, department heads, administrative staff, and the families of patients were encouraged to discuss problems, complaints, or suggestions with the administrator. In exercising the second device, the administrator regularly toured the hospital, observing employees at work and asking patients questions about the food, their opinions about their care, and the like. If the responses seemed to be of special consequence, the administrator would discuss problems with the appropriate department head.

INTERDEPENDENCY OF OPERATIONS

Because the total efforts of a hospital are directed toward patient care, we will now briefly consider this total process. Each patient's care is somewhat unique and his treatment is determined by his physician. The physician will instruct or direct the nurse in the specific care of his patient, and the nurse will execute the doctor's orders.

The nursing department therefore "represents" the physician and is the key department in a hospital; other departments exist to assist the nursing department in providing the kind of care each patient is to receive. However, the nursing department, in turn, depends upon the effectiveness of the other departments for assuring the prescribed patient care. For example, if a physician

292

prescribes a diet, he will instruct the patient's nurse, who will transmit the request to the dietetic department. If a physician wants to diagnose his patient more thoroughly, he will tell the nurse to arrange for specific tests that will be conducted by either the X-ray or the laboratory department.

The effectiveness or ineffectiveness of the service units will eventually be expressed in the immediate care which the nurse renders. If the physician or the patient should be dissatisfied, this displeasure is often directed toward the nurse, who might voice this complaint to the units directly involved or to her supervisor or the director of nursing. The latter, in turn, might approach the administrator, and the administrator would then take the necessary action to effect more efficient performance by the service units.

Because individual treatment is entailed, the nursing service's demands upon the other departments will require flexible responses. In the hospital under discussion, for example, the dietetic department must prepare between 250 to 300 trays for every meal. Because a physician may request special diets for certain patients, or may change certain diets from meal to meal, this information must not only reach the dietetic department, it must also be implemented—and sometimes almost as soon as the request is made. This process must be executed without mistakes: patients must receive the proper meals on the proper schedule. The nurse, who will check the tray, will see that the dietitian corrects any mistakes; but this can delay the patient's meal, or, if the dietetic department must make adjustments for many patients, the meals may be served cold.

The general operation of this hospital was not significantly different from that in most others; primary reliance upon department heads for the administration of their departments is the generally accepted operational approach in most hospitals. Therefore, at the time the new hospital administrator took office, its decision making system was essentially unplanned in that each department head planned and administered his department as he judged best.

EVOLUTION OF THE NEW SYSTEM

The system which was eventually developed (see Figure 12–1, pages 294–295)[2] resulted from the new administrator's efforts to cope with a series of problems which soon became apparent.

[2] Not all of the departments are shown on the schematic; for a complete list see Figure 12–2, p. 309.

Figure 12–1
THE NEW HOSPITAL MANAGEMENT SYSTEM

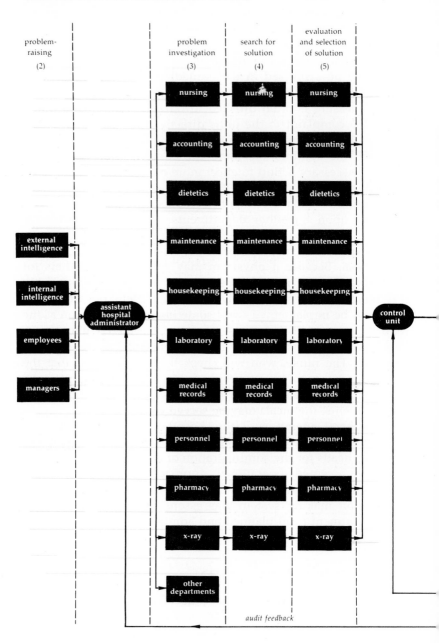

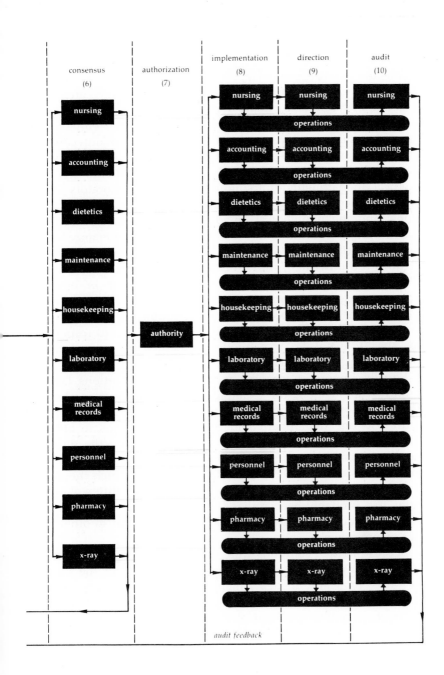

The new strategy was that as management problems arose "non-departmental" mechanisms would be designed to handle them. Our exploration of the process by which the system was accomplished will illustrate some of the problems and the mechanisms that were subsequently designed to cope with them—along with a consideration of submanagerial reactions to these innovations.

The first problem which came to the administrator's attention was that of solutions by many department heads and supervisors which were imparted as verbal instructions to their employees. Departmental procedures and policies were usually unrecorded, and only those supervisors, department heads, or employees who had worked in the department a long time knew them fully. The medical departments—nursing, X-ray, and laboratory—had written procedures, but these did not cover their entire operations; and the nonmedical or administrative areas—personnel, purchasing, accounting, housekeeping, and maintenance—had very few written procedures. Of course, when policies and procedures are unwritten, individuals cannot be expected to know the policies and procedures of other departments or how to adjust to external departmental requirements; nor can it always be ascertained that procedures exist for coping with all expected situations. When department heads were asked about responses for specific events, it was frequently learned that no solutions had been prepared in advance.

Equally important was the fact that verbal solutions lacked uniform application; for example, the purchasing department treated various departments differently, applying a certain procedure to one department and different procedures to others. This practice created feelings of favoritism among the departments, in part because no solution inventory was kept. Department heads could not always recall the way in which they had handled past situations, and, if an event recurred, different solutions had probably been utilized. This sometimes caused confusion for subordinates, which could at times extend to other departments as well.

Because written solutions were seldom issued, the new administrator—ultimately responsible for the operation of the hospital—was unaware of departmental modes of operation, and responses to queries about hospital procedures—from the medical staff, or visitors, or the relatives of patients— were not always meaningful. Although the administrator could not have judged the adequacy of all technical procedures, even if they had been recorded, a system of written procedures would have at least supplied ready information on the hospital's activities. Without a

296

record of solutions, the administrator also found it difficult to exercise effective control. It could not be established that solutions were being properly followed, nor could solutions be properly reviewed without written records.

To cope with this situation the hospital administrator stipulated that all procedures and policies had to be in written form. The department heads were told to record the established or customary policies of their departments, and, if new operating problems were indicated, to record their newly devised solutions; further, if interdepartmental procedures or policies were unwritten, the affected departments did not have to comply with them. If, for example, the head of purchasing instructed a member of the nursing department to follow an unwritten procedure, that individual was under no obligation to carry out the instruction.

Departmental employees were notified of this general administrative rule. The administrator also indicated that, in all future misunderstandings between departments, no support would be given to a department which had not reduced its procedures to written form. Disciplinary action for ignoring a verbal instruction would not be upheld, particularly if it had emanated from another department.

Finally, the administrator's office was to receive a copy of all procedures and policies for the purpose of information and review, and operating manuals were prepared for all procedures and policies which were interdepartmental in nature.

INTERDEPARTMENTAL CONTROVERSY

Another management problem, which soon became apparent, was interdepartmental controversy. An early symptom of this state (that appeared during the administrator's first month of office) was the complaint of the dietetic department head that nurses entered the kitchen area to make up trays for patients. The complainant suggested that the hospital administrator inform the director of nurses that nurses were not to be allowed in the dietetics area.

The administrator questioned the nursing head about the matter and was told that the dietetic department had refused to change some patients' diets. The head of the dietetic staff countered with the information that her department had recently instituted the policy that no lunch menus would be changed after 11:00 A.M. The director of nurses then pointed out that physicians often visit patients between 11:00 A.M. and noon, and that, because of the dietetic department's new policy and because new diets are sometimes requested by the physicians during that interval, the only alternative was for the nurses to attend to the matter personally.

Because of the time involved and because the nurses were away from their floors, the director of nurses believed that all alterations in diets should be made by the dietetic department. She also said that she had become aware of the dietetics policy only after several nurses had phoned for dietetic changes after 11:00 A.M. If this *was* the policy, she questioned its wisdom. The dietetic department head then observed that if diets were changed while trays were being delivered to the patient area—between 11:00 A.M. and noon—the entire process would be delayed and the food would not remain warm.

This was a clear case of a department verbally changing its policy and not informing the medical staff, the nursing service, or the administrator: the new policy had not been recorded. The dietary department had merely decided this change would be best for its operation and had proceeded to implement it.

Indeed, the major reason for all hospital controversies was the fact that, from time to time, departments modified their procedures and thereby affected the operations of other departments; the initiating departments then expected the other departments to accept the new procedures automatically. Some of these changes were written out and others were verbal; some had been approved by the former administrator while others had not; but, by one means or another, the other departments were only eventually informed that they were expected to conform to the changes.

In many instances departments refused to cooperate and expressed either vocal or behavioral dissatisfaction, sometimes merely ignoring the new "policy" and operating in the traditional manner. When controversy arose, the previous administrator had been placed between contending department heads, each of whom alleged that the other was withholding cooperation or pursuing programs that were inconsistent with overall organizational goals. Discussions at such times became highly emotional, and, in extreme cases, the personal relationships between department heads deteriorated.

The practice had been that the administrator (or the assistant administrator) would informally reprove the department heads with the observation that everyone should work together, that they were team members whose concern was the patient and not individual departmental development. This had little or no effect. As one department head described the situation:

In the past, each department more or less went its own way. A kind of feudal system existed in which the hospital represented a series of principalities, loosely organized under the aegis of the hospital administrator. Each department was possessive about its own jurisdictional rights and privileges. Occasionally two or more would informally reach some accommodation over certain types of changes. This represented a treaty of sorts between respective dukedoms. An implicit struggle between departments continued over budget allocations, with each attempting to maximize its own departmental development. Hence, each exercised continual pressure upward toward the hospital administrator in relation to requests for additional equipment, space or personnel for programs that each honestly felt would improve overall departmental performance.

In the previous administration no systematic endeavor had been made to come to grips with the problem of suboptimization. Each department pursued its own objectives and no organizational machinery had been provided for evaluating the total hospital effect of any interdepartmental decision; department heads would develop new policies but would make no attempt to determine their total effect. Even when the former administrator had approved changes, there had been no data on whether a net payoff could be expected. The general position was that if a suggested policy produced an improved operation in one department the total efficiency would also be increased. The administrator had also assumed that all other operations would remain unchanged. In short, the belief had been that if each department improved its operations, the total effectiveness of the hospital would progress by that degree.

The only time the administrator had met the problem of suboptimization was when one department head would object to a procedure initiated by another department—or would refuse to comply with the procedure. If the controversy was brought to the administrator's attention, the effects of the new procedure would be reviewed. However, this was not done systematically; the two department heads would be given the opportunity to present their cases, then the administrator would make the decision.

COMMUNICATION

Absence of effective communication within the total administrative process was another problem: department heads did not know how decisions were being made, neither those by the hospital administrator nor those by other department heads. Although some decisions were made upon the advice of department heads, most top managerial solutions were made unilaterally and were then announced to the department heads, most of whom had not participated in the process (although they were nevertheless expected to conform).

The top management decision making process was regarded as mysterious and secretive by the administrative and medical staff. Department heads were not informed about the problems with which decisions were to cope; and often they did not know from which area of the hospital the problems were derived. For example, budgetary limitations had caused the past administrator to decide that no new personnel would be hired, but department heads wondered if the ruling had been directed toward their respective operations. Had they hired an excessive number of personnel? Or was this an indirect criticism of their supervision?

Department heads often did not know *how* a problem had been solved. If they had not been consulted, who had been? Were any data collected? Were alternative solutions reviewed? What criteria were utilized to evaluate these solutions?

Solution construction at the top administrative level was not uniform. At times it seemed that some decisions were arbitrarily directed at certain individuals, and that other decisions were capricious and not thoroughly reasoned through. In some situations the administrator had responded impulsively, and at times emotionally, without considering the decision's total impact.

This mystery that surrounded decision making at the top level created anxiety among the staff. Not only were they unaware of the method for arriving at decisions, they were unable to predict decisions that would adversely affect their operations. Although department heads and supervisors had the authority to operate their departments, and were responsible for them, they were still expected to conform to the decisions of higher authorities, and it was felt that this only made their operations and responsibilities more difficult. As a result, there was a serious lack of confidence in the logic and in the objectives of many decisions made by the administrator or assistant administrator.

The assistant administrator resigned soon after the new administrator took office because it had become apparent that many of his decisions had been ineffective. Plant improvements, which had been his responsibility, had exceeded the budget, or had not worked properly, or had to be redone—all of which was apparent to the administrative staff. Although not all of his decisions had been poor, it was the mistakes that were constantly discussed via

300

the hospital "grapevine." As the number of poor decisions accumulated, the respect of the submanagers had decreased; and it was on this basis that the submanagerial staff justified its noncompliance with many of his decisions. The rationale seemed to be that since the assistant administrator's ability was questionable, there was little reason for following his directions.

The assistant administrator became increasingly aware of this attitude and found that it was increasingly difficult for him to get his ideas and decisions accepted. Moreover, the declining respect of the submanagers produced antagonism and frustration in the assistant administrator, which also affected his interpersonal relations with the administrative staff.

ORGANIZATIONAL POLITICS

There was no agreed-upon method for introducing change into the organization; instead, formal and informal strategies were utilized which depended primarily upon the individual and the situation. Because many of the changes that department heads wanted to make required capital expenditures, the administrator's approval was mandatory, and this was sought by the department head's "closeting" with the administrator to present and "sell" his proposition. If approval was given, the department head could then purchase the necessary equipment or material and introduce it into his department.

If a department head desired to introduce changes that would affect other departments, and also wanted to obtain their cooperation, he would use the same approach. He had to not only "sell" his proposition but also persuade the administrator that other department heads should conform with his suggestion. If this conformity or cooperation was later refused, the department head would return to the administrator and propose additional action to force compliance. Usually, it was only at this point that the administrator would call the uncooperative department head into the office to explain the new policy; and, because it was an approved policy, he was told that he would be expected to follow it. Thus, the administrator was virtually committed to action; the circumstances made it difficult to "back away" without losing face.

Two issues are involved here: the merit of the solution and the authority of the administrator. In effect, the uncooperative department head was questioning the authority of top management, and this, of course, the administrator could not accept; administrators cannot permit department heads to question each action approved by top management. As a result, once this point was reached, there was a tendency to *insist* that policies be followed, even those of questionable or doubtful merit.

Middle management was confronted with the chronic political question of who can exercise the greatest influence over the administrator. Because the budget was limited, the "influential" department heads were presumably able to win a greater share of the capital budget, which meant a more rapid development of their departments *vis-à-vis* the other departments.

Department heads exercised different degrees of influence; why, and in what manner, was not entirely evident, but one reason seemed to have been psychological—the administrator personally got along better with some department heads than with others. In cases where a department head had "oversold" a proposal (which subsequently proved to be less beneficial than had been originally asserted), the administrator would become suspicious of further proposals by the same department head. Some department heads had opposed the administrator's directions, or had attempted to isolate their operations from the rest of the hospital, and were therefore not looked upon with favor.

But the department heads themselves often did not know why some of them were more influential than others. It was a "political" situation, and they generally realized they had to defer to the administrator if they were to achieve their goals; they had to ascertain the administrator's attitudes toward the many operations of the hospital and adjust their proposals and approaches accordingly. Moreover, an analytical review of past administrations disclosed the same pattern: with each administrative change a different group of influential department heads had emerged.

EFFECT OF THE CONSENSUS PROCEDURE

The new administrator, as we have indicated, responded to the problems of suboptimization, interdepartmental cooperation, communication, and introducing organizational change by having department heads submit their solutions to all the departments that would be affected, directly or indirectly, by new solutions (the consensus step in Figure 12–1). This process was required so that the other departments would become fully informed of the proposed solutions, and it also permitted the amendment or modification of solutions in order to adjust and coordinate interdepartmental operations. It was further stipulated that all new interdepartmental policies and procedures would be tentative or suggestive (rather than authoritative) until all department heads had agreed to them. A policy would be authorized only when the administrator believed that an acceptable solution had been reached, and the policy would then be binding upon all hospital operations and departments.

Once the department heads understood that policies would have to be cleared to affected departments and returned for mutual consultation, it was found that they could broadly determine the effect of any suggested solution upon the operation of their own departments. During the process of reaching a consensus it also became clear, however, that a department head often had little awareness of the *total* effect of his proposed solution. Because of the technical complexity of a hospital's operation, department heads represented a reservoir of specialized knowledge within their areas of operation.

After proposals had been reviewed — and if the heads of smaller units (such as physical therapy) believed they would have no negative effects — approval was usually automatic. Because it was the larger departments that were most often affected by these decisions, the department that suggested a policy would generally seek the approval of these larger operating units: nursing, dietetics, housekeeping, laboratory, and X-ray (these were also the departments that exercised major responsibilities or were allocated the highest budgets). If these departments accepted a proposal, the probability of its ultimate acceptance was almost certain. At departmental meetings, however, each department head had an equal voice and each could comment freely.

Upon the receipt of a suggested solution the department heads would review it in terms of its feasibility: they would determine if there were any technical or medical reasons why the solution would not work in their particular area. If the proposal violated medical standards, it would be rejected; or if it was medically acceptable but difficult or impossible to execute because of departmental procedures or capabilities, it would also be denied. For example, a suggested pharmaceutical solution was to reduce its service from twenty-four hours to twelve in order to reduce its operating cost (a legitimate objective) and to resolve the difficulty of acquiring and providing qualified personnel during the evening and early-morning hours. However, the head of nursing pointed out that physicians sometimes change their patients' prescriptions during these hours and that nurses could not comply with these changes if the pharmacy were closed. The pharmacy remained open.

Feasible solutions were then reviewed in terms of whether

303

they were "good" or "bad." If a solution would facilitate a department's operation, its managers would view it favorably; if it required a rearrangement of procedures, or made it difficult for activities to be performed on time (such as a doctor checking a patient during visiting hours), or necessitated additional personnel, objections would be raised.

Rarely was a solution accepted without discussion, and usually at least one department would believe that a solution was not entirely beneficial to its operation. For the most part, such differences would be resolved by appropriate modifications of the original solution: a section might have to be amended; exceptions might have to be written in; or a segment might have to be deleted so that an accommodation could be reached.

Department heads eventually began to review written solutions with facility. They would enter meetings prepared with changes that they wanted made part of the solutions that were scheduled for discussion (although no vote was taken at departmental meetings). Discussions took on the character of a bargaining procedure and they often continued until the affected parties reached an accommodation, largely through the mutual search of alternative possibilities. A give-and-take attitude prevailed, each department head adjusting to the others on the basis of the changes he would make in his operation in order to reach an agreement.

The hospital administrator, who was the chairman of these meetings, encouraged discussion. However, if a problem involved two or more departments, and the meeting was not productive, the administrator would suggest that the dissenting individuals get together and work out their difficulties before the next meeting. (Eventually, a limitation was set on the amount of time that could be spent considering a solution at department head meetings.) It was understood that if the department heads were unable to reach an understanding within a reasonable time (perhaps two weeks), the administrator reserved the right to determine the final solution. This provision was used to avoid indefinite opposition or discussion, and, in the four and one half years during which this mechanism has been in effect, the administrator has had to exercise it only once or twice.

On the whole, the department heads performed reasonably and responsibly, and perhaps a major reason for this was that they wanted to maintain the clearance mechanism, which meant that the decision making process would continue in their own hands. They did not want to return to the former approach, in which decisions emanated from the administrator's office without their

304

participation or consultation. Clearance was looked upon as a protective device; the long-run view was that unless a suggested solution had a drastic and adverse effect upon a department there was little reason for strenuous opposition. Moreover, if a department rejected solutions on insufficient grounds there was every likelihood that its solutions would be similarly rejected. The attitude was that reasonable actions would assure the needed cooperation of other departments.

Most of the department heads realized that one of their most serious problems was the attainment of interdepartmental cooperation, and also that the consensus step was the means for achieving harmonious behavior (which had been lacking in the past). They also realized that vigorous opposition to new policies—or even the lack of agreement—would discourage the administrator, who might then dispense with the consensus component and revert to unilateral and "secretive" top management decisions. Departments were encouraged and gratified by their new ability to incorporate into decisions those features or objectives which they believed were important.

Further, the consensus step was a rational, systematic mechanism in which they had confidence, and the discussion of solutions produced greater individual understanding of the total hospital operation. The maintenance superintendent began to learn more about nursing; the nursing department head began to appreciate the technical aspects of heating and plumbing. With increased knowledge, attitudes became more tolerant: the nursing department did not insist that the maintenance department immediately correct each defect that every nurse might find.

Moreover, with greater general information there was less departmental orientation and greater willingness to see problems and solutions from a total hospital perspective. Department heads came to realize that they were responsible not only for their specific operations but, indirectly, for the operation of the entire hospital. Solutions that originated in a certain department were codified accordingly, so that a set of personnel, purchasing, housekeeping, and nursing policies was gradually compiled. These policies, in effect, became the policies of the hospital.

The department heads, however, did not view the clearance mechanism as ideal; for one thing, it required them to attend weekly meetings and to consider discussions of problems that were often not related to their departments. Many felt their time was being taken from more pressing business within their departments. The traditional proprietary attitude toward their departments was of course not entirely removed, and, although they sometimes enjoyed participation in decision making as it related to other departments, some were still desirous of managing without organizational constraints.

At the outset the submanagers submitted solutions on a voluntary basis. Some, however, refrained from submitting solutions because they were reluctant to have others determine their departmental operations. Indeed, the submission of a solution sometimes provided an "opening wedge" for a rather thorough investigation by other departments: questions could be raised as to why the solution had been needed, other alternatives might be suggested, and so forth. Some managers saw that this kind of discussion could lead to an embarrassing analysis of present operations; still others offered solutions only because interdepartmental problems had become so pronounced that they had little alternative.

Department heads were permitted to suggest procedural changes in any area of the hospital's operation; their attention was not restricted solely to their own areas. However, each department head evidently recognized the "exclusive" aspects of his colleagues' departments because very few such proposals were submitted.

To a degree, some of the managers' early hesitancy in proposing solutions can be attributed to their inexperience in writing solutions. Several department heads had trouble with composition; or their grammar was faulty; or their solutions may have been ambiguous or incomplete. Such people, however, were helped by the new assistant administrator, who reviewed their solutions with them to assure that they accurately expressed their intent.

The problem that arose in using the new system for the development of managers was caused by educational limitations. Two department heads were physicians, and others were also college-trained, but several had only four years (or less) of high school; and it was this last group which presented training difficulties. This group had not had extensive experience in written communications, conference leadership, or in reviewing the literature in their fields, and it was highly apprehensive of the reactions of the college-trained toward its solutions. They knew that their solutions had merit, and that they were personally accepted, yet they were uncertain of formulating solutions, especially in their analytical and communication aspects. The college-trained personnel had little difficulty because they had long ago acquired the basic skills demanded, and they readily adjusted to the management system.

The new administrator had begun by assuring all the administrative staff that even though new and perhaps experimental administrative procedures would be introduced, no manager would be discharged as long as he made a reasonable effort to adjust. Furthermore, before the introduction of any new administrative techniques, department heads were to have the opportunity for reviewing them. No one was ever discharged; any who left did so voluntarily.

Considerable counseling was required. In the short run it would have taken less time if the administrator had solved some of the problems instead of explaining the solution process to the department heads who had been assigned these problems. However, in the long run, if department heads were to assume the problem solving responsibilities of their areas, they would have to be trained. The administrator therefore worked closely with department heads in developing solutions, especially during the first year. Facility was eventually developed, and less time was spent in counseling the administrative staff in the formulation of solutions.

The reluctance to enter solutions into the system because of educational shortcomings gradually disappeared. After two or three solutions had been presented, department heads with little educational background felt sufficiently confident to utilize the mechanism as it was needed. A few department heads, however, postponed using it in their desire to maintain "autonomous" departments.

As had been half-expected, a strong administrative service— the purchasing, personnel, and maintenance departments— emerged to provide services for what can be thought of as the line divisions: nursing, laboratory, dietetics, and housekeeping (the major departments for personnel and actual hospital operations). Because the solution constructions of the administrative service units are directed toward the operation of the entire hospital, it is of course necessary that they be accepted by the line units if their solutions are to become operational. It was the decision making system that provided the basis for this acceptance and that permitted these units to exercise considerable initiative and to formulate solutions. Under the old administration this development would have been extremely difficult or unlikely because the line divisions could have effectively opposed the introduction of such changes.

Some line managers still felt that the service units were overly ambitious and were exploiting the new system, but the administrator asserted that everyone was permitted to review and accept solutions, and that line managers had ample opportunities to construct their own solutions. This feeling against the service units was personal rather than organizational, but it demonstrated that the system could resolve even the traditional line-versus-staff problem. (After this has been accomplished, the staff official can move fairly rapidly in introducing new policies.)

The consensus machinery was regarded in one of two ways by the department heads: one group viewed it as a means for securing the cooperation of other departments; the second group viewed it as a defensive device that could be used to block or modify proposals they opposed. The second group, which demonstrated little initiative in the submission of solutions, was also the group which attempted to maintain autonomous operations. Personal rather than organizational factors seemed to determine the group with which a department head identified. Large line operations, such as X-ray and laboratory, exercised much more solution initiative than did such other large operations as nursing, housekeeping, and dietetics. The business office, an administrative staff unit, was one of the least productive units until 1964.

Figure 12-2 (page 309) illustrates the interdepartmental solution output. Over the four-and-one-half-year period, personnel, maintenance, and purchasing were high-producers; dietetics, nursing service, and housekeeping (to which most of the employees are attached) were relatively unproductive.

EMPLOYEE PARTICIPATION

The new administrator soon realized that many changes would have to be introduced and that the established modes of performance would have to be altered. Unless employees accepted these changes, and quickly, efforts to improve the operation of the hospital would be seriously delayed. Nor would only the administrative staff have to accept changes; it would perhaps be even more important to modify the employees' basic behavior patterns. To effect the changes, the clearance mechanism provided that department heads would hold departmental meetings with their employees and review suggestions as they were received. Department heads were also required to submit weekly summaries of their meetings which set forth the solutions that had been considered and the employee reactions.

Moreover, when departmental solutions were discussed it was expected that the department heads would serve not only as representatives of their units but also as spokesmen for their

Figure 12 – 2

INTERDEPARTMENTAL SOLUTION OUTPUT

	1960	1961	1962	1963	1964	Total
Top Management	10	8	3	5	1	27
Anesthesis	—	—	—	—	—	0
Auxiliary Board	—	—	—	—	—	0
Accounting	3	—	1	1	5	10
Admitting	—	2	2	1	3	8
Dietary	—	—	2	4	1	7
Emergency Service	—	—	—	—	—	0
Maintenance	1	3	3	5	1	13
Housekeeping	—	3	3	3	—	9
Laboratory	6	—	5	1	1	13
Laundry	1	1	1	—	—	3
Medical Records	—	—	—	1	1	2
Medical Staff	3	1	7	6	—	17
Nursing Education	1	—	—	—	—	1
Nursing Service	3	—	1	2	1	7
Personnel	9	4	4	10	5	32
Pharmacy	1	2	1	—	—	4
Physical Therapy	—	—	—	—	—	0
Purchasing	4	1	6	1	—	12
Volunteer Service (started in 1964)	—	—	—	—	1	1
X Ray	4	—	2	1	—	7
Public Relations	2	2	2	2	2	10
Inhalation Therapy	—	1	1	—	—	2
Cardiology	—	—	3	3	—	6
Medical Education	—	—	1	1	—	2
Out-Patient	—	—	3	—	—	3
Social Service	—	—	1	1	—	2
Total	48	28	52	48	22	198

employees. For the most part, if a department head had conducted a successful meeting with his employees, he could accurately
report their opinions and list the reasons why some favored a
solution, why others did not, and so forth. Because the administrator would sometimes find it was more important to know
employee reactions than those of the department heads, a repre-

sentation function was introduced into the decision making process.

The effectiveness of imposing changes upon employees without their participation is dubious. In the past, threats or the exercise of discipline (particularly upon professional employees, such as nurses or X-ray and laboratory technicians) more often led to resignations than to conformity. Furthermore, these employees were in critical supply, and, because they could easily acquire similar positions in other metropolitan hospitals, coercive techniques resulted in an increased shortage of personnel in a hospital that was already understaffed. Alternative techniques had to be found to gain professional employee cooperation.

Professional employees expected to participate in the decision making process, even if this were limited to their departmental problems, and they were usually quite outspoken in their criticisms. In addition, the former administrator's attempts to discipline the professional staff had met with opposition from department heads and supervisors, who were (at least to this extent) employee-oriented: department heads and supervisors took a proprietary interest in their operations, which of course included their employees. Further, the high degree of specialization in the hospital and the protracted training required to develop professional skills meant that the loyalty of employees — and that of the administrative staff — was directed toward their respective professions and associations rather than to the organization which employed them.

For example, the director of nursing held an office in the League of Nurses and the head dietitian held a position in the local dietetics association. Moreover, the hospital performed a teaching function in the professional areas of nursing, X-ray, and anesthesiology which tended to reinforce this professional attitude. Criticism of professional employees was viewed as an attack not only upon the individual but also upon the profession. This demonstrated professionalism seemed to be a reflection of the attitude exhibited by the medical staff, whose loyalty was given primarily to the profession.

The departments in which meetings had been regularly conducted and whose heads and supervisors had been accustomed to leading or participating in discussions on mutual problems had no problems of employee participation. The nursing department, for example, had always considered nursing problems at its meetings, and suggestions which now related to other hospital operations represented no significant innovation. The reactions of professional employees were similar to those of the

310

department heads, once they were consulted on matters. Through the consensus device, the hospital achieved a high measure of cooperation from professional employees, and without using coercive methods.

It was quickly learned that only professional employees on the floor were sufficiently aware of certain situations to evaluate or cite the limitations of various solutions; even department heads were not cognizant of some of the facets of their operations. The professional employees were therefore important sources of valuable information which was reported by their superiors at departmental meetings so that appropriate modifications could be made. Employee participation also worked rather well in clerical departments, such as admissions, medical records, and accounting, and in the administrative offices of personnel and purchasing.

However, the participation of employees in the decision making process was not uniformly successful; it was unsatisfactory in the nonprofessional areas of dietetics (kitchen employees), housekeeping, and laundry. The department heads in these operations did not hold regular meetings, and, when meetings were held, they were not conducted effectively; few responses were elicited from these employees. The managers had no experience in holding meetings nor did they know how to encourage employee cooperation; they lacked discussion and conference skills. But perhaps the primary reason why participation did not work efficiently here was the caliber of the employees: these work forces were the lowest-paid in the hospital; they were classified as unskilled labor; and they were predominantly women, many of whom were elderly. Traditionally, these employees did not expect to participate in any formal discussion of departmental problems, and they were most reluctant to do so. They seemed to be comfortable with an authoritarian form of supervision and to feel that they were not competent to make formal observations about their operation.

As a result, the method employed to gather information in the nonprofessional areas was informal. The heads and supervisors made the rounds in their departments, encouraging and listening to "complaints." This interaction usually did not relate to the merits of a proposal but rather to the consequences it might have for the individual, and it was on the basis of such information that the supervisors had to construct an evaluation of employee reaction. Conversely, top management's considerations were communicated in the same manner, through the departmental grapevine.

Because unskilled labor in this urban area was in surplus supply, and because workers could be easily hired and trained, few problems of cooperation arose from unskilled employees. Although it was hoped that eventually the unskilled labor group would participate more fully, the level of participation remained relatively minimal.

The new administrator was generally satisfied with the employees' participation, however, and changes were introduced into the total operation at a more rapid rate than in the previous administration. Moreover, there were indications that employees conformed once the decisions had been authorized. Department heads and supervisors reported that employees liked the approach principally because the method of introducing changes was now predictable. Problems were raised; solutions were submitted and then discussed with employees; and eventually each department head would have his department adapt to a solution's implementation. No decision came as a complete surprise, and the rationale of each decision was understood. This understanding encompassed the problem's origin, the alternative solutions considered, and the reason why the selected solution had been judged the best. Employees, and particularly professionals, were not required to comply with decisions solely because individuals in positions of authority had made them.

The hospital administrator was therefore successful in designing and installing a decision making device which the organizational participants accepted as the appropriate method for introducing change. If a system is favorably received, the changes introduced via that system should be accepted; and this proved generally true. Although all employees did not agree with every solution, they were pleased with the system and they found that it was equitable. They had the opportunity to voice their opposition, and they were confident that their representatives would present their views at the departmental level. They consented to the rules of the game, win or lose, a point that was emphasized at the internal departmental meetings.

In meetings with his employees, a department head would summarize the results of a recent administrative meeting and would also report on the success or failure of their particular departmental proposals. If they had lost a point or if a decision had gone against them, he would recall their past decisions that had been ratified and would anticipate their future achievements. He would encourage his department to cooperate with the decision (even if it were negative) because compliance would obtain greater long-run departmental and hospital benefits.

312

Another device for adjusting employees to impending change was piecemeal implementation of certain solutions. This suggestion presented no problem at department head meetings, and the department which had proposed such a solution usually agreed to such implementation.

For example, one of the first solutions approved was the establishment of centralized hiring in the hospital's personnel department. In the past, most department heads had performed this task themselves and they were not convinced that the proposed hiring system could provide enough qualified personnel. They therefore suggested that it be applied initially only to the unskilled and clerical sectors, from which, if it became successfully established, it could be expanded to the professional areas. This method was acceptable to the personnel department. Once the procedures were established, and the professional departments were assured of the capability of the personnel department, all hiring responsibility was transferred to personnel.

MANAGERIAL INITIATIVE

It had been made clear at the outset that department heads could formulate solutions whenever problems arose, submit them to the assistant administrator, and have them placed on the departmental meeting agenda for discussion. After the first year of operation it was found that most solutions were coming from only a few department heads, although there were clear indications that many problems existed within or between departments, and the system was therefore altered to enable the administrator or assistant administrator to assign specific problems for solution. Steps 2 and 3 were introduced (see Figure 12–1). Further, when the problem-raising step was designed, the medical staff, managers, and employees were encouraged to raise problems. Patients (and their families) were systematically surveyed about their hospital stay and any coincident problems. These problems were thereupon assigned to department heads, who could no longer decide whether or not to work on a problem.

Under the previous administration the initiative exercised by department heads had varied considerably. Some displayed a high measure of initiative, searching for improved methods of operation and requesting the introduction of new materials and equipment. In other departments, procedures and operations had not changed for several years; supervisors merely maintained operations by making certain that adequate personnel, equipment, and material were available.

In other situations—where problems may have existed but where the previous administrator had been too busy or unaware of them—little action of any kind had been taken; the administrative staff and employees had accepted these situations, adopting the attitude that a measure of ineffectiveness was to be expected or that hospital operations were so complex that one could not strive for a completely efficient organization.

There had been no systematic way of raising problems, assigning them, and getting action—although rather glaring hospital problems had been discussed between the former administrator and the department heads. Department heads who were made aware of problem areas by the administrator would speak of more pressing tasks, or would express the hope of eventually applying corrective action. However, unless the situation arose again and the administrator again voiced concern about it, corrective actions were seldom taken. Or department heads might agree to take action but would not always follow through, thereby increasing the possibility of the situation's recurrence.

Nor had there been machinery for transferring the problems of one part of the operation to the appropriate problem solving personnel. Thus, although patients may have voiced dissatisfactions to the cashier at the time they paid their bills, these complaints could not be formally registered and processed for correction. If a problem was especially significant and of frequent occurrence, the former administrator might insist that the department heads give it their full attention and solve it, but this was an isolated act of judgment, and the problem might or might not be transmitted to the administrative staff. The possible exception here was in the medical staff, the major source of problems; persistent application to the administrator would eventually secure the desired correction of a hospital procedure.

Individual responsibility for problem solving had differed widely under the previous administration. One group of department heads seemed to manage its operations autonomously and seldom communicated with the administrator except to request capital equipment. The administrator usually did not know exactly what these department heads were doing or how they were handling problems. On the other hand, some department heads brought every problem to the administrator for solution, thus involving top management in departmental problems and, in effect, having the administrator perform the tasks of department heads.

The administrator was soon overburdened with work, perhaps spending one or two hours with a department head in exploring possible solutions. It was not unusual to find several individuals in the outer office waiting for their appointments. The administrator, as a result, could not readily turn to more significant areas, such as long-range hospital development.

One of the reasons, of course, why the new administrator assigned problems to department heads was to assure their actual solution. If a supervisor approached the new administrator with a departmental problem he would be informed that the responsibility for solution rested with the department head and not with the administrator. He would also be informed that, after he had formed its solution, the administrator would review it with the other department heads.

The department heads did not regard the assignment of problems as favorably as they did the consensus procedure, maintaining they had insufficient time for solving the problem that had been assigned to them. Upon investigation, however, it was found that they had been performing activities that were not problem solving in nature. The administrator stressed that these other tasks would have to be delegated so that a department head could spend his time in problem solving; if there was still a lack of time, additional administrative staff would be assigned to help with the solution of problems. With increased understanding of the nature of the problem solving function, department heads have gradually ceased to perform detailed nonmanagerial tasks.

The implementation step (step 8 in Figure 12–1) is primarily the responsibility of the department heads and supervisors, who will instruct employees about the new policies and procedures at regular department meetings and/or in training periods especially arranged for this purpose. (Implementation involves putting the new solutions into effect.)

The implementation step serves as a constraint upon the system. On the basis of the hospital's experience, there is reason to believe that an organization can incorporate solutions only at a certain rate. The hospital averaged one interdepartmental solution per week (Figure 12–2), and a limit to the speed for introducing solutions seemed to be imposed by the rate of employee learning that had to accompany changes. The rapidity with which organizational employees adjusted to solutions was an uneven process because not all units were able to learn at the same rate.

Under the previous administration the decision process itself was the primary constraint upon how quickly the organization changed or improved. Because it was an inefficient system, however, few solutions had been processed and employees had little difficulty in adjusting to them. Under the new system, and because the decision making process increased the number of solutions produced, the required adjustment time became the new constraint. As of this writing, no administrative techniques have been developed to cope with the problem of the learning rate.

The new administrator quickly discovered that department heads used different criteria for selecting the best solutions to problems. Instead of using the objectives of the hospital, they seemed to apply personal criteria which would enhance either their departments or their personal positions. This practice was most evident during the sessions when solutions were being evaluated, as department heads openly expressed personal opinions, preferences, or dislikes; it was not unusual for a department head to reject a solution because it did not conform to his accustomed way of working, or to his training, etc. In short, the dissimilar criteria used to evaluate solutions made the resolution of differences among department heads difficult.

As a result, the administrator insisted that supervisors select and review all new departmental policies on the basis of the hospital's goals—improvement of patient care at the lowest cost—and that only this dual criterion would be used to evaluate solutions. The fifth step in the management decision making system was thereby introduced (see Figure 12–1). No attempt was made at a rigorous definition of "improved patient care," the administrative staff being content to accept the opinions of the professional staff (especially those of physicians and nurses) in evaluating alternatives and selecting the best procedure with the patients.

The new administrator saw that the lack of rigorous analysis in the formulation of solutions posed another managerial problem: no quantitative or factual analyses accompanied solutions. The third and fourth steps of the decision making system were therefore introduced, requiring the problem-solver to investigate the causes of each problem and to search for solutions systematically in terms of the organizational objectives. Solutions were therefore to be submitted to the assistant hospital administrator, and, if he should decide that an analysis had been incomplete, he could ask that the problem-solver rework the solution.

Although forms were designed for facilitating the analysis of problems, little stress was placed upon this aspect of the system. One reason for this was that most of the department heads had no accounting background, which made it very difficult for them to calculate the payoff of solutions, and particularly their costs.

316

(Indeed, it would be most unusual if the managerial staff of the average hospital were equipped with the statistical, mathematical, and other tools necessary for this systematic analysis.) But it was a major forward step when department heads were able to write up solutions and explore them at department head meetings.

Operational solutions had seldom been produced in the past; in fact, workable solutions had been so few that this stabilization of the decision making process proved highly productive.

(If operations are inefficient at the outset, a systematic approach can furnish a significant payoff. Then, after total hospital operations are programmed, solution analysis can be raised to a more sophisticated level; but progress in this direction cannot be pressed until the medical staff has been formally incorporated into the decision making process, and this has only recently been attempted. Sophisticated analytical upgrading involves sending many administrative individuals back to school, a process that also has begun.)

Initially, department heads did not spend much time in searching for solutions; they relied on personal experience instead. Therefore, in addition to its medical library, the hospital developed an administrative library and subscribed to periodicals in associated hospital areas. This provided ready reference sources for department heads, and, in time, this resource was increasingly utilized by management (although some department heads did not consult this material).

The authorization step was also introduced into the decision making process (see Figure 12–1) so that operating personnel would no longer be uncertain whether a policy or procedure were official or unofficial. In the past, especially with verbal instructions, personnel sometimes doubted that certain instructions had been properly authorized, and they had been reluctant to accept them. The recourse, in such situations, was to check with the administrator to make sure that the change had been approved. However, the implementation of authorized policies had thereby been delayed and the administrator had been burdened with issuing frequent verbal assurances.

As with "improved patient care," the new system did not attempt a definition of the authority of the administrative personnel; instead, authority was incorporated into the solutions as they were constructed. Past administrators had handled questions of jurisdictional authority upon vertical and horizontal levels. However—along horizontal lines—it had not been clear where the assistant administrator's authority ended and where departmental authority began, or where departmental authority ended and where supervisory authority began. It was equally difficult to draw a sharp distinction along vertical lines, and an example of this was that the authority of the purchasing manager and that of the dietetics manager were not distinguishable.

The precise establishment of jurisdictions was not attempted because the process would have been extremely lengthy, requiring a thorough examination of all hospital activities for determining the proper administrative responsibilities of each manager. An even more important reason was that hospital activities would henceforth be constantly modified, with the new decision system perhaps shifting activities among departments. Because of this dynamic quality a static organizational allocation of authority would have been even more difficult to establish. The problem of departmental responsibilities was therefore treated as any other problem that required a solution.

For example, one problem was whether the nursing or the housekeeping department would be responsible for preparing the rooms for incoming patients (formerly assigned to the practical nurses because infections or communicable diseases necessitated special procedures). This situation was carefully reviewed, and both departments agreed that, with proper instruction, the maids could perform this activity; these duties were then transferred to the housekeeping department, an action which altered the jurisdictional lines. Then the budget of each department was adjusted accordingly, for this had been a basic part of the departmental agreement. The housekeeping budget was increased and the nursing budget was decreased to equalize the respective expenses and savings.

If each department head knows the solutions that have been formulated, each will know his responsibilities. Using this approach, the administrator held the administrative staff accountable for its assigned activities but was able to shift responsibility among the administrative staff so as to obtain more effective hospital results. As more solutions were produced, more precise lines of administrative authority could be drawn.

The final step in the decision process, the auditing of solutions, was introduced (see Figure 12–1) to determine if employees were conforming properly. The monitoring of solutions (by the administrative staff) meant that employees would be observed in the performance of their work and the results of their efforts would then be evaluated.

However, the audit of solutions was made voluntary and was left to the discretion of the department head who had initiated a

318

solution. The administrator did not press for the audit because the assumption was that the solutions were acceptable and that the employees usually observed them. However, it would have been better and more conclusive to have hired an additional department head with qualifications that would have enabled him to serve as the internal intelligence unit. His primary responsibility would have been to monitor all decisions.

SPECIAL CONSIDERATIONS

Other factors — in addition to formulating specific responses to managerial problems — were considered in the design of the decision making system, and one of the underlying objectives of the overall process design was to define, standardize, and install effective management practices. Initially, each department head had had a different conception of the performance and nature of his job and all had therefore performed dissimilar tasks. The head of the maintenance department had done maintenance work; the controller had explained the charges to patients or their families; the assistant administrator had attended to construction and renovation tasks. In order to eliminate random and erratic managerial activities, it had then been decided that the central or primary function of the managers was the solution of organizational problems (in the manner we have described). The department heads were told that problem solving was their essential function and that they had no other duties; that their performance of other tasks would mean they were not performing their jobs.

Another goal of the system was to objectify and depersonalize the decision making process, or to establish a real distinction between the system and the individuals who participated in it. Before the development of the system the administration of each department seemed to have been governed by the motivation, aptitudes, interests, attitudes, experience, education, skills, and temperament of each department head. These personal attributes had varied widely from department head to department head, and, in large measure, they caused the randomness of the original management process.

The new approach was that planning the decision making process around specific tasks would deemphasize the personality variables of department heads and that the decision making function would standardize the work pattern. As long as the personality of a department head entered into his decisions, the confidence of subordinates, colleagues, and superiors would be largely determined by their evaluations of the personality of that individual. Decision making, under these conditions, would be a highly personal process. If there were a lack of confidence in a department head, there would usually be a corresponding uncertainty about his decisions.

Thus the standardized decision making system was initiated in the hope that confidence need not be solely a confidence in individuals; it could also be placed in a system or plan. If this endeavor were successful, the personality variables of each department head would become less significant in terms of the decision output, and interpersonal differences within the organization would also be reduced. Moreover, a regular and predictable decision process, it seemed certain, would ensure less arbitrary and capricious results than those produced through the often irregular and unpredictable discretion of each decision-maker.

GENERAL REACTION

The system was accepted by most (but not all) of the administrative staff members, and some of the reasons for this acceptance have already been given. But there are other reasons also. The administrative staff was ready for a change; it was known that a new administrator would soon take office and that, as is usual in such circumstances, innovations would be made. Further, there seemed to have been a general realization that the hospital administration could be improved upon.

Another set of reasons for the staff's acceptance of the system was its provision for a more orderly, predictable, and rational process of administration—plus the fact that under the former administrative process the submanager frequently found himself "the man in the middle,"[3] subjected to conflicting and unresolvable pressures from the medical staff, employees, other departments, and higher administration. Some of the old decisions had appeared to be whimsical and unpredictable; and queries about problems within and between departments often went unanswered by higher administration. On the one hand, managers

[3] For discussions of this phenomenon see Fremont A. Shull, Jr., and Delbert C. Miller, "Decisions of the Man in the Middle," *Selected Readings in Management* (2d series), Fremont A. Shull, Jr., and André L. Delbecq (eds.) (Homewood, Ill.: Richard D. Irwin, Inc., 1962), pp. 465–472; and F. J. Roethlisberger, "The Foreman: Master and Victim of Double Talk," *Management of Human Resources*, Paul J. W. Pigors, Charles A. Myers, and F. T. Malm (eds.) (New York: McGraw-Hill Book Company, 1964), pp. 117–129.

had been assigned the responsibility for maintaining an effective departmental operation; on the other hand, they felt surrounded by an unstable situation which they were unable to control. To a large extent, the new system removed the everyday frustrations faced by the middle managers (although a few of them did not "accept" the system and therefore had difficulty in adjusting to it).

The resignation of the assistant administrator has already been mentioned. Personable and persuasive, he had been able to operate effectively in an unplanned and unstructured administrative setting; and, because of his highly developed communication skills, he had been able to influence the previous administrator, the board of trustees, and the department heads, and win their acceptance for many of his ideas and proposals. He had accomplished this on a person to person basis, "selling" his proposals by cultivating these various individuals and by spending time in their offices. However, this approach became less effective as time went on.

In an unplanned administrative process, interpersonal administrative cooperation can be achieved only in such a manner; because the assistant administrator had been in a highly unstructured situation, his political skill had therefore emerged as the major influence. However, after the new system had been installed, the effectuation of administrative cooperation was an inherent part of the system. Highly developed interpersonal skills were no longer needed.

The supervisor in charge of surgery was another who did not adjust to the new process. Over a period of time, this individual had developed an almost entirely autonomous unit, divorced from other hospital operations, and he had been able to exercise a very high degree of control over it. When the new system was introduced, this supervisor was required to participate in cooperative decision making and to submit all decisions (which were largely intradepartmental in nature) to the director of nursing. Because this had not been required in the past, the supervisor resented the requirement as an "undue" interference and eventually resigned. This was a case of "empire building" within a large administrative unit, and one that had ignored the interdependent needs of all the operating units, which again reflected the unstructured situation.

The case of the financial manager was similar. Because he had been able to exercise considerable control over capital expenditures he had also been able to exert indirect influence over departmental development. But, under the new system, expenditures were incorporated into solution constructions, and he could no longer use his veto power without fully justifying such action. The previous administrator had rejected various proposals because the financial manager had believed the hospital lacked the financial capability to undertake them, a process—and use of power—that other department heads had resented.

The financial manager had been able to build his position of organizational power because of his unique position, in this case by handling the organization's finances. Furthermore, he could not adjust to the new process because he tended to become involved in the detailed work of his department, and he subsequently resigned. Fundamentally, he was not a problem-solver; he preferred to concentrate upon the preparation of financial reports, a subfunction that could have been performed by his clerical personnel.

The laundry department head also had difficulty with the system, but this was caused by a lack of inherent intellectual skills. He could not operate effectively in the new system because he did not have the ability to analyze situations. Nevertheless, he made a reasonable effort, but he eventually chose to resign.

The managers who resigned had been favorably regarded by the previous administrator. The assistant administrator had been on good terms with the administrator and with the board of trustees, and had received a relatively high salary. The financial manager had always been very busy, knew a great deal about what was occurring in the hospital, also had a high standing with the administration, and had also been paid a high salary. But the performance of both these individuals was not efficient under the new system. Conversely, the supervisor of the blood bank had been considered a manager of questionable administrative ability, and his interpersonal relationships with others on the administrative staff had been poor. Yet, under the new system, this supervisor proved to be an excellent administrator and one who produced many effective solutions.

The new system obviated the necessity for "selling" personal effectiveness to top management and it permitted more equitable and accurate evaluation of the unassuming, or less personable, or less persuasive department heads. The new emphasis on productivity instead of on personality won favor with the administrative staff. Nor could the new system engender favoritism.

Although the system worked as a handicap on department heads who were not educationally equipped to perform decision making duties, it tended to increase the rewards of the college-trained group—the group which exercised the greatest initiative, produced the most solutions, and participated to the greatest extent in the entire process.

SOME RESULTS OF THE NEW SYSTEM

The new decision making system gave the new administrator more effective control over the managerial process, and, although the new system was not completely optimum, it proved to be productive. It was planned, installed, and subject to control. The administrator knew what submanagers were doing, was able to detect weaknesses and difficulties, and could correct the system as the need arose. Figure 12–2 shows the 198 *interdepartmental* decisions that were produced in four and one half years, all in accordance with the plan.

This study demonstrates that it is possible to introduce an administrative decision making system that is distinctly unlike the bureaucratic system which it replaces. The success of this project also indicates that such systems can be designed not only for hospitals but for all other organizations as well. Even when early results are somewhat less than had been expected, there is every reason for confidence that an operational decision making system can be obtained and continually improved upon.

This hospital experience demonstrates that—since the performance of the top management function is continuous—a system's redesign is accomplished through constant review and by timely modifications to meet new problems. The hospital we have considered is now in the process of extending the system to the medical staff, which will present special problems and which will certainly be a lengthy process. Even here, however, the early indications are that the medical staff has approved and accepted the process and is beginning to operate effectively within it. But, because the primary emphasis had been on the design of an operational system and on the construction of its major components, little effort has so far been spent upon the plan's refinement. The reason for this is that until a *total* system can be developed, including all the managerial and medical staff, complete preciseness is necessarily precluded, or at best tentative.

The managerial technology employed in the hospital is relatively unsophisticated; regression analysis, system simulation, linear programming, and similar techniques have not been employed. This, of course, need not always be the case; but, because gross inefficiencies seemed to exist at the outset, even a basic or unsophisticated decision making technology was able to render a large payoff.

323

As the immediate hospital problems are solved, a more sophisticated technology may become warranted or necessary, which would again tend to support the position that organizational decision making must be viewed as a total systems process. There would be little merit in using complicated tools for two or three decision making steps in one problem if the other problems, or steps—or hospital areas—are not also included in the decision process. For example: disturbed by high costs, the former administrator had hired a consulting firm that devised a complex standard-cost budget; however, because no provision was made for executing this budget—or even for handling the problems that would affect the budget—it was never used as intended.

Some aspects of this new management system were unexpected; for instance, its installation was a lengthy process. As each stage was introduced, continual encouragement and explanation were required, until the managerial staff gradually conformed. This same process has been even more pronounced with the medical staff. And the upgrading of managers has also been a very gradual process.

Many problems remain: a complete control apparatus for top management is yet to be developed; performance standards for the total system have not yet been established in terms of the problems to be solved and their relative values; the auditing component has not been refined. Yet, with continuous top managerial effort, these problems will be faced and an ever-improving system will evolve. The present system is flexible and ensures growth; a good beginning has been made.

SUMMARY

This hospital case study demonstrates the feasibility of planning, installing, and controlling a planned decision making system. Its system was designed in terms of the management problems that emerged. The program proved to be highly acceptable to the administrative staff and the employees because the system has, in the main, alleviated the management problems it was designed to solve.

QUESTIONS FOR DISCUSSION

1. Do you think the administrative problems faced by the newly appointed hospital administrator were in any way unique? Explain.

2. Are there administrative problems in a hospital that are not generally found in a business?
3. Do you believe that the department heads had excessive autonomy under the previous administrator? Using the bureaucratic approach, how could the previous administrator have exercised greater personal control over operations?
4. When the authority to make capital expenditures is highly centralized under a bureaucratic structure is there a tendency for top management to be overly concerned with budgeting? Who assumes the responsibility for other decision making activities?
5. What problems can arise when solutions are not recorded?
6. Under the previous administrator, department heads were frequently admonished to work together. Explain why this appeal failed to produce interdepartmental cooperation.
7. Why is the "political" problem of submanagers (who can exercise the greatest influence over top management's decisions?) an inherent characteristic of the bureaucratic system?
8. Why is a balanced development between processes and techniques more likely if the management function is treated as a total system?
9. Why do individuals prefer an "open" decision making process to a "hidden" decision process?
10. What additional improvements would you make in the hospital system? Explain.

SUGGESTED READINGS

BENNIS, WARREN G.; BENNE, KENNETH D.; CHIN, ROBERT (eds.). *The Planning of Change: Readings in the Applied Behavioral Sciences.* New York: Holt, Rinehart & Winston, Inc., 1961.

BURNS, THOMAS, and STALKER, G. M. *The Management of Innovation.* Chicago: Quadrangle Books, Inc., 1962.

LEAVITT, HAROLD J. *Managerial Psychology* (2d ed.). Chicago: University of Chicago Press, 1964.

LIPPITT, RONALD; WATSON, JEANNE; and WESTLEY, BRUCE. *The Dynamics of Planned Change.* New York: Harcourt, Brace & World, Inc., 1958.

RONKEN, HARRIET O., and LAWRENCE, PAUL R. *Administering Changes.* Boston: Harvard University Division of Research, 1952.

STRAUSS, GEORGE, and SAYLES, LEONARD R. *Personnel: The Human Problems of Management.* Englewood Cliffs, N.J.: Prentice-Hall, Inc., 1960.

VROOM, VICTOR H. *Some Personality Determinants of the Effects of Participation.* Englewood Cliffs, N.J.: Prentice-Hall, Inc., 1960.

13

INTERORGANIZATIONAL COOPERATION

We have thus far considered only a system of *intra*organizational cooperation, but the welfare of individuals can also be increased through a process of cooperative *inter*organizational actions between two or more organizations. Although there are many opportunities for joint action in our society, and although the advantages of cooperative action among organizations are very clear, it would seem that such action has seldom been achieved with complete success. This would seem to derive, in part, from an inability to design acceptable and productive decision making systems.

In the international field, whether one reviews decision making systems among allies or potential enemies, the effectiveness of the present processes is highly questionable. On our own federal level, improvements are needed not only within but between the congressional and the executive branches of the government. From an administrative point of view, Congress and the President are cast in top managerial roles: they must attempt to ascertain that departments established to execute national policies are making the decisions that are consistent with obtaining certain objectives. On the local level, urbanization almost demands that metropolitan communities work together, but local governmental units have so far been unable to devise efficacious intermanagement systems.

This chapter will therefore show how the conceptual framework for designing intraorganizational decision making systems might be applied to interorganizational efforts. Similar advantages would accrue: more decisions, with greater payoffs, would be produced in shorter periods of time, which would lead to greater individual welfare. Moreover, a planned decision making system may be the only feasible way, in certain situations, to obtain the cooperation of two or more organizations.

Six broad areas will be considered:

1. Conditions under which cooperation would be mutually advantageous;
2. Problems that top managements might face in the design of such a decision making system;
3. The design process;
4. Its applications;
5. A comparison of the proposed decision making system with the present approaches to interorganizational decision making; and
6. The advantages of planned interorganizational decision making.

ADVANTAGES OF INTERORGANIZATIONAL COOPERATION

The possibility for mutual gain must exist for two or more organizations before joint cooperation can be effectuated, and it is here that economies of scale, more productive technologies, and increased specialization (in addition to the considerations listed in Chapter 2) make cooperation highly desirable.

Economies of scale are achieved when the size of an operation increases and the cost per unit of output decreases, with the result that there is a greater payoff per unit of resources input. Indeed, varied technological and market configurations require a certain magnitude of operation if full efficiency is to be realized.

More productive technology is related to economies of scale in that a certain volume of units may have to be produced if the full economies of certain equipment are to be realized. If, for example, educational television is to be utilized most effectively, many schools must cooperate in the program; it is doubtful that one or two high schools would consider it beneficial to establish an exclusive educational television facility.

If advantage is to be taken of such marketing efficiencies as large sales forces, warehouses, and distribution facilities, or mass television advertising, the product must be sold on a mass scale. The European Common Market is an example of this principle: tariffs and import quotas are reduced, and the flow of goods between European countries is further encouraged through the establishment of more efficient selling agencies, such as supermarkets and large department stores.

Similar economies of course accumulate on the buying side of the market. Independent farmers and grocers have organized their buying in order to take advantage of volume discounts. If funds must be raised through the sale of stocks or bonds, or through lines of credit from financial institutions, the cost of obtaining the funds is lowered for large borrowing units because the risk to the lender is reduced. The cost of selling stock for established and reputable organizations is also lowered.

A similar factor applies in the labor market. Large units can afford to use specialized and expensive labor skills, as in product research and development, but small organizations may be unable to hire the services of highly skilled managers. However, if small organizations can establish efficient systems of cooperation, they may still be able to compete effectively with large, integrated economic units.

Cooperative action is also productive in acquiring greater power. Units with mutual interests may seek to exercise political power in order to secure beneficial legislation, but, to accomplish this, they will have to group together, in a farm bureau or a manufacturing association perhaps. On the international level, smaller countries may have to create a single military force in order to protect themselves against larger countries, or to exercise more influence in international affairs. Because of the nature and cost of modern weaponry, many countries do not have the economic base for maintaining a modern military establishment, and the creation of NATO, SEATO, and other alliances is one response to this problem.

Group effort is often desirable even when diverse units seek a single or similar goal. For example, if a community is faced with the problem of achieving racial integration, the top managers of various local organizations will realize that all units must cooperate if this goal is to be attained. The problem really consists of designing a decision making mechanism that will incorporate the community's economic, religious, political, educational, and social institutions into a single action device. The United or the Community Fund is another example of this kind of endeavor.

Cooperative organizational action may also be necessary when a group of organizations has a common purpose but diverse means for reaching this end. For example, a national objective is the maintenance of peace, and the departments of defense, state, agriculture, and commerce all work toward this goal. However, because these units are distinct, or relatively autonomous, the matter of coordinating their activities is significant, and here we are confronted with the problem of suboptimization between

328

organizations: if their efforts are not successfully integrated, they may proceed at cross-purposes, and duplications or imbalances in efforts can negate the potential, overall effectiveness. Conversely, organizations may have unlike objectives but the same means: in collective bargaining both managements and unions desire to maximize the welfare of their respective memberships, which are different, yet both utilize the same productive process.

Another situation in which interorganizational cooperation is advantageous is in preventing several autonomous organizations, with dissimilar but nonconflicting objectives, from pursuing policies which would result in nullifying the others' welfare or objectives. (This is another aspect of the suboptimization problem.) Each community that dumps its sewage in a river can adversely affect the water supply of another downstream community; or industries can cause harmful air pollution for the residents in several locations.

Under any of the above situations, if the top managements from different yet mutually affected organizations recognize the potential benefits of their cooperation and decide to confer, they would still be confronted with the task of designing an effective interorganizational decision making mechanism that could solve their mutual problems.

PROBLEMS IN
DESIGNING AN INTERORGANIZATIONAL
DECISION MAKING MECHANISM

Top management, in addition to solving the problems it ordinarily encounters in constructing an organizational design, will also have to resolve questions that arise from factors that are unique in the interorganizational sphere. These factors are (1) limited cooperation, (2) the size of each organization and the number involved, (3) the production and distribution of utility, and (4) the problem of mixed authorities and sovereignties.

LIMITED COOPERATION

When parties consider the design of a decision making machinery for achieving a limited amount of cooperation, they should recognize, at the outset, that cooperation may be restricted because of the nature of their total relationship, and that cooperative, competitive, and conflictual factors can be intermixed.

Cooperative action is defined here as a system of interdependent behavior which clearly produces increased utility, and

329

which is distributed in such a manner that it is mutually advantageous to the parties who act jointly.

In a competitive relationship the production of utility is independent but its distribution is interdependent, limited, and divisible. In the typical competitive business situation, the production functions of company A and company B are separate. However, they both sell in the same market, and consumers can exercise an option between them, but each company can adopt independent strategies in order to increase its share of the total market. An increase will almost necessarily decrease the share received by the competitor, and it will also alter the relative welfare return to each organization.

A conflictual state is one in which two or more individuals or organizations desire an object of utility which is both limited and indivisible — as two individuals striving for the same promotion. The object of utility may be produced by either party, by both, or by a third party. In a case of theft, the stolen object has been produced by one individual and removed by another; in a horse race, all the entrants may contribute to the purse but the winners take all; and a war may involve a struggle between countries A and B over which shall occupy country C. Competitive situations become conflictual when one competitor attempts to acquire the total available welfare.

A mingling of cooperation, competition, and conflict among organizations will maximize the total utility of the individual memberships. In both inter- and intraorganizational relations, such a mingling or interaction among participants is natural because of the circumstances in which the parties find themselves, because of the objective they are attempting to achieve, or because of the means they have for attaining their objectives. In the case of two individuals seeking the same promotion (as long as their conflict remains within the confines of socially acceptable behavior), probably the only way in which the problem will be resolved is by one individual winning and by the loser leaving the field. On the other hand, price competition in the marketplace has long been viewed as economically desirable, while the advantages of cooperative behavior are of course manifold.

If the situation is dynamic, it is important that the organizations be able to realize when certain forms of interaction are no longer beneficial, so that they can shift to another pattern. No one form of behavior is necessarily more profitable than other forms under all circumstances, nor is total utility always increased by cooperative interactions. In fact, organizations often have a mixed relationship with one another: although in some

330

areas of activity it may be highly desirable to cooperate, it may be mutually advantageous to compete — or even contest — in other areas. For example, the Soviet Union and the United States may find it mutually beneficial to cooperate in the exchange of cultural activities and to compete in their efforts to reach the moon.

This intermixed behavior should present no difficulties if the parties can clearly separate both the objects of mutual benefit and the activities needed to obtain them from the other aspects of their independent activities. However, it is also possible for the conflictual or competitive aspects to destroy cooperative efforts, and it may at times be very difficult to maintain a separation between cooperative and competitive activities. Or conflict between two organizations may grow and engender so much distrust that even limited cooperation is unattainable.

The time factor is another element that can limit the extent of cooperation between any two organizations. Top managers may think in terms of an immediate, planned decision making mechanism, but the potential payoff from such cooperation may have to be projected over several years, becoming profitable only long after the design and installation costs have been amortized.

Restricted organizational resources can also limit cooperation by constituting a constraint on the resources that can be devoted to such effort; for example, countries that enter into defense alliances may have minimal military capability. Thus the nature of the relationship between the parties, the available time, and the available means may limit the extent of cooperation that can exist between organizations, and the design of decision making machinery must weigh these limitations.

SIZE AND NUMBER OF ORGANIZATIONS

The second problem that is unique in designing an interorganizational decision making process relates to the size of the organizations and the number involved. If the organizations are large, there will be many suboperations, which can lead to suboptimization. The designer must therefore provide that interorganizational decisions will not adversely affect suboperations. For example, two organizations may have relatively effective productive facilities and may decide to take advantage of economies of scale by merging their marketing functions; as a result, marketing costs may be reduced but inefficiencies may appear in the production areas. When inter- and intraorganizational activities are integrated, productive operations should be maintained at all organizational levels.

331

Another aspect of size is that more individuals are involved as systems expand. Information must then be processed through additional relay points, and the possibility of error therefore increases. Information can also be delayed, lost, or garbled, and it becomes more cumbersome to bring interested or affected parties together for the purpose of obtaining consensus. Further, the effective control of the decision making processes becomes a problem because added control units are necessary, and this, in turn, makes the control of the entire decision making process more difficult for top management.

PRODUCTION AND DISTRIBUTION OF UTILITY

The third unique aspect of interorganizational design, which also requires attention, is the production and distribution of the mutual welfare which this cooperation is expected to create. Machinery must be established that will assign the obligations of each organization and distribute the rewards that each will receive; and, to maintain the system of cooperation, the distribution must be equitable. If an organization believes it has been assigned more obligations and less rewards than the other participating organizations, it may leave the relationship.

There is little question that an interorganizational relationship requires a more precise agreement-making step (that must be worked out in the decision making design) than does an intraorganizational agreement. The reason for this, of course, is that the potential payoff for all participants may not be as clear, or as great, as it is in an intraorganizational system, particularly if the cooperation is of a limited nature. Because the parties have less to lose if the former type of cooperative relationship should fail, each party may press harder for what it thinks is a proper share of the rewards of cooperation. This can make agreement among the organizations more difficult. If there is also a likelihood that the parties may dissolve their relationship, the agreement-making machinery should be strong enough to maintain the cooperative relationship.

MIXED AUTHORITIES AND SOVEREIGNTIES

The fourth factor in the design of an interorganizational decision making mechanism relates to the problem of multiple authority. Participating organizations are separate, autonomous, legally constituted units. Insofar as their cooperation requires the expenditure of funds, the incurring of debts, or entering into con-

332

tracts, the appropriate officials in each organization will be required to authorize such arrangements. Even if the organizations should establish a single, legally constituted organization, the officials of the constituent units will still remain legally responsible. Unlike an organization with a single authority, there would now be multiple authorities, and each organizational unit would have to agree not only to the terms of cooperation but each would also have to authorize the agreement. As a consequence, authorizers will be most cautious about the terms of their consent, so that multiple authorization can increase the difficulty of reaching agreements.

In the intraorganizational setting the authorization step was defined as the formality which meets the pertinent legal requirements, but it was also recognized that individuals with this authority have the organizational power to coerce participants who breach organizational agreements and internal units that refuse to comply with these agreements. In a situation of multiple authority, however, organizational power is more diffuse; coercion is likely to be much less effective if a participating unit refuses to cooperate.

The following hypothetical case of a planned decision making system between organizations will illustrate or suggest how all of these various problems can be resolved.

DESIGNING AN INTERORGANIZATIONAL DECISION MAKING SYSTEM

Our illustration of the design process will consider a two-organization model. Business organizations A and B have decided to establish a joint product research and development division. Although both companies market a similar line of products, their small size had made them unable to afford an independent product development unit. Figure 13–1 (page 334) shows how a limited interorganizational decision making system might operate.

The top of the schematic represents company A's decision making system, the middle segment is company B's, and unit C is the joint decision making process for the new product development operation. (We will also assume that all three designs and processes are the same as in our basic model [and unit C also has its own control unit and its own authorizer, and solves its problems in the same manner as the parent unit].) The establishment of the decision making mechanism for the product development unit is, in fact, very similar to the process an integrated organization goes through when it expands its system; it is largely a matter of adding additional decision making lines or channels.

Figure 13–1

A Two-Organization Decision Making System
Utilizing a Third (Joint) System

(CU represents the sensory or intelligence control units)

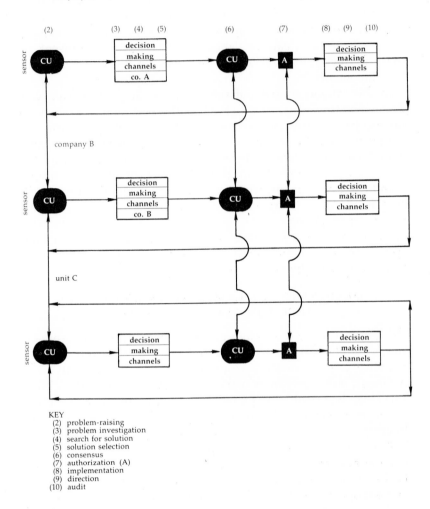

KEY
(2) problem-raising
(3) problem investigation
(4) search for solution
(5) solution selection
(6) consensus
(7) authorization (A)
(8) implementation
(9) direction
(10) audit

However, the top managements in A and B must determine specific facts before they can establish unit C: they must establish the area of mutual gain and ascertain that such an undertaking would be worthwhile. In this case, the development of new products will increase the sales volume of both organizations, which, in turn, will increase their profits. The production and

334

marketing facilities of companies A and B must then be found to be sufficiently complementary, so that solution of a range of product development problems will also be mutually beneficial.

Further, the parties must determine the investment necessary for establishing the unit and the division of its cost. One of the advantages of planned decision making is that, at the outset, both the cost and the risk can be minimized by installing only the decision making apparatus of the new unit; there is no need for the parent organizations to hire scientists and engineers. As will be explained, companies A and B can decide upon the actual activities which this unit will perform and can underwrite them on a decision by decision basis. As the decision-makers of organizational unit C produce solutions which are accepted by the parent organizations, the activities of the new unit will gradually be expanded. If the unit is successful, it will become self-financing, thereby reducing both the cost and the risk to both companies. (In fact, one reason why a cooperative undertaking is even possible is that the initial investment can be significantly minimized.) At this initial stage, there will be only the minimal cost of hiring the decision-makers required for establishing the new unit's operations.

The sharing of this cost will be negotiated between the organizations, and, because in this case the initial costs are relatively small, reaching an agreement should not be difficult. In addition, the top managements will have to agree upon the individuals who will be hired to perform the decision making duties. The established mechanics of selecting managerial personnel and training them in the decision making machinery will be applied here, by either or both of the organizations, as long as each has the right to veto any selection.

In considering how the decision making machinery of unit C can be integrated with those of A and B, we shall, for the most part, treat those aspects of the design that differ from intraorganizational decision making. Because the organizational objective of unit C has already been defined, we can now review the second step, that of problem-raising. There are three potential sources of problem inputs into the new unit: companies A and B can raise problems that relate to product development (which will be assigned to the new unit), and unit C may also have its own sensory apparatus for detecting problems. If A and B have external and internal sensory devices which are also attuned to product development problems, unit C will have additional major sources of problem inputs.

As for internal sensory devices in the parent organizations, the marketing departments, and specifically the salesmen, may suggest leads for major efforts in the development of new products, based upon customer responses or upon a knowledge of competitors' activities. The external sensory apparatus of A and/or B may also suggest or conclude that there is a consumer need for a product that is not presently being produced.

The sensory apparatus in the parent organizations would pick up product development problems and send them to their control units (the same as for any other problem), and the control units, following their usual procedures, would classify all incoming problems by the management unit to which each should be assigned (in this case, the control units of A and B would know that all product development problems are to be assigned to unit C). The decision making control unit of the product development division would operate in the same way as the A and B control units, receiving, classifying, assigning, scheduling, routing, and controlling all problems assigned to it.

The A and B control units could maintain, as part of their master schedules, a record of all problems assigned to and solved by the product development unit. Each company would therefore know not only what problems had been assigned to unit C but what problems had been assigned by the other company, along with their schedules for completion. Because each parent organization is limited in what it can manufacture and market, constraints will have to be built into the screening processes of their control units so that unit C will not be assigned developmental problems that are unfeasible for either company to produce.

Also, if it were found that one organization assigns more problems to the unit than the other, and the latter believes it is not receiving an equitable utilization of unit C, some agreement will be necessary for establishing assignment priorities. Problem input to unit C may then be restricted to problems that, when solved, will be equally beneficial to both organizations, and both control units would then have to agree upon the problems that would be assigned to unit C. The guide for establishing priorities would be no different from those for the intraorganizational design: both organizations would want the new unit to undertake the solution of problems that have the greatest economic payoff. If appropriate inspection devices were provided, this screening of problems could also be left to the discretion of C's control unit.

Once a product development problem has been received and assigned by control unit C, the investigation of its causes and the selection of its solution (after all solutions had been evaluated)

336

would be performed in the intraorganizational setting (steps 3, 4, and 5). The output of the solution would be in terms of an increased sales volume, the input would relate to the cost of product development, and the payoff would represent the difference between the two. (In the formulation of such solutions, one potential difficulty is whether the unit C decision-makers are permitted to collect data from companies A and B. If A and B are competitors, they may refuse to disclose all their data for fear of revealing vital or confidential information. In such cases, however, data can be classified as to use.)

Two problems are involved in achieving consensus (step 6) among companies A and B and unit C: (1) the contribution and return each organization will receive through unit C's solutions, and (2) the existence of a multiple net organizational payoff. As for the first consideration, unit C, after formulating its solutions, . would estimate the cost and the payoff of solutions and submit only those that have an aggregate payoff. However, A and B must still agree on their obligations and returns: when a solution is implemented, how much of its cost will each contribute, and how much of its payoff will each receive?

It is best if the parties agree upon a fixed formula to meet this problem at the time that unit C is established. A and B might decide that each will pay half of every solution's cost and share equally in utilizing any new products produced. The products could also be patented by both organizations and the royalties divided, etc. An alternative method is that in which the parties negotiate their contributions and return as each solution is submitted. This, however, is time-consuming and tends to reduce the number of solutions that can or will be agreed upon.

Still another method is an agreement by A and B that unit C, at its own discretion, will incur the cost of a proposed solution. Unit C would then attempt to "sell" its solution to A and/or B at a price that will cover its costs. (However, this means that unit C must be relatively autonomous in the expenditure of funds, and this would depend upon its proven achievements.) For example, if unit C developed a new product which could return a net aggregate gain of $1 million, the parties might decide that company A will receive $400,000, company B $400,000, and unit C $200,000, and, after several such solutions, unit C might have built up sufficient funds to develop other solutions. (Eventually, since solution payoff is to be distributed to the membership of all participating organizations, this will include the members of unit C.)

In the decision making system of a single organization, the

statement of what the participants will create and what they will receive in the distribution of the increased payoff does not have to be as explicit as it must be in an interorganizational system; even if every individual is not completely satisfied with a proposed solution, top management can still authorize it. However, in an interorganizational arrangement, which requires multiple authorization, each organization (as we noted in another connection) will probably insist that its expected contribution and return be detailed before it will approve a solution.

Having deduced a solution's cost and payoff, unit C would then have to calculate the expected payoff for each organization according to the formula for distribution. If a solution's aggregate cost is $50,000, and if organizations A and B have agreed to share half the cost, each would pay $25,000. Then, if the total sales output of the new product is $250,000 — with A receiving $100,000 and B $150,000 (derived from their sales) — B would have captured 60 per cent of the market and A only 40 per cent. Organization A's return from the solution would be $75,000 and B's return would be $125,000, or the output minus the cost. Upon completion of its calculations, the C control unit would clear its solution to the control units of companies A and B (step 5), which, in turn, would clear the proposal to all of the affected units in each organization for establishing the existence of a net organizational payoff.

Suboptimization should be avoided in unit C's solutions. One must assure that the product and development solutions of unit C do not negatively affect the operating units (such as sales and production) of the parent companies, and in this context the suboptimization problem on an inter- and intraorganizational level is similar. In the example of the $75,000 payoff for A and $125,000 for B, the net result, after this solution had cleared, might emerge as follows:

Organization A		*Organization B*	
Product development	$75,000	Product development	$125,000
Finance	− 5,000	Finance	− 5,000
Production	−60,000	Production	−75,000
Net	$10,000	Net	$ 45,000

The parties would have to adopt guidelines for the conditions under which they would proceed with a given proposal; for example, what they will do if they differ over the prospects of a net payoff. Unit C could request a meeting to determine if any

338

adjustments can be made in the solution so as to make it mutually acceptable (if organizations A and B are comparatively large, some form of representation could be employed). Or the parties may hold to a rule that a net payoff has to exist for each organization before they are obliged to cooperate; or each could be provided with the right of veto, so that if neither finds a proposal acceptable it must be rejected. They could also agree that either party can undertake development of a specific product on its own if the other rejects the plan, and, in such a case, that the former organization has sole possession of such a product.

If the parties accept the condition that a proposal must provide an aggregate net payoff for both organizations, they would proceed with the solution and divide the profits which were produced. For example, the product development division may suggest a research proposal that organization A decides will result in a negative payoff of $100,000, but for which B calculates an expected net payoff of $500,000. The result would be that a $400,000 net payoff would be anticipated between the two organizations. If the parties can agree on a formula for redistributing the $400,000 between them, it would still be possible to think in terms of an aggregate net payoff.

The long-run operation of unit C may indicate different welfare results for each cooperating organization. As marketable and profitable products are developed, the group with superior marketing facilities may be able to increase its sales to a greater extent than the other, thereby achieving a distinct competitive advantage. It may therefore cease to be in the latter's interest to maintain a cooperative relationship, and it would withdraw from the arrangement. Over time, in a mixed cooperative and competitive relationship, the disadvantage of cooperation will sometimes outweigh the advantages.

The problem of multiple authorization (step 7) is solved by having each participant, A, B and C, authorize the solution. Upon completion of the consensus step, the accepted solution is sent to the individual in each organization who has the right of authorization. He will approve the funds for executing the solution, which will be allocated from affiliated organizations A and B to the budget of unit C.

The implementation and direction of unit C's solutions (steps 8 and 9) is the same as in an intraorganizational situation if the action takes place within its jurisdiction. In C's utilization of solutions, or the direction step, the sensory apparatus of companies A and B would presumably detect and notify unit C of the states to which it is to respond.

Unit C could execute the audit (step 10) of its solutions and send the results to the parent organizations so that their control units could evaluate the audits in terms of expected payoff (although each company should be free to conduct an independent audit if it so desires). Fundamentally, the monitoring problem is the same here as it is in the intraorganizational situation. If either of the parent organizations thinks there are "bugs" in unit C's operation, these questions and problems can be raised in the manner we have described.

In summary, reviewing the total design of this hypothetical case, we can note that it was established to take advantage of economies of scale. As for the special problems in interorganizational design, we can also note that the fact that companies A and B were competitors did not prohibit cooperative action in limited areas. Even though A and B were assumed to be small organizations, if each had effective internal control units, the addition of the independent unit would not have imposed a significant burden upon these parent units. The problem of the production and distribution of utility was resolved by the conditions that had been agreed upon in determining a solution's acceptability. We can also note that planned problem solving tends to minimize the risk of organizational cooperation by minimizing the initial cost, and that, with multiple authorization, the problem of mixed authority is satisfactorily resolved.

APPLICATIONS

Depending upon the number, size, purpose, means, and dispersion of cooperating organizations, different interorganizational decision making designs may be required. We will therefore turn to very large cooperating units that have a single ultimate authority but mixed organizational means. For example, a goal of the United States is the maintenance of international peace, and it will be assumed that the responsibility for achieving this objective rests with three primary organizations: the defense, state, and intelligence departments. The design of an interorganizational system would be for the purpose of preventing the suboptimization which could result if these departments were permitted to pursue independent courses of action with only limited organizational capabilities: the defense department having only military means, the intelligence department only informational means, and the state department having political, economic, psychological, and other means.

Figure 13–2 is a broad decision making design that we will

Figure 13–2

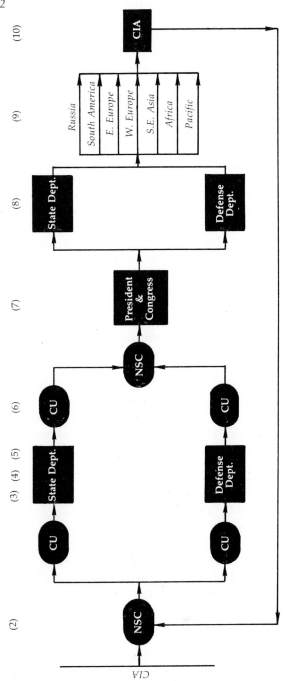

assume represents the single rational objective, based upon "top management's" definition that the common objective of these three governmental units is maintaining peace. (This is step 1 in our process; the other nine stages will be outlined briefly.)

Now assume that the Central Intelligence Agency (CIA) is assigned the responsibility for surveying the external environment of the system and for providing the sensory apparatus for the other two units. The CIA would send the problems it has detected to a central control unit, similar to the National Security Council (NSC), which would classify, schedule, assign, and control the incoming problems. Military problems would be assigned to the defense department; diplomatic, psychological, economic, ideological, and social problems would be assigned to the state department (provided it had facilities for executing operations in these areas). Problems that had both military and diplomatic aspects would be redefined by the central control unit so that the participating organizations, the state and the defense departments, could work on the parts for which they have special capabilities. The problems would then be sent to the control units of each organization, which in turn would reclassify them and send them to the respective subcontrol units. Each problem would be channeled to the management sector in each department that had been established for solving certain types of problems.

Each organization would produce solutions (steps 3, 4, and 5) that would be returned to the master control unit, or the NSC, which would then be cleared to all affected units. These units, in turn, would calculate the effects of the solutions and retransmit these amplified data to the NSC, which would compute the total net organizational payoff (step 6). If a payoff seemed to be assured, the solutions would be cleared to the individuals who could authorize them, the President, congressional committees, and so on (step 7). After a solution had been authorized, it would be returned to the proper organization for implementation (step 8).

Let us assume that operations directed at the maintenance of peace are divided along geographical lines and that solution utilization may have to be exercised under individual field directors (step 9). For example, operations might be divided into world areas, such as Eastern Europe, South America, Russia, Africa, and so forth; and a single director might be in charge of each area with the responsibility for applying the relevant solutions produced by the defense and state departments. Audits of the consistency of actual field results with the expected results could be conducted by field directors of the state and defense departments and by the CIA (or intelligence unit). If discrepancies are noted, particularly by the intelligence unit, a problem would be triggered, looped back, and fed into the NSC, which would again process it in the manner just described.

Another situation that requires interorganizational cooperation occurs when many separate organizations join together to achieve a common but limited purpose, for example, a trade association. One approach to the problem of the number of members involved is to have the association solve organizational problems in an intraorganizational manner except for the authorization step, where the solution can be distributed to all members for their approval (and under the stipulation that the association will effectuate only those solutions approved by the majority of its members).

PRESENT MODELS

Traditionally, three general models have been used to obtain interorganizational cooperation: (1) the bureaucratic, (2) the exchange, and (3) the representative. The decision making aspects of each of these models can be compared with the planned model, but we will first review the bureaucratic approach.

THE BUREAUCRATIC MODEL

When the bureaucratic system is used, interorganizational cooperation is usually achieved through a merger, which is a matter of combining separate organizations under a central authority. A new organizational chart is drawn which redefines lines of managerial authority and responsibility, and organizational activities are regrouped under the appropriate managerial jurisdiction. A single overall bureaucratic structure is formed.

As organizations merge, they increase in size, and the bureaucratic organization attempts to meet this problem with the technique of decentralized authority.[1] Although submanagers are granted authority to administer comparatively large divisions within the total organization, and in terms of their own discretion, they are nevertheless constrained to work within the broad policies formulated by top management. They are expected to achieve certain results on their divisional level, based on predetermined top management forecasts relating to sales, costs, and

[1] For a treatment of this technique see Ernest Dale, *The Great Organizers* (New York: McGraw-Hill Book Company, 1960), pp. 84–109 and 143–174.

profits. In addition, centralized staff services, such as public or industrial relations, are provided to assist the divisional manager in his operations; but the success of divisional operations fundamentally depends upon the ability of the submanager. If he does not produce the results which top management expects, he may be replaced by another manager.

Several deficiencies inhere in the bureaucratic approach to achieving interorganizational cooperation. First, there is considerable risk in using the bureaucratic approach; for example, the top managements of cooperating organizations are given only one choice: to merge or not to merge. The decision to merge is generally thought to be permanent, and, once organizations are so incorporated, if the potential benefits from interorganizational operations are less than had been anticipated it is extremely difficult to return to autonomous units without seriously impairing organizational effectiveness.

Cooperating organizations, under the bureaucratic model, relinquish their rights to decide how they will operate. One of the central features of the bureaucratic model is unity of command. If it is not known in advance how the centralized authority will be utilized in the creation and the distribution of utility, it of course cannot be known that this authority will seek the greatest benefits for the participating membership—one of the basic risks which attaches to any grant of unrestricted authority.

(Planned decision making, on the other hand, provides that each organization will retain its authority and will be able to review every proposed solution, which guarantees that the organizational interests of each will be enhanced. Each organization also has the option to veto. Divisibility of choice is maintained in that the organizations decide not only upon cooperating but also can determine all the subsequent conditions of cooperation.)

One cannot credit the claim advanced by advocates of bureaucratic cooperation that after a merger is carried out there will be no drastic changes in the benefits and privileges of the organizational participants. The history of mergers is replete with examples of individuals achieving ultimate authority and overriding organizational power, of turning this authority to ends unlike those that had been promised, with the result that many submanagers and organizational participants have lost former benefits.

To utilize the bureaucratic approach in obtaining interorganizational cooperation, the potential benefits must appear so attractive that, despite the chance for abuses, the possibility of net

344

individual payoff will still remain. Unfortunately, however, as organizations expand in mergers the advantages of interorganizational cooperation are often lost because of administrative inefficiencies. This is particularly true when a system of centralized authority is maintained since the problem solving load of top management can become overwhelming. The decentralization of authority can, at times, cope with the problem of organizational size, but centralized controls and highly competent submanagers are still required. Decentralization has not been universally successful.

Another disadvantage of the bureaucratic form of interorganizational cooperation is the length of time required to effectuate the merger of two autonomous organizations, a disruptive process in itself. Not only must a new organizational chart be drawn up, but submanagers must learn and acquire a new behavioral process, and, through experience, ascertain their new areas of authority and responsibility. Past informal decision making patterns are often broken and only gradually reestablished. Because authority and its delegation will depend solely upon top management, a period of adjustment is necessary before submanagers will be able to determine their superiors' expectations.

For all of these reasons, proposals to merge under a single, centralized authority usually meet with considerable opposition, as did the establishment of a unified defense department, and the Soviet Union's centralized control of economic activities.

THE EXCHANGE MODEL — mutual benefiracal

The exchange model also provides for interorganizational cooperation. Under this form, the various organizations agree upon the conditions for cooperation: the obligations that each will undertake and the benefits that each will receive; and these conditions are then specified in a contract. This model restricts the decision process to the consensus step; agreement is absolutely essential, and if it is not reached there is no basis for cooperation and subsequent action. The exchange model works well under certain conditions, and it probably cannot be improved upon when these conditions exist. One general example in which the conditions are fairly obvious is the competitive market situation.

The exchange model has distinct advantages over the bureaucratic model as a decision making approach to interorganizational cooperation; it provides less risk and greater choice. Its

345

agreements usually imply narrowly limited organizational consequences; and the parties can enter into relatively short-run arrangements, within a specified time limit, and renew the agreement if they desire. The arrangement is much like a trial experiment; if it proves to be unsatisfactory to either of the parties it need not be repeated.

When the potential benefits of interorganizational cooperation have a temporary nature, the flexibility of the exchange model provides a tool or means for taking advantage of such situations. To assure that organizational interests will be served, the parties can stipulate the conditions under which they will cooperate.

The exchange model, however, is not without disadvantages, one of which is that the environment of the negotiating parties may be monopolistic rather than competitive. The desirable attributes of the exchange model should be the same as those of a planned decision process: freedom of choice, minimized risks, and maximum individual utility—which are dependent upon a competitive, freely "negotiable" environment. To the extent that monopolistic characteristics are present, these features or utilities will tend to be diminished; for example, through superior bargaining power one of the parties can reduce the other's area of choice. If one of the negotiators has greater bargaining power—of an economic, political, or social nature—he can force the other party to accept undesirable terms of economic, political, or social exchange. Under such circumstances, the exchange model takes on many attributes of the bureaucracy.

Another limitation of the exchange model is that it is not a very effective means for collective action among a large number of organizations in gaining a common objective. By and large, it is restricted to a two-party cooperation: a buyer and a seller, or two nations negotiating an agreement. In the absence of a directing authority, it is highly improbable that several autonomous individuals and/or organizations can come together, and, through individual negotiations, devise a single plan of effective group action. When common group action is required and when many organizations are involved, as in the political sphere, such objectives as defense, improved education, or a highway system must be achieved by decision making mechanisms other than the exchange model. Thus the effective use of this "negotiating" model is usually restricted to situations in which only two organizations are involved.

Nor is the exchange model an efficient device for executing a highly interdependent plan of action, a conclusion most vividly supported by a classic example from the textile industry. Before

346

the invention of spinning and weaving machinery, cloth was manufactured through the process of an exchange system: a merchant would purchase wool and would then negotiate with different individuals to perform one of the various operations for converting it into cloth. One group would weave the wool, another group would card it, another would bleach it, another would dye it, while yet another group would cut it. At each step in this integrated production process, the merchant "put it out" for that specific operation.

The inefficiencies of the putting-out system came from the logistics involved. The partially finished goods had to be transported from one location to another, which made for idle time, transportation costs, damage, and loss. Also, production units were not wholly dependable: the dyers may have done a competent job but the weavers may have been inexperienced; so that it was difficult for the merchant to control the quality of his product. Nor did he have any assurance of the capacity of the productive process. Without long-term contracts, weavers who formerly had been willing to work were free to acquire better contracts from other merchants—so that it was also difficult for the merchant to predict the quantity of his product. The central factory system, a bureaucratic process, developed because it had a coordinator in management that could exercise effective control over the productive process in terms of both the quality and the quantity of the product (a situation in which the bureaucratic decision making mechanism proved superior to the exchange model).

The exchange form of interorganizational cooperation presents further limitations when a complex technology is involved. It is extremely difficult to draw up a contract between two organizations that will incorporate all of the possible contingencies which the parties may subsequently face. Defense contracting and subcontracting are examples of this difficulty. When a group of companies joins with the government to produce a weapons system that may eventually cost several million (or billion) dollars, an initial agreement cannot be drawn up that will solve (or even foresee) all the problems which might arise. Consequently, the defense department has sometimes authorized "cost-plus" contracts under which the participating companies produce the product and the defense department underwrites the cost. These contracts are often felt to be undesirable because the defense department cannot exercise effective control over costs. And occasionally the parties have used a system of continual renegotiation, but this also has proved unsatisfactory.

347

Another shortcoming of these bargaining models is that they do not engender "group consciousness" of the possibilities for mutual gain through collective action. (The exchange form, instead, emphasizes individual gain as exhibited in its "buyer beware" atmosphere, and, within a rather permissive context of legal, economic, or moral constraints, it permits each party to attempt to take the utmost advantage of the other during the negotiations.) Even the bureaucratic system endeavors to develop a "team spirit" in the form of loyalty to the company or political unit because it is a most important psychological incentive in group achievement. In its absence, individuals and/or organizations will wrangle among themselves to maximize their immediate gains and will thereby jeopardize the long-run benefits of group cooperation.

The problem of enforcing agreements is another drawback in the exchange model. If no legal enforcement apparatus exists, the parties may be reluctant to enter into an arrangement because each cannot be assured that the other party or parties will meet its obligations. In diplomatic negotiations, for example, the only binding element is the mutual self-interest perceived by the parties themselves. If at any time either party sees no further benefits from the proposed arrangement, it can negate the agreement by a refusal to continue. But in the buyer-seller relationship, laws and courts will guarantee the compliance of the contracting parties.

The last limitation that we will consider in the exchange approach is that there is no search for a mutually optimum solution. Emphasis is largely confined to the consensus step of the decision making process (a disadvantage that will be treated below in our evaluation of the collective bargaining relationship).

In summary, then, the exchange model represents an effective decision making mechanism for effectuating interorganizational cooperation under certain circumstances, primarily in the competitive market situation, but it has basic and significant limitations.

THE REPRESENTATIVE MODEL

We have listed the representative model as the third decision making approach to interorganizational cooperation. This model provides, by means of a "constitution," that the participants will elect representatives for making the actual decisions, that they delegate their right to determine the conditions of mutual cooperation. The need for representation arises, of course, when

348

the participants are very numerous. The participants also agree that they will submit to their representatives' decisions, whose authority is also defined in the charter. If many representatives are involved, majority rule may be utilized. For example, a certain group may organize a trade association to prevent the passage of harmful legislation or to encourage the passage of favorable legislation, and it will draw up a constitution that states the manner in which its representatives are to be elected, the minimal obligations of the membership, and the limitations on the authority of the representatives.

The representative model is advantageous insofar as it provides for collective action and simultaneous single choice by a large number of people. It also enables individual selection of representatives and thus maintains a measure of individual self-interest within the group.

Some limitations of this approach, however, are that choices may be restricted to alternatives selected entirely by the representatives, that the membership does not participate in making substantive decisions, and that individuals cannot determine the conditions under which they will cooperate. At the very minimum, a two-party system is necessary for giving the voters at least two alternatives to choose from. A corporation, for example, is legally a representative decision making form: individuals are elected to a board of directors to represent the economic interests of the stockholders and to administer the corporation. However, in most cases only one slate of officers is submitted to the stockholders, so that a truly meaningful or formal choice is precluded. And, whatever its form, another disadvantage of the representative system is the danger—if the majority-rule mechanism is used—that minority and individual interests will be disregarded.

Furthermore, as these organizations become larger and undertake more activities, the representatives may establish administrative agencies for performing some of their activities. This delegation of authority can lead to a further dilution of the participants' control of the total operation; and this is particularly true if administrative agencies are established along bureaucratic lines. There is then the possibility that the representative form will in turn take on bureaucratic characteristics with the actual decision making devolving to a relatively small group of administrators. An oligarchy might eventually evolve if these agencies become divorced from the organizational participants and begin to assume an existence of their own, striving to satisfy their own administrative ends rather than the welfare of the membership. Thus the representative system of decision making can break down between the voter and his representative, between the representative and the administrative official, and between the administrative official and the agency worker.

This development, in fact, seems to be exemplified in many corporations: stockholders elect boards of directors, who in turn delegate the stockholders' authority to administrative officials or management. Because of the complexity of the organization and the bureaucratic form that is most frequently used, these administrative officers have acquired a large degree of organizational autonomy, and it is questionable whether in exercising their authority they actually make decisions that only or primarily reflect the economic interests of the stockholders. No doubt there are areas in government where this same phenomenon occurs, where there is no longer a connection or relationship between the actual decision-makers and the individuals they "decide for."

Another shortcoming of the representative form relates to numbers. As the number of voters increases, the significance of each vote tends to decrease. In the political sphere, except for very close elections, many people feel that their ballots carry little weight. Moreover, with the sprawl of urbanization and its proliferation of small suburban communities, voters must consider two alternatives: the greater efficiency of large political units or the greater individual control over small political units. It may well be that individuals prefer to tolerate inefficiencies if they can exercise greater control.

We can see from the above that the best decision making mechanism for interorganizational cooperation will depend upon many and various conditions — on the advantages and disadvantages of the mechanism itself and on the objectives of the cooperative effort — and that an intermixture of forms can be employed. It still remains to be said, however, that planned decision making, under proper circumstances, can provide benefits which the present forms do not. In some circumstances, both the representative and the negotiating models could be significantly improved if more explicit planned procedures were introduced. Let us look at the collective bargaining relationship and see how, through increased planning, improvements could be made.

REDESIGNING THE COLLECTIVE BARGAINING DECISION MAKING PROCESS

As presently conducted, the collective bargaining process is an intermixture of the bargaining, bureaucratic, and representative

350

forms. Management, one of the negotiating parties, is structured on the bureaucratic process, and the union is structured on representative lines. The nature of the relationship is structured upon bargaining.

The manner in which decisions are reached can be described rather briefly. At the expiration of a labor contract, a union has formulated its demands and submits them to management. These demands relate to improvements which the union would like to see incorporated into the new labor agreement: increased wages, reduced hours of work, greater fringe benefits, and various restrictions on management's control over changes in work processes and job content. If the parties are unable to agree, the union may call a strike in an effort to force an agreement.

But, after a union contract is signed, many of its provisions may be effectuated through a grievance procedure (usually part of every labor agreement), and this procedure — from a decision making point of view — can be thought of as another form of the audit because it can be used to establish whether or not the agreement is being properly effectuated. A union employee can then raise a grievance if he believes that his rights, as expressed in the agreement, have been violated. The grievance may eventually be resolved by a neutral third party, an arbitrator, who has been granted authority by the parties to render a final and binding decision.

However, the only steps in the management-union bargaining process which the parties have seriously considered are the consensus and audit steps. Therefore, because the parties have not planned the other phases of the process, the collective bargaining process suffers from many of the defects that are found in the bureaucratic system. If the parties had planned a total procedure for solving their mutual problems, significant benefits would accrue and many of the disadvantages in the present collective bargaining relationship would be minimized or, perhaps, eliminated.

PLANNED DECISION MAKING
IN THE COLLECTIVE BARGAINING PROCESS

A brief examination of the feasibility of planned decision making in the collective bargaining process should help us better understand the adaptive potential of the planned system. Initially, both management and union officials must define their mutual organizational objectives when they plan their decision making process, and of course both parties have the same economic

351

objective: an increased aggregate return to the factors of production. For management, this means increased profits per unit of capital invested; for labor, an increased return in wages and salary per unit of labor worked.

Figure 13–3 depicts the decision making process as it relates to collective bargaining. As part of the sensory apparatus, all management officials, union officials, and employees would be able to raise problems, which would be submitted to the control unit and handled in the regular manner; that is, they would be assigned to management officials who would search for the best organizational solutions. Once a solution was formulated, the consensus step would clear the solution not only to all of the management officials but also to all of the union officials, and ultimately to all of the employees. The union officials would be permitted to review the proposed solution, and union and management officials would then have to agree on how the increased payoff would be distributed among the factors of production — or perhaps a permanent formula would have been negotiated, as in the Scanlon Plan.

The Scanlon Plan provides that labor's return for increased organizational productivity will equal its percentage of the total production cost. (If — at the time the Scanlon Plan was introduced — labor costs were 30 per cent of the total production costs, labor would receive 30 per cent of the value of any increased productive efficiency.) Or the parties may decide to negotiate the distribution on a decision by decision basis if, in the formulation of a solution, a very precise accounting can be made of the factors which provide the major contributions to increased efficiency. For example, if a large capital investment is required to effectuate a solution but only minor contributions are made in the job content, capital would receive the major portion of the value that was derived from such a solution.

If the consensus step is stalemated, with the parties unable to reach an agreement after repeated attempts, they could provide that a neutral third party, or arbitrator, would make the final decision. If considerable risk were involved in a solution, the arbitrator's authority could be restricted or conditioned in terms of the solution's cost or consequences. For example, proposals that involved an initial investment of more than $1 million or a layoff of 5 per cent of the work force would be ruled outside the arbitrator's authority.

The area of agreement could of course also be limited to solutions that clearly affect both factors of production: if management wants to invest its funds in government bonds, no union agree-

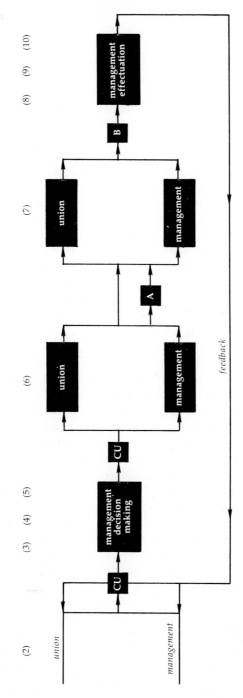

Figure 13–3

PROPOSED DECISION MAKING SYSTEM FOR THE
COLLECTIVE BARGAINING PROCESS

(2)   (3)   (4)   (5)   (6)   (7)   (8) (9) (10)

union

management

management
decision
making

CU

union

management

A

union

management

B

management
effectuation

feedback

KEY:–CU:
Control Unit;
A: Arbitrator;
B: Budget.

353

ment would be needed; or if the union wants to raise membership dues, management need not agree.

Solutions can have negative as well as positive consequences for the parties, affecting labor by necessitating changes in job content, transfers, and even layoffs, and affecting stockholders by financial loss. However, portions of the increases in payoff can be funded to meet negative consequences in much the same way that management sets aside funds for depreciation, contingencies, and surplus. Labor's reserve or depreciation fund could be spent for pensions, severance pay, and retraining programs: the severance fund would help ensure better between-job subsistence; the pension fund would provide for eventual retirement; and the retraining programs would help labor maintain its technological proficiency. A labor contingency reserve could also be set aside for unpredictable risks, such as a short-term layoff. Surplus funds — after withdrawals for any adverse results of solutions — could be expended for increased employee benefits.

The clearing of solutions to the employees could be accomplished jointly by management and union officials. Management would presumably hold meetings for explaining solutions to the affected employees, and union officials (even though they would already have been fully informed of all details of the solutions) could be present at that time. Also, union officials could explain proposed organizational changes at union meetings, where, if any official believed a proposal was unfeasible, or extremely risky, he could object to it (in the same way as other management officials) and ask for a consensus meeting; or he could participate in meetings that would be arranged with management officials. In such a context, the union officials would clearly be a part of the total administrative decision making staff.

The two parties should thus be able to work out any problem that affects the distribution of benefits, particularly if the solutions will provide a net organizational payoff. There is also every reason for believing that union officials would not oppose solutions suggested by management — or be negative participants in the consensus step — if solutions would clearly benefit the employee sector of an organization. If they *were* to act so irresponsibly, they could reasonably be expected to be replaced.

After a solution is accepted it would be sent to the union and management officials who have, or have been delegated, the authority to approve them. The solution would then be implemented and directed by management; and, in the auditing step, both the union and the management officials would receive reports on the organizational results. If these results were objec-

354

tionable, to either the union or to management, a problem could be raised and the solution would be reconstructed so as to produce improved organizational results.

Let us now visualize two levels of decision making for planning the collective bargaining procedure. The first level would be top management (the top officials of both the union and the management), which would design, institute, maintain, operate, and audit the interorganizational decision machinery. (This machinery, which could be incorporated into the labor agreement, would be essentially procedural in that it would stipulate how decisions should be made. Moreover, the parties would always be able to renegotiate the basic system in order to achieve a design that would maximize organizational payoff—upon the same criteria used in selecting an intraorganizational design [see Chapter 9].)

The second level of decision making would be comparable to submanagement, and it would relate to the *actual* construction of new solutions, the work to be performed, wages, hours, etc. (These issues would be solved on a solution by solution basis, which would make collective bargaining a continuous process.)

If the operation of all the decision making steps are planned, greater advantages should accrue to both parties. When the parties define their mutual economic objectives, they emphasize their common interests rather than their differences. When union officials are able to raise problems, the union has an additional apparatus for handling employee problems, particularly in terms of the environment external to the collective bargaining relationship. Currently, however, union officials can raise problems only in the form of demands upon management. (An important distinction should be noted here: raising a problem implies that a search will be made for a solution; a demand implies that a solution has already been found.) A planned process should decrease the number of union demands as steps 3, 4, and 5 continually search for optimal solutions to all problems that have been raised.

The parties now have no assurance that the agreements they have reached are optimum. For example, of twenty possible alternatives, union and management might agree upon ten, and it is probable that one of the ten solutions will render a greater payoff than the other nine; yet the search for only *one* agreeable solution may result in choosing an alternative that will *minimize* payoff. The planned approach would provide not only for a mutually agreeable solution but for that solution which promises the greatest benefit for both parties. This approach also induces

355

labor to discover and use its most productive applications and thereby increase its return. Management, under the present system, is mainly concerned with the optimal use of capital.

Another advantage of the planned approach is that the consensus or agreement step permits simultaneous consideration of the contributions and the returns—those of labor and those of capital—in terms of increasing the welfare of both groups. In the present form of collective bargaining, each party submits its demands to the other and then each separately considers these demands—both in a rather isolated and narrowly selfish context. If the parties are unable to agree, the union can strike and the employer can discharge the workers in question.

There are several consequences for both parties when their demands are considered separately, but, fundamentally, the result is an irrational bargaining process. Although the function of an economic bargain is the determination of the economic value of a product or service, the exact mutual obligations and considerations of the bargaining parties must also be assessed for establishing the value of that which is being exchanged; and the parties must weigh these mutual considerations against their obligations. The only rational way to determine the wage of labor is by ascertaining the value of its contribution; similarly, the only way to determine whether management is receiving an appropriate return is by comparing wages with the labor services contributed.

In almost any bargaining situation in which either party wants to alter the terms of exchange, demands for increased returns are usually coupled with the understanding that increased output will be rendered. If an automobile dealer seeks a higher than average price for his product, he must offer the buyer special items of value, such as an air-conditioner, a radio, or the like; on the other hand, if the buyer wants to pay a lower price, he must forgo these items. It is this adjustment of obligations and considerations that enables the bargainers to arrive at a mutually agreeable solution. (However, if the mutual demands are unrelated, there are no certain criteria for judging whether a set of demands is justifiable.)

The mutual or respective separation of union and management demands, we must also note, tends to encourage union and management irresponsibility. When a union merely stipulates demands, it does not assume responsibility for increasing (or even for producing) the value of its products or services, and therefore its demands need not recognize the conditions or necessities of the actual situation. Management acts or reacts in the same manner, pressing unrealistic demands on the employees because it does not intend to grant additional compensation.

However, the most serious consequence of separate demands is that the parties must use economic coercion rather than economic reason for achieving agreement. The union threatens to strike or the employer threatens to fire if their demands are not met, which is clearly a wasteful and conflictual approach. Although economic force is usually available to all bargainers (a housewife could boycott or even picket a store that has put exorbitant prices on its products), this approach is not usually productive. One advantage of a planned system is that it can, and must, treat all of the bargaining aspects simultaneously and reasonably. A solution that would increase labor's productivity must at the same time consider the increased return as the result of labor's added productivity. Rather than rely upon economic force, both parties should search for the true economic value of the labor factors.

As for the implementation step, management frequently has difficulty in introducing operational changes because of union opposition; however, if the union had participated in the decision making process, it would have to encourage such changes. Continuous conflict, moreover, can introduce restrictive features into organizational operations that may prevent effective adjustments to external environmental changes, adjustments which are necessary for maintaining and increasing the welfare of both labor and capital. Finally, the inability to audit solutions systematically can result in labor's being subjected to poor management decisions, which could reduce total labor welfare.

In summary, then, planned collective bargaining would substantially reduce the conflict and controversy that currently take place; it is a real alternative to the strike-and/or-discharge techniques for maintaining management-union cooperation; its emphasis is on mutual interests and not on differences. It is a rational process, and a process that discounts extraneous determinants (such as personality or status) as decision making factors. It enables effective participation of unions and employees in the decision making process while it maintains effective techniques for achieving operational decisions. Most importantly, planned decision making in collective bargaining can significantly increase the individual's economic return—whether stockholder or employee—not only by removing the drawbacks which now exist but by serving as a positive and constructive alternative.

357

SUMMARY

The design of an interorganizational decision making system should consider: (1) conditions under which cooperation would be mutually advantageous; (2) problems that top managements may face in designing such a system; (3) the design process itself; (4) the system's applications; and (5) the unique advantages of planned interorganizational decision making.

Traditionally, three models have been used for obtaining interorganizational cooperation: (1) the bureaucratic, (2) the exchange, and (3) the representative. Each model has certain advantages and limitations, but planned decision making, a fourth alternative, can provide perhaps greater advantages and significantly reduce the limitations.

QUESTIONS FOR DISCUSSION

1. Is the design of interorganizational decision making systems a less-developed art than the design of intraorganizational systems? Explain. Do you believe that designing interorganizational systems will become more, or less, important in the future? Explain.
2. Under what conditions is interorganizational cooperation advantageous?
3. Are interpersonal relations—on an individual or a group basis— usually of only one nature, or are they an intermixture of cooperative, competitive, and conflictual factors? How would you evaluate the family?
4. What factors determine the admixture of cooperation and competition in a relationship, and does competition lead inevitably to conflict? In the marketplace? In foreign relations?
5. Why is the design of the consensus step more important in an interorganizational context than in an intraorganizational setting?
6. Review the hypothetical unit C, the product development unit, and redesign the schematic (Figure 13–1) to add additional autonomous units to the two-parent organization.
7. Develop a community decision making schematic for achieving effective racial integration.
8. Assuming that the collective bargaining relationship could be effectively redesigned, do you believe that union and management officials might favor this, or might disapprove?
9. What control measures do you think should be applied to administrative governmental agencies to assure the execution of the goals of Congress and the President?
10. In terms of decision making models, why should the initiation of government regulation of economic activities be approached cautiously? What two decision making systems are involved?

SUGGESTED READINGS

BARNARD, CHESTER I. *Organization and Management.* Cambridge, Mass.: Harvard University Press, 1948.

CYERT, RICHARD, and MARCH, JAMES G. *Behavioral Theory of the Firm.* Englewood Cliffs, N.J.: Prentice-Hall, Inc., 1963.

DAHL, ROBERT A., and LINDBLOM, CHARLES E. *Politics, Economics and Welfare.* New York: Harper & Row, 1953.

MARCH, JAMES G., and SIMON, HERBERT A. *Organizations.* New York: John Wiley & Sons, Inc., 1958.

SNOW, C. P. *The Two Cultures and the Scientific Revolution.* London: Cambridge University Press, 1959.

WOODHAM-SMITH, CECIL. *The Great Hunger.* New York: Harper & Row, 1963.

14

INDIVIDUALISM WITHIN THE ORGANIZATION

One criticism that may be made of a planned decision making system is that it might reduce or even eliminate the middle manager's individualism and organizational freedom, especially since, in the bureaucratic setting, he is frequently viewed as a self-directing person who exercises considerable personal initiative and discretion. His role is often believed to be one of self-actualization and expression—in its most idealistic interpretation, that of "the captain of his ship." Therefore, as we say, there may be apprehension that a planned system would adversely affect these desirable attributes.

Although the middle manager's job content, under a planned model, would still differ from that of other employees', his job would nevertheless be formulated along "employee" lines. Just as the middle manager plans, directs, and controls the work of the employee, his own work would be similarly planned, directed, and controlled. The middle manager, under a planned decision making system, would be treated as any other employee. He would no longer be free to administer organizational units in any manner he personally deems best.

But even if the organizational payoff is greater under the planned approach, will it really be worthwhile for the middle manager to change from the bureaucratic to the planned system if, in this process, he loses his organizational individualism? This chapter will demonstrate that the traditional image of the middle manager as an economic individualist is a delusion and that, instead of lessening the manager's "autonomy," planned decision making will enlarge and justify it.

THE MIDDLE MANAGER MISCONCEIVED
AS AN ENTREPRENEUR

The popular image of the middle manager as an economic individualist, as we have suggested, warrants close examination. In
the bureaucratic conception the submanager's role often is conceived to have characteristics that are almost identical with those
of the entrepreneur, and, on the surface, this belief seems to have
merit. The stockholders or owners of an enterprise in fact delegate a portion of their property rights, through the board of
directors and top management, to the middle manager, and the
middle manager would therefore seem to perform an entrepreneurial or ownership function in the enterprise.

But the real entrepreneur is, first of all, self-employed; and an
excellent example is the farmer who owns and controls his land.
A farmer cannot be arbitrarily deprived of the land he owns,
but he can sell it or even give it away. All feasible decisions for
its use are his alone, but we can assume his decisions will be
toward maximizing his profits from its ownership. We can also
assume that this maximization will be more probable if he increases his output and reduces his costs. And if he concentrates
upon his tasks, uses good judgment, makes cautious expenditures, weighs alternatives judiciously, and invests his money in
his farm, he will probably be able to acquire more land and
further increase his profit. On the other hand, if he is lazy, care-
less, or extravagant, he can lose his property.

Now to turn back to our middle manager. We have implied
that if certain assumptions are made in structuring his organizational prerogatives in a bureaucracy, his role can be thought of as
entrepreneurial: if his authority is clearly defined and fixed in a
specific organizational area, his position would seem to be comparable to that of the farmer who possesses defined and permanent property rights. Therefore, once such a manager has been
assigned a unit, no change would ordinarily be made in its size
or functions without his consent; and his delegated authority
would mean that only he can make the decisions which govern
its operation; nor (ideally) would his superiors, colleagues, or
subordinate managers interfere in his administration of this area.
There would seem to be no company policies or procedures that
would prevent his deciding upon actions that might improve or
maximize his unit's payoff.

The manager has also been granted the right to enter into
contracts for the purchase or sale of organizational property
which, in his judgment, will lead to unit profits. He exercises full

361

control over the resources connected with his unit; and he can hire, direct, reward, and discharge his employees. As a pseudo-entrepreneur, the middle manager is willing to accept the risk in his decisions, for top management will reward and punish him solely on the basis of his unit's results. If his unit meets its objectives, he will be rewarded with a promotion or bonus; if his unit's results are negative, he will be penalized by the loss of certain benefits (or by the loss of his job).

It follows from these assumptions that the successful middle manager should enjoy all the economic benefits of an entrepreneur. He will have a large measure of personal economic freedom; no person or group will direct his economic activities; he will be economically self-directing and self-determining; and free to decide, direct, and correct the actions of those who are part of his unit. He seems to be almost self-employed, and able to build or develop his unit along whatever lines he chooses, advancing in prestige and recognition. Part of the American Credo, as it related to the economic development of our country, was that great significance and importance attached to the entrepreneurs who "built" this country — who built the railroads, the steel mills, the automobile plants — and we see that the successful modern manager also partakes of this in the form of community esteem.

The middle manager also partakes of another entrepreneurial quality: the economic power to dominate or direct economic resources in terms of his personal judgment; he is "the boss." There is also a more subtle status differential between a manager and an employee that requires or expects employees to exhibit a certain measure of respect toward their managers — in addition to following their instructions. Finally, the fact that employees can be discharged for various reasons — including insubordination — makes a manager appear more than ever like an entrepreneur.

Along with a high salary and job security, then, the middle manager's role frequently is assumed to include the traditional values and benefits of the entrepreneur: economic freedom, independence, self-direction and self-development, individualism, power, status, and recognition.

A COMPARISON OF THE ENTREPRENEURIAL AND MIDDLE MANAGEMENT ROLES

The belief that planned decision making would diminish the organizational individualism of the middle manager therefore rests on two suppositions: (1) that the manager achieves an

362

entrepreneurial role through the delegation of property rights and (2) that his authority in the bureaucratic structure is actually allocated in the manner described above. But all that can be said of these suppositions is that they are as idealistic as they are unfounded. How, then, is the role of the middle manager really established, and how does it compare with the role of the true entrepreneur?

We must begin this answer by saying that the authority of the entrepreneur and the authority of the middle manager are not at all alike. The former authority is defined in ownership rights which are established through the purchase of property; the latter authority is defined by one's superiors and is merely delegated. The middle manager is not an owner of property; but the property rights of the entrepreneur are fixed, and, unless changed by legislation or the courts, they are absolute and permanent. The authority rights of the middle manager are conditional and can be changed by his superiors at any time and for any reason, or he may be delegated only the most limited authority because his superiors may intend to make all the decisions. Unlike the self-employed role, in which certain rights inhere, no real or enforceable rights inhere in the middle management role. (A group of middle managers—who are categorized as "staff personnel"—can only advise; they have no authority at all, and are found in the personnel, engineering, accounting, finance, systems, operations research, legal, and market research departments.)

The entrepreneur's rights are relatively clear and are defined by law; but the authority rights of the middle manager tend to be ambiguous, not only because they are often changed but primarily because the delegation device is usually not completely clear in just what rights it has allocated. The entrepreneur, again, has no superior and he exercises sole jurisdiction over his operation, but the middle manager is subject to all instructions from his superiors. Higher management, on its own initiative, can intervene in any activity at any time and not violate the rights of its submanagers; but one entrepreneur cannot so impose upon another entrepreneur without violating his property rights and incurring legal liability.

Further, the middle manager is usually vitally concerned with the activities of his colleagues, but the operation of the entrepreneur is independent of other producers. The middle manager must be aware of the activities outside his area of jurisdiction in order to integrate his operations with those of the rest of the firm, and it is (in part) this interdependent aspect of organizational activity that makes his authority ambiguous and contingent. If top management believes the coordination of the activities of two or more departments is a problem, it can intervene and provide a solution, which again curtails the authority of each submanager.

In this matter of the interdependent process, Leonard Sayles quotes a successful manager as saying:

My people get directed (as to what they should be doing) on the basis of pressures: pressures from people doing work for them and for whom they are working and from whom they must get certain approvals. These pressures determine the priorities in a manager's job; they direct his attention; they even force his attention. You see we live on the basis of communication—a man's ability to keep in touch with all the parts of the organization that can affect him.

I have a terrible time trying to explain what I do to my wife. She thinks of a manager in terms of someone who has authority over those people who work for him and who in turn get his job done for him.

You know she thinks of those nice neat organization charts too. She also expects that when I get promoted, I'll have more people working for me.

Now all of this is unrealistic. Actually I have only eighteen people directly reporting to me. These are the only ones I can give orders to. But I have to rely directly on the services of seventy-five or eighty other people in the organization if my work is going to get done. They, in turn, are affected by perhaps several hundred others—and I must sometimes see some of them too—when my work is being held up.

So I am always seeing these people—trying to get their cooperation, trying to deal with delays, work out compromises on specifications. Again when I try to explain this to my wife, she thinks that all I do all day is argue and fight with people.

Although I am an engineer trained to do technical work I really don't have to understand much about the technical work going on here.

What I have to understand is:

1. How the organization works—how to get things through the organization (and this is always changing, of course) and

2. How to spot trouble—how to know when things aren't going well.[1]

[1] Leonard R. Sayles, *Individualism and Big Business* (New York: McGraw-Hill Book Company, 1963), p. 24. Copyright © 1963, and used by permission of McGraw-Hill Book Company.

Staff officials will often provide the middle manager with advice and counseling in many aspects of his operation. Although the middle manager does not always have to accept all of this advice, he must always give it serious consideration because the staff can appeal his refusal to a higher company official. Staff managers are therefore another intervening force in a manager's operations.

It is apparent, then, that the direction a middle manager can exercise over an organizational activity is highly problematical, often depending upon the activities of other managers, his superiors, and the staff officials; it is also apparent that the middle manager does not have the entrepreneur's individual and independent control. He has no unlimited right to purchase and sell, being restricted by item and price, and the approval of his superiors is necessary before significant purchases can be made. Nor does the manager really have sole control over his employees: higher approval is usually required before employees can be hired, rewarded, or discharged. Finally, the decisions a submanager makes must be within the constraints of the organizational policies and procedures, which further narrows his prerogatives and his exercise of discretion. Often, indeed, the middle manager is considered to have no decision making authority at all, merely interpreting the policies made by top managers, who are viewed as the only true decision making segment of the organization.

The middle manager's operation is generally under continual review by his superiors, and the performance data of his unit are regularly forwarded to higher management—which is a form of indirect control. Moreover, because computers can almost instantaneously classify and evaluate great quantities of data, top management can take a rather active part in administering subunits. Authority, in fact, is becoming increasingly *recentralized*,[2] so that much of the authority the middle manager once had is now being withdrawn. Top management may also demand that submanagers keep it informed of their plans, or clear all major decisions, thereby retaining full veto power.

However, the legal difference between the entrepreneur and the middle manager is perhaps the most significant. The entrepreneur is the legal owner of the enterprise that provides his income; the middle manager is legally an employee, an agent of the owner, who has been hired to work for a salary and who can be discharged. To the entrepreneur accrue all the legal rights of an owner, to the middle manager all the legal rights of an em-

[2] Gilbert Burck, "Management Will Never Be the Same Again," *Fortune* (August, 1964), p. 199.

ployee. Although the middle manager may have been delegated the right to exercise a part of the entrepreneurial function, this does not change his legal status as an employee. Insofar as any employee (manager or nonmanager) is assigned the duty of utilizing the owner's property, he is, legally, only an agent of the principal.

The middle manager is an employee who is economically dependent on higher management, which will decide his economic welfare as long as he remains in the organization; and, in the bureaucratic setting, the top manager determines the middle manager's duties, the rewards he will receive, and so on. Although the duties of the middle manager are different from those of the employee, his treatment or relative position is not significantly different. He, too, must be responsive to top management. Walter Guzzardi has observed:

> To determine how to conduct himself when it comes to direct dealings with the boss summons up every ounce of the young man's managerial judgment. One man says he will always have trouble deciding "how hard to fight, how much to rein in emotion. Sometimes your boss expects you to talk back. When he says, 'Stop, I've had enough,' should you really stop? Or does he expect you to bring it up again?" For this man there is no formula: he weighs each situation on its own merits, deciding "how hard to fight" in accordance with the depth of his own conviction. Nor, looking back, is he always sure he was right.
>
> . . . In the formal relationships with his superiors that fall outside of the detailed discussion of business problems, the young executive must often pay proper respect to ceremony. If he is based in the provinces, he spends more time than he likes in meeting airplanes and attending social affairs. He entertains company brass a good deal, and the weight of protocol can become heavy and tedious. Especially in smaller towns and cities, where he is usually only a transient, he is often involved in some aspects of community life that may not interest him very much.[3]

Thus the role of the middle manager and that of the entrepreneur are really quite dissimilar. Legal and economic determinants require a large measure of organizational conformity by the middle manager. In order to avoid discharge and to maintain his job security, he must carefully follow top management's instructions.

There is little doubt that abuses occur in the relationships

[3] Walter Guzzardi, Jr., "Man and Corporation," *Fortune* (July, 1964), pp. 202, 204. Courtesy of *Fortune* magazine.

between superior and subordinate or higher and lower management. Higher management can make almost any demands it desires, interfere in the middle manager's job at almost any time, and withdraw whatever managerial authority it chooses. Under the bureaucratic system, responsibility and authority are rarely equal, and the middle manager may be held responsible for results that he did not effect or change. Because superiors are clearly able to grant rewards or to mete out punishment on a personal basis, discrimination, favoritism, and servile dependence upon the favor of higher management can easily result.

An additional factor that adversely affects the middle manager's "autonomy" is the politics of organizational life, or the competition that often exists among middle managers for the superior's favor. As one manager observed: "The politicians always want to be the ones the boss talks to. Each falls all over himself trying to show how important he or his department is in making profits."

Our earlier assertion that the nature of the middle managerial role is essentially that of an employee is supported by many observations, and at least two reliable studies suggest that the middle manager is really a conformist rather than an individualist. William Whyte notes that the individualistic mythology is too removed from the reality of everyday life. To make a living, one must do what others tell him to do. The traditional concepts of the Protestant Ethic, such as thrift, hard work, and self-reliance, no longer apply in the organization. "Most [middle managers] see themselves as objects more acted upon than acting — and their future, therefore, determined as much by the system as by themselves."[4]

David Riesman has also commented on the conformity of the middle manager and on his "other-directedness":

> [He is] psychologically dependent on others for clues to the meaning of life. He thus fails to resist authority or fears to exercise freedom of choice even where he might safely do so.
> . . . [W]ork is seen as a network of personal relationships that must be constantly watched and oiled. Increasingly, both work and leisure call on the same sort of skills — sociability, sensitivity to others' feelings and wants, and the exercise of taste-preferences freed from direct considerations of economic advantage.[5]

[4] William H. Whyte, Jr., *The Organization Man* (New York: Simon and Schuster, Inc., 1956), pp. 5, 17, and 395.
[5] David Riesman, *Individualism Reconsidered* (New York: Free Press of Glencoe, Inc., 1954), pp. 106, 110.

Although the organizational chart may formally designate specific authorities and responsibilities for the middle manager, because he is economically dependent on higher management he may never exercise his full, granted authority but may defer to his superior's attitudes, prejudices, or informal directions in order to maintain his economic welfare. The freedom to exercise organizational authority is meaningless if one's job is thereby jeopardized.

THE BUREAUCRATIC IMAGE OF THE MIDDLE MANAGER

The fact that the middle manager does not actually behave in a manner consistent with his entrepreneurial image is not surprising when the bureaucratic structure is viewed more closely. It is not the intent of the bureaucratic form to create and maintain the economic individualism of the middle manager. On the contrary, insofar as the middle manager has been delegated decision making discretion, it has been done only in the belief that this will increase organizational objectives, or profits. If top management could formulate an alternative approach (such as the computer or planned decision making) that would increase profits and yet not specify this form of delegation, it would readily accept such an alternative.

In the traditional bureaucratic view, exemplified in the military, the church, and governmental agencies, there is little support for a belief that the middle managerial image is that of the individualist; the ideal image is rather that of the team player, subservient to a greater good and highly disciplined. Top management lays down the broad policies and procedures for the organization, and the middle manager interprets and executes them in the manner that top management desires. The submanager is not to act independently because such action would jeopardize more important plans. For example, top military officials cannot permit regimental or company commanders to use their forces as they see fit, and the military's image of the middle manager is therefore one of obedience and strict conformity to the rules and regulations.

Eugene Schneider has considered the bureaucracy from a normative viewpoint. He notes that:

> [I]ndustry finds in bureaucracy a means for creating and maintaining a continuous and rigid discipline over its personnel at all levels. The need of industry for the coordination of many diverse tasks . . . demand[s] a close supervision of work, a

rigid obedience to rules, and the suppression of many natural human impulses.

[B]oth worker and official are economically dependent on the bureaucracy, and consequently are necessarily submissive to the demands of the organization.[6]

The belief, therefore, that the middle manager exercises an entrepreneurial role in the bureaucratic structure is almost entirely a myth, and the concept of the "self-employed" middle manager is an unrealized ideal, a normative concept. Organizationally, legally, and economically the middle manager is an employee.

INDIVIDUAL AUTONOMY OF MIDDLE MANAGEMENT AS A FAULTY ORGANIZATIONAL OBJECTIVE

If it *were* possible to structure the bureaucratic organization so as to provide more autonomy for the middle manager, it would probably be fashioned in the manner described earlier in this chapter (pp. 361–362): authority would be decentralized; there would be no interference with the middle manager's administration of his unit; etc. However, the feasibility of such a structure is highly questionable, and, because there could be no machinery for coordinating the operations, it is doubtful that such an organization could long remain operative; it would be as if there was not just one organization but as many organizations as there were middle managers. Each subunit would proceed alone, with an apparent lack of concern for the other units; sales managers might be selling products that production managers did not have in supply; and so on. Such an arrangement would quickly falsify the principle that an organization is a system of cooperative action. Leonard Sayles emphasizes that we must be realistic:

Contemporary fiction, sermons, and social science have become enamored of their moans over the fate of the individual in the large organization. Unfortunately, the eagerness with which the term "organization man" has been adopted has resulted in substantial confusion, a good portion of which stems from its original promulgation. The essence of organization, of organizational behavior, involves learning to follow routine procedures. Of necessity the organization must be a predictable system of human relationships, where rhythm and repetition are

[6] Eugene V. Schneider, *Industrial Sociology* (New York: McGraw-Hill Book Company, 1957), p. 80. Copyright © 1957 by McGraw-Hill Book Company.

369

the vital components. This may come as a rude shock to those who think of managers as constantly improvising new activities. Chester Barnard once commented candidly that during a year as president of the New Jersey Bell Telephone Company he had to make only one decision that was, in fact, a real choice between alternatives. The preponderant elements of organizational behavior consist of matters such as Joe's knowing that he must check Bill's activities two or three times a week, must be available when Al gets into trouble, and must sit with his boss at least an hour a day to work through plans for the following day. The combination of work-flow imperatives and personality needs provides the raw material for these predictable and rhythmical patterns of interaction.

It must be remembered that in speaking of an organization we imply some degree of permanence — the need for predictable repetition, self-maintenance, assured continuity, and regulated activity. Only when the regular business of an organization is functioning properly — following the routines *of acquisition, processing, and distribution (of ideas, materials, or paper) — can individuals apply, or are they likely to be permitted to apply, their rational, creative talents to the challenge of new, unsolved problems. Imagination, innovation, and intellectual vigor cannot prosper where individual energies are fully utilized in handling recurring crises.*[7]

Not only, then, can the question of feasibility be raised, but also the more important question of objectives. Can the middle manager's personal desire for organizational autonomy and economic individualism be posited as the primary goal of an organization? The answer, of course, is in the negative. If we accept the assumption that the purpose of the organization is to increase the welfare of all organizational participants, the personal values of the middle manager cannot take precedence over those of all other participants. For example, if a personal goal of a middle manager were adversely to affect the profits a corporation could make, the stockholders would certainly be unwilling to minimize their potential profits so that one middle manager might be satisfied.

The middle manager is an agent of the owner and he is obligated to serve the ends of his principal; he cannot usurp them. Nor can top managers renounce the trust that stockholders placed in them in delegating control over all operations so that organizational objectives might be achieved. If employees were sub-

[7] Sayles, *op. cit.*, pp. 180–181.

jected to the economic individualism and autonomy of middle managers—who pursued these two objectives as separate goals—employees might also suffer a loss of extrinsic and intrinsic benefits. Obviously, these various groups would not forsake their interests to further those of the middle manager.

THE DILEMMA OF THE MIDDLE MANAGER

Although no one ever asked or expected the middle manager to assume the entrepreneurial role he so admires, and even though assumption of this role is totally unfeasible, the illusion has nevertheless persisted, and with unfortunate consequences. The dilemma of the middle manager is that his ideological aspirations are inconsistent with his circumstances: he is legally, economically, technologically, and socially an employee, yet he tends to regard himself as an entrepreneur.

Ideological determinants are beliefs and doctrines on how a role ought to be enacted or conducted and what rewards should attach to it. They are idealized images in the minds of individuals, and they are manifested in every sphere of society. Some people believe, for example, that there should be no governmental regulation of economic activity, or that equal political opportunities should exist for all, yet neither belief may be logically possible or attainable in any recognizable form.

For the most part, the middle manager continues to believe in the values of the Protestant Ethic. He believes that he is entitled to a measure of economic autonomy because he is a manager and because he adheres to the value of individualism, and, if he is not free (or not permitted) to behave as an entrepreneur, the organization should be restructured so that he can. He rejects his employee status. The conflict between one's real organizational role as an employee and his self-image as an entrepreneur is, unfortunately, irreconcilable; but one cannot—simultaneously—be both an employee and an entrepreneur.

Before the industrial revolution the values that attached to the entrepreneurial role were consistent with the realities of our nation's economy. Most of the economic population was self-employed, self-sufficient, and self-determining, and therefore independent. But the industrial revolution changed our agrarian society into a highly interdependent, organized, urbanized, "employeeistic" society, and a cultural lag resulted insofar as the traditional ideological values of the agrarian society changed more slowly than the form of our economy.

How does the middle manager resolve the conflict between

371

ideology and reality—between his desire to be an entrepreneur and the reality of his role as an employee? The conflict is essentially psychological, and four defense mechanisms are used, singly or in combination: (1) rejection, (2) projection, (3) sublimation, and (4) acceptance of reality.

In the first approach, rejection of reality, the middle manager assumes he is an entrepreneur and acts out this assumption in an appropriate imagery. Rather than view other managers, or superiors, or colleagues as individuals with whom he must cooperate, he regards them as constraints on the expression of his individuality and he resists "interference" by them. He maintains rigid jurisdictional lines, asserts that only he can make decisions that affect "his" operation, and continually inspects the organizational "boundaries" to be assured of their integrity.

The following case illustrates this mechanism in a manager's response to what he felt was an interference.

> *Late one afternoon this man found out that the amount of money that his division was to contribute to corporate research was being determined by the chief of the company's research organization. Not without a trace of grim pleasure, he says, "I blew my stack. I called a meeting that started at ten o'clock that night. At three in the morning I called the research chief, woke him up and told him, 'The hell with that research budget of yours. We're not going to put in a nickel.' The next morning the company president called me into his office. I held out my hand and said, 'Go ahead, rap my knuckles. But nobody can spend my division's money without my approval. If they can, then you can't hold me responsible for the p. and l.' He admitted I was right, but he said, 'You might have been a little more diplomatic with Peter.' I guess I might have—but I sure got results fast."*[8]

Through the use of this rejection mechanism the middle manager can ignore corporate procedures and policies and pursue his own lines of action. One submanager did this and later said:

> *We threw their [company headquarters] book of procedures out of the window. We didn't have time to explain and justify everything to St. Louis. . . . So on our own we spent $2 million, and we filled out the forms afterward. There was hell to pay at the time, but it worked. If it had gone sour, I would have been fired for sure.*[9]

[8] Guzzardi, *op. cit.*, pp. 202–204. Courtesy of *Fortune* magazine.
[9] Guzzardi, "At the Crucial Points of Decision," *Fortune* (September, 1964), pp. 162–163.

Or the manager can assume he is free to do anything he has not been explicitly forbidden to do. In those decision areas where it is not clear what the company policy is—or that there is a policy—rather than clear decisions with his superior the manager will proceed on his own, interpreting company instructions to mean he is permitted to use the maximum amount of personal discretion. In his relations with other managers this manager may insist on his point of view, may consistently refuse to accept the advice of staff officials, and may resent and resist all attempts to change his operation. His resentment might be expressed in the form of discourtesy, refusal to attend conferences (too busy), or weak enforcement of procedures originated by staff officials.

Individualism pursued without compromise will, in all likelihood, result in the loss of one's job. Because of this danger, the middle manager may also attempt to maintain his value system by projection, the second defense mechanism, which takes the form of a ritual. On one hand, the manager achieves a measure of organizational and economic success; on the other hand—under circumstances which will not adversely affect that success—he also maintains his self-image of rugged individualism without undue risk.

This is one of the traditional functions of ritual. When a set of values that has been incorporated in behavior as a consequence of change becomes inoperative, and when these values cannot be used without a significant reduction in personal benefits, individuals may seek to maintain them by acting them out in the form of play. Games, plays, literature, etc., often symbolize the entrepreneurial situation.

In one form of projected ritual, the novel, the individual can picture himself as the hero or as the leader of men. Moreover, on the *non*fictional level, many managerial readings portray the middle manager as if he is indeed an entrepreneur: he is told how to manage his employees, how to exercise good judgment, and how to take risks. Implicit in much of this literature is the concept that the middle manager is free to do whatever he pleases to maximize the profits of the organization. Although not explicitly stated, it would appear that the purpose of such literature is to perpetuate a set of highly personal values rather than to provide realistic guides for managerial behavior.[10] In addition, there has been a recent reaction against the concepts of human relations, employee participation, and committees; and some of these writers now proclaim that it is the strong, self-directed

[10] For a review of the function of managerial ideology, see Reinhard Bendix, *Work and Authority in Industry* (New York: John Wiley & Sons, Inc., 1956).

middle manager (by virtue of his wisdom, initiative, and aggressiveness) who makes, or will make, the organization successful.

Rituals are also performed in management associations and miscellaneous meetings: managers meet with their colleagues and relate incidents of their handling or direction of situations and operations. Thus, as a group, they reinforce their self-esteem. In their daily interactions they assume proprietary attitudes toward their operations. The middle manager may habitually talk about "his" department, division, employees, or building as if he actually possesses that area of the organization. He may oppose proposals, even though they are good for the company as a whole, because he feels "his" employees will find them unsatisfactory.

This mythology is also enacted in management conferences and training sessions. Management development programs frequently use a case approach in which middle managers role-play as if they are top managers: what would the top manager do under certain circumstances; what decisions would he make; how would he direct General Motors? The make-believe is even promoted in speeches by top officials of many organizations, who may allude to the desirability of individuals exercising freedom and initiative in their work. However, and significantly, it is somehow understood that this encouragement is not to be taken seriously.

Another form of projection is the transfer of the emotion caused by organizational constraints (which prevent the exercise of individual freedom) to an object that cannot "strike back." Caught in this self-induced conflict, the middle manager must suppress his hostility toward the constraints, and particularly his hostility for higher officials, but a scapegoat will help him rationalize his inadequacies. A favorite object is the government, and a disaffected manager can join political action groups which criticize government regulations, direction, control, and dominance, or communism, fascism, liberalism, etc. He can be "pro-freedom." The government or "the unions" can become a substitute for his organization, or "Washington" can take the place of the home office or his superiors. Suppressed aggression towards higher management, staff officials, or other "interferences" can be diverted by opposition to any of these straw men.

Projection is not a completely satisfactory device, however, because the basic conflict is always present and the organizational reality must be continually faced. The escape is only temporary.

The third defense mechanism for resolving the conflict between myth and reality is sublimation. If one cannot exercise individuality in his job, he can search out areas in which his unacceptable impulses can be expressed in socially acceptable forms. He can channel his drives toward his possessions: his yard, his car, his home, etc. His yard may be the "best" in the neighborhood, or his furniture may be highly individual. He can become a real "boss" in his church, or can purchase stock so that he can discuss the progress of "his" company. Finally, with increased leisure, he can pursue such hobbies as gardening, boating, fishing, or painting, in which he can express himself as freely as he desires.

The fourth approach to this dilemma is for the middle manager to accept the reality of his position: his employee status *and* his organizational environment. If he accepts the ideology of organizational adjustment, which William H. Whyte calls the "social ethos," he becomes an organization man. He will accept directions and will concentrate on the skills of "getting along"; he will become sensitive to the wishes of his superiors and the organization's managerial mores in dress, manners, and mode of speech. Thus the conflict between reality and ideology is apparently resolved by such an acceptance of reality, but there is the drawback that the manager must relinquish his individualism for a group-directed organizational ideology.

Individualism, in and of itself, is a desirable trait, but can it be preserved within an organization? We will subsequently see that planned decision making not only maintains the individuality of the middle manager but actually enhances it. Furthermore, a planned system will not permit the fiction that the middle manager has an entrepreneurial role in the organization, a belief which the bureaucratic structure fosters by allowing unrealistic defense devices to continue. The planned system brings the conflict between illusion and reality to the fore and compels the individual to understand the true nature of the conflict. The myth must be relinquished, although many may do so reluctantly.

MAINTENANCE OF THE ILLUSION

We may have been tempted to conclude that adjustment to organizational reality (the fourth reaction, above) is the sensible or proper solution on the basis that, ultimately, if the middle manager is to resolve his dilemma, he must simply accept the reality of his situation. Yet none of the four psychological mechanisms we have considered will satisfactorily resolve the conflict, and each can lead to negative side effects.

Because of the nature of the conflict, we may wonder why the middle manager would attempt to maintain—in reality or in myth—the ideology of economic individualism, and with such persistence. One reason, of course, relates to the inherent values in the entrepreneurial role, especially when they are contrasted with those in the employee role. The entrepreneur is recognized as being autonomous, self-sufficient, free, and self-determining; the employee as subordinate, dependent, directed, frequently immature and irresponsible. The middle manager therefore necessarily imitates the entrepreneur, as he necessarily rebels against the pressures that lead to dependency and immaturity. Furthermore, the entrepreneurial role represents a desirable ideal, a model that one can aspire to rather than expect to attain, and people require ideals and normative guides for behavior, which, after all, is ideology's role in society.

Conformity and dependency, we have said, are not acceptable alternatives to the ideology of individualism, and the manager tenaciously holds to his image of individuality because it represents a set of highly desirable values. Indeed, the person who wants to grow or to realize his potential will strive for independence. So the problem of creating an efficient or optimum organizational structure, which incorporates all of the most desirable values, remains; we have seen that the bureaucratic structure fails to create or incorporate this.

INDIVIDUALISM THROUGH PLANNING

Planned decision making can be looked upon, in some respects, as the "constitution" of an organization, guaranteeing those rights which are believed to be most important and making them part of every decision making process. Our analysis has shown that this can be done whenever values are consistent with or supplementary to the efficient operation of an organization.

Individual participation in the decision making process is provided by the clearance-feedback mechanism, which is a form of voting representation in the decisions being made. The mechanism also provides freedom of speech, permitting individuals to express their reasoned views upon proposed solutions. Individuals are also able to raise grievances through the problem-raising mechanism. Individual obligations extend to only those decisions which have been properly made, as defined by the decision process itself. Finally, the planned system need never be regarded as complete; it can, in fact, be continually redesigned and continually improved.

376

The decision making mechanism lends itself to the incorporation of due-process procedures that will protect the individual from an arbitrary loss of job or organizational benefits, and it can also provide that no discriminatory punishment will be applied. (The logical place for such a provision is the auditing step, where an independent organizational unit — comparable to the Inspector General's Office in the army — could be created to protect the rights of the individuals.)

In a planned decision making procedure, a measure of economic autonomy is possible for the middle manager in that he can exercise a proprietary attitude toward his assigned organizational problems. Fundamentally, he wants to make his own decision; moreover, if his solutions really have merit, they will be accepted and utilized in this planned procedure.

The middle manager does not enjoy comparable rights under the bureaucratic construct. He has little freedom of speech; and in company meetings and interpersonal relations with superiors he will be overly circumspect and guarded because candid expression could involve him in serious organizational difficulty. Real freedom, of course, cannot exist when an individual must be ever conscious of his behavior because of the fear that he will displease his superiors. He is frequently precluded from raising problems; "star chamber" devices often measure his contribution; he is usually unable to determine the reward or punishment criteria which affect his welfare; and he has no organizational machinery that will protect his rights and benefits.

No limits are placed on his obligations in the bureaucratic model: he may even (indirectly) be compelled to undertake duties in the political or social sphere which do not relate specifically to his job. Apart from the fact that he can quit his job, there is no satisfactory constraint on his superiors' exercise of organizational power. The bureaucratic system, in fact, gives rise to so many coercive abuses that it often becomes an organizational jungle,[11] devoid of a code of behavior. Because this system does not protect the individual from the abuses of power, it tends to produce timorous and ingratiating middle managers.

Individual freedom and autonomy can flourish only when the social process is orderly. Only when decision making procedures are explicit, when rights are defined and upheld, and when limitations are placed on the personal use of power can the individual be protected from managerial excesses, assert his organizational rights, and exercise individual autonomy.

[11] For more on this point, see Melville Dalton, *Men Who Manage: Fusions of Feeling and Theory in Administration* (New York: John Wiley & Sons, Inc., 1959).

The entrepreneur remains economically free because a set of laws works unremittingly to that end, but organizations that are ruled by men — as distinct from law — will always be abusive, and near-dictatorial power will be limited only by individual consciences. A basic advantage of planned decision making is that it *is* a system of laws or rules, a system that supplants the traditional "system" of arbitrary direction or abuse, that largely eliminates organizational power politics, and that necessarily assures the middle manager of his organizational rights. An additional advantage is that it provides — and requires — measurable performances in terms of the value of the decision output. Top managers cannot attempt to intimidate middle managers without obviously disrupting the decision making and the productive systems, which is the ultimate constraint on every exercise of organizational power.

Planned decision making encourages individualism because it first of all deals realistically with the nature of the organization and the nature and role of the middle manager, so that he need no longer rely on myth or empty ritual for preserving his individuality. It resolves the ideological conflict. In order to increase his welfare the middle manager must face the personal and organizational realities; if he perpetuates an unrealizable objective, he is much less able to develop techniques that will incorporate attainable goals into the decision process. Planned decision making will provide the manager with a more meaningful role that can lead to individual growth, and his new role — and image — will be analogous to that of the legislative lawmaker.

One can incorporate intrinsic benefits for organizational participants into the planned system, but, because the nature and purposes of organizations vary, their systems and their benefits can also vary. Organizations will have to experiment and redesign their decision making systems so that they appreciably increase individual net payoff and so that benefits are formulated in a manner that is consistent with total organizational payoff. As this study has attempted to illustrate, planned decision making is primarily a tool by which top management can discover, test, and revise organizational states that will provide increasingly greater welfare for all participants.

SUMMARY

The criticism that a planned decision making system might harmfully reduce organizational individualism is totally inaccurate. Indeed, the belief in this kind of individualism is posited on the mistaken assumption that the middle manager is an entrepreneur; in reality, however—legally and economically—he is only an employee.

The dilemma of the middle manager is based upon this misconception and confusion of roles, and his ideological aspirations are therefore inconsistent with his organizational circumstances. He attempts to resolve this conflict by (1) rejecting his organizational role, (2) projecting his value system, (3) sublimation, or (4) acceptance of reality. But it is only through a planned decision making system that the value of individualism can be incorporated into ongoing organizational activities.

QUESTIONS FOR DISCUSSION

1. Why do we like to believe that the middle manager is the "captain of his ship"?
2. It is sometimes asserted that employees (nondecision-makers) prefer routine, directed jobs and do not want to participate in the decision making process. Evaluate this assertion.
3. How—since the effective use of modern technology requires large, highly interdependent and tightly controlled systems of behavior—can the traditional values of economic individualism be maintained while these modern techniques are exploited?
4. What is the value of social images and rituals?
5. Give examples of the political ideology and its ritual.
6. How does the image of the middle manager in the economic organization differ from that of the middle manager in the military organization?
7. Why is law a basic component of individual freedom? Can freedom flourish in the absence of an orderly legal process? Explain.
8. Is it true that organizations ruled by men, as distinct from law, will always be abusive? Explain. Does power always corrupt? Explain.
9. Why are individuals reluctant to relinquish certain self-images even though they know they are false? Why do our self-perceptions tend to be more favorable than the perceptions others have of us?
10. The political formulation of national policies often introduces conflicts between ideological, economic, and technological determinants. Give examples of these conflicts and explain the differences between these determinants.

SUGGESTED READINGS

ARGYRIS, CHRIS. *Personality and Organization.* New York: Harper & Row, 1957.
DALTON, MELVILLE. *Men Who Manage: Fusions of Feeling and Theory in Administration.* New York: John Wiley & Sons, Inc., 1959.

HARRINGTON, ALAN. *Life in the Crystal Palace*. New York: Alfred A. Knopf, Inc., 1959.

MERTON, ROBERT K., *et al.* (eds.). *Reader in Bureaucracy*. New York: Free Press of Glencoe, Inc., 1952.

RIESMAN, DAVID. *Individualism Reconsidered*. New York: Free Press of Glencoe, Inc., 1954.

SAYLES, LEONARD R. *Individualism and Big Business*. New York: McGraw-Hill Book Company, 1963.

WHYTE, WILLIAM F. *Men at Work*. Homewood, Ill.: Richard D. Irwin, Inc., 1961.

WHYTE, WILLIAM H., JR. *The Organization Man*. New York: Simon and Schuster, Inc., 1956.

PART FIVE

EVALUATION
OF
THE BUREAUCRATIC
MODEL

15

REDESIGNING THE BUREAUCRATIC SYSTEM

Because most business, educational, political, welfare, or non-profit organizations follow the bureaucratic form of decision making, top management would have to modify this system significantly in order to increase its solution payoffs. On the basis of our analyses in the preceding chapters, we can now recognize or anticipate potential and existing management problems, we can suggest appropriate solutions, and we can also apply these concepts and techniques to an examination and redesign of the bureaucratic system.

The primary emphasis of this chapter will be upon problem recognition. Before top management can install an improved decision making machinery it must recognize the managerial shortcomings that exist in its organization and realize that they can be rectified. Too often, however, unacceptable managerial practices are endured either because they are not realized or because no solutions seem to be available (and this includes the attitude that gross managerial inefficiency is an inherent and necessary part of organized activity).

In all likelihood the redesign process will be problem-oriented: top management will work upon those segments of the decision making system that currently are the most inadequate. Before we consider these specific problem areas, however, we will review the characteristics of the bureaucratic model.

CHARACTERISTICS OF THE BUREAUCRATIC MODEL

Planning the formal organizational decision making process in the bureaucratic system—usually referred to as "organizational

382

planning"—is generally limited to stipulating the manner in which authority is to be exercised. The organization itself is divided into separate operating subunits that are classified along functional, product, or geographic lines. A manager or supervisor is appointed for each of these units and is delegated the right to determine how each unit will operate. The size of the unit to be managed, particularly in relation to the number of its members, is a crucial variable for determining the number of managers (the "span of control" problem). The authority of the organization is integrated by structuring positions of authority in a chain-of-command sequence: one manager may supervise the first line managers and in turn be supervised by a higher manager, until, at the apex, a chief executive will exercise ultimate authority over all submanagers. This is the hierarchical or pyramidal structure.

The authority of every submanager is usually defined. A *functional* definition of authority specifies the activities which a manager has the right to determine and the point where one submanager's authority ends and another's begins. In addition, authority can be defined in *financial* terms, by the amount and the nature of expenditures a manager may authorize. Or authority can refer to the *kind of decisions* managers may make: top management will formulate broad operating policies which may affect many operating units; middle managers will interpret these policies in relation to their operating units; and first-line supervisors will apply middle management's interpretations to their respective units. Decisions of great significance, such as those on pricing policies, are usually reserved for top management, and decisions that apply to more than one operating unit or that cut across lines of authority are determined by the official who has ultimate authority over these units.

For the most part, the bureaucratic model does not make a rigid distinction between the authority of a superior and that of his subordinate manager. The higher manager has the right of intervening in any problem or decision making activity that affects the units within his overall authority because he is held responsible for the results of their operations. Subordinate managers are therefore obliged to follow their superiors' instructions, and the latter—at their own discretion—can contravene any decisions made by subordinates. Consequently, the submanager's authority within or over his unit is often a rather uncertain quantity. If higher management takes an active role in the operation of subunits, the authority of lower managers is further qualified. In such a manner are the problem solving activities of many organizations said to be "centralized."

Therefore, for any organizational activity, a decision and its execution may involve many and various levels of management, eluding any constant definition of an authority relationship between superior and subordinate managers; and we must conclude that, by and large, authority is seldom fixed and final. Although authority can also vary with the kind of problem or decision to be made, in some organizations programs will evolve with definite grants of authority to subordinates, in which superiors will not intervene; but this practice may not be consistent throughout these organizations. For example, in very large organizations top management may restrict its decision making to a few major areas and permit middle managers great discretion in the other areas, yet these middle managers may not allow similar freedom of decision to the lower managers.

It is of course difficult to adhere rigidly to a definition of authority between superiors and subordinates because each manager is accountable for the results of the unit for which he is responsible, but obviously, if one of these units is being mismanaged, higher management will intervene to correct the situation. This, however, is not the only reason for intervention in the bureaucratic system, and the authority of every manager is conditional and contingent upon the discretion of his superior.

In addition to defining authority, planning a bureaucratic system frequently includes providing staff officials to assist line managers or others who have organizational authority. Staff officials, although chosen for their technical competence, are usually not given organizational authority but are restricted to making recommendations to line managers, so that the relationships here tend to be rather ambiguous. Theoretically, staff officials can make recommendations to line officials for achieving organizational goals, and the latter are supposed to accept these recommendations—but they also have the authority to reject them. Some line officials will accept most staff suggestions while others will tend to reject them.

Then too, some staff officials have access to higher line officials, who might accept staff suggestions and then insist that lower line officials carry them out. Consequently, differences between line and staff officials can be appealed to higher line officials, and, for that matter, disagreements between line officials on the same level can be appealed to the line official who has the authority of adjudication.

Goals are frequently established both for the organization as a whole and for the subunits, and a time limit is set for their achievement. For example, the sales division may be told to

384

increase sales volume by 10 per cent in the coming year and this objective might then be "subdivided" along geographic lines so that each subunit in the sales division will increase its output by 10 per cent. Sometimes these objectives are explicitly defined in quantitative terms while at other times they may be general, with neither a time nor a quantitative dimension.

When the performance of any manager is evaluated, the goals for the unit (or units) for which he is responsible are considered. Information is collected and reports are submitted to higher management for evaluation. For example, sales officials receive data for the sales volume of subsales units within their division. If all their units have been instructed to increase sales 10 per cent in a given year, at the end of that year it is easy for higher sales managers to determine the extent to which units have achieved this objective. The manager in charge of sales can take whatever action seems warranted against the manager and the unit which is not fulfilling its quota increase. If the performance of a unit is chronically poor, its manager may be removed; if it is operating successfully and meeting its objectives, its manager may be rewarded by a salary increase or promotion.

UNMANAGED MANAGEMENT

To what extent is the decision making process managed in the bureaucratic system? If we would measure the process according to the ten steps this book suggests, we would find that the bureaucratic system has only one planned decision step: authorization. Some of the other nine steps may be performed to some extent, but only partially and not in sequence. Further, there is no designed machinery for coordinating management's decision making activities. Although authorization is a necessary phase in every management model, it is only one small aspect of total planning effort.

Systems of authority and decision systems are not synonymous, and the bureaucratic model fails to provide a *total* decision system by failing to stipulate how organizational solutions are to be constructed, the decision making tasks of the managers, the manner of performance, the definition of an organizational problem and its solution, and how its system is to be integrated, installed, maintained, and controlled. The bureaucratic model therefore provides no assurance that productive solutions will emerge, which is the essential purpose of every management system.

If the decision making process, in whole or in part, is left to the discretion of individual managers, it becomes highly individualistic. Each manager can decide how the problem solving process will be carried out for the unit within his allocated sphere of authority. Each manager can decide upon which problems he will work, and how many. Each decides through which problem solving steps he will proceed and what techniques he will use for any step. Each, upon his own criteria, selects and implements his own solutions. All this can happen unless a superior intervenes—perhaps only on the basis of his organizational rank—and performs or directs these activities according to *his* individualistic manner.

If authority has been formally delegated in an unplanned system, the success of the managerial process will be determined by the ability of the individual managers. But because the bureaucratic model is not a complete decision making system, chronic managerial problems can persist. The following section will consider the practices which cause mismanagement, but it should be kept in mind that not all of these shortcomings are true of all bureaucratic organizations or of all managers who operate within them. Furthermore, although a bureaucracy is for the most part incompletely planned, it can be improved upon or redesigned so that poor managerial practices can often be replaced by the more positive techniques of a total system.

PROBLEM INDICATORS

In organizations structured along bureaucratic lines, to what particular events should top management be attuned that might indicate managerial problems and the necessity for redesign? One of these areas is the nature and quantity of the organizational problems that submanagers are working on. Because there is no systematic problem-raising machinery within the bureaucratic apparatus, the mechanics of inputting problems into the management system depends entirely upon the individual managers. If managers do not exercise initiative, few problems will be investigated. Raising a question for a subordinate manager to solve is not a systematic procedure but essentially (in this case) a function of the relationship between superior and subordinate managers.

Few bureaucratic organizations have a highly developed sensory apparatus that scans their environments in order to detect problem areas or opportunity states. Although many organizations have staff units that carry out economic and market analyses, these units—as with problem-raising—are not integrated into the decision making process. They do not automatically feed in environmental problems nor do they trigger programmed solutions.

When a manager is only one of many, he is often isolated from his organization's external environment. Except for events which he may personally observe or experience, he may be totally unaware of areas in the organization's environment and therefore omit them from his deliberations. Or recurring problems may go unsolved because the manager does not know of them, ignores them, or does not search for them. Although events may change drastically inside and outside the organization, outmoded forms of response may continue to be used.

Through the use of computers, many organizations are introducing operational techniques of rapid data collection, recording, and reporting, so that, theoretically, management can take all necessary corrective actions. We find, however, that the problem-raising step in decision making is still rather primitive, and that although management receives many data it is doubtful that this information is correctly evaluated for raising the problems it reveals.

We saw much earlier that an important function of the intelligence unit is screening the data on external and internal events, pointing out the problem areas, and triggering the problem solving mechanism. Therefore, even though data processing procedures have improved and managers are receiving data more rapidly, there is no indication that more problems are being solved. If the manager is inundated with reports, records, and data, screening can become unmanageable; he may be forced to spend his time searching through data for problems which he has little time to solve.

In the bureaucratic system each manager can determine his problem solving workload. If he is satisfied with the current operations, he may not raise problems but may instead instruct employees in the established procedures of the organization, doing no problem solving at all. In such cases an organization receives no output from such a manager. Nor, in such a system, are the other organizational participants — employees, consumers, suppliers, and stockholders — encouraged to raise problems which they believe to be significant either to themselves or to the group as a whole. Problem-raising is usually left entirely to the discretion of the individual managers.

When staff managers raise a problem to assist a line manager in the performance of his job, the line manager may choose to ignore the suggestion. If there is no agreement within the organization as to what constitutes an organizational problem, problem interpretation is also left to the individual manager. As a result, one manager may view a situation and believe that operations are functioning satisfactorily; another may interpret the same situation as one that contains a variety of problems which require immediate response and correction. Two different managerial reactions are therefore not merely matters of individual initiative but results of perception or recognition. If each manager has a different concept of an organizational problem, each will raise a different number of problems. Some may respond only to situations which threaten organizational effectiveness—which is a different behavior from searching for areas of improvement and continually rearranging and modifying work procedures.

Under this model, then, problem-raising tends to be geared to what managers are willing to undertake as problems rather than to actual problems in the external and internal environments. (Staff officials have even raised nonexistent problems merely to justify their organizational positions.) In the absence of an effective sensory machinery, it is characteristic of the bureaucratic system to respond tardily and incompletely to the changing environment.

Upon finding any of these problem-raising inadequacies, top management should consider the appropriate definition for organizational problems and the establishment of a sensory or intelligence unit.

COORDINATION AND INTEGRATION

The absence of machinery for coordinating managerial activities is another possible disadvantage of the bureaucratic system. Therefore, if it appears that the managerial staff is not working well together, this aspect of the system should also be considered by top management. An organization that has 1,000 managers who, by and large, function independently of one another can already be in the midst of very serious problems.

It will be recalled that the control unit of our programmed model had the primary responsibility for coordinating decision making activities. After organizational problems were raised, they were sent to this unit, which recorded the receipt of such problems, classified them as legitimate or irrelevant, and checked for existing solutions. Solutions were then activated by the unit. The organizational location of problems was also determined, as well as their priority, and problems were routed, assigned, and

388

scheduled (all this recorded on a master control board), and then dispatched—along with advice on the proper tools—to problem-solvers, who were obliged to work on them. The control unit later followed up its assignments, and checked solution content and analysis before arranging the consensus procedure.

In the bureaucratic system, although managerial action is coordinated through the chain of command or the hierarchy of authority positions, no blueprint is provided for achieving integration. It is difficult to postulate how, from a set of authority relationships, a systematic integration of managerial behavior can spontaneously emerge. The bureaucracy has no control units for integrating decision making activities, no problem transfer or assigning machinery, and no procedure for assuring that new problems in the external environment will be transferred to the appropriate problem-solver.

If, for example, a production problem originates with a consumer (in the sales area), how could this problem be transferred to the production area? At best, it would flow upward in the organization: the consumer would relate his problem to a salesman, who in turn would notify his superior, and so on up the chain of command until it reached a high official in production, who would presumably transfer the problem downward. This problem, to be worked on, would have to flow through a series of organizational communication linkages, and at the discretion of each manager.

Within such a framework, problems would be lost, forgotten, or delayed. Moreover, when an operating unit raises a question or problem about the operation of another unit, criticism is inferred by the latter unit, which may respond defensively or merely ignore the problem. At times, problems will be transferred horizontally; for example, directly from the sales department to an operating manager in the production department, but with no assurance that production will take action. Further, managers often do not know to whom a problem should go.

In the programmed system, as we have said, submanagers are assigned the problems upon which they are expected to work; in the bureaucratic model the manager selects his problems. As a result, the latter may select only those problems in which he is interested, or which he feels competent to handle; he may ignore or screen out all others. For example, a plant manager might spend all his time on problems which concern plant equipment, ignoring those which relate to personnel, costs, etc., and, if his experience and interest are in the area of equipment, this is only a natural reaction. Indeed, reviews of managerial performance confirm that managers are primarily concerned with specific types of problems and devote their time to these.

Top management, then, by leaving too much to individual discretion, risks the possibility that the individual manager will select unimportant problems and ignore more significant problems. Even apart from whether these problems are successfully solved, it is apparent that the overall welfare of the organization does not greatly increase by this process.

Because the bureaucratic system has no screening mechanism that can evaluate problems by their relative importance, it has no priority system by which managers can be directed to an organization's most meaningful problems. If top management reserves the function of problem solving, and if the required time exceeds the available time, an increasing number of problems will be left unsolved. Furthermore, such an organization may have a few overworked executives at the top and a nonutilized managerial staff, an imbalance of the utilization of total managerial time that can easily occur when there is no systematic scheduling of time and problems.

Finally, bureaucracies do not keep a master record of decision making activities. Even when managers assign problems to lower managers, this is usually done verbally. If the submanager has several assignments, or becomes busy with other tasks, the original problem can be forgotten. Therefore, an initial step that top management should consider in redesigning the bureaucratic model is the introduction of control units.

QUALITY OF MANAGERIAL DECISIONS

If the competency of managerial judgment is questioned, top management may want to review the process by which certain solutions were devised. But the bureaucratic model has no predetermined designation of steps, sequence, or proper techniques. For technique, a manager may employ intuition, experience, or the advice of employees or staff officials. He may omit some crucial steps, or may decide not to investigate the problem at all because he assumes he knows the causal factors. He may also use poor techniques for isolating the causal variables, or he may not consider all of the factors.

For example, in examining a problem of sales decline a manager might concentrate wholly on the psychological aspect of sales and ignore the economic determinants, which might be critical in this situation. Or he might concentrate on the internal environment and ignore the external environment as a source of

390

determining factors. Biases might also affect his considerations so that he is comfortable working with only two or three determinants, or he may not have the skills to isolate the determinants. He might not even be aware of variables and might rely, instead, on his personal judgment.

Another common error under this system is that managers may carry out an incomplete search for alternative solutions to a problem. Often—in professional literature or in the technology—there are "answers" for the best solution of certain problems, but managers sometimes disregard these sources and rely on rather limited knowledge or experience.

The bureaucratic system does not always require that only organizational objectives be used in deciding upon solutions. Under programmed decision making, with a calculated payoff for any alternative, organizational goals are the only criteria that can be used. Submanagers are thus provided with a solution comparison form for each solution and the control unit can easily check the calculations.

Managers in a bureaucratic system may knowingly or unknowingly select alternatives which serve only their personal ends, not those of their organization. Even though a manager attempts to be impartial in selecting an alternative, personal value judgments may be the basis for his selection between alternative lines of action. Furthermore, the submanager may not calculate the payoff of the alternatives and may forgo ascertaining the cost (or input) and the results (or output). In some situations the payoff of the alternatives cannot be predicted, although considerable risk is involved, and here the manager must make a choice that is based only upon his personal judgment. (However, this is quite different from a manager's making no endeavor to evaluate each alternative in relation to organizational goals.)

The bureaucratic form, in short, has no device for making sure that a manager has used the designated objective as his criterion for selection of a decision. To improve the quality of submanagerial decision making, top management must stipulate the tasks and the techniques that its managers will perform.

CONSENSUS

Top managers may also contend with situations for which submanagers are unable to work out effective cooperative relations between their units, and this is symptomatic of the need for a more explicit agreement-making machinery. The sixth step in our decision making model is an organizational consensus to help ensure the optimum solution for the organization. However, the bureaucratic apparatus has no machinery for clearing solutions through the organization so that total organizational payoff can be calculated: each decision-maker is responsible for his unit's operation and may not (and need not) concern himself with the operation of other units; it is as if each manager were in business for himself.

The problem of suboptimization is particularly difficult in a bureaucratic system. Because managerial rewards are usually based on the achievement of the subobjectives for each unit, each manager will attempt to reach these goals to the best of his ability; but these subgoals often conflict with each other as well as with the goals of the organization. Managers are not required to relate their decisions to those of other managers, nor need they, as a group, evaluate the effects of a decision upon the other units. Even if a manager receives an informal reaction from another manager on a proposed or an operating solution, the former need not modify the decision he had been granted the authority to make; he must modify a solution only if a superior so directs him. The total organizational net payoff is not calculated by a control unit.

Much of what has come to be known as "organizational politics" derives from these circumstances. The bureaucratic model seems to encourage managerial competition and conflict, rather than cooperation, for attaining organizational goals.

The bureaucratic model has no explicit agreement-making machinery for relating the work of the manager and that of employees, no device for assuring that—after a solution is reached—the employees will follow it. The assumption of the bureaucratic model is that subordinates will comply with all instructions; but when, as often happens, subordinates do not follow directives, how does the bureaucratic organization achieve employee acceptance of its decisions? Managers always have the right to discipline and (to some extent) reward employees; but the organizational motivating factor in the bureaucratic system is not integrated with the decision making process: employees are not rewarded by the extent of their compliance with decisions; they do not share in the decision payoff.

An employee might therefore follow a new decision only to the extent of not providing adequate grounds for being discharged. Here again, the responsibility for employee conformity is that of each individual manager, and apparently each manager must possess sufficient "leadership skills" for ensuring acceptance; but unfortunately these skills have never been isolated nor evaluated

392

in terms of their real effect upon employee behavior. In effect, then, the manager must achieve cooperation by whatever means he can. Moreover, because of union constraints or a short supply of labor, the sanctions available to the manager may not be wholly successful.

Staff personnel (who have been given no official authority) also have the problem of persuading line officials to accept their solutions; and again we find an assumption that line officials will always accept "good" solutions from the staff. However, experience again indicates that this is not always the case, so staff officials also must rely upon "leadership skills" for "selling" their solutions to line officials — and, like the managers, without the benefit of explicit sanctions or any guides for successful techniques.

Generally, in the bureaucratic model, employees do not participate in the decision making process even to the extent of signifying that they understand (or don't understand) a proposed solution. There is no systematic clearance and feedback machinery between managers and nonmanagers. Our programmed model, on the other hand, suggested that before a solution was implemented it should be cleared through the affected employee segment so that the employees would understand the decision, their new responsibilities, and the changes they must make in their accustomed tasks.

Suboptimization, intraorganizational bickering, line and staff controversy, and employee opposition would seem to be glaringly symptomatic of the need for effective clearance, agreement, and feedback machinery. Control units can certainly help perform these tasks in the bureaucratic model.

SOLUTION EFFECTUATION

Another problem area to which top management should direct its attention is the manner in which solutions are effectuated. Bureaucratic authorization does not always insist that the final solutions to problems be in a specific form, and there appears to be no agreement that the end product of the decision making system is an organizational solution. Therefore, one manager may rely wholly on verbal instructions and another may issue lengthy memoranda (which may be difficult to interpret). Under these circumstances a subordinate cannot always know that a solution has been officially authorized: the manager may be expressing an opinion, or merely commenting on a problem area — or stating official policy. It is therefore a moot question

393

whether employees can be relied upon to exercise unfailing discretion and follow the proper instructions.

Moreover, because many instructions are verbal and because managerial solutions directed to employees are not always recorded, misunderstandings arise over the nature of the instructions, and even whether they were or were not issued. Furthermore, a manager will probably not be able to recall all of the many instructions he has given over a long period, particularly if he has directed them to many different subordinates. In addition, if instructions are lengthy or technical, the employees may forget the exact instructions or may not understand them, thereby making such decisions progressively ineffectual.

Conflicts over authority can arise if managers give instructions directly to employees instead of through the chain of command, and staff officials also can exceed their positions by taking direct measures. Employees may therefore be subjected to conflicting instructions and be uncertain which they should follow, especially if these officials can exercise direct or indirect sanctions against them for failing to comply. We find that the mechanics of good communication simply cannot be performed if there is no adequate machinery for doing this.

Failure to achieve effective solutions can also result from the way in which managers implement solutions. They may not plan the effectuation of new solutions in advance, and, as a result, a unit may be expected to meet extra demands at inappropriate times, perhaps during its busiest work schedule. Or different aspects of a solution may not be properly integrated. For example, new equipment may have been purchased but plans had not been made for training employees in its use. Or the manager may not have considered the time it will take to complete the adjustment, or he might have assumed that adjustment and compliance will be immediate. Another possibility is that the manager may not have estimated the cost of the implementation. Further, if more than one unit must implement a solution—engineering, sales, and personnel, which is a frequent combination—the bureaucratic system can seldom provide a ready-made control unit for coordinating these efforts.

In the ninth step of our programmed model, direction, we saw that an inventory of written solutions is essential for efficient decision making. But because many organizations do not maintain such an inventory, a recurrent problem might be solved repeatedly. Implementation, directing, and auditing would also be more difficult than need be, and it would be unlikely that such an organization could quickly adjust to contingencies. The

394

failure to maintain an inventory precludes the detection of faulty decision making; clearance is not possible; and managerial performance cannot be accurately recorded. However, because organizations frequently record data which are not nearly as important as decisions, this failure is not because of any cost involved but merely because it is not required that managerial decisions be recorded. Without an inventory of well-defined solutions, the manager and his employees do not have a ready source of responses when their working environment changes.

The tenth step in the programmed decision making system, the audit, is not a consistent part of bureaucratic solutions; however, because managers in the latter system have the right to audit their own solutions, there would be a real question of their validity even if this procedure were regularly performed. There could be no real assurance that managers would actually evaluate their solutions, comparing the estimated and the actual payoff for each. Moreover, ineffective solutions might be applied after the environment of the organization had changed (although we saw how the audit findings in the planned system help determine the new problem inputs). Finally, if there is no requirement that all solutions be periodically audited, employee compliance cannot be ascertained or guaranteed.

An important human relations aspect accompanies the systematic auditing of solutions. If, upon completion of an audit, disciplinary action must be taken, it can be accomplished judiciously. However, in the bureaucratic organization a manager might audit only certain solutions or only the behavior of certain employees, which can give rise to feelings and accusations of discrimination. If a manager should ignore some violations and overemphasize others, arbitrary favoritism and discrimination would be the result.

If any of the above deficiencies exist in solution effectuation, top management must specify how each task is to be executed, and the provision for an independent audit of solutions is of particular importance for assuring appropriate control and feedback.

UNPREDICTABLE MANAGERIAL BEHAVIOR

When top management considers the redesign of its system, it may find it is difficult to isolate a common negative pattern in submanagerial behavior which hampers the selection of proper remedies. But when managers are permitted to determine how they will perform their jobs, and, indirectly, those of their subordinates, random managerial behavior should be the first pattern to be investigated because organizational effectiveness will be equally random. Thus, because the bureaucratic model employs no systematic search for a single, optimum procedure in performing decision making activities, an organization with one hundred managers would have some who interpret their roles correctly and perform their tasks effectively, a large middle group which probably performs some tasks well but others less efficiently, and a few managers who consistently tend to misinterpret their managerial roles. Such a distribution can be critical: if there are too many ineffective managers, the organization may easily fail.

MAINTENANCE OF THE BUREAUCRATIC MODEL (MANAGEMENT DEVELOPMENT)

Maintenance of the bureaucratic model usually entails determining the required number of managers and the authority of each, and then finding the right manager for each position. Management development programs perform this staffing task of selecting, training, and evaluating personnel.

Most organizations have some form of a management development program, yet the basic philosophy of these programs is that the source of management problems resides in the manager himself. Consequently, top management believes the optimum course is to acquire better managers through improved selection, training, and evaluation techniques. It is indeed ironic that top management errs by not employing the same logic for solving managerial problems that it uses for solving nonmanagement problems.

If an organization is beset by inefficient decision making results it would seem that it should evaluate its formal decision making plan by noting the policies, procedures, methods, standards, objectives, or projections to be utilized in the formulation of its organizational decisions. An examination of how these plans are implemented, and whether appropriate personnel and equipment have been acquired to implement and direct these plans, would also seem to be necessary. Finally, the organization should evaluate an actual situation by comparing managerial performance with its plans.

The source of the problem seems to be in the initial plan. Top management usually concentrates on the implementation phase of a problem and on the acquisition of qualified managers; however, if its initial plan is incomplete or poorly designed, its implementations, directions, and controls will also be faulty. Frequently, but incorrectly, the blame is placed upon an individual manager; the truth is that the management design should receive closer inspection and evaluation.

OPERATION OF THE SYSTEM

There is every reason to believe that a prime cause for the difficult and inefficient operation of the bureaucratic system is that it does not provide an appropriate allocation of managerial labor for coping with the problem input load. This problem is compounded by permitting managers to select their own tasks, which may be nondecision-making in nature. However, we have assumed from the very beginning that the problem solving function is uniquely managerial, and in a dynamic situation every organization survives only by solving problems. When managers carry out tasks other than problem solving, many critical problems will go unsolved (if sales managers engage in selling, or if research managers perform research, or if personnel managers interview new employees). The manager is then only another nondecision-making employee.

Under the bureaucratic model, because a manager is responsible for the operations of his unit, he tends to perform tasks which in his opinion lead to attaining the unit's assigned objectives. A sales manager, for example, may try to compensate for falling sales within his jurisdiction by entering the field and actually selling. Although he may be advancing the objectives which have been assigned to his unit, he may not be performing his essential task: determining the causes for the unfavorable situation and the best corrective changes his unit can make to optimize the situation. Managerial productivity is also lessened if middle managers are assigned nondecision-making tasks by higher management, such as time-consuming clerical tasks which less skilled individuals could easily perform.

Higher managers can also discourage problem solving by middle managers if they reserve this function for themselves. This situation will vary among higher managers in a bureaucratic organization because top management may have different concepts of what its subordinates should do. In one instance a top manager may delegate authority and accept the solutions which his subordinates design for their respective units; but another top official may not have confidence in his subordinates and will therefore discourage their problem solving activities. Thus there can be a misallocation of managerial resources within an organi-

397

zation: some managers may be overworked and unable to solve all the problems at hand, and others may be performing non-managerial tasks.

CONTROL

The control or audit of managerial behavior in a bureaucratic system is generally limited to periodic personal evaluations and reviews of the performance by each manager's unit (submanagers' rewards are essentially a matter of top management's subjective judgment). There is, unfortunately, no device for checking on the quality or quantity of each manager's decisions; and this again is in contrast to the programmed procedure, which permits higher managers, control units, other managers, and employees to review solutions before their implementation.

This does not mean that a bureaucratic system has no checkpoints. A solution that requires a sizable expenditure or a budgetary adjustment may first have to be cleared by higher management. Line officials can review and question the solutions of staff officials. However, although occasions for these (and other) checks may exist, those who examine the solutions may apply personal criteria in their final selections.

It is very difficult to measure the efficiency of the decision making function in a bureaucratic system because decisions are not usually evaluated in terms of the organizational payoff per unit of output (decisions), therefore conclusions about bureaucratic decision making are usually only deductive. The measure of managerial effectiveness is the efficiency of the operating subunits: if managers achieve their subobjectives within the allowed costs, it is assumed that they are operating effectively. Yet there *is* a difference between the two forms of measurements: the decisive factors in measuring managerial effectiveness are not only the results of an operation but also the specific actions or decisions of each unit manager.

In the examination of a unit's operating results a lack of accurate measuring and auditing mechanisms makes it exceedingly difficult to isolate the effect of a manager's decisions from the effects of other determinants. Operating results can be attributable to causes that are external to a unit, or they can reflect the decisions of a higher manager, of staff personnel, or of employees. But the basic objection to using only a unit's operating results as a standard is that it is a gross measurement; it is not sufficiently precise for evaluating the contribution of the manager in charge. A unit can actually have very positive operating

398

results under a very poor decision-maker: if there were a great demand for a product, sales might increase without any effort being made by the sales manager (an external cause). To state all this in its basic form, measurement of a manager's performance—rather than his unit's performance—is undeniably the better measurement of managerial achievement.

Because the managerial reward system in the bureaucratic model is not adapted to encouraging effective decisions, it tends to encourage differences rather than cooperation. Moreover, if a manager is rewarded according to the progress of his unit, he can be expected to take whatever measures are necessary to achieve a "good record," no matter how these measures may conflict with the efforts of other managers.

We have seen, then, that many managerial shortcomings will necessarily occur if management's decision making system is not fully planned, and we have considered some of the potential problem areas. Although we have treated the bureaucratic model rather extensively, the redesign of any system requires top management to stipulate the behavior it expects, to be able to detect when these expectations are not being achieved, and to take appropriate action.

GENERAL CRITICISM OF
THE BUREAUCRATIC MODEL

Although this chapter has been primarily concerned with the redesign of the bureaucratic system, we should also consider some operating aspects of this model.

Its decision making is often carried out in a "concealed" fashion, the reason and method for arriving at solutions being frequently unknown because the process remains within the mind of the decision-maker. This "mystery" is particularly disconcerting to nondecision-makers, who, if they are to have confidence in the procedures they must follow, should know that solutions have been derived through a rational procedure. Nor can the bureaucratic system's nondecision-makers have such assurance if authoritative directives are promulgated without explanations.

There is no inherent or necessary reason for concealing any organizational process; indeed, the less open the process the less confidence individuals will have in its decisions. Political decisions in the United States are generally quite explicit and subject to public review; the construction of federal legislation, for example, is a fairly open process. Because people want to know not only the decisions they are expected to follow but the way in which these decisions were reached, they will suspect a decision of being irrational if this process is closed or secretive.

There should of course be confidence in the individuals who have the authority to make decisions, but if the decision-makers are incompetent, biased, or impulsive, reasonable men cannot be expected to follow their decisions. If subordinates (as in Herman Wouk's *The Caine Mutiny*) are dependent upon an almost absolute authority, and have no checks or balances or redress, and are seriously affected by temperament and emotion and all the other factors which enter into personal decision making, the effects are bound to be more than just unpleasant. Such circumstances are obviously not ideal conditions for optimum attainment of organizational goals.

However, there is a difference between reliance upon a decision making system and reliance upon decision-makers; and the U.S. Constitution (which was considered as a decision making system in Chapter 1) may help us see this distinction. Americans assume that as long as political decisions are made in the manner stipulated by the Constitution, these decisions will be relatively effective regardless of the individuals in the governmental apparatus. The bureaucratic system, on the other hand, depends on the wisdom of the decision-makers rather than on a system.

One hundred years ago, when most activities were carried out on a personal level or in a family context, organizational decision making forms were not as complex (or perhaps as critical) as they are today. Organizational behavior has since become increasingly complex and subject to bureaucratic control: nonmanagers — in their various capacities of citizens, consumers, stockholders, employees, parents, and students — must depend upon the wisdom of managers for their well-being. There is little doubt that the proponents and users of the bureaucratic model seek a rational, impartial, responsive, and responsible management system, and that the welfare of the organizational members — whether stockholders or employees — is of primary concern; but the model provides rather ineffective machinery for meeting this objective. The fault is therefore not in its objectives but in its technology of implementation. If an impersonal decision making system is desired, organizational machinery must be designed that can assure a managerial behavior which will produce the desired objectives.

Nothing at all is gained by personal criticisms of top management for the failings of our prevailing management system. Top government officials, top corporation executives, and university presidents — these perhaps more than any other groups — are

400

acutely aware of the shortcomings of the bureaucratic system. If improved designs are available, top managements will surely utilize them.

The technology required for designing more effective management systems has been developed only within the past twenty years. Computers, systems engineering, and operations research are some of the components the analyst must consider as he designs an operational, totally integrated management system that will provide, maintain, and increase the satisfactions and personal values which the members of every organization seek.

SUMMARY

Because the bureaucratic model is essentially an unplanned decision making process, serious and persistent management problems arise. Top management must be sensitive to all existing and potential problem areas; it must investigate their nature; and it must provide appropriate corrective measures so as to obtain a more explicit decision making plan. Even apart from the inefficiencies of the bureaucratic model, because its decisions are usually made in a "concealed" manner, it is unlikely that non-decision-makers—those who are most affected by these decisions—will ever have complete confidence in the bureaucratic form.

QUESTIONS FOR DISCUSSION

1. How do you account for the widespread use of the bureaucratic model?
2. Is the conclusion valid that the bureaucratic process is an unplanned system? Explain.
3. Distinguish between a system of authority and a system of decision.
4. Do you believe it is feasible to fix the authority relationship between superior and subordinate managers in the bureaucratic model? Explain.
5. Describe the bureaucratic model's sensory apparatus and the tasks it performs.
6. How, in the bureaucratic system, can a manager avoid working on problems?
7. Is it possible for a manager to believe he is solving many problems even though his solution output is negligible? Explain.
8. Can there be an integrated set of authority relationships and an uncoordinated decision making system? Explain.
9. How are new decision making techniques, such as operations research, introduced into the bureaucratic system?

10. As long as its decision making process is concealed, do you believe that, in the long run, nondecision-makers will ever be satisfied with the bureaucratic form? Explain.

SUGGESTED READINGS

BLAU, PETER. *Bureaucracy in Modern Society,* New York: Random House, Inc., 1956.
———. *The Dynamics of Bureaucracy: A Study of Interpersonal Relationships in Two Government Agencies* (2d ed.). Chicago: University of Chicago Press, 1963.
BLAU, PETER, and SCOTT, W. RICHARD. *Formal Organizations.* San Francisco: Chandler Publishing Company, 1961.
DAVIS, RALPH C. *The Fundamentals of Top Management.* New York: Harper & Row, 1951.
GUEST, ROBERT H. *Organizational Change.* Homewood, Ill.: Richard D. Irwin, Inc., 1962.
LIKERT, RENSIS. *New Patterns of Management.* New York: McGraw-Hill Book Company, 1961.
MERTON, ROBERT K., *et al.* (eds.). *Reader in Bureaucracy.* New York: Free Press of Glencoe, Inc., 1952.
THOMPSON, VICTOR. *Modern Organization.* New York: Alfred A. Knopf, Inc., 1961.
WEBER, MAX. *The Theory of Social and Economic Organization,* A. M. Henderson and Tallcott Parsons (trans.). New York: Oxford University Press, 1947.

16

CASES

This chapter presents a series of cases in decision making processes, for the most part in subunits of ongoing organizations, as occasions for student analysis and discussion. Chapter 15 was concerned with potential management problem areas, but this chapter will deal with actual situations. In analyzing the cases, it will be noticed that variability occurs and that different management problems will appear in different organizational contexts; and occasionally the same problem will reappear.

Our purpose in simulating these organizational situations is to give students the opportunity to design alternative, detailed, and integrated decision making systems. Students need not restrict their considerations to the ten-step system presented but may design their own appropriate organizational machinery. It should be recalled that the particular system explored throughout the text was meant to demonstrate how a system can be designed. The author's experience with student designs indicates that they are capable of creating a wide variety of plans.

It may at first appear that sufficient data are not presented to permit students to create such designs; however, sufficient information is given so that specific questions can be evaluated:

What management problems appear to be present?
What additional data are needed to assure that these are the
  critical problems?
What methodology could be used to acquire additional data?
What alternative designs could be considered?

Whether or not extensive case material is presented, the classroom can be used as a laboratory in which student teams can explore the possibilities of utilizing alternative decision processes under various problem inputs. They can also select and explore organizations in which they have participated and design appropriate systems for them.

The data presented in these cases are restricted to decision making processes. In some instances the history of specific decisions are reviewed so as to indicate the pattern of the system; in others, a more general review is presented. All of these cases report actual situations.

A MARKETING DEPARTMENT (A)

The organization chart for the marketing department of this large corporation is shown in Figure 16–A1. The firm is a standard bureaucratic organizational structure and the director of marketing delegates various responsibilities to his three subordinates: the directors of product sales, field sales, and sales administration. These directors, in turn, have delegated responsibilities to their subordinates. Job descriptions have been prepared that set forth the broad responsibilities of each director and manager, and an organizational manual contains procedures and methods for handling routine personnel and administrative problems; but these documents do not describe the decision making flow within the organization.

The firm's immediate system for decision making is hard to classify because it has many variations and is at times fully hidden. Figure 16–A2 (pages 406–407) shows the schematic of the present flow of the decision process. There are no written procedures or forms for controlling, directing, or designing the decision process. For a better understanding of the system for the organization as a whole—and for the marketing department in particular—the corporation's equivalent of the nine decision making steps (2 through 10) will be outlined.

PROBLEM-RAISING

Information flows into the marketing department from many sources. Major sources for external environmental information are salesmen's reports, sales statistics, management contacts with the public, and marketing research; major sources for internal environmental information are expense and profit statistics, budget information, and problems from related functional de-

Figure 16 – A1

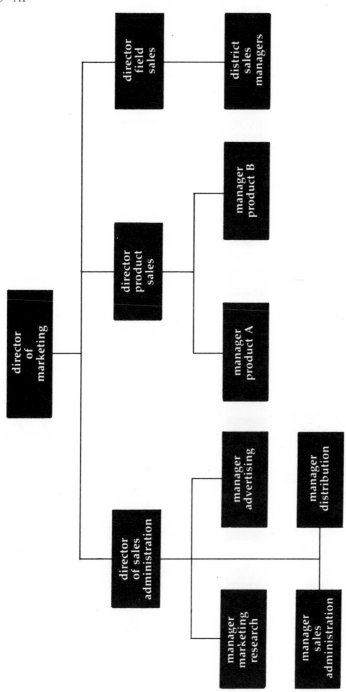

Figure 16-A2
DECISION PROCESS FLOW IN THE MARKETING DEPARTMENT

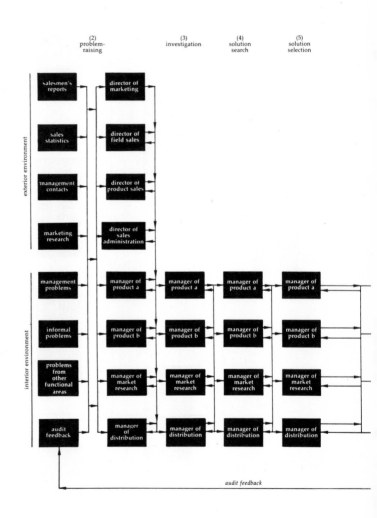

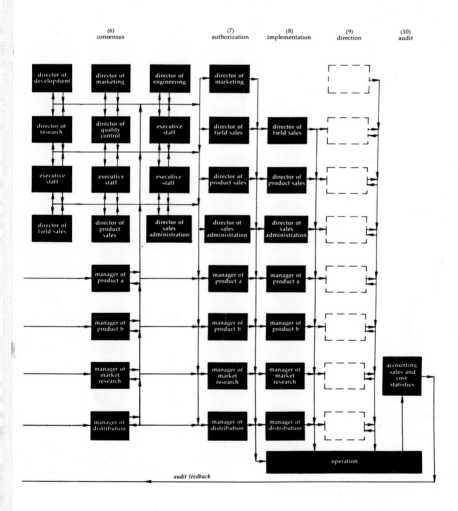

partments. The information is adequate but its flow into the decision making process is not; there is no control unit or central point through which all incoming data and problems must pass.

Some information is programmed to enter specific areas of the organization, some information has no entrance provision, and still other data are broadcast across the departments. Salesmen's reports about specific products go primarily to the product manager. Marketing research information is frequently distributed to all directors and managers. Sales statistics, budget information, and sales expense information are also widely distributed, although managers must report on their specific activities. Problems from related departments might enter the system anywhere.

Managers analyze all of the incoming data for problems. If a problem enters the organization at a high managerial level, it will be sent down the hierarchical structure to lower levels with instructions to investigate or to solve, and these problems receive disproportionate attention or emphasis in comparison with problems that are input at lower levels. If a problem enters the organization at a lower point, it can be solved at that level or can be sent to a higher level. Problems can therefore be raised in all parts of the system.

There is little control over the work on specific problems. Each manager works independently and investigates the problems he has discovered or those he has been assigned. In the investigation process, however, there is a large intermanagerial flow of ideas and assistance.

SEARCH FOR SOLUTIONS

The manager who investigates a problem also searches for solutions, and problems are sometimes accompanied by suggestions for solution, but this is not a well-defined or differentiated step. Frequently, solutions are devised from personal experience, and, as a result, few alternatives may be considered.

SELECTION OF THE SOLUTION

Selection is performed by the manager who carried out the problem investigation and the search for solutions, but this step is not separated in the decision process and is often performed at the time a problem is raised. Seldom is there extensive evaluation of alternative solutions before selection is made; subjective judgment and experience are heavily relied upon; payoff is rarely calculated.

CONSENSUS

The consensus step is not a formal part of the decision making process, but, informally, considerable managerial interaction occurs in this area. The company has a tendency toward committee rule, which requires internal "selling" of an idea to many people, and several methods are employed: memoranda are sent to all concerned; preliminary reports are circulated to affected people; attempts are made to persuade influential managers.

One of the difficulties in obtaining a consensus is that those who oppose a solution are not required to submit alternative payoff calculations, and simple lack of support can prevent a solution's coming to the attention of superiors in the organization. Because there is no central clearing mechanism for obtaining a consensus, managerial time is wasted in this informal process. Managers also seem to be more concerned with achieving an agreement among themselves than with finding solutions that provide the greatest organizational payoff.

AUTHORIZATION

Authorization can take place at any organizational level, depending on the significance of the particular solution. If the person who creates a solution does not have the authority to authorize it, he submits it to his superior, who, after reviewing the situation, can authorize or reject it or send it to a higher level for authorization. The authorizer need only be convinced of a solution's "correctness." Also, it is not always clear who has the responsibility for authorizing particular solutions.

Authorization is often verbal or in the form of a brief memorandum, and it is sometimes difficult to determine the intended disposition of a solution.

IMPLEMENTATION

The responsibility for implementing a solution is delegated down the chain of command to the manager or the person in charge of the affected area. Implementation is largely ignored during the decision making process; the problems of implementation are usually confronted only after a solution has been authorized.

DIRECTION

The corporation and the marketing department have no systematized inventory of decisions. Solutions are scattered through various files or committed to memory. It is usually possible to find supporting reports and files for reconstructing a solution, but it is very difficult to reconstruct or deduce the conclusions. Routine solutions, such as price schedules and distributor policies, are kept in written form, but there is no formal procedure for assuring that the appropriate solutions (in any area) are being utilized. However, informal checks on decision utilization are generally a part of the established practices for this operation.

AUDIT

There is no audit of decisions that compares expected payoffs with actual payoffs, nor is the budget revised during the year that new decisions are adopted and applied. The accounting system produces analyses of sales cost, budget, and profits, and distributes these statistics throughout the marketing department. The budget system is used to evaluate the performance of the marketing management, and efficient sales and expense performances are rewarded by increased pay and promotions, but no attempt is made to evaluate decision making performance.

QUESTIONS FOR DISCUSSION

1. What does Figure 16 – A2 indicate about the information flow?
2. When the market research department transmits its information to all of the directors and managers, what is likely to occur in terms of problem-raising?
3. What can happen when problem investigation, search for solution, and solution evaluation are not separated in the decision process?
4. Evaluate the firm's consensus procedure.
5. When solutions are passed up the chain of command for approval, and the authorization is verbal, what problems arise for the sub-managers?

AN ELECTRONICS DIVISION (B)

The next case concerns an electronics division of a company. Figure 16 – B (pages 412 – 413) is an inspection device showing how ten specific problems were solved: *yes* and *no* denote the performance or omission of each decision step. There is no planned decision making mechanism in this organization and no problem-raising machinery for dispatching problems through predetermined channels so that planned action can be taken. The following description of how one problem was handled will indicate this company's general decision making program.

The problem, an overrun of the estimated cost for developing and producing an electronic triggering device, was brought to the attention of the divisional general manager in a memorandum from the corporation's cost accounting department. In citing the magnitude of the overrun (by labor category and material) and suggesting that the division had not followed the proper estimating and budgeting procedures, the memorandum indicated the problem (step 2) and suggested its causes (step 3). The construction of the solution was as follows:

1. A copy of the memorandum was sent to the engineering, administration, and manufacturing managers, and they were instructed to answer the charges within a week.
2. A joint engineering and manufacturing memorandum was drafted in defense of the division's actions. It indicated the customer's lack of specification on purchase orders, enumerated the technical problems encountered by the engineering and manufacturing departments, and stressed that the division was striving to establish a proper budgeting operation.
3. An assistant to the manager of the administration department was hired with the responsibility of budget establishment and monitoring.

The only steps of the decision making process which were performed by the division itself were step 6 (a consensus was reached within the division between the department managers in drafting the memo) and step 7 (the appropriate department head authorized the hiring of a budget manager).

At present, there is no definition of what a manager's role should be, except for the general statement that he is "responsible for all activity in the area of communications." There is much confusion in the present decision making system primarily because there is neither a methodology nor a set of standards by which the system can be administered.

Figure 16–B indicates a random sample of decisions which have been made and of problems which have been raised in this organization. The matrix for the project problems lists four decisions that were reached (1, 2, 3, and 4) and one problem upon which no further action was taken (5); the matrix of organizational administrative problems lists only decisions that have been made and implemented.

Figure 16-B

PERFORMANCE AND NONPERFORMANCE RECORD
FOR THE TEN DECISION MAKING STEPS

Project Problems	Defining Objectives (1)	Problem-Raising (2)	Problem Investigation (3)	Search for Solution (4)
1 *Purchase of additional computer forms*	*yes*	*no*	*no*	*yes*
2 *Military specifications applied to commercial unit*	*yes*	*no*	*no*	*yes*
3 *Manpower shortage in manufacturing area*	*yes*	*yes*	*no*	*no*
4 *Purchase of unmodified tooling*	*yes*	*no*	*no*	*no*
5 *Message computer overran budget†*	*yes*	*yes*	*no*	*no*
Total	5	2	0	2

Organizational Administrative Problems

	Defining Objectives (1)	Problem-Raising (2)	Problem Investigation (3)	Search for Solution (4)
1 *Addition of publication section*	*yes*	*no*	*no*	*no*
2 *Initiation of recruiting campaign*	*yes*	*no*	*no*	*no*
3 *Decision to bid on lem trainer*	*yes*	*yes*	*no*	*no*
4 *Addition of a planning section*	*yes*	*no*	*no*	*no*
5 *Hiring of departmental assistants*	*yes*	*no*	*no*	*no*
Total	5	1	0	0

*Only one solution proposed.
†Problem introduced but no action taken.

412

Evaluation and Selection of Solution (5)	Consensus (6)	Authorization (7)	Implementation (8)	Direction (9)	Audit (10)	
1 yes	no	yes	yes	yes	no	6
2 yes*	no	yes	yes	yes	no	6
3 yes*	no	yes	yes	yes	no	6
4 yes	no	yes	yes	no	no	4
5 no	no	no	no	no	no	2
4	0	4	4	3	0	24

1 no	no	yes	yes	no	no	3
2 no	no	yes	yes	yes	no	4
3 yes	yes	yes	yes	yes	no	7
4 no	no	yes	yes	no	no	3
5 no	no	yes	yes	no	no	3
1	1	5	5	2	0	20

413

1. Evaluate the Figure 16–B decision grid as an inspection device for ascertaining how effectively the decision making process is being performed. What are its advantages and its limitations?
2. What do the figures in the extreme right column indicate?
3. What do the *total* figures indicate?
4. What additional information is needed in order to know how decisions are made in the engineering and manufacturing divisions?
5. Does Figure 16–B help indicate the problems that require further investigation? Explain.

ANOTHER ELECTRONICS DIVISION (C)

Our third case is that of an electronics division that operates in a staff capacity within the total organization. It submits proposals and recommendations to the company's line offices, which decide whether or not to implement them. Here we are most interested in the division's internal decisions and in the process by which they are reached.

The objective of the company, of course, is to produce certain products at a profit, and the output of the electronics subsystem must contribute to this goal. However, the subsystem output has never been defined in these terms, and a survey of the eighteen people employed in this division revealed diverse ideas on its nature. Most tended to interpret the output in terms of their assigned duties: estimators should estimate, central records personnel should maintain orderly records, and so on.

As for raising problems, the division has no systematic input through a formal sensing device for either internal or external problems. This is done entirely on an informal, verbal basis.

Nor are solutions recorded. If a problem reappears, individuals may recall a solution but may not remember all of the events to which it is to apply, which may necessitate solution reconstruction. Neither is there a systematic search for alternative solutions; behavioral changes are resented, and, as a result, that solution is applied which best conforms to the present procedure. Further, solution evaluation and selection are usually based on an individual's opinion.

Organizational consent or agreement is based on authority; there is no consensus process. The divisional leaders commit

414

their subordinates to tasks whose scope and implications may not be realized. Nor are solutions defined completely or in detail.

Authorization is also faulty, or omitted, because it is assumed that the superior will "go along with" a solution. Because previous solutions had not been recorded, repeated verbal authorizations of the same solution are necessary, yet the effects of its implementation can never be anticipated with any certainty. Implementation is not only exceedingly difficult, but serious repercussions often develop at this late stage.

Because solutions are not written, they are not a completely dependable guide in the direction step. The individuals who carry them out can interpret their instructions rather loosely, or they will constantly ask the manager for additional instructions. Audit and feedback (generally in the form of complaints) follow no formal procedure; if there are no grievances, then all is assumed to be going well.

The cost of the present system in annual wages and salaries is approximately $100,000, but there is no way of measuring its yearly output. And, again because decisions are not recorded, there is no measurement or means for determining previous outputs.

QUESTIONS FOR DISCUSSION

1. What problems arose in this division because solutions were not recorded?
2. Evaluate the use of complaints as an auditing device.
3. To what extent is it necessary that all individuals understand and accept their particular unit's output?
4. At what point in the decision making process does one determine whether or not the output of a particular operating unit will contribute to profits?
5. What management problems are indicated if solutions that conform to existing operations are selected merely because it is difficult to install new solutions?

A STRUCTURES ENGINEERING UNIT (D)

This case deals with the structures engineering unit of an aircraft manufacturer. The manner in which three problems were solved will be reviewed in order to indicate the management process.

415

PROBLEM 1

A \$600,000 contract was granted by the Department of Defense so that the company could engage in a sixteen-month study of the use of beryllium in equipment structure (beryllium is a lightweight, flexible, and very expensive metal). The contracts division then notified the company's strength department that it was authorized to begin the study.

To acquire some beryllium for testing, the department head ordered a part made of beryllium from an outside company, after obtaining verbal approval from the director of systems technology for this purchase. Because the strength department was to conduct this study, it had been sent the authorization notice; however, the weights and loads departments were also involved but they had not been officially notified.

It is not known if the output of this project was ever defined, but advancement of the structural beryllium technology can be assumed from the defense department's request for bids. The study (and the problem raised) was to find an effective method for determining the strength, weight, and load characteristics of beryllium structures in equipment applications. It can also be assumed that the department head carried out the problem-raising and investigation processes, although again there is no certain indication that they were performed as separate steps or given full and proper consideration. But it is certain that a search for alternative solutions was not performed.

It later appeared that the decision to purchase beryllium for experimental testing of structural characteristics may have been an error because other solutions would have met the contract requirements equally well. For example, an analytical analysis of beryllium characteristics may have been justified because of the high ratio between the cost and the effectiveness of the result; or a compromise between analytical and experimental findings could have been another acceptable alternative (although it would have required the purchase of test material). At any rate, there was no calculation of the payoff for the single solution considered.

The result was that the purchased material and its testing encumbered most of the \$600,000, so that the company had to finance the expenses involved in reducing, compiling, and summarizing the test data. The fact that the company was itself interested in the technological findings eased the consequences of the overrun.

Implementation had been accomplished at almost the same

time that authorization had been given to purchase the beryllium parts. The department head at that time had instructed the advanced-design supervisor to write a request for the test instrumentation that would be placed on the beryllium specimen. There was evidence of a clearing procedure on the supervisory level, although the heads of the weights and loads departments did not accept the solution. An implementation schedule was prepared by master planning after the bid was submitted, but this was in very general terms and it was not revised to include the purchase of beryllium. Direction (step 9) was undertaken by the department heads but it was not a major factor since only a single solution was involved. The utilization of the decision making steps for this problem is shown below:

1	2	3	4	5	6	7	8	9	10
1	5	7	*	8	?	10	2	?	3

*Was not performed.
?No information.

The top line of the grid represents the suggested sequence for performing the problem solving steps and the second line illustrates the actual sequence. Note that step 5 (selection [in this case there were no alternatives]) was performed in place of step 2. Authorization, implementation, and audit were done somewhat haphazardly, after the solution had been selected. Raising the problem and analyzing it (steps 2 and 3) took place only after the preliminary audit indicated an overrun condition. Step 4 (search for alternative solutions) was not performed.

PROBLEM 2

The second problem situation arose in one of the weekly meetings of the company's contract change board, which was discussing necessary product modifications. An operations analysis representative said several squadron commanders had informed him that an aircraft the company was designing would be more desirable if it could carry a greater amount of fuel for long-distance flights. It was therefore decided to propose the installation of two auxiliary 300-gallon wing-mounted fuel tanks, and an engineering change proposal was prepared for a month of analysis (by the engineering design and structures engineering groups) and submitted to the air force.

The decision to incorporate the external wing fuel tanks was made in the following manner. After the objective of providing an increased fuel source was discussed, the board members agreed to a feasibility analysis for the additions because they believed the air force would accept this change. The chairman of the contract change board then asked the heads of the weights and loads departments to analyze the proposal and make recommendations. Detailed analysis was begun by the departments on the basis of this verbal direction, but no alternative solutions were evaluated, such as the feasibility of a single fuselage tank or the advantages of using jetison tanks.

When the analysis was completed, the design group sought an engineering change approval before it submitted its findings and recommendations. However, the strength division head refused to authorize the change because no clearance had been arranged. His department had not been notified of the problem and had learned of it only after the problem had been solved.

The loads department therefore estimated the wing strength factors (which should have been estimated by the strength department) and decided that no strength problem existed. However, when it received the loads department's strength analysis, the strength department discovered serious errors that necessitated reanalyses of the weight problem by the loads and weights departments.

The defense department did not authorize the retrofit incorporation of the external fuel tank, but its approval would have been more likely if alternative fuselage proposals had also been presented. At any rate, the following grid shows the decision steps that were taken (and their sequence) in deciding to increase the aircraft's fuel capacity. (The implementation, direction, and audit steps were omitted since the proposal was not accepted.)

	1	2	3	4	5	6	7	8	9	10
Loads Dept.	1	2	3	*	5	*	†			
Strength Dept.			3	*	5	6	†			

*Not performed.
†Authorized but not signed.

Note that steps 1, 2, and 3 were performed in the correct sequence and that step 4 (alternative solutions) was again omitted. An attempt was then made to obtain authorization, but, because no strength clearance had been granted, this resulted in a feed-

418

back to and through steps 3, 5, 6, and 7 in order to obtain the strength department inputs.

PROBLEM 3

This problem originated in the manufacturing department's quality control final assembly unit with the discovery that aircraft wing panels frequently buckled. Quality control prepared a trouble report form which brought this problem to the attention of the strength department head, who turned it over to his supervisor in charge of aircraft projects. This supervisor verbally requested assistance from the weights department for estimating the effects of installing structural support brackets to prevent future buckling. (A preliminary consideration of increasing the gauge of the panel structure had been ruled out by the strength department before the consultation with the weights department.) It then took several weeks for the weights department to relay the required information to the strength department.

Finally, after receipt of the desired information, the strength engineer completed his analysis and presented his data (on an engineering design form) to his supervisor, the strength department head, who approved it—although no clearance had been obtained from the weights department head. An engineering order was then sent to the corporate budgets group for the assignment of a time-charge number, and after this was accomplished, authorization was confirmed by the telephone call of a budgets representative to the strength department head. The latter then instructed his staff to revise the engineering drawings by incorporating the brackets. There is no evidence of further direction by the department, and no official audit was made.

QUESTIONS FOR DISCUSSION

1. How should the control unit perform when a problem must be solved by more than one operating unit?
2. Does a decision making pattern seem to emerge from the three problems in this case?
3. Will a research and development division require a decision making system that is different from that of the marketing or manufacturing divisions? Explain.
4. Would an interorganizational decision making design be required between the Department of Defense and major contractors? Explain.
5. What auditing procedure would you suggest for the structures engineering unit?

A DRUG COMPANY SALES DEPARTMENT (E)

This case considers a scanning problem which arose from a company's sales practice of generously supplying physicians with new drug samples for their clinical use and trial. Physicians became acquainted with the drugs, evaluated them, and eventually prescribed them. The problem was how to reduce the distribution of samples after the physicians had begun prescribing certain drugs; and there was no scanning device that could discover when this stage was reached.

For example, reports eventually reached the sales manager that physicians had been frequently prescribing a new drug, but the company had not received restocking orders for the quantity that had supposedly been prescribed and sold. The volume of mail from physicians in praise of the drug and the salesmen's reports of repeated success in obtaining prescriptions induced the sales manager to hire a research firm to discover why the company's sale of this drug was not increasing.

The research firm soon discovered that physicians were receiving excessive samples of the drug through the company's mailings and from the visits of salesmen. Therefore, when the samples began to accumulate in the physicians' offices, they gave them to the local pharmacies, which used the samples for filling prescriptions. The delay in discovering the problem caused an estimated sales loss of $75,000.

QUESTIONS FOR DISCUSSION

1. To prevent the recurrence of this problem, what activities would you require of the intelligence unit?
2. Is this situation indicative only of a scanning problem, or should other decision making stages also be reviewed?
3. What kind of triggering device would indicate when physician support of a new drug is adequate for a specified sales volume and when the distribution of free samples should be reduced?
4. Was an outside consulting firm necessary in this situation?
5. What control problems were present in this case?

AN ASSEMBLY PLANT (F)

The following case is of special interest because one phase of its decision making system is planned—the quality of the product—while the other phases are unplanned. It also illustrates the possibility of a gradual extension of a planned system.

The concept of operational output is vague, and the process is lightly regarded at the plant level, but the watchwords "quality," "costs," and "safety" are frequently advanced in bulletins, posters, and orders to supervisors. Aside from these abbreviated indications of the firm's objectives, each member of the lower managerial hierarchy must determine or "sense" the organizational goals (at least as they apply to him) from policy statements, experiment, and experience. The philosophy is that if everyone does his part, company goals will be achieved.

In general, there is little coordination of decision making efforts, and communication is not effective. It is not uncommon to find that two or more people are independently engaged in solving the same problem, yet neither the problem-solvers nor their superiors are aware of this duplication. Occasionally a problem-solver will be deeply involved in a pressing problem only to find that it has just been solved by someone else, or that there is a long-established solution which has been set aside and forgotten. Solutions and revised methods are seldom reported to all of the affected personnel.

Efforts to improve the performance of each department often lead to revisions of operating procedures, and this has a considerable impact on the procedures or operations of other departments. However, the lack of communication frequently means that other departments will not be notified of the revisions in time to plan the necessary adjustments.

For the most part, except for very important problems, problem solving is done informally. The authorization step is extremely vague and undefined; in fact, in nearly all cases the solutions constructed by staff officials are effectuated with no authorization whatever—by the problem-solver convincing a foreman that the proposal is "sound."

On the other hand, if an expenditure is involved, formal authorization is almost an absolute requirement. When the services of maintenance personnel are needed, the amount of authorization can vary daily. Occasionally the work is actually done with no authorization, and with the labor charged to another account, but even very minor jobs are often accompanied by a work order and a detailed cost estimate, and are processed through administration.

A major exception to the general approach occurred when a problem reporting and problem solving program was established in the company's quality control headquarters. Quality defects and quality problems (the latter are usually discovered in the quality audit or the testing program, which in effect is a problem-raising section) are reported to the local assembly plants. Problems are also raised through the analyses of dealers' complaints and through the charges for work performed under the new-machinery guarantees.

All problems are specified in a Product Problem and Corrective Action Status Report, and the assembly plants are given ten working days to rectify the error and report back to headquarters. Because of the time limit, a special form was employed for assigning problems to higher and middle managers in the second, third, and fourth levels of the managerial hierarchy. This has proved to be an effective problem solving system; for a brief time, however, more importance was placed on getting a quick response to headquarters than on solving the problem.

The Product Problem and Corrective Action Report has a companion form, the Product Problem Computation, which allows for systematic and standard computation of each problem. The computations are used primarily for determining the cost of the additional efforts required by the solution; there is no indication of the gain or payoff of the solution.

At the time the assembly plants were making the adjustments for handling these problem reports from headquarters, it was decided to expand the system by having the local managers raise, assign, and solve problems in a similar manner. An assignment sheet and a disposition and status form were devised to aid in controlling this system. Although the system was initiated with enthusiasm, the timing was poor because it coincided with the early production and acceleration stages of a new model. Because this was the busiest period in the production year for all members of management, the local program was set aside in order to deal with more urgent problems.

QUESTIONS FOR DISCUSSION

1. When new managerial practices are to be introduced at the plant level, what top management problems may arise?
2. In terms of quality control problems, what management control problems arose in this case?
3. When a management system is introduced piecemeal, as was attempted here, what problems can arise?
4. What form of plant-level control unit would you suggest for allocating problem inputs from the headquarters control unit?
5. What are the problems in this case that such a plant control unit would solve?

AN INDUSTRIAL ENGINEERING DEPARTMENT (G)

This case and the schematic in Figure 16-G (page 424) concern the industrial engineering department of a brewery. Unlike the other cases, this one illustrates a fairly systematic decision making system that is currently in use as well as the effectiveness of the system in terms of its decision output. As with the preceding case, this case will also demonstrate that firms can introduce planned decision making procedures in certain areas of their operations. These are procedures which relate to an overall company effort in one area, such as quality control, or to one departmental operation.

EXPLANATION OF FIGURE 16–G

(1) Problems may arise from any source, but they must flow through the organizational authority relationships to the individual problem-solvers (the industrial engineers). The problem-solvers do not usually know the sources of the problems, but they must come from one of these areas: (a) union organizations, (b) any department, (c) any problem-solver, or (d) any individual in a higher position of authority.

(2) Problem assignment is made by the department director; he may decide to solve the problem himself or to assign it to his assistant. (a) The assistant will determine whether he will solve the problem or will assign it to a section leader. (b) The section leader will review the problem to decide whether he will solve it or will assign it to an industrial engineer.

(3) Since the industrial engineer cannot reassign a problem, he must develop a solution, but, because all major problems are classified and assigned on an annual basis to specified department personnel (control board technique), the engineer must fit the new problem into his schedule.

The work schedule is flexible so that it can allow for added and higher-priority work assignments during the year. For example, the industrial engineer might be given a special assignment of helping one of the higher ranking problem-solvers—the section leader, the department assistant, the department director, or a vice-president—or he might be temporarily assigned to a different department. The problem he had been working on will be seriously affected by these disruptions if his schedule is not sufficiently flexible.

(4) At this point the operating department is informed of the problem under study in order to obtain authority to talk to the

Figure 16–G
SCHEMATIC OF A PRESENT DECISION MAKING PROCESS

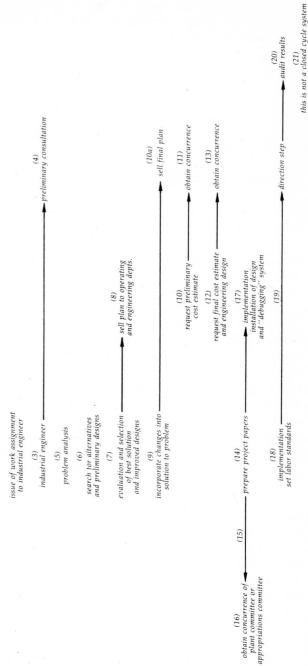

various operating foremen involved. This step also informs the operating foremen's supervisors of the study in their area.

(5) The analysis procedure is generally in the hands of the industrial engineer (unless he is a new employee); therefore the procedures of any two engineers may vary considerably.

(6) The number of alternative solutions developed is also left to the discretion of the industrial engineer: he may study ten alternatives or none, depending only upon the particular engineer involved.

(7) The solution with the highest rate of return on invested capital is usually selected (see Exhibit 16–G, pages 426-427). If alternative solutions appear worthwhile, they are also included in the proposal to higher management.

(8) The final plan must be accepted by the operating department. The engineering department will then review it for feasibility of installation.

(9) Any changes in the plan are incorporated here.

(10) The plan is sent to the engineering department for a preliminary cost estimate.

(10a) The plan is again reviewed with the operating department.

(11) The cost estimate is reviewed by the operating department.

(12) The plan is then sent to the engineering department for a final cost estimate and final design.

(13) The final design and the cost estimate are reviewed with the operating department, which then signs them.

(14, 15, 16) The industrial engineer prepares the formal project papers for the plant committee if an expenditure is less than $10,000. The papers are sent directly to the appropriations committee for all expenditures of more than $10,000.

(17) After the funds for the project have been authorized, a series of events are initiated in the engineering department for installing the facilities. The operation of the new installation is checked out by the engineering department, which "debugs" it and sets it operating at the predicted level of efficiency.

(18) The industrial engineer checks on projected labor requirements and the establishment of labor standards.

(19) The new operation and labor standards are either accepted by the operating department or it requests the vice-president and the general plant manager to have additional work performed by either department, so as to improve the installation, before it will accept the responsibility for its operation.

Exhibit 16-G

SUMMARY OF ANALYSIS (STEP 5)

I. REQUIRED INVESTMENT

1	Cost of project	$_____	1
2	Disposal value of assets to be retired by project	$_____	2
3	Capital additions required in absence of project	$_____	3
4	Investment released or avoided by project (2 + 3)	$_____	4
5	Net investment required (1 - 4)	$_____	5

II. NEXT-YEAR ADVANTAGE FROM PROJECT

A. Operating Advantage
(Use first year of project operations*)

		Increase	Decrease	
6	Assumed operating rate of project (hours per year)	_____		6
	Effect of Project on Revenue:	Increase	Decrease	
7	From change in quality of products	$_____	$_____	7
8	From change in volume of output	_____	_____	8
9	Total	$_____ A	$_____ B	9
	Effect of Project on Operating Costs:			
10	Labor	$_____	$_____	10
11	Material	_____	_____	11
12	Overhead	_____	_____	12
13	Total	$_____ A	$_____ B	13
14	Net increase in revenue (9A - 9B)		$_____	14
15	Net decrease in operating cost (13B -13A)		$_____	15
16	Next-year operating advantage (14 + 15)		$_____	16

B. Nonoperating Advantage
(Use only if there is an entry in Line 4)

17	Next-year capital consumption avoided by project:		17
	A Decline of disposal value during the year	$_____	A
	B Next-year allocation of capital additions	$_____	B
	Total	$_____	

C. Total Advantage

18	Total next-year advantage from project (16 + 17)	$_____	18

III. COMPUTATION OF URGENCY RATING

19 Total next-year advantage after income tax (18 - tax) $_____ 19
20 Chart allowance for project (total of column F, below) $_____ ** 20

(Enter Depreciable Assets Only)

Item or Group	Installed Cost of Item or Group A	Estimated Service Life (Years) B	Estimated Terminal Salvage (Per cent of cost) C	Chart Number D	Chart Percentage E	Chart Percentage × Cost (E × A) F
	$					$
					Total	$_____

21 Amount available for return on investment (19 - 20) $_____ 21
22 Urgency rating (21 ÷ 5) · 100   %_____ 22

---

*For projects with a significant break-in period, use performance after break-in.

**Since the chart allowance does not cover future capital additions to project assets, add an annual proration of such additions, if any, to the figure in Line 20.

(20) The audit of operations is made by the standards department, and the system is set up in the following manner. The industrial engineering department sets the labor standard and the base against which it is to be measured; that is, cases per man-hour, square feet cleaned per man-hour, pallets per man-hour, etc. The foreman reports the total units to the cost accounting department, which applies the rate to the units to determine the standard man-hours allowed. The actual labor hours reported by the foreman to the labor control department (for verification of total hours reported against total time-clock hours) are then sent to the cost accounting department, which compares actual labor hours to standard man-hours on a by-shift basis. The summary (or variance) reports are investigated by the standards department.

(21) This is not a closed cycle system at present. The problems raised by labor variances do not feed back to the industrial engineering department.

SOLUTIONS OF THREE PROBLEMS BY THIS SYSTEM

Problem 1: Increase speed on can line by 50 cpm.

Schematic Step Number	Explanation	Date of Action
1	by industrial engineer	11/19/57
2	sent to section leader	11/19/57
3	industrial engineer assigned problem	11/19/57
4	talk to plant manager	11/25/57
5-10a } 11-13 }	analysis	11/25/57 to 1/8/58
10	request preliminary cost estimate	12/23/57
14	prepare project papers (proposed savings $32,000, return 62%)	2/7/58
15	unknown	
16	unknown	12/22/58
17	implementation	
18	not required, no change	
19	operating department accepts can line changes	1/23/59
20	audit by industrial relations (actual savings $66,000 due to added sales)	9/10/59

Problem 2: Union complaint of slippery tile floors because of alkali from bottle soakers.

Schematic Step Number	Explanation	Date of Action
1	by letter to superintendent of packaging	10/14/58
2	letter given to section leader	10/14/58
3	letter given to industrial engineer	10/22/58
4-13	analysis	10/22/58 to 4/27/59
14	prepared project papers, proposed savings $99,000 (range $43,000 to $158,000), return 25%	6/15/59
15	unknown	
16	unknown	
17	implementation	4/14/61
18	labor to clean soakers eliminated	4/14/61
19	operating department accepts new alkali reclaim system	4/14/61
20	audit by industrial relations (actual savings $190,000 due to reduced price of alkali)	5/16/62

Problem 3: Increase speed on can line by 50 cpm (same line as in Problem No. 1).

Schematic Step Number	Explanation	Date of Action
1	problem raised by industrial engineering	9/11/59
2	sent to section leader	9/15/59
3	industrial engineering assigned problem	9/15/59
4-13	solution offered (solution offered 100% return on investment, so section leader wrote new work assignment to himself and then submitted project to department director)	9/17/59

14	department director wrote project papers (projected savings $18,000, return 100%)	10/6/59
15	unknown	
16	unknown	
17	implementation	1/29/60
18	not required, no change	
19	operating department accepts can line changes	2/26/60
20	audit by industrial relations (actual savings $29,000 due to increased sales)	7/13/60

CALCULATION OF NET PAYOFF
FROM THIS PROBLEM SOLVING SYSTEM

An analysis of the elapsed time in the solution of the three problems yielded the net payoff data shown below:

1. Average elapsed time per solution: 1.6 years.
2. Number of problems one problem-solver can work on simultaneously: 3.
3. Average time per problem-solver: .53 years.
4. Average payoff per problem: $100,000.
5. Average payoff per problem-solver per year: $186,680.

QUESTIONS FOR DISCUSSION

1. What improvements would you make in this decision making procedure?
2. How does the decision making procedure of this case differ from the basic design presented in this book?
3. Is there a control unit operation in the industrial engineering department?
4. In this system the industrial engineer solves the problem and the engineering department implements it. Do you think this is a satisfactory arrangement? Explain.
5. Evaluate the payoff of this system. Do you think that if this system were extended to marketing it would be equally productive, or is industrial engineering unique because its problem potential is greater?

INDEX

87–88; staffing of, 258; types of, 263–265

Cost: of the audit, 187; as criterion for selecting decision making techniques, 212; of implementation, 177–178; of a solution, 69, 138, 140–141, 229

Crawford, Meredith, 16

D

Dale, Ernest, 343*n*

Dalton, Melville, 377*n*

Data: for auditing a solution 119, 186–187; collection of, 125 142; for controlling the management system 268–276; on the environment, 51–53, 124–131; interpretation of 126–129; for making decisions 138–143 151–153; for selecting a management system, 221–225; sorting of, 125–126

Decision making, 2–4, 30–31; assignment of, 172–174; in a bureaucratic system, 385–386, 399–400; characteristics of, 32–34; as essential task of management, 37–38; evaluation of, 36–37; as a function of the organization, 4, 11–12, 26, 29, 36–37; group, 35–36; organizational *vs* individual, 34–35; as problem solving, 32; specialization in, 20–21, 32, 87, 96–97, 149–150, 253

Decision making models, 6–10; *see also* Management systems

Decision utilization, 30–31

Decision making techniques, 7, 132, 197–216; criteria of selecting, 199–207; list of, 199; mechanics of selecting, 207–211; review of availability, 198; stage for use of, 198–199; technological change in, 211–214

Decision making systems: *see* Management systems

Decisions, definition of, 32; *see also* Solutions

Defining organizational objectives (Step 1), 50, 99–116; *see also* Objectives

Deutsch, Karl W., 258–259

Direction procedure (Step 9), 81–83, 180–186; applied to the organization, 181–186; in a bureaucratic system, 393–394; definition of, 180; in a marketing department, 409–410

Distribution, of organizational welfare, 101–102, 158–159, 161–165, 167; guides to, 164; in interorganizational systems, 332, 337–339, 352–354

Drucker, Peter F., 10

Drug company sales department, case study of, 420

E

Efficiency, of an organization, 110–111, 162–163

Electronics division, case study of, 410–413, 414–415

Ellis, David O., 27*n*

Employees: acceptance of a decision, 154, *see also* Consensus; acceptance of organizational change, 154–159, 244–245; individual welfare of, 104–105, 109–113; management's concept of, 157–159, 162; motivation of, 101, 155–165; participation of, in a hospital system, 308–312; *see also* Membership, of an organization

Entrepreneur: characteristics of, 361–362, 376; compared with the middle manager, 362–369

Environment, 18–19; organizational adjustment to, 23-26, 28, 129–131, 181–186, 274–275; as source of problems, 51, 118, 119–120; *see also* External environment and Internal environment

Evaluation, of the management system, criteria for, 221–233

Exchange model, of interorganizational cooperation, 345–348

External environment, 24, 51, 120–123, 183; definition of, 120

F

Feasibility: as criterion for evaluating the management system, 221, 226–227; as criterion for selecting decision making techniques, 200–202; of a solution, 143, 303

"Fire-fighting," 145–147

Flow charts, 16, 19

Forms: design of, 53–54; use of, 54, 65, 69, 70, 271, 316